WORLD
CHEESE
BOOK

WORLD CHEESE BOOK

EDITOR-IN-CHIEF
JULIET HARBUTT

CONTRIBUTORS

ANDROUET • MARTIN ASPINWALL • VINCENZO BOZZETTI • KEVIN JOHN BROOME

RAN BUCK • SAGI COOPER • DIANNE CURTIN • JIM DAVIES • SHEANA DAVIS

ANGELA GRAY • RIE HIJIKATA • RUMIKO HONMA • KATIE JARVIS • MONIKA LINTON

GURTH PRETTY • HANSUELI RENZ • RICHARD SUTTON • WILL STUDD

KATE ARDING • AAD VERNOOIJ • STÉPHANE BLOHORN

DK INDIA
Senior Art Editors Ivy Roy, Ira Sharma
Art Editor Era Chawla
Assistant Editor Saumya Gaur
Senior Editor Nidhilekha Mathur
Deputy Managing Editor Bushra Ahmed
Managing Editor Alicia Ingty
Managing Art Editor Navidita Thapa
DTP Designers Satish Chandra Gaur, Anurag Trivedi,
Manish Chandra Upreti
Pre-production Manager Sunil Sharma

DK UK
Managing Editor Dawn Henderson
Managing Art Editor Christine Keilty
Senior Jacket Creative Nicola Powling
Producer, Pre-Production Rebecca Fallowfield
Senior Producer Jen Scothern
Art Director Peter Luff
Category Publisher Peggy Vance

2009 Edition
DK UK **Project Editor** Danielle Di Michiel
Senior Art Editor Elly King
Editorial Assistants Shashwati Tia Sarkar, Erin Boeck Motum
Designer William Hicks
Managing Editor Dawn Henderson
Managing Art Editor Christine Keilty
Senior Jacket Creative Nicola Powling
Senior Production Editor Jennifer Murray
Production Controller Alice Holloway
Creative Technical Support Sonia Charbonnier

DK INDIA **DTP Designers** Dheeraj Arora, Preetam Singh, Jagtar Singh
Senior Designer Tannishtha Chakraborty
Design Manager Romi Chakraborty
Head of Publishing Aparna Sharma

First published in Great Britain in 2009 by Dorling Kindersley Limited
80 Strand, London WC2R 0RL

A Penguin Random House Company

This revised edition published in Great Britain in 2015 by Dorling Kindersley Limited
2 4 6 8 10 9 7 5 3 1
001 – 262224 – June/2015

A CIP catalogue record for this book is available from the British Library

ISBN 978-02-411-86-57-2

Printed and bound in China

A WORLD OF IDEAS:
SEE ALL THERE IS TO KNOW
www.dk.com

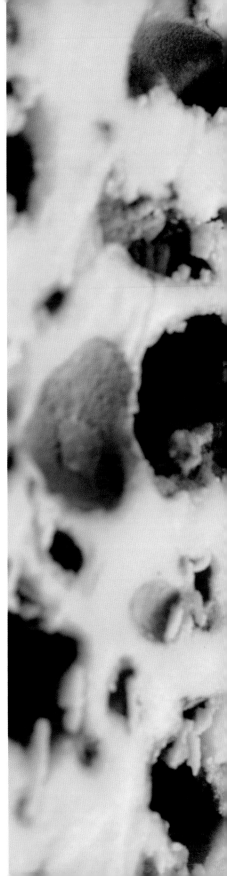

CONTENTS

Introduction

Evidence of cheesemaking has been found dating back to 2800BCE, but the discovery of cheese would have come about as a happy accident. Any milk left to warm by a fire or stored in a sack made from the stomach of an animal would have soured, causing the milk solids (the curds) and liquid (the whey) to coagulate and separate, allowing man to learn that his most precious commodity, milk, could be preserved in the form of cheese and, eventually, that rennet, an enzyme found in the stomach of the milk-producing animal, was the coagulant.

The Story of Cheese

Now, some 5,000 years later, cheese is made all over the world with all kinds of milk, from reindeer's milk in Lapland, to buffalo's milk in Australia, and yak's milk in the Kingdom of Bhutan. The miracle of cheese is that, although milk tastes virtually the same the world over, the diversity of textures, tastes, and aromas of cheese is almost infinite, and virtually any cheese can be made anywhere in the world. The size, shape, and milk of a cheese, however, has been determined by such diverse external forces as historical events, centuries of experimentation, religious orders, and the terrain, while the nuances of texture and taste are influenced by the raw materials – the type and breed of animal, the soil, the grazing, the climate, microclimate, and ingenuity of the cheesemaker.

European cheeses owe much to the Greeks' knowledge and, later, the Romans, who built on that knowledge and took their recipes for making cheese across Europe to feed their legions as their Empire spread – a legacy clearly seen throughout Europe to this day. The Middle Ages saw the proliferation of monastic orders across Europe and into Britain and Ireland, particularly the Benedictine and, later, the Cistercian monks, who developed the cheeses we

know today as Trappist or monastery cheeses, of which Maroilles of Northern France was probably the first.

Historically, a cheese's size was determined by the amount of milk available and the proximity to the nearest market. Hence, mountain cheeses tended to be large, with the farmers combining their milk to make slow-ripening cheeses they could sell at the end of the summer months when the cows returned to the valleys. Those made in the valleys and near large markets would have been smaller, quicker to ripen, and sold at weekly markets. Shape was determined by the sophistication of the maker and the raw materials available to make the moulds – whether woven grass, fired clay, or wood.

Today, Europe's traditional cheeses are typically made in designated areas by various artisan producers whose combined volume is sufficiently high that the cheese can be found around the world. Classic examples include raw milk Camembert de Normandie (see p44), made by only ten producers and Parmigiano-Reggiano (see p128), made by around 400 producers. Artisan cheeses developed in the last 35 years or so, however, tend to be invented by individual cheesemakers and are often hard to find outside their region or country of origin, even if made in large volumes.

The ancient art of cheesemaking is lovingly depicted in this colourful Swiss wood engraving.

The Raw Materials

The individual identity and personality of a cheese is determined by a number of facts of nature.

The climate and landscape, including the minerals in the soil, affect what flora grows, and therefore what a milk-producing animal eats, thereby influencing the subtle flavours of the milk. Even the most unobservant cannot fail to see and smell the difference between fresh grass, wild clover, and meadow flowers compared with compacted feed, silage, or turnips. Minerals also affect the speed of ripening, the texture, and flavour of the cheese.

The animal and its grazing habits add another dimension. The comfort-loving cow is largely found on rich plains, lush valleys, and sunny mountain pastures. Goats, unlike cows and sheep, are browsers, tearing sparse but aromatic flora from hedgerows, craggy peaks, rock-strewn valleys or, when the opportunity arises, from the farmers' carefully manicured garden. The resulting milk is herbaceous, like a crisp, white wine infused with herbs, becoming like marzipan or ground almonds with age.

The sweet, almost caramel, taste of ewe's milk has been valued in Europe and the Middle East for thousands of years. The numerous breeds adapt to almost any climate, some surviving on seemingly nothing, yielding but a few litres of milk a day imbued with the essence of the wild, aromatic herbs, grasses, and flora that form their diet.

The breed of animal can also be a factor. Compared with the high volume yield of the Friesian, for example, milk from Jersey or Guernsey cows is less but has larger fat globules that produce a richer, smoother deep Monet-yellow cheese, and the sweet, mellifluous milk of the Montbéliarde cow is renowned throughout the Savoie region of France.

The microclimate of both the milk and the cheese room provide the finishing touch. Tiny colourful, wind-born moulds and yeasts treat each new batch of protein-rich curd as a canvas on which to create their daily masterpiece, while the naturally occurring bacteria prefer the seclusion and warmth of the interior to work their magic. These convert the sweet milk sugars, lactose, into lactic acid and so begins the fermentation process. Once an accident of Nature, most have been harnessed by cheesemakers to ensure the end result is more predictable. These microflora, along with the subtleties inherent in milk, are lost when the milk is pasteurized and must be re-introduced in the form of a cocktail of bacteria known as a starter culture. Regrettably these laboratory-produced cultures cannot emulate the complexity provided by Mother Nature.

How Cheese is Made

Cheesemaking equipment and methods vary from cheesemaker to cheesemaker but the basic principles involved have remained unchanged for thousands of years.

1 The milk Ideally, milk is pumped straight from the milking parlour to the dairy where it is checked and tested to ensure it is pure and clean. It may then be pasteurized, typically at 73ºC (163ºF) for 15 seconds. The milk is transferred to a vat and heated until it reaches the acidity level required for the type of cheese being made.

2 Coagulation or curdling Once the acidity reaches the desired level, a special cocktail of lactic bacteria or starter culture is added. This both converts the lactose to lactic acid and contributes to the flavour, aroma, and texture of the cheese. (Too much or not enough acidity results in imperfect cheeses.) Most cheeses are made by adding rennet (derived from the stomach of a milk-fed animal) or another coagulant to make sure the protein and fat in the milk bond and are therefore not lost in the whey.

Curdling is the fundamental step in cheesemaking, as the degree of coagulation determines the final moisture content of the cheese and this in turn affects the speed of the fermentation process.

3 Separation of curds and whey The freshly formed curd looks like white jelly, while the whey is a yellow-green liquid. Gently separating the curds from the whey creates soft, high-moisture cheeses, while cutting the curds expels more whey and produces harder cheeses. The finer the curd is cut, the harder and finer-grained the final cheese. The whey is drained off once it reaches the desired acidity.

4 Shaping and salting The curds are then piled into moulds or hoops and may be pressed before being turned out of their moulds. Once out of the mould, the cheese is rubbed or sprinkled with salt or soaked in brine before being placed in a cold room or cellar to age.

5 Ageing and the *affineur* The ageing process is the art and science of cheesemaking as it brings out the character of the milk and the unique flavours attributed to the grazing. A good *affineur*, a person who ripens cheeses, can nurture the simplest cheese to yield every nuance of flavour. Artisan cheeses vary from day to day, depending on the grazing, the season, the conditions in the cheese room, and the cheesemaker; so unlike wine, cheese has a vintage every day, which is what makes it so extraordinary and wonderful.

FRESH CHEESES
(See pp10–11)

AGED FRESH CHEESES
(See pp12–13)

SOFT WHITE CHEESES
(See pp14–15)

SEMI-SOFT CHEESES
(See pp16–17)

Understanding Cheese

There is no universal system for identifying cheeses. Instead, every cheese-producing country has its own system using technical terms such as semi-hard, semi-cooked, pressed uncooked, smear-ripened, or washed-curd that are all but meaningless, and confusing, to cheese lovers.

By contrast, this book uses the Editor-in-Chief's easy-to-grasp system of identifying cheese types, based on the type of rind a cheese grows and its texture.

The way it works is that the amount of moisture, or whey, that is left in the cheese determines not only the texture of the interior, but also the type of rind and moulds the cheese will grow. There is the odd exception that crosses two of these categories, but most are very obvious.

The Editor-in-Chief's system (see pp10–23) identifies seven different types of cheese:
Fresh, Aged Fresh, Soft-White, Semi-Soft, Hard, Blue, and Flavour-added.

Using this system, with just a glance and a gentle squeeze you can categorize 99 per cent of the cheeses you meet, whether from a French market, a New York cheese shop, or elsewhere. With a little practice, you can assess a cheese's basic character, strength of flavour, how it will behave when cooked, and even its ripeness and quality.

HARD CHEESES
(See pp18–19)

BLUE CHEESES
(See pp20–21)

FLAVOUR-ADDED CHEESES (See pp22–23)

Denomination and Designation of Origin

Some cheeses have legally protected names linked to their provenance. Certifying the origin of a cheese recognizes its *terroir* (French) or *tipicità* (Italian), acknowledging that the unique character of each traditionally made food is a result of a complex interaction of soil, plant life, and climate, combined with traditional production methods and raw materials – a combination that cannot be replicated elsewhere. There are various national systems, such as the French AOC (Appellation d'Origine Contrôlée) and the Italian DOC (Denominazione d'Origine Controllata), as well as the European Community-created PDO (Protected Designation of Origin) for traditional regional wines and food made throughout the EC.

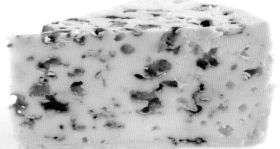

In 1666, Roquefort was the first cheese to be protected by law, the forerunner for the AOC system in France.

Using this Book

This book will open up a world of exciting cheeses for cheese fans. The core of the book is formed by chapters cataloguing cheeses from each country, detailing their origins, tasting notes and how best to enjoy them, with prominent and important cheeses explored in greater depth. The information box included with each cheese entry, explained here, contains information that is key to understanding the identity of the cheese.

Region
Some cheeses are made all over a country, while others are made by various producers in specific regions. Where three or fewer producers make the cheese in a specific location, a city or town is also listed. The region can reveal much about the *terroir* of a cheese, which dictates the type of animals found there and their grazing environment.

Age
This gives the age or range of ages in which a cheese is at its best.

Weight and Shape
Some cheeses are made in one weight and shape only, but most are produced in a range, which we have listed wherever possible.

Size
This gives the dimensions of a cheese, usually measurements such as diameter (D), height (H), length (L), or width (W), depending on its shape. Where there is a range of sizes, a range of dimensions is given. In some cases, where the range is not known, the dimensions of the pictured cheese are given.

Milk
This gives the type of animal whose milk is used to make the cheese. In some cases, a cheese may be made from a mix of milk from different animals, depending on the season and availability.

Classification
Each cheese is categorized as one of the seven types described in the Editor-in-Chief's system (see pp10–23).

Producer
Up to three producers are listed for artisan cheesemakers. "Various" indicates that the cheese is made by more than three producers.

Pecorino Siciliano PDO

This cheese is documented as far back as 900BCE, when Odysseus meets the Cyclops Polyphemus in Homer's *Odyssey*. As in ancient times, this cheese is still handmade using lamb's rennet.

TASTING NOTES Yellow and sometimes studded with whole black peppercorns, it is firm and friable with a pungent, salty, full, and long-lasting flavour.

HOW TO ENJOY Serve young cheeses with vegetables; aged ones with bread and olives or grated over pasta.

ITALY Sicilia	
Age 4–12 months	
Weight and Shape 4–12kg (9–26½lb), wheel	
Size D. 14–38cm (5½–15in), H. 10–18cm (4–7in)	
Milk Ewe	
Classification Hard	
Producer Various	

Name
The name of a cheese is always given in the language of the cheese's origin, followed by any designation of origin status, if it applies.

Introduction
This describes the cheese in terms of its identity, giving useful information about its makers and origins.

Tasting Notes
These describe the aroma, flavour, texture, and finish of the cheese.

How to Enjoy
This offers suggestions on how best to enjoy the cheese, including cooking ideas and, in many cases, wine accompaniments.

Map
A quick reference to the country that produces the cheese. The black dot indicates the general location or region of the cheesemaker. Where there is no black dot, the cheese is produced all over the country.

Photograph
For ease of recognition, this shows a cheese as it is sold. Generally, the photograph shows both the exterior and the interior of the cheese.

Scale
This symbol provides an at-a-glance visual guide to the approximate or largest size of the cheese in relation to an average-sized hand. Where the symbol is missing, the sizing information was unavailable, or the cheese is soft and sold in tubs or pots.

Fresh Cheeses

NO RIND · HIGH MOISTURE CONTENT · MILD · FRESH · LEMONY

Ready to eat within a few days, or even hours, of being made, fresh cheeses are so young that they barely have time to develop any more than a whisper of the milk's potential flavour, so the taste is typically described as lactic or milky, sweet, lemony, refreshing, citrus or acidic. This does not mean they are bland. On the contrary, the skill of the true craftsman can coax the subtle flavours from the milk; the sweet, grassy notes of cow's milk; the aromatic, herbaceous character of goat's milk, with its hints of white wine and crushed almonds; the richness of ewe's milk that suggests Brazil nuts, caramelized onions, and roast lamb; or the leathery, earthy undertones of buffalo's milk.

HALLOUMI

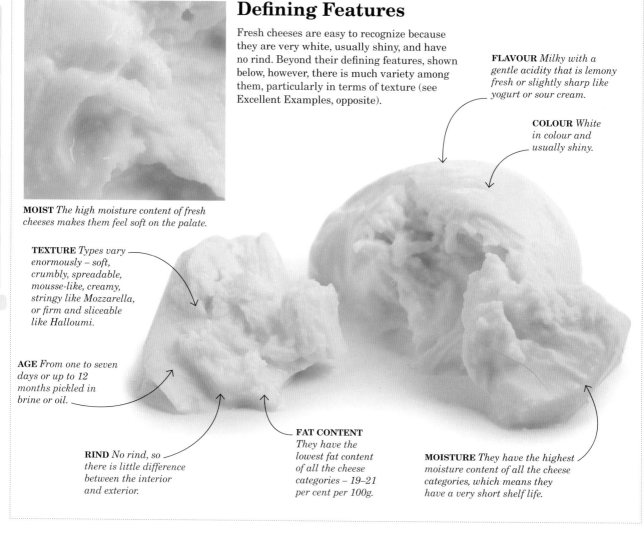

MOIST *The high moisture content of fresh cheeses makes them feel soft on the palate.*

Defining Features

Fresh cheeses are easy to recognize because they are very white, usually shiny, and have no rind. Beyond their defining features, shown below, however, there is much variety among them, particularly in terms of texture (see Excellent Examples, opposite).

FLAVOUR *Milky with a gentle acidity that is lemony fresh or slightly sharp like yogurt or sour cream.*

COLOUR *White in colour and usually shiny.*

TEXTURE *Types vary enormously – soft, crumbly, spreadable, mousse-like, creamy, stringy like Mozzarella, or firm and sliceable like Halloumi.*

AGE *From one to seven days or up to 12 months pickled in brine or oil.*

RIND *No rind, so there is little difference between the interior and exterior.*

FAT CONTENT *They have the lowest fat content of all the cheese categories – 19–21 per cent per 100g.*

MOISTURE *They have the highest moisture content of all the cheese categories, which means they have a very short shelf life.*

How They're Made

The most common fresh cheeses such as fromage frais or cottage cheese are made by heating the milk then adding a starter culture of bacteria that will cause the milk to curdle. Excess whey is then drained off and the loose curd is put into cheesecloth or small moulds for a few hours before being turned out and salted. A similar process, shown here, is used to produce fresh cheeses from whey, such as Ricotta.

Firstly, the whey, *left over from making hard cheese, is heated with a little vinegar to raise its acidity and cause the protein to rise to the surface in tiny lumps.*

Once firm, *the curd lumps are scooped into open-weave basket moulds.*

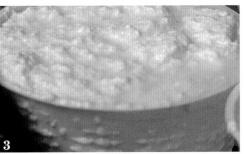

The curds *are left to drain slowly. The yield is very low, only a few ounces from a gallon of whey.*

The fragile curds *are turned over once in the basket and when removed will bear the imprint of the mould.*

Excellent Examples

Halloumi
A harder, denser texture than other fresh cheeses because the curd has been "kneaded". The brine it is preserved in gives it a salty tang. (See pp262–63)

Ricotta
A soft, moist, fragile whey cheese. (See p134)

Feta
Dense, creamy, and crumbly in texture, it is preserved in brine, giving it a salty taste and texture. (See pp258–59)

Mozzarella
Because the fresh curd is placed in hot water, this cheese is very elastic and can be stretched and formed into different shapes. (See pp118–19)

Mascarpone
Sweet in flavour, it is made by heating cream rather than milk. (See p121)

How to Enjoy

UNCOOKED The microscopic fat globules trapped in fresh cheeses absorb and concentrate the flavours of the other ingredients, transforming the simplest and often the easiest dishes into classics like Feta in a Greek salad, cream cheese with smoked salmon or Mascarpone in tiramasu. Consequently, fresh cheese is used to add texture to a recipe rather than to give it additional flavour. Fresh cheeses destined for the cheeseboard are often decorated, rolled, or dusted in ash, herbs, or spices to enhance their appearance and flavour.

COOKED Fresh cheeses are at their best when grilled or baked in classic dishes, such as Feta in spanakopita, Ricotta in ravioli, or Mozzarella on pizza. However, their high moisture content and loose texture means they fall apart or split in sauces and become tough when grilled too long.

WITH DRINKS With their high acidity, fresh cheeses are best with crisp white wines or cider. For a non-alcoholic alternative, try apple juice or elderflower cordial. However, when fresh cheeses are combined with other ingredients, choose a wine that complements the more dominant flavours.

Aged Fresh Cheeses

THIN, WRINKLED RIND · GRAINY TO CREAMY · WHITE, GREY, AND BLUE MOULD

As the name implies, these are fresh cheeses that have been allowed to age and dry out in special temperature- and humidity-controlled caves or cellars, where a multitude of moulds and yeasts are encouraged to grow on the rind. The best-known are made in the Loire in France; they are the small rounds, pyramids, cones, bells, and logs you see in small, straw-lined, wooden boxes on rickety tables in French markets, but are increasingly made around the world. These creamy and aromatic cheeses are mostly goat's cheeses and often covered in ash, herbs, or spices, or wrapped in vine or chestnut leaves, over which the moulds grow. When made with cow's, or ewe's milk, the texture is softer, the moulds less aggressive, and the taste creamier and sweeter.

CLOCHETTE

Defining Features

Their distinctive thin, wrinkled rinds are coated with a myriad of moulds and yeasts (the most dominant of which are splashes of steely grey or blue moulds called *Penicillium glaucum*), and dusted with a thin layer of white *Penicillium candidum* or *Geotricium candidum*. Thinner cheeses develop a softer rind with less mould and become almost runny just beneath the rind. As it ages the cheese develops a texture some call "claggy" and coats the roof of the mouth.

WRINKLES *As the cheese matures, wrinkles deepen and the interior becomes flaky.*

MOISTURE *They lose moisture and shrink as they age. After about four weeks 50 per cent of their original weight is lost.*

AGE *They are considered ripe from 10–30 days.*

FAT CONTENT *They have a fat content of 22–23 per cent per 100g.*

RIND *The thin, wrinkled rind is dusted with white mould and blotches of grey and blue.*

TEXTURE *As the cheeses age, the texture inside gradually changes from moist and slightly crumbly to dense, compact, flaky and brittle.*

COLOUR *Since most are made with goat's milk they have a very pale, almost white, interior.*

FLAVOUR *Creamy when young, they become nutty like ground almonds, and turns intensely goaty and sharp as the cheese ages.*

How They're Made

When left to age naturally, usually in cool cellars, the protein-rich surface of fresh cheese attracts a range of natural microflora, each contributing to the ripening process. In the hands of a competent *affineur,* they will age gracefully and be sold at varying stages of ripeness depending on the tastes of the clientèle. Each will develop its own individual character that is influenced by the cheesemaker, animals, grazing, season, and microclimate in which they are made and ripened. The following is a general outline of the stages through which these cheeses pass.

1 **The delicate,** *pure-white curd is carefully hand ladled into individual moulds and then topped up until they are almost overflowing. The weight of the curd gradually forces the expulsion of the excess whey.*

2 **Once the level** *of the curd has dropped, the base of each cheese is sprinkled with salt to speed up the expulsion of the remaining whey.*

3 **After a few hours** *the cheeses are firm enough to retain their shape and are turned out onto draining trays. At this stage it is a fresh cheese.*

4 **Gradually** *over the next few days the cheese develops a soft, thin, almost opaque rind that gradually shrinks and becomes wrinkled.*

5 **Within 9–12 days** *a layer of white* Penicillium candidum *develops, followed by a pale-blue mould that darkens and covers the cheese.*

How to Enjoy

UNCOOKED The texture and rind of the various aged fresh cheeses do not lend themselves to spreads or dips but no cheeseboard is truly complete without one of these attractive, rustic-looking cheeses.

COOKED Chèvre Salad is ubiquitous throughout France, but is not, as so many chefs think, simply a "goat's cheese salad". In fact it is made with an aged fresh cheese, typically Crottin de Chavignol (see p54), which is sliced, drizzled with olive oil, and grilled on rounds of baguette. To use any other type of goat's cheese is a travesty since you will not get that wonderful nutty, aromatic flavour characteristic of these cheeses when grilled or baked.

WITH DRINKS A crisp, white Sauvignon Blanc, Viognier, or Rosé is perfect, especially if it is from the same area as the cheese. Alternatively, a light ale or beer brings out the nutty side of the cheese and the taste of the hops.

Excellent Examples

Valençay
The rind of this truncated pyramid is encrusted with a dusty blue-grey mould. The goat's milk interior is a bright white. (See p96)

Clochette
This bell-shaped example from France has a rind that is dusted with a fine white mould. (See p51)

Sainte-Maure de Touraine AOC
This french log has a pure white grainy interior which contrasts against the wrinkled, ash grey exterior. (See pp92–93)

Ketem
Based on French-style aged fresh cheeses, Israel's Ketem illustrates the growing popularity of this cheese type. (See p264)

St Tola Log
This Irish cheese is produced in a large log shape and has a silky, creamy texture. (See p223)

Soft White Cheeses

VELVETY WHITE RIND · CREAMY INTERIOR · MUSHROOMY TASTE

Camembert de Normandie and Brie de Meaux are the best-known examples and the inspiration behind the variations produced around the world. Soft white cheeses typically have a white crust, a slightly grainy to almost runny texture, and a wonderful aroma of mushrooms. The mildest cheeses hint of sweet hay and button mushrooms; the strongest taste like creamy, wild mushroom soup with the peppery bite of dandelions on the finish, and an earthy aroma reminiscent of cool cellars and mushrooms warmed in butter. Those made with ewe's milk have a subtle sweetness with just a hint of roast lamb or lanolin, while those made with goat's milk taste of almonds or even marzipan.

CAPRICORN GOAT

Defining Features

Factory-made varieties tend to have a thick, velvety rind that seems more like a wrapping than an integral part of the cheese. In contrast, artisan examples grow a thinner, white crust that can be stained with reddish pigments or yellow-grey blotches of mould. The coat protects the cheese from drying out and speeds up the ripening process hence why they are sometimes called mould-ripened cheeses.

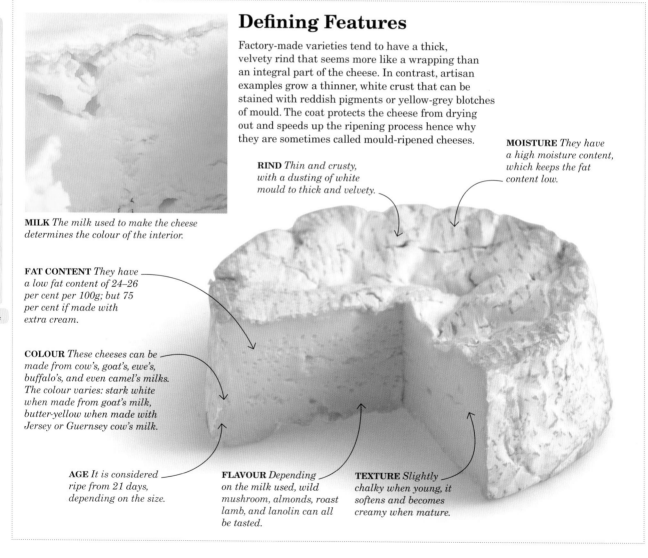

MILK *The milk used to make the cheese determines the colour of the interior.*

RIND *Thin and crusty, with a dusting of white mould to thick and velvety.*

MOISTURE *They have a high moisture content, which keeps the fat content low.*

FAT CONTENT *They have a low fat content of 24–26 per cent per 100g; but 75 per cent if made with extra cream.*

COLOUR *These cheeses can be made from cow's, goat's, ewe's, buffalo's, and even camel's milks. The colour varies: stark white when made from goat's milk, butter-yellow when made with Jersey or Guernsey cow's milk.*

AGE *It is considered ripe from 21 days, depending on the size.*

FLAVOUR *Depending on the milk used, wild mushroom, almonds, roast lamb, and lanolin can all be tasted.*

TEXTURE *Slightly chalky when young, it softens and becomes creamy when mature.*

How They're Made

To achieve their almost-liquid texture, soft white cheeses must retain a high percentage of whey. This means that the curds must be scooped gently into the moulds. During this part of the process only the weight of the curd is used to lightly press out the excess whey. The surface of the cheese is then enveloped in a white, velvety *Penicillium candidum* coat that is made up of millions of microscopic mushrooms of the penicillin family. This is where the mushroomy aroma and taste originate.

1

The floppy, jelly-like *curd is scooped from the vat and put layer upon layer into the round, high-sided hoops, or moulds, until full.*

2

Once firm, *the cheese is turned out of the moulds, a disc is placed on top of each one, gently pressing out any remaining whey.*

3

After receiving *a sprinkling of salt they are moved to a room where the white mould, and sometimes others, is introduced.*

4

The mould is naturally *attracted to the moist, protein-rich surface, and gradually spreads over the entire the cheese.*

5

After two weeks *its velvety white coat has formed. Colourful moulds may appear but most cheesemakers prefer only the purest white.*

How to Enjoy

UNCOOKED These wonderful cheeses are at their very best when served at room temperature with crusty bread and a glass of wine.

COOKED A popular recipe involves baking a small soft white cheese in an oven for about 15 minutes and scooping out the molten interior with chunks of bread or raw vegetables. These cheeses also grill well; try some on a croissant layered with roasted peppers or sweet chutney, but cut off the rind around the sides because it will become dry and a little bitter.

WITH DRINKS The French serve cider or calvados with Camembert, Chardonnay with Brie de Meaux, and Champagne with Chaource. As a general rule, goat's or ewe's milk variations work very well with similar wines. Alternatively, try a tawny Port with a strong soft white. A hoppy pale ale (rather than a bitter beer) works with the milder, sweeter cheeses.

Excellent Examples

Brie de Melun
Like most Bries, Brie de Melun has a strong mushroom flavour, but is less well known than Brie de Meaux. (See p41)

Camembert de Normandie
France's other famous soft white comes packed in wooden boxes. Ripe examples have pink or brown-tinged rinds. (See p44)

Flower Marie
This is a unique ewe's milk cheese from England, with a soft rind and a refreshing lemon flavour. (See p181)

Brillat-Savarin
Extra cream added to the milk triples its fat content to 75 per cent per 100g and gives this cheese a wickedly rich feel. (See p42)

Capricorn Goat
One of England's first soft white goat's cheeses, it has a stark white interior typical of goat's milk cheeses. (See p174)

Semi-Soft Cheeses

THIN AND DRY TO ORANGE AND STICKY RIND · MILD TO PUNGENT · RUBBERY TO RUNNY

Semi-soft cheeses vary in appearance and texture more than any other cheese type, but can be divided into two styles. Dry rind cheeses ripen slowly and range from springy, mild, sweet, and nutty with barely formed rinds to rubbery, floral, and pungent with thick leathery rinds. When made with goat's milk, they are mild and nutty, with a hint of marzipan. Those with a sticky orange rind are called washed-rind cheeses and are softer and have a pungent, savoury, farmyardy, smoky, and even meaty taste and aroma. They tend to be grainy, with a softening just under the rind when young, and become soft and supple with age. The washed-rind type includes those known as Trappist or monastery-style.

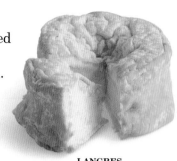

LANGRES

16

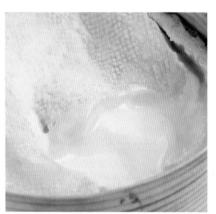

LIQUID *Some washed-rind cheeses are almost liquid when ripe.*

Defining Features

All semi-soft cheeses are washed in brine to discourage unwanted moulds. Dry rind types develop anything from a thin, relatively bland-looking rind to a colourful coat of grey mould, splashed with red, yellow, and white moulds, over a pinkish leathery rind. Washed-rind examples that are regularly treated with brine have wet, sticky, pale orange to russet-red rinds. The more they are washed, the softer, stickier, and smellier the rind.

FLAVOUR *Depending on the rind, some are buttery and mellow, while others are smoky and meaty.*

FAT CONTENT *They have a fat content of 24–30 per cent per 100g.*

RIND *They vary from barely formed to a thick, leathery grey coat, or one that is shiny, sticky, and orange.*

AGE *It is considered ripe from three weeks to three months.*

COLOUR *The interior can vary from a pale straw colour to creamy yellow in colour.*

TEXTURE *Both dry and washed-rind cheeses soften greatly. The texture of semi-soft cheeses ranges from rubbery and elastic to supple or even runny.*

MOISTURE *They retain a lot of moisture as they are only lightly pressed, if at all. Washing seals the rind and also locks in moisture.*

How They're Made

Semi-soft cheeses are washed in numerous ways, each creating a different style of rind. Those soaked in brine for a few hours or days and then left to dry out develop a pale, barely formed to thin pink-tinged leathery rind. Splashing or spraying the cheese creates a thin, sticky, pale orange rind, like the Stinking Bishop example shown here, but they become stickier and brighter with more frequent washing. Those dipped in, or wiped with, brine by hand are called smear-ripened.

2

Perforated moulds *let the whey drain from the curd, although some semi-soft cheeses can be lightly pressed.*

4

Any white mould *that grows is knocked out by the washing process and, after five to six weeks, the rind becomes very soft.*

1

Rennet is added *to the milk to coagulate it. Along with the starter culture, this separates the curds from the whey.*

3

Once removed *from its mould, it is bound with a thin strip of wood and hand washed with a mix of brine and perry (or fermented pear juice).*

5

The final cheese *develops a thin, sticky golden rind, and the texture is so soft that it literally oozes out when it is cut.*

How to Enjoy

UNCOOKED Mild semi-soft cheeses such as Edam or Havarti are classic breakfast cheeses, while the stronger varieties are essential on any cheeseboard.

COOKED The dry rind cheeses are superb when grilled because their rubbery texture stretches but holds its shape – but for the same reason they do not work well in sauces. Washed-rind cheeses, however, melt superbly in sauces, though a little goes a long way. When they

are baked whole, they become sweeter and more savoury, which makes them an amazing starter.

WITH DRINKS The milder cheeses need a Chardonnay, a light red like Merlot, or beer, but more acidic wines will make the cheese taste sour. The pungent washed-rind cheeses are superb with beers, ciders, and sweeter grape varieties such as Riesling or Gewürztraminer. These wines highlight the fruity, sweet meadow-flower character that is usually hidden beneath their farmyardy aroma and taste.

Excellent Examples

Taleggio
The fine, dry rind feels gritty and has patches of grey and white moulds. A stamp of quality and authenticity marks its rind. (See pp136–37)

Stinking Bishop
This washed-rind cheese is splashed or rubbed in brine mixed with perry. It is named after the pear variety used to make the perry. (See p198)

Langres
Frequent washing and ripening in very humid cellars creates the bright colour. The rind shrinks and wrinkles as it ages, and can also be finely dusted with mould. (See p62)

Edam
Edam is a washed-curd cheese (see p19) and has a sweet flavour, a rubbery texture, and a very thin, barely formed rind dipped in a protective coat of red wax. (See p228)

Vacherin Mont d'Or
The thick rind of this cheese protects the moisture in the interior, and as a result the interior is a runny liquid. (See p243)

Hard Cheeses

ROUGH OR POLISHED RIND · CRUMBLY TO BRITTLE · COMPLEX FLAVOURS

The large wheels, cylinders, and drums of hard cheese found in all traditional cheesemaking countries are typically made with cow's, goat's, or ewe's milks. Their rinds range across the spectrum from smooth with polished rinds to rough and pockmarked like the moon's surface. Flavours grow complex as they mature; very old hard cheeses such as Parmigiano-Reggiano and Dry Jack become granular, giving the cheese a crunchy feel in the mouth. Classic ewe's milk hard cheeses, such as Manchego and Pecorino, have a dense, slightly grainy texture with an oily-yet-dry feel in the mouth, a characteristic sweet, caramelized onion flavour, and an aroma reminiscent of roast lamb or wet wool. Hard goat's milk cheeses have a subtle almond taste.

MANCHEGO

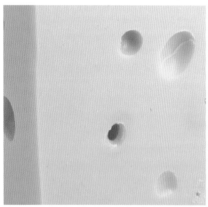

BUBBLES *The holes in Swiss-style cheeses are formed by gas bubbles created when the cheese is moved to a warm room for secondary ripening, activating the starter culture.*

Defining Features

Hard cheeses can vary greatly in appearance. Traditional hard British cheeses are clothbound drums or tall cylinders. The Dutch and Swiss tend to make large boulders or wheels with polished or waxed rinds. Spanish cheeses usually bear the imprint of plaited reeds or the wooden moulds in which they were drained. Producers in France and Italy make hundreds of different hard cheeses, from smooth barrel-shaped Pecorino to enormous wheels of Beaufort, with its thin, tough rind.

FLAVOUR *When young they are slightly sharp or buttery sweet; with age they dry out and the taste intensifies, becoming fruity and tangy.*

COLOUR *This varies with the seasons – pale when animals are hay-fed in winter, but brighter yellows come with fresh summer grazing.*

MOISTURE *The amount of whey expelled determines the texture. The more moisture removed, the longer the maturation, and more complex the final flavours.*

TEXTURE *This category ranges from textures that are creamy, to flexible, through to brittle.*

FAT CONTENT *They have a fat content of 28–34 per cent per 100g.*

AGE *Considered ripe from a few weeks old to three years.*

RIND *This varies enormously from thin and leathery to very hard and thick. Some types are waxed, polished, or bound in cloth.*

How They're Made

Hard cheeses fall into one of two categories. Pressed uncooked cheeses are lightly pressed for a few hours and eaten from one week old when still mild and springy. Cooked and pressed cheeses are heated in the whey and then pressed. Different temperatures give various results. Other methods include milling the curds between cutting and pressing to expel extra whey and create a finer texture; soaking in brine to achieve a thick rind; or washing the curds in hot water to scald them, creating a supple texture.

1

After the coagulation process, *the cheese curd is sliced using different-sized giant combs with knife-sharp wires.*

2

When making washed-curd *cheeses, such as Gouda, hot water is added to the vat of curd, which gives the cheese a sweeter taste.*

3

Some cheeses, *such as Parmigiano-Reggiano, are placed in brine baths for up to 21 days, where the salt draws out more of the whey.*

4

Pressing is often *carried out by hand. The pressure is increased gradually to avoid loosing too much whey too quickly.*

5

To prevent moisture loss *as they ripen, some cheeses are sealed with wax, wrapped in cloth, or sometimes rubbed with lard.*

How to Enjoy

UNCOOKED The most versatile of any cheese type, hard cheeses are ideal for cheeseboards. They can also be shaved or grated into salads, dips, and dressings, for instance Parmigiano-Reggiano in pesto.

COOKED Hard cheeses play an integral role in the culinary history of the country where they are made. Thermized cheeses (see Emmentaler, right) such as Gruyère and Beaufort become stretchy when heated, making them perfect for grilling or fondues rather than in sauces. Others melt completely, while very hard cheeses such as Parmigiano-Reggiano simply dissolve, adding flavour but not texture; both these styles are excellent when added to sauces, pasta, and soups.

WITH DRINKS Their high fat content and stronger, more intense taste marries best with red wines. They absorb the rough edges of young wines or soften the tannin in wines such as Cabernet Sauvignon or Barolo. White wines bring out the fruitier nature of the cheese, while beer and cider, with their natural acidity, make equally good companions.

Excellent Examples

Manchego DOP
The interior has tiny eyeholes and an oily sheen typical of hard ewe's milk cheeses. The wooden board on which it is drained makes the ridges on its base. (See pp160–61)

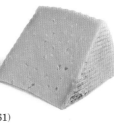

Emmentaler
The milk is heated to 54°C (129°F), a process known as thermizing, resulting in sweet, fruity flavours and an elastic texture. (See p240–41)

Grana Padano PDO
Curds cut into rice-sized pieces give this cheese a brittle texture. It has a thick, hard rind from soaking in brine for 21 days and tastes sweet, like ripe pineapple. (See p120)

Cheddar
Cheddar curds are cooked at 40°C (104°F), then milled before being pressed to create a smooth, very creamy texture and a savoury, raw-onion tang. (See pp178–79)

Mimolette
This cheese has a dry crust that is often attacked by harmless cheese mites, creating a rind like a rusty cannonball. (See p67)

Blue Cheeses

STICKY TO CRUSTY RIND · STREAKED WITH BLUE MOULD · SPICY TANG

Blue moulds are members of the penicillin family but, unlike white moulds, they pefer to grow inside a cheese. They create a seemingly endless array of wonderful cheeses from dense, buttery Stilton to sweet Gorgonzola with its luscious, gooey texture and spicy tang. Ewe's milk blue cheeses such as Roquefort retain the sweet, burnt-caramel taste of the milk that offsets the sharp, salty, steely blue finish. Most European blues are wrapped in tin foil, ensuring their rinds remain damp and sticky and develop a multitude of moulds layered on them, while traditional British blues have rough, dry, crusty, orange-brown rinds, often splashed with blue and grey moulds.

STILTON

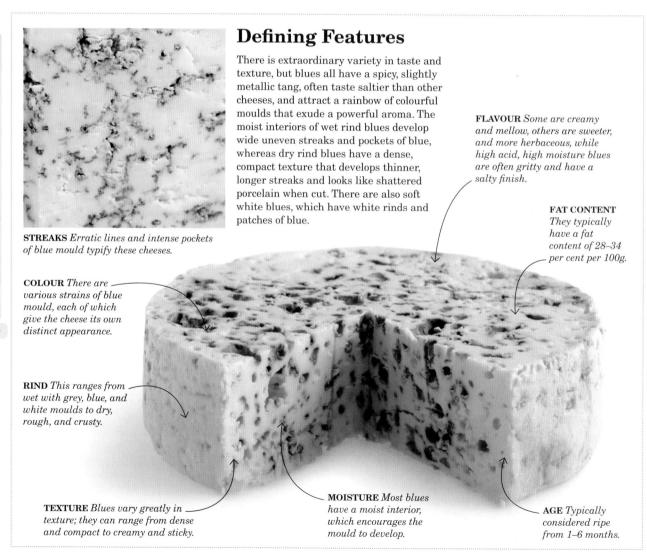

STREAKS *Erratic lines and intense pockets of blue mould typify these cheeses.*

Defining Features

There is extraordinary variety in taste and texture, but blues all have a spicy, slightly metallic tang, often taste saltier than other cheeses, and attract a rainbow of colourful moulds that exude a powerful aroma. The moist interiors of wet rind blues develop wide uneven streaks and pockets of blue, whereas dry rind blues have a dense, compact texture that develops thinner, longer streaks and looks like shattered porcelain when cut. There are also soft white blues, which have white rinds and patches of blue.

FLAVOUR *Some are creamy and mellow, others are sweeter, and more herbaceous, while high acid, high moisture blues are often gritty and have a salty finish.*

FAT CONTENT *They typically have a fat content of 28–34 per cent per 100g.*

COLOUR *There are various strains of blue mould, each of which give the cheese its own distinct appearance.*

RIND *This ranges from wet with grey, blue, and white moulds to dry, rough, and crusty.*

TEXTURE *Blues vary greatly in texture; they can range from dense and compact to creamy and sticky.*

MOISTURE *Most blues have a moist interior, which encourages the mould to develop.*

AGE *Typically considered ripe from 1–6 months.*

How They're Made

Cheeses were once ripened in caves, stone cellars, or barns, which were havens for blue moulds in particular. They entered the warm interior through cracks in the rind and grew in the gaps in the fresh curd. Today, the blue mould is typically added to the milk in powder form, and then the young cheese is pierced to allow air to enter and the mould to turn blue. Soft style blue cheeses are injected with moulds because they are too soft and dense for the mould to spread naturally.

2

Blue cheeses *are never pressed. The curd must remain loosely packed, leaving space for the blue mould to grow and spread.*

4

After a few weeks, *the cheese is pierced with rods to create tunnels in the curd. Exposed to air, the blue mould flourishes in these gaps.*

1

Along with *the starter culture, penicillin mould is added to the warm milk or sometimes, as shown here, to the freshly formed curd.*

3

After two or three weeks, *the sides of some types of blue cheeses are scraped smooth to cover any cracks before being rubbed with salt.*

5

To check the texture *and the even spread of the blue mould, a grader will remove some cheese with a cheese "iron" and then replace it.*

Excellent Examples

Stilton
This cheese has the dry rind typical of many British blue cheeses. The dense buttery interior forces the blue mould to develop as thin broken streaks. (See pp192–193)

Roquefort
The famous ewe's milk blue has a loose, moist interior, allowing *Penicillium roqueforti* to grow *en masse* as thin streaks and large scattered pockets. (See pp82–83)

Gorgonzola
Thick, blue-green streaks and scattered patches fill the interior. Its thin wet, sticky rind, finely dusted with mould, typifies traditional European blues. (See pp108–09)

Bavaria Blu
This is a soft white-style blue. Pockets (rather than streaks) of blue result from injecting blue mould directly into this creamy, dense cheese. (See p234)

BLUE CHEESES

21

How to Enjoy

UNCOOKED Blue cheeses are essential on any cheese platter and, with the exception of the brie-style blues, also add another dimension to salads, especially when crumbled over flageolet beans, walnuts, and peppery rocket dressed with honeyed vinaigrette. Walnut bread is especially good with blue cheeses, and a drizzle of honey brings out the subtlety of the cheese.

COOKED Stir small amounts into pasta, soups, and sauces to elevate dishes into classics like celery and Stilton soup; pasta with pinenuts and Gorgonzola; or grilled steak with blue cheese sauce.

WITH DRINKS Try a Tawny or late-bottled-vintage (LBV) Port rather than a richer vintage or less complex ruby Ports, as they tend to overpower the majority of blue cheeses. If Port is not to your taste, a sweet or dry Riesling can make a perfect partner. Match the dessert wine Sauternes only with the very sharp, salty, steely blues, such as Roquefort, with its sweet undertones.

Flavour-added Cheeses

COLOURFUL AND EXOTIC RINDS · HARD OR SEMI-SOFT · SAVOURY OR SWEET

With their bright colours, the vast array of flavour-added cheeses stands out on deli counters across the world. Smoked cheeses have existed since man learnt to make hard cheeses and stored them near their wood fires. In the 16th century, Dutch cheesemakers incorporated the exotic spices brought back from the East Indies into Edam and Gouda, producing a tantalizing mélange of flavours. Today, most flavour-added cheeses are well-known hard cheeses blended with fruit, spices or herbs, and shaped into a round.

HEREFORD HOP *Its rind is encrusted with toasted hops*

Defining Features

Flavour-added cheeses can be divided into four distinct types. Natural smoked cheeses have a golden brown to caramel-coloured rind but the internal colour is not affected. Traditional-style examples (based on the original Dutch method where the ingredients are matured with the fresh curds) absorb and intensify the aroma and essence of the added ingredients. Rind-flavoured cheeses have various ingredients, such as vine leaves, toasted hops, or grape-must, pressed into the rind. The majority, however, are re-formed cheeses, where a young cheese is broken up, blended with added ingredients, then re-formed.

A fine grey-white mould grows across the cheese, emphasizing the nettles.

Yarg Cornish Cheese
Probably the best-known British example of a rind-flavoured cheese, its elegant rind of interwoven forest-green nettles imparts a subtle flavour. (See pp200–201)

Wensleydale with Cranberries
The most successful re-formed flavour-added cheeses blend young, low-acid cheeses with sweet, dried fruit. Here, the young hard cheese Wensleydale has been crumbled up with cranberries. (See p204.)

Taramundi
This traditional-style Spanish cheese has a semi-soft texture and is made by adding local crushed walnuts and hazelnuts. (See p162)

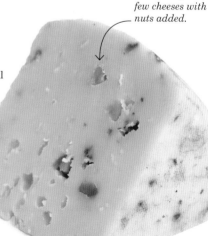

One of only a few cheeses with nuts added.

After pressing, the re-formed cheese is softer than the original.

How to Enjoy

UNCOOKED The choice of flavours to add to cheese is limited only by the imagination of the cheesemaker. Flavour-added cheeses with dried fruit are typical served in place of dessert, while only those with garlic, herbs, chives or that are smoked work in salads. Weird combinations such as those with chocolate, sticky toffee pudding, or fruitcake are curiosities best left to those who enjoy experimenting with unconventional flavours.

COOKED Traditionally-made semi-soft or hard flavoured cheeses behave like their unflavoured counterparts when cooked and can add character to basics like baked potatoes or pasta – smoked cheeses work especially well for this. Additional ideas can be found under the entries for individual cheeses.

WITH DRINKS Beers nicely complement savoury-flavoured cheeses with onion, chives, garlic, oak smoke, and chilli, while the sweet dessert cheeses are better with cider or Chardonnay. The tannin and red berry flavour of red wines tends to clash with all but the hard cheeses like Cheddar with Garlic or Gouda with Peppercorns.

How They're Made

Smoked cheeses are matured over natural fires. Traditional flavour-added cheeses are made by adding the flavour ingredients to the curd of semi-soft and hard cheeses. Rind-flavoured cheeses are covered with the flavour ingredient after the cheese has been pressed. Re-formed cheeses are made by breaking up the curd of a young hard cheese, blending it with different flavours, then re-forming and pressing it.

Herbs & Garlic

Fresh herbs can deteriorate within a cheese's damp interior, so they are mostly used dried. Examples include sage, nettles, basil, rosemary, and lavender. Garlic and chives are also popular.

Nagelkaas means "nail cheese". This refers to the shape of the cloves studded in its interior.

Nagelkaas

This traditional-style flavour-added cheese from the Netherlands is based on a Gouda recipe and uses cloves. The orange colour comes from adding annatto (a natural dye derived from the *Bixa orellana* seed), and provides an attractive contrast to the dark cloves. (See p229)

Nuts

Nuts are not commonly used, but walnuts are sometimes added to fresh cheeses as they have a high acidity and ripen quickly.

Wonderful smoky bacon taste, and nut-brown rind.

Idiazábal

A great example of a natural smoked cheese, Idiazábal was traditionally stored in the rafters of shepherds' huts in Northern Spain, where the young cheeses would absorb the smoke from the wood fires. Today, they are cold-smoked in special rooms over a few days. (See p155)

Spices

Cumin, caraway seeds, black or red peppercorns, paprika, and cloves are widely used as they make natural partners with the savoury tang of hard cheeses.

Dried Fruit

Adding fruit is a modern trend. The most popular are candied citrus, dried berries, apple flakes, figs, and apricots.

The Perfect Cheeseboard

There are no hard and fast rules to determining a cheese category or type, but some guidance can enable you to create an amazing and memorable cheeseboard. If you are having your cheeseboard with a meal, make sure you enjoy it after the main meal but before dessert.

ACCOMPANIMENTS

Chargrilled vegetables, **dried fruit**, **apples**, and **pickled walnuts** work well with almost all cheeses.

Celery and **grapes** can be enjoyed with blues and strong hard cheeses.

Crusty or **fruity bread**, rather than biscuits, allow you to experience the texture and feel of the cheeses in your mouth.

THE BASICS

Buy the cheeses as near to the time you want to eat them as possible – they will not improve in a fridge.

Shop somewhere that encourages you to taste.

Support your local cheesemakers.

Search for medal winners and the AOC, DOC, or PDO label on European cheeses.

Remove the cheeses from the fridge at least an hour before serving so that they come to room temperature.

THE BOARD

An elegant **wooden board**, **chunk of driftwood**, or **wicker basket** lined with linen cloth gives the cheese a fresh and natural appearance.

Slate looks great; **marble** or **granite** is marvellous, but is often very heavy.

Decorate the board with some wild flowers, herbs, or seasonal leaves.

Alternatively, prepare individual plates with small chunks and wedges of cheese.

FLAVOUR-ADDED
Yarg Cornish Cheese pp200–201

SEMI-SOFT
Taleggio pp136–137

QUINCE

AGED FRESH
Sainte-Maure de Touraine pp92–93

DRIED FIGS

24

THE CHEESES

One superb large cheese is better than three or four small wedges, which can be in danger of drying out quickly.

Colour and shape should come from an interesting combination of cheeses, not from the garnishes.

Allow around 55g (2oz) of each cheese per person.

Offer diversity by choosing cheeses with different textures. Use the classifications on pages 10–23 to give you an idea of the range of textures available.

For variety of flavour, provide at least one goat's or sheep's milk cheese, rather than relying only on cow's milk cheeses.

Pre-cut a couple of wedges to show guests how it's done. You could remove the rind from blue or hard cheeses to avoid anyone cutting across the wedge instead of into smaller wedges.

THE WINE

The union of cheese and wine has moved writers to fill endless columns with riveting descriptions of distinguished or disreputable marriages, but there really is no right or wrong. Some combinations simply make the senses whirr, while others definitely do not.

Fresh, **Aged Fresh**, and **Soft-White** cheeses prefer dry, crisp fruity wines and ciders that won't dominate.
Semi-soft cheeses, especially washed rind, need a feisty, aromatic white or *eau de vie* to pair with their sweetness.
Hard cheeses pair well with red wines. The harder and darker the cheese, the heavier, richer, and redder the wine.
Blue cheeses work superbly with sweet pudding wines or aromatic whites. The sweetness cuts through the sharpness of the cheese.
Flavour-added cheeses work with different types of wines, it really depends on what flavour has been added.

HARD
Berkswell p171

SOFT WHITE
Camembert de Normandie p44

BLUE
Valdeón p164

SPRIG OF ROSEMARY

FRESH
Innes Button p183

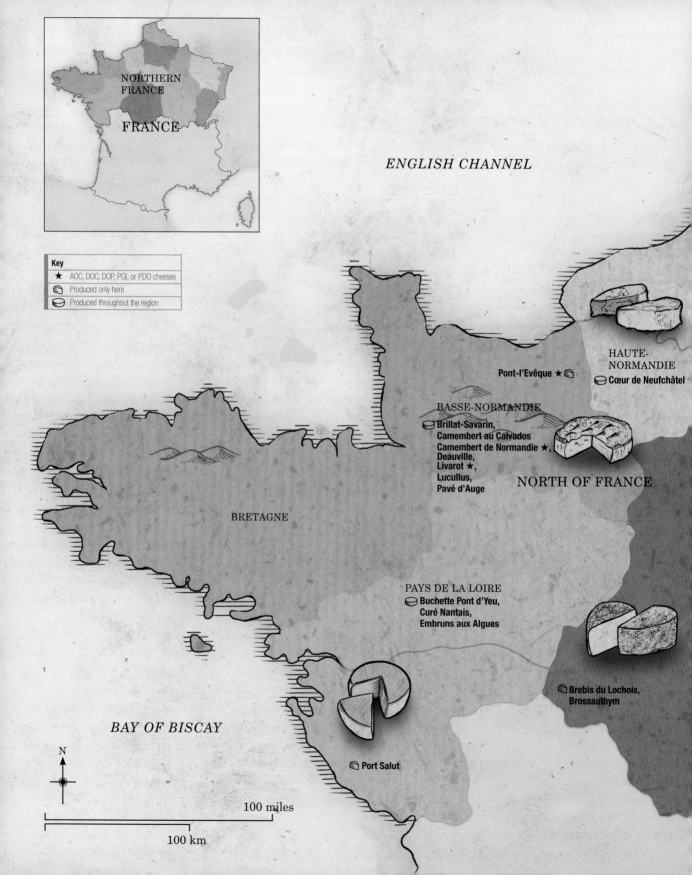

NORTHERN
FRANCE

FRANCE

Key

★ AOC, DOC, DOP, PGI, or PDO cheeses

🪚 Produced only here

🫓 Produced throughout the region

ENGLISH CHANNEL

HAUTE-
NORMANDIE

Pont-l'Evêque ★ 🪚   🫓 Cœur de Neufchâtel

BASSE-NORMANDIE

🫓 Brillat-Savarin,
Camembert au Calvados
Camembert de Normandie ★,
Deauville,
Livarot ★,
Lucullus,
Pavé d'Auge

NORTH OF FRANCE

BRETAGNE

PAYS DE LA LOIRE

🫓 Buchette Pont d'Yeu,
Curé Nantais,
Embruns aux Algues

🪚 Brebis du Lochois,
Brossauthym

BAY OF BISCAY

🪚 Port Salut

N

100 miles

100 km

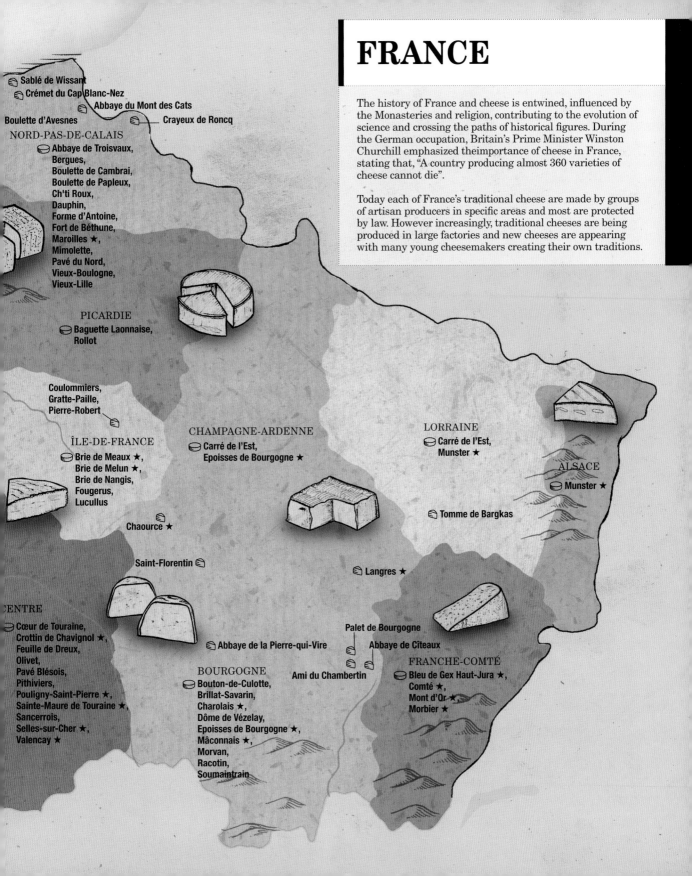

FRANCE

The history of France and cheese is entwined, influenced by the Monasteries and religion, contributing to the evolution of science and crossing the paths of historical figures. During the German occupation, Britain's Prime Minister Winston Churchill emphasized the importance of cheese in France, stating that, "A country producing almost 360 varieties of cheese cannot die".

Today each of France's traditional cheese are made by groups of artisan producers in specific areas and most are protected by law. However increasingly, traditional cheeses are being produced in large factories and new cheeses are appearing with many young cheesemakers creating their own traditions.

Sablé de Wissant
Crémet du Cap Blanc-Nez
Abbaye du Mont des Cats
Boulette d'Avesnes
Crayeux de Roncq

NORD-PAS-DE-CALAIS

Abbaye de Troisvaux,
Bergues,
Boulette de Cambrai,
Boulette de Papleux,
Ch'ti Roux,
Dauphin,
Forme d'Antoine,
Fort de Béthune,
Maroilles ★,
Mimolette,
Pavé du Nord,
Vieux-Boulogne,
Vieux-Lille

PICARDIE

Baguette Laonnaise,
Rollot

Coulommiers,
Gratte-Paille,
Pierre-Robert

ÎLE-DE-FRANCE

Brie de Meaux ★,
Brie de Melun ★,
Brie de Nangis,
Fougerus,
Lucullus

CHAMPAGNE-ARDENNE

Carré de l'Est,
Epoisses de Bourgogne ★

Chaource ★

Saint-Florentin

LORRAINE

Carré de l'Est,
Munster ★

ALSACE

Munster ★

Tomme de Bargkas

Langres ★

CENTRE

Cœur de Touraine,
Crottin de Chavignol ★,
Feuille de Dreux,
Olivet,
Pavé Blésois,
Pithiviers,
Pouligny-Saint-Pierre ★,
Sainte-Maure de Touraine ★,
Sancerrois,
Selles-sur-Cher ★,
Valencay ★

Abbaye de la Pierre-qui-Vire

BOURGOGNE

Bouton-de-Culotte,
Brillat-Savarin,
Charolais ★,
Dôme de Vézelay,
Epoisses de Bourgogne ★,
Mâconnais ★,
Morvan,
Racotin,
Soumaintrain

Ami du Chambertin

Palet de Bourgogne
Abbaye de Cîteaux

FRANCHE-COMTÉ

Bleu de Gex Haut-Jura ★,
Comté ★,
Mont d'Or ★,
Morbier ★

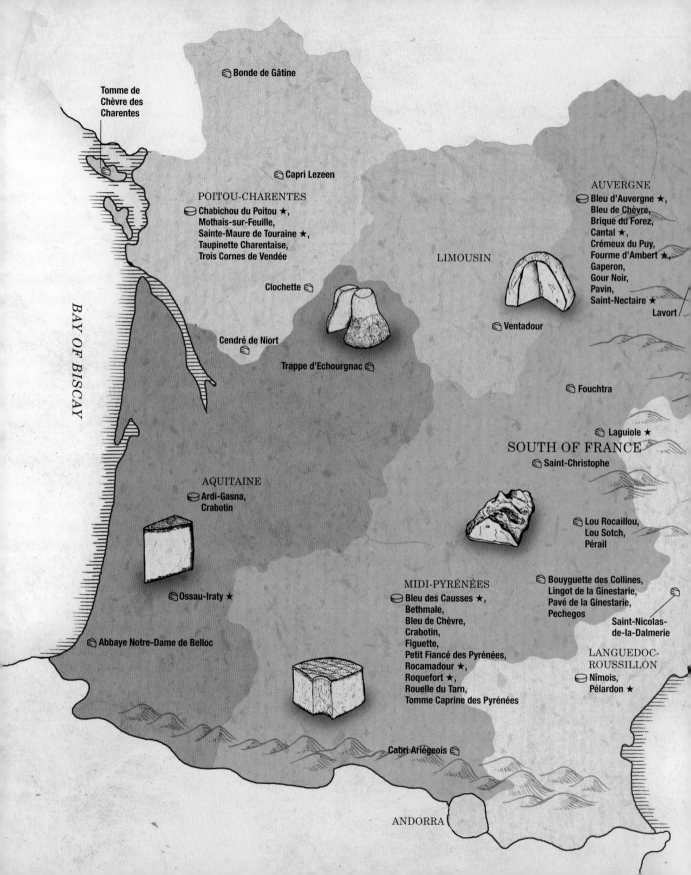

Tomme de Chèvre des Charentes

🧀 Bonde de Gâtine

🧀 Capri Lezeen

POITOU-CHARENTES
🧀 Chabichou du Poitou ★,
Mothais-sur-Feuille,
Sainte-Maure de Touraine ★,
Taupinette Charentaise,
Trois Cornes de Vendée

Clochette 🧀

🧀 Cendré de Niort

Trappe d'Echourgnac 🧀

AUVERGNE
🧀 Bleu d'Auvergne ★,
Bleu de Chèvre,
Brique du Forez,
Cantal ★,
Crémeux du Puy,
Fourme d'Ambert ★,
Gaperon,
Gour Noir,
Pavin,
Saint-Nectaire ★

LIMOUSIN

🧀 Lavort

🧀 Ventadour

🧀 Fouchtra

🧀 Laguiole ★

SOUTH OF FRANCE

🧀 Saint-Christophe

🧀 Lou Rocaillou,
Lou Sotch,
Pérail

AQUITAINE
🧀 Ardi-Gasna,
Crabotin

🧀 Ossau-Iraty ★

🧀 Abbaye Notre-Dame de Belloc

MIDI-PYRÉNÉES
🧀 Bleu des Causses ★,
Bethmale,
Bleu de Chèvre,
Crabotin,
Figuette,
Petit Fiancé des Pyrénées,
Rocamadour ★,
Roquefort ★,
Rouelle du Tarn,
Tomme Caprine des Pyrénées

🧀 Bouyguette des Collines,
Lingot de la Ginestarie,
Pavé de la Ginestarie,
Pechegos

Saint-Nicolas-de-la-Dalmerie

LANGUEDOC-ROUSSILLON
🧀 Nîmois,
Pélardon ★

🧀 Cabri Ariégeois

BAY OF BISCAY

ANDORRA

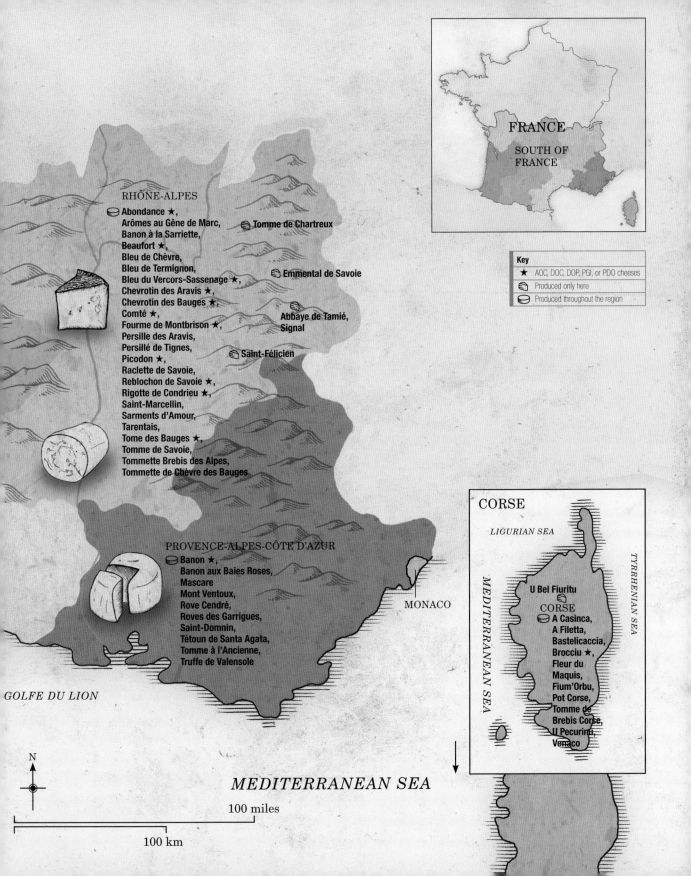

FRANCE

SOUTH OF
FRANCE

Key
★ AOC, DOC, DOP, PGI, or PDO cheeses
Produced only here
Produced throughout the region

RHÔNE-ALPES
Abondance ★,
Arômes au Gêne de Marc,
Banon à la Sarriette,
Beaufort ★,
Bleu de Chèvre,
Bleu de Termignon,
Bleu du Vercors-Sassenage ★,
Chevrotin des Aravis ★,
Chevrotin des Bauges ★,
Comté ★,
Fourme de Montbrison ★,
Persille des Aravis,
Persillé de Tignes,
Picodon ★,
Raclette de Savoie,
Reblochon de Savoie ★,
Rigotte de Condrieu ★,
Saint-Marcellin,
Sarments d'Amour,
Tarentais,
Tome des Bauges ★,
Tomme de Savoie,
Tommette Brebis des Alpes,
Tommette de Chèvre des Bauges

Tomme de Chartreux

Emmental de Savoie

Abbaye de Tamié,
Signal

Saint-Félicien

PROVENCE-ALPES-CÔTE D'AZUR
Banon ★,
Banon aux Baies Roses,
Mascare
Mont Ventoux,
Rove Cendré,
Roves des Garrigues,
Saint-Domnin,
Tétoun de Santa Agata,
Tomme à l'Ancienne,
Truffe de Valensole

MONACO

GOLFE DU LION

CORSE
LIGURIAN SEA

MEDITERRANEAN SEA

TYRRHENIAN SEA

U Bel Fiuritu
CORSE
A Casinca,
A Filetta,
Bastelicaccia,
Brocciu ★,
Fleur du
Maquis,
Fium'Orbu,
Pot Corse,
Tomme de
Brebis Corse,
U Pecurinu,
Venaco

N

MEDITERRANEAN SEA

100 miles

100 km

Abbaye de Cîteaux

The Abbey of St Nicolas de Cîteaux was founded 900 years ago, but it was only in 1925 that the resident Trappist monks began to make this delicious and exclusive cheese. It is rarely found outside the region because only 60 tons of it are made each year from the milk of 70 Montbéliarde cows.

TASTING NOTES This sweet, smooth, and creamy cheese with a greyish-yellow rind is worth seeking out. It is relatively mild compared with other washed rind, Trappist-style cheeses.

HOW TO ENJOY It is delicious served with fruity and light red wines, such as a Beaujolais or a Bourgogne.

FRANCE Dijon, Bourgogne	
Age 2 months	
Weight and Shape 750g (1lb 10oz), round	
Size D. 18cm (7in), H. 4cm (1½in)	
Milk Cow	
Classification Semi-soft	
Producer Abbey of St Nicolas de Cîteaux	

Abbaye du Mont des Cats

Produced since 1890 by monks at the Abbey of Saint-Marie-du-Mont in northern France, Mont des Cats is a semi-soft, washed cheese made from the milk of cows from neighbouring farms.

TASTING NOTES The thin, leathery, orange rind covers a pale yellow, supple, elastic interior. The cheese melts in the mouth with a subtle, yet pronounced, milky flavour and the rustic aroma of hay.

HOW TO ENJOY It is delicious, washed down with beer or a light, fruity wine, such as a Loire red or a dry white cadet.

FRANCE Godewaersvelde, Nord-Pas-de-Calais	
Age 2 months	
Weight and Shape 2kg (4lb 6oz), round	
Size D. 25cm (10in), H. 3.5cm (1½in)	
Milk Cow	
Classification Semi-soft	
Producer Abbaye du Mont des Cats	

Abbaye Notre-Dame de Belloc

This rich, fermier cheese, made from the milk of a local red-nosed breed of ewes, is one of the last few "Abbaye" or Trappist cheeses produced by monks at an abbey in the traditional way.

TASTING NOTES Its long ageing period gives it a very rich taste, with a pronounced caramel-like, fruity flavour. Beneath its crusty, greyish-brown rind, the paste is firm yet supple and softer than most other ewe's milk Basque cheeses, with a surprisingly mild scent.

HOW TO ENJOY Avoid strong red wines that might mask the flavour; try sweet whites, such as Pacherenc du Vic-Bilh.

FRANCE Urt, Aquitaine	
Age Best around 6 months	
Weight and Shape 5.5kg (12lb), round	
Size D. 25cm (10in), H. 8.5cm (3½in)	
Milk Ewe	
Classification Hard	
Producer Abbaye de Belloc	

Abbaye de la Pierre-qui-Vire

This Benedictine abbey in the Yonne region was founded in 1850 by a priest named Dom Muard. Since 1920, it has also become known for its delicious, semi-soft, washed cheese. It is similar to Epoisses, and is made from the milk of the monks' herd of 40 cows.

TASTING NOTES The brick-red rind covers a soft, smooth, and supple cheese that has a distinct country taste and a strong aroma.

HOW TO ENJOY As part of a cheeseboard or mix into mashed potatoes and grill. Serve with any lively, full-bodied red Burgundy, such as Beaune.

FRANCE Bourgogne, Saint-Léger-Vauban	
Age 6–10 weeks	
Weight and Shape 200g (7oz), round	
Size D. 10cm (4in), H. 2.5cm (1in)	
Milk Cow	
Classification Semi-soft	
Producer Abbaye de la Pierre-qui-Vivre	

Abbaye de Tamié

At the Abbaye of Tamié, in the Savoie mountains, the incumbent monks produce a cheese that is similar to the well-known Reblochon (see pp74–75) but not as strong. The finished product is sold wrapped in blue paper decorated with the white cross of Malta.

TASTING NOTES This semi-soft, washed cheese has an orange-coloured, thin leathery crust; supple, springy texture; and a mild, sweet, milky taste.

HOW TO ENJOY This elegant, subtly flavoured cheese stands proudly on a cheeseboard, served with a light and fruity red, white or rosé Savoie wine, such as an Apremont or Mondeuse.

FRANCE Savoie, Rhône-Alpes	
Age 1–2 months	
Weight and Shape 750g (1lb 10oz), round	
Size D. 18cm (7in), H. 4.5cm (2in)	
Milk Cow	
Classification Semi-soft	
Producer Abbaye de Tamié	

Abondance AOC

AOC-protected since 1990, this hard cheese is produced by various cheesemakers using milk from three breeds of native cows, which are renowned for their excellent milk: Montbéliardes, Tarines, and Abondance. To sustain the quality and flavour of the milk, the cattle are not fed silage or any other fermented fodder.

TASTING NOTES This strong-smelling cheese has an immediate, subtle taste that can be light or full flavoured, depending on the season and producer.

HOW TO ENJOY Pair this smooth and supple cheese with a local white wine, preferably a dry one, or a Beaujolais.

FRANCE Rhône-Alpes	
Age Best around 2–3 months	
Weight and Shape 5kg–15kg (11–33lb), wheel	
Size D. 40–46cm (14–18in), H. 7.5–10cm (3–4in)	
Milk Cow	
Classification Hard	
Producer Various	

A Casinca

Robust, almost wild, Corsican goats roam freely over vast landscapes, infusing their milk with various natural aromas. A hand-moulded delight, A Casinca is one of the best washed-rind cheeses that they produce.

TASTING NOTES Although it has a pronounced taste and a rather strong smell, A Casinca is by no means unrefined. Ageing and the gentle climate improve it, creating a unique nutty flavour.

HOW TO ENJOY For an exotic taste, serve A Casinca with a white wine, such as Condrieux, which is made from grapes grown in sunny climates.

FRANCE Corse		
Age 1½–4 months		
Weight and Shape 400g (14oz), round		
Size D. 15cm (6in), H. 3cm (1in)		
Milk Goat		
Classification Semi-soft		
Producer Various		

A Filetta

The name reflects the roots of this artisanal cheese; *a filetta* means "fern" in the Corsican language. As an added reminder of its provenance, this semi-soft cheese is most often produced decorated with a fern leaf on top.

TASTING NOTES This truly original taste, tinged with fern and the smell of a cellar, which can be a bit strong for some palates, is definitely worth a try. The grazing is quasi-wilderness, so this cheese has more personality and more natural flavour than many others.

HOW TO ENJOY Perfect served with a fig jam to offset its trademark sharpness and with a Corsican red or white wine.

FRANCE Corse		
Age About 6 weeks		
Weight and Shape 350g (12oz), round		
Size D. 10cm (4in), H. 3cm (1in)		
Milk Ewe		
Classification Semi-soft		
Producer Various		

Ami du Chambertin

Raymond Gaugry created this artisan cheese in 1950 as an accompaniment to the famous wine, Gevrey Chambertin, that is made close by. Although the cheese is made in a modern creamery, much of the work is done by hand.

TASTING NOTES The rind is washed with local Marc de Bourgogne brandy, giving it an orange colour and a powerful taste. The paste has a mouth-watering, creamy texture.

HOW TO ENJOY Ami du Chambertin is best appreciated with a glass of Gevrey Chambertin or a Chassagne Montrachet – delicious wines that have a long finish and are very flavoursome.

FRANCE Brochon, Bourgogne		
Age 2 months		
Weight and Shape 250g (9oz), round		
Size D. 8.5cm (3⅓in), H. 4.5cm (2in)		
Milk Cow		
Classification Semi-soft		
Producer Gaugry dairy		

Ardi-Gasna

Ardi-Gasna means "sheep's cheese" in the Basque language, so it's no surprise that this hard cheese comes from the milk of ewes grazing on alpine pastures high in the Pyrénées. It can be eaten all year round, but the best cheeses are made using milk from lush spring or summer grazing.

TASTING NOTES It grows sharper with age, but even the youngest cheeses have a sophisticated, nutty taste and a pleasant aroma.

HOW TO ENJOY A fruity red wine is the perfect match for a young cheese. Pair sharper ones with full-bodied reds. Serve with jam, honey, or walnuts.

FRANCE Aquitaine		
Age 2–24 months, best at 5 months		
Weight and Shape 5kg (10lb), round		
Size D. 32.5cm (13in), H. 7.5cm (3in)		
Milk Ewe		
Classification Hard		
Producer Various		

Arômes au Gêne de Marc

This fermier cheese is produced using an ancient method of curing and preserving. A ripe cheese is placed in a barrel of marc – the damp skins, pips, and stalks of pressed grapes – that slowly permeate the cheese.

TASTING NOTES It has a strong and bittersweet flavour that is distinctly yeasty. As the cheese ages, its texture evolves from creamy to hard.

HOW TO ENJOY This cheese is an ideal partner to a light Beaujolais-village or a sweet dessert wine such as Muscat de Beaumes de Venise.

FRANCE Rhône-Alpes		
Age 1 month		
Weight and Shape 80–120g (3–4oz), disk		
Size D. 6–7cm (2½–3in), H. 2–3cm (¾–1in)		
Milk Cow		
Classification Aged fresh		
Producer Various		

Baguette Laonnaise

Made at a distinctive creamery or industrially produced cheese, Baguette Laonnaise is usually brick shaped but can also be found resembling a baguette. This feature, and the fact that it is produced in the city of Laon, gives the cheese its name.

TASTING NOTES It has a moist, red, washed rind and a highly pronounced flavour that is similar to that of the Maroilles.

HOW TO ENJOY You can eat this semi-soft cheese alongside all very full-bodied red wines of substance and character, and you could even wash it down with a glass of beer.

FRANCE Picardie		
Age 2–3 months		
Weight and Shape 450g (1lb), brick		
Size 15cm (6in), H. 4.5cm (2in)		
Milk Cow		
Classification Semi-soft		
Producer Various		

Banon AOC

A speciality of the mountains of Lure in Provence, this cheese is sold rustically wrapped in layers of chestnut leaves and bound with raffia. The Banon has benefited from status AOC since 2003.

TASTING NOTES When young, the flavour is mild and lactic, becoming slightly nutty with age. As the leaves dry, moulds develop softening the paste and the flavour becomes more nutty with a distinct goaty tang.

HOW TO ENJOY This cheese is a real pleasure to share with friends. Serve with any fruity and lively red and white, and rosé Provençal wines.

FRANCE Haute-Provence
Age 2 weeks–2 months
Weight and Shape 90–120g (3–4oz), round
Size D. 6–7cm (2½–3in), H. 2.5–3cm (1in)
Milk Goat
Classification Aged fresh
Producer Various

Banon aux Baies Roses

Provence has a history of making goat's cheese that can be traced back to the Roman times; some even claim that the 'Banon' cheese was enjoyed by the 1st-century Roman emperor, Antoninus Pius. This fresh variation is decorated with pink peppercorns (*baies roses*), the dried berries from the Baies rose plant.

TASTING NOTES The mild, nutty flavour of this cheese is counterpointed by the sweet, distinct anise character of the pink peppercorns.

HOW TO ENJOY This beautiful-looking addition to the cheeseboard can be served with a fresh rose to decorate.

FRANCE Haute-Provence
Age 2–8 weeks
Weight and Shape 90–120g (3–4oz), round
Size D. 6–7cm (2½–3in), H. 2.5–3cm (1in)
Milk Goat
Classification Fresh
Producer Various

Banon à la Sarriette

The Provençal climate provides perfect growing conditions for some of the most wonderful aromatic flowers and plants, such as lavender and thyme, that subtly flavour the milk of the grazing goats. In this version of the region's Banon, the herb savory creates yet another layer of flavour.

TASTING NOTES The herb has a strong sharp flavour; its pungency adds a new dimension to this creamy, slightly nutty cheese.

HOW TO ENJOY Serve with an aromatic wine, such as a Gewürztraminer.

FRANCE Rhône-Alpes
Age 2–8 weeks
Weight and Shape 90–120g (3–4oz), round
Size D. 6–7cm (2½–3in), H. 2.5–3cm (1in)
Milk Goat
Classification Fresh
Producer Various

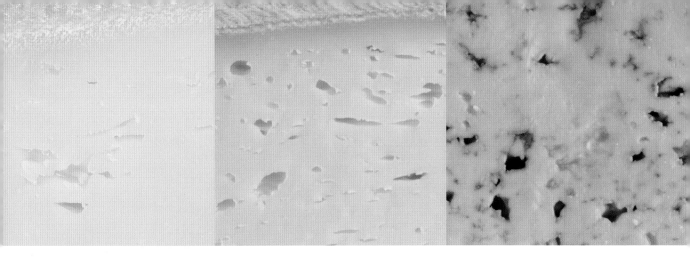

Bergues

This *fermier* cheese is named after the town in which it originated, and is still produced at Bergues in Flandres, around 12km (7.5 miles) from the Belgian border. It is a very popular cheese throughout northern France.

TASTING NOTES During the curing stage, this semi-soft cheese is repeatedly washed with brine and beer. This gives it a sharp, distinctive flavour against its supple and elastic texture.

HOW TO ENJOY It can be grated, grilled, or baked with vegetable dishes, soups, and pasta, and it is best enjoyed when washed down with a chilled beer.

FRANCE Nord-Pas-de-Calais	
Age 2 months	
Weight and shape 2kg (4lb 6oz), round	
Size D. 20cm (8in), H. 4.5cm (2in)	
Milk Cow	
Classification Semi-soft	
Producer Various	

Bethmale

Produced in the Pyrénées, Bethmale is one of the region's best-known cow's milk cheeses and is named after the village where it is made. It has a royal seal of approval, too, as it is said to have been favoured by King Louis VI in the 12th century.

TASTING NOTES The flavour of Bethmale differs depending on how it is produced. Industrial varieties are very mild, while *fermier* varieties have a more pronounced taste.

HOW TO ENJOY Pair this cheese with all fruity and robust wines of Fitou, Corbières, Roussillon, and Madiran.

FRANCE Midi-Pyrénées	
Age 3–4 months	
Weight and Shape 5kg–7kg (11lb–15lb), round	
Size D. 30–40cm (12–16in), H. 4.5–7.5cm (2–3in)	
Milk Cow	
Classification Hard	
Producer Various	

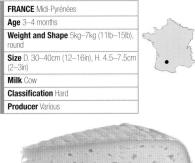

Bleu d'Auvergne AOC

Named after the province in which it originated, Bleu d'Auvergne has been AOC protected since 1975. It is similar to Roquefort, but this cheese is made using cow's rather than ewe's milk.

TASTING NOTES This blue cheese has a very sharp, engaging flavour and is best when made with milk from herds that have grazed the lush summer and autumn mountain pastures.

HOW TO ENJOY This is a delicious addition to salad dressings or hot pasta dishes, or served with chicory, nuts, and raw mushrooms alongside a robust red or sweet white wine.

FRANCE Auvergne	
Age 2–3 months	
Weight and Shape 2.5kg (5½lb), drum	
Size D. 20cm (8in), H. 10cm (4in)	
Milk Cow	
Classification Blue	
Producer Various	

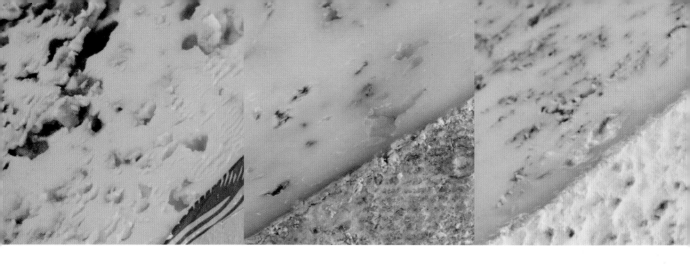

Bleu des Causses AOC

Like Roquefort, this cheese is ripened in natural caves called *fleurines* in the limestone plateaus of the Causses. Bleu des Causses is made with cow's milk and is aged longer than most blues. It has been AOC protected since 1979.

TASTING NOTES The flavour differs depending on the season in which it is produced. Ivory-yellow summer cheeses are milder than the stronger-tasting, white winter cheeses.

HOW TO ENJOY It is excellent in salads and on cheeseboards, and goes well with all lively, well-balanced red wines that have an aromatic note, such as Cornas, Lirac, and Jurançon.

FRANCE Midi-Pyrénées
Age 3–6 months
Weight and Shape 2.3kg–2.6kg (5lb 3oz–5lb 13oz), drum
Size D. 18–20cm (7–8in), H. 7.5–10cm (3–4in)
Milk Cow
Classification Blue
Producer Various

Bleu de Chèvre

As a blue goat's cheese, Bleu de Chèvre is a rare thing. Most French blues are made with cow's milk and a few, such as Roquefort, are made using ewe's milk. This cheese is produced on only a handful of small farms, mainly in the mountains, so it is little-known outside the region.

TASTING NOTES Bleu de Chèvre is dense with erratic patches of blue. It melts in the mouth with a subtle but herbaceous tang from the goat's milk, but is milder than cow's and ewe's milk blues.

HOW TO ENJOY Eat with fresh figs and a glass of sweet Muscat de Beaume de Venise.

FRANCE Auvergne, Rhône Alpes, Midi-Pyrénées
Age 2 months
Weight and Shape 3.6kg (8lb), round
Size D. 19cm (7½in), H. 10cm (4in)
Milk Goat
Classification Blue
Producer Various

Bleu de Gex Haut-Jura AOC

Granted AOC status in 1977, this unusually dense, almost hard, blue cheese is produced in small, traditional dairies using milk from cows grazing the pastures of the Jura mountains.

TASTING NOTES The yeasts and moulds in the mountain grasses and flowers pass through the milk into the cheese, giving the soft interior a speckled blue appearance and a slightly bitter, savoury flavour. Eat it after wiping off the white powdery mould covering it.

HOW TO ENJOY Serve as the locals do with boiled potatoes and a fruity, regional red wine – a Beaujolais or Burgundy.

FRANCE Franche-Comté
Age Around 2–3 months
Weight and Shape 5–6kg (11lb–13lb 3oz). wheel
Size D. 30cm (12in), H. 7.5–10cm (3–4in)
Milk Cow
Classification Blue
Producer Various

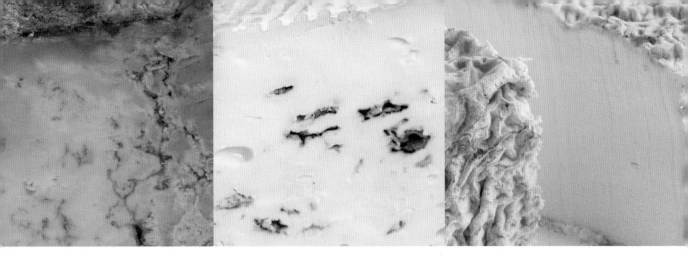

Bleu de Termignon

This blue cheese is produced to very precise specifications. Just four producers make it in summer using milk of cows that graze 1,300m (4,265 feet) up the mountain pastures of the French Alps. The spare, irregular blueing is not the result of piercing, but of wild moulds entering through cracks in the rind.

TASTING NOTES Beneath the rough, crusty, brown-gold rind is a dense, yet crumbly interior with a strong, almost spicy, tang and earthy, refined flavour.

HOW TO ENJOY Team this tasty blue with a glass of Chignin Bergeron or a mellow wine, such as a Tokay.

FRANCE Rhône-Alpes		
Age 4–5 months		
Weight and Shape 7kg (15½lb), drum		
Size D. 29cm (11¾in), H. 15cm (6in)		
Milk Cow		
Classification Blue		
Producer Various		

Bleu du Vercors-Sassenage AOC

AOC protected since 1998, this cheese is named after the town of Sassenage where, in the 14th century, subjects were ordered to pay their taxes in cheese. Unlike most traditional blues, it is lightly pressed, which gives it a more supple texture.

TASTING NOTES The rind is thin, leathery, and brown, the paste pale yellow, dense yet soft, and marked with irregular thick streaks and blue patches. Delicate for a blue, it has a slightly bitter aftertaste.

HOW TO ENJOY Eat alongside a glass of robust, lively Beaujolais-Villages and Côtes-du-Rhône-Villages.

FRANCE Rhône-Alpes		
Age 2–3 months		
Weight and Shape 5–6kg (11lb–13lb 4oz), wheel		
Size D. 15cm (12in), H. 7.5cm (3in)		
Milk Cow		
Classification Blue		
Producer Various		

Bonde de Gâtine

Produced in the marshy Gâtine area of Poitou, the Bonde de Gâtine is a high-quality *fermier* goat's cheese that requires two litres of milk to make just one 400g (14oz) cheese. It has a thin wrinkled rind, which is dusted with blue, grey, and white moulds.

TASTING NOTES The paste has a pronounced acidity and saltiness which melts in the mouth, leaving behind it a rich aftertaste.

HOW TO ENJOY Team with a dry and fruity wine, such as a Sancerre Blanc, which complements the creamy, acid, and fruity flavours.

FRANCE Gâtire, Poitou-Charentes		
Age 6–10 weeks		
Weight and Shape 400g (14oz), drum		
Size D. 4.5cm (2in), H. 7cm (3in)		
Milk Goat		
Classification Aged fresh		
Producer Patrick Cantet		

Beaufort AOC

Of all the great cheeses of the world, Beaufort encapsulates everything that is magical, traditional, and truly awesome about cheese, and demonstrates how, in a harsh and rugged terrain, man has worked alongside Mother Nature and adapted to the rhythm and demands of the seasons.

In the 14th and 15th centuries, the local church and landowners of the Savoie-Beaufortain in the French Alps, instigated a widespread programme to remove much of the woodlands and create mountain pastures. These pastures – as colourful, and spectacular as a Monet painting – are unploughed and unfenced, and contain thousands of different species of wild herbs, meadow flowers, and grasses. These provide the native Abondance and Tarine cows with fresh grazing in summer, and aromatic hay in winter. The resultant milk is sweet, nutty, aromatic, and complex.

It takes the milk of about 35 cows to make one Beaufort cheese. Because of this, herdsmen have, since ancient times, combined their milk, forming cooperatives, and shared the tasks of herding, milking, cheesemaking, and maturing.

Cheese produced in the lush summer pastures is known as Beaufort *d'Alpage*; those produced from a single herd that graze above 1,500m (4,921ft) are called Chalet *d'Alpage*, and are some of the largest artisan cheeses in the world. Winter cheeses, known as Beaufort *d'Hiver*, are paler, as they are made when the cows enjoy a more concentrated diet of hay cut from the summer pastures.

Beaufort is protected by the AOC label, and can only be made in an area covering approximately 450,000 hectares (1112 acres) in the Rhône-Alpes' Beaufortain, Tarentaise, and Maurienne valleys, as well as a section of the Val d'Arly.

TASTING NOTES Young Beaufort is firm but not hard. It melts in the mouth, and has a rich, sweet, complex flavour. The Chalet *d'Alpage* is aged longer and has more honeyed, aromatic notes and a long, savoury tang that hints of meadow flowers.

HOW TO ENJOY This is not a cheese to melt on toast or put in a sandwich (although both would be heaven), and certainly not to be bought in miserable thin slices! It should be eaten in generous mouthfuls accompanied by a bottle of the best Pinot Noir you can afford. Fresh walnuts, grown throughout the Savoie, also make a great partner. Beaufort's rich sweetness is also excellent with Champagne, as well as Chardonnay, and Riesling, but avoid dry whites that take away its flavour.

The milk *comes from the Tarentaise and Abondance cows, whose diet is strictly controlled.*

FRANCE Rhône-Alpes	
Age 5–18 months	
Weight and Shape 20–70kg (44lb–154lb 3oz), round	
Size D. 35–75cm (14–27½in) H. 11–16cm (4½–6in)	
Milk Cow	
Classification Hard	
Producer Various	

A CLOSER LOOK

Beaufort has been protected by the AOC label since 1968, resulting in strict control of each stage of production. This includes the milk used, which is never pasteurized, the distinct concave shape, and every aspect of its maturation.

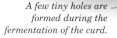

A few tiny holes are formed during the fermentation of the curd.

The rind is rubbed with brine enriched with scrapings from old cheeses and whey, creating a grainy, russet crust that protects the cheese from drying out.

The inward curving sides are a result of the beechwood belt that circles each cheese as it matures.

Exterior

COAGULATION This process only takes 20–30 minutes. The curds are then cut and the temperature raised to scald the milk and to squeeze out moisture from the curd. The curd is piled into cloth and carefully removed from the cauldron.

PRESSING The curd is encircled with a *cercle*, a "belt" made of beech, and pressed for 20 hours. The cheese is turned regularly during this time.

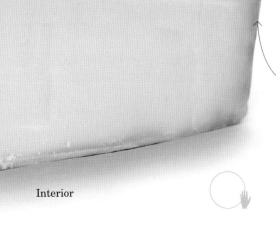

During its maturation, small horizontal cracks appear near the edge as the rind dries faster than the interior.

Interior

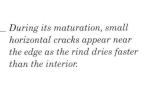

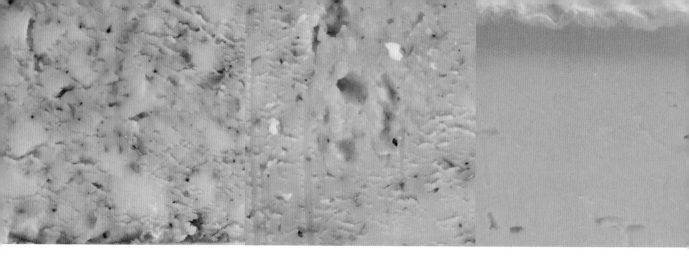

Boulette d'Avesnes

In the past, this *fermier* cheese was made exclusively from buttermilk; nowadays, it is made with the fresh curds of Maroilles and mashed with parsley, tarragon, cloves, and pepper. It is shaped by hand, dyed with peppery annatto and dusted with paprika.

TASTING NOTES The paprika from the rind gives it a hot peppery bite, while the semi-soft, ivory-coloured paste adds a spicy, herbaceous, and sharp flavour.

HOW TO ENJOY Pair with any strong, full-bodied red wines, such as Cahors. A shot of gin will also bring out its unusual combination of flavours.

40

FRANCE Flandre-Hainaut, Nord-Pas-De-Calais	
Age 3 months	
Weight and Shape 200–300g (7–10oz), cone	
Size D. 7.5cm (3in), H. 10cm (4in)	
Milk Cow	
Classification Flavour-added	
Producer Pont du Loup, Fauquet, and Leduc	

Boulette de Cambrai

Made by hand in Cambrai, near the Belgium border, where it has long been popular, this cow's milk cheese is a delicious combination of fromage frais, tarragon, parsley, chives, and seasoning. Unlike Boulette d'Avesnes, Boulette de Cambrai is always consumed fresh.

TASTING NOTES This fresh rindless cheese is mildly aromatic and has a deliciously herby flavour, but it will become bitter if allowed to age for too long.

HOW TO ENJOY Spread on crusty bread and pair with a light and fruity red wine, such as Beaujolais.

FRANCE Nord-Pas-De-Calais	
Age 1–5 days	
Weight and Shape 280g (10oz), cone	
Size D. 7.5cm (3in), H. 10cm (4in)	
Milk Cow	
Classification Fresh	
Producer Various	

Bouton-de-Culotte

Bouton-de-Culotte, or "trouser buttons", are small Mâconnais that are stored during the autumn for winter use. By winter the rind becomes dark brown and hard and this goat's cheese can be grated into the local fromage fort.

TASTING NOTES It has a very distinct goaty taste that hints of ground nuts, feels dry in the mouth, and has a sharp, tongue-tingling finish.

HOW TO ENJOY Enjoy this cheese with all the powerful full-bodied vintages of Mâconnais and Côte Chalonnaise.

FRANCE Bourgogne	
Age 2 months	
Weight and Shape 60g (2oz), tiny drum	
Size D. 5cm (2in) base, 4cm (1½in) top, H. 3.5cm (1.5in)	
Milk Goat	
Classification Aged fresh	
Producer Various	

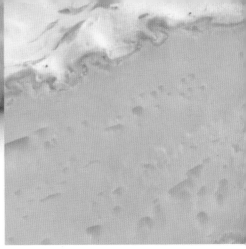

Bouyguette des Collines

The pale ivory, soft, wrinkled rind of this hand-formed goat's cheese is decorated with a sprig of rosemary, making it a very attractive addition to a cheeseboard. Its thin rind means the paste breaks down very quickly and becomes soft and creamy.

TASTING NOTES Bouyguette des Collines has a slight taste of thyme and rosemary. Initially the cheese is smooth, then, after 20 days of maturing, its flavour becomes more pronounced.

HOW TO ENJOY It is best paired with a dry white wine, such as Sancerre, Riesling or Chinon, but is also good with a rosé.

FRANCE Tarn, Midi-Pyrénées	
Age 2–3 weeks	
Weight and Shape 150g (5½oz), oval	
Size L. 20cm (8in), H. 4cm (1½in)	
Milk Goat	
Classification Aged fresh	
Producer Segalafrom	

Brebis du Lochois

This modern, French ewe's milk cheese comes from central France (a region traditionally associated with goats), where the flock grazes on very good pastures. Cheeses that are dusted with ash are called Cendré Lochois.

TASTING NOTES Lochois has a tender and generous paste, as well as a smooth buttery flavour and herby aromas. The beech ashes give it a somewhat smoky and woody character.

HOW TO ENJOY It tastes delicious served with figs and jam and goes very well when paired with white wines from Touraine, such as Sancerre or Montlouis.

FRANCE Touraine, Centre	
Age 2 weeks	
Weight and Shape 110g (4oz), round	
Size D. 7.5cm (3in), H. 2.5cm (1in)	
Milk Ewe	
Classification Aged fresh	
Producer Brebis du Lochois	

Brie de Melun AOC

Unlike other Bries, the coagulation of the curd in this cow's milk cheese is very slow, since it relies mainly on lactic fermentation rather than rennet. This produces a very thick curd, and eventually a thick, crusty white rind with red, yellow, and brown pigments and moulds.

TASTING NOTES It can be sold fresh, when sour yet sweet, or when fully mature, when it has a very fruity flavour and a strong scent of fermentation.

HOW TO ENJOY It can be enjoyed with all red wines of Burgundy, Bordeaux, and Côtes-Du-Rhône that are lively, full-bodied, and have bouquet.

FRANCE Ile-de-France	
Age Best around 2 months	
Weight and Shape 1.5kg (3lb 5oz), wheel	
Size D. 24cm (9½in), H. 3.5cm (1½in)	
Milk Cow	
Classification Soft white	
Producer Various	

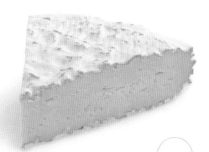

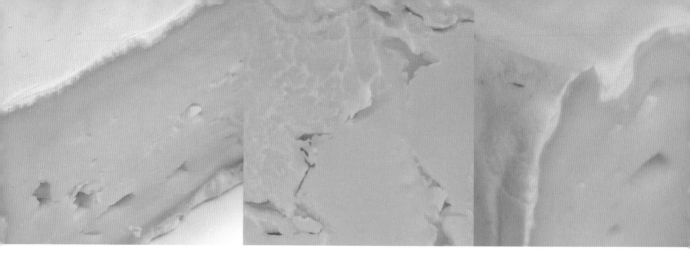

Brie de Nangis

Originally made in Nangis, south east of Paris, this Brie almost disappeared when superseded by Brie de Melun. However, it has since been revived by a single producer in Tournan-en-Brie and remains true to the original. It is at its best when made from milk from cows grazed on spring and summer grass.

TASTING NOTES Like Brie de Melun, this Brie has a white mould rind and a soft, creamy paste. Unlike Brie de Melun, it has a very fruity, rather than savoury or meaty, flavour.

HOW TO ENJOY Pair this Brie with a glass of lively, full-bodied Bourgogne, Bordeaux or Côtes-du-Rhône.

FRANCE Ile-de-France	
Age 4–5 weeks	
Weight and Shape 1kg (2¼lb), round	
Size D. 23cm (9in), H. 5cm (2in)	
Milk Cow	
Classification Soft white	
Producer Rouzaire	

Brillat-Savarin

Although named after a renowned 18th-century gourmand and food writer, Brillat-Savarin was in fact created in the 1930s by Henri Androuët, a famous cheesemaker and *affineur*. This triple-cream cheese with a fat content of 75 per cent for every 100g (3½oz) is not for the dieter.

TASTING NOTES When young, it has no rind and a texture like thick crème fraîche; if eaten once it has developed its thin white coat, the paste will have softened to become luscious, creamy, and soft.

HOW TO ENJOY It goes well with all light fruity wines, in particular Champagnes with some character.

FRANCE Basse-Normandie and Bourgogne	
Age 2–4 weeks	
Weight and Shape 500g (1lb 2oz), round	
Size D. 12cm (5in), H. 3.5cm (1½in)	
Milk Cow	
Classification Soft white	
Producer Lincet	

Brique du Forez

This traditional cheese from the Auvergne region takes its name from its brick-like shape. It is characterized by a thin white rind that develops a blue-grey hue. It used to be made using a mixture of cow's and goat's milk, but now it is made solely with cow's milk.

TASTING NOTES The white mantle smells mushroomy and sharp, while the interior is creamy and almost runny, with a nutty flavour and a long finish in the mouth.

HOW TO ENJOY Team this creamy cheese with light and fruity white, rosé, and red wines of Auvergne, Roanne, and Beaujolais.

FRANCE Auvergne	
Age 2–3 months	
Weight and Shape 350–400g (12–14oz), brick	
Size L. 12–13cm (5–5½in), W. 3.5–5.5cm (1½–2½in), H. 2.5cm (1in)	
Milk Cow	
Classification Soft white	
Producer Various	

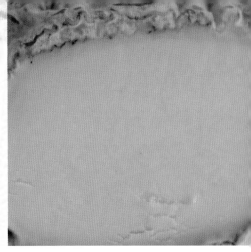

Brocciu AOC

This famous Corsican fresh cheese is made by unusual production processes: whey is added, rather than discarded, during the process, giving it a unique taste in addition to some precious nutrients. It is then drained in small rush baskets – *canestres*.

TASTING NOTES Fresh Brocciu is mild tasting and creamy; however, ripened Brocciu (also referred to as Brocciu Pasu) is strong and a little spicy.

HOW TO ENJOY Brocciu can be used in many recipes, including salads, omelettes, and cheesecakes. It is delicious served with just salt, sugar, rosemary, or honey, and a light wine.

FRANCE Corse	
Age 2–3 days	
Weight and Shape 675g–1.3kg (1½–3lbs), basket	
Size Various	
Milk Ewe	
Classification Fresh	
Producer Various	

Brossauthym

This is a unique cheese because it is thought to be the only ewe's cheese produced in the Loire region. Flavoured with thyme, it has a natural rind and oval shape, and it makes a decorative addition to any cheeseboard.

TASTING NOTES This fresh cheese is tasty, thyme-flavoured, and has a mellow, melt-in-the-mouth finish.

HOW TO ENJOY Serve with aromatic red wines, such as a well-structured Ajaccio or a full-bodied Patrimonio.

FRANCE Touraine, Centre	
Age 1 month	
Weight and Shape 225g (8oz), oval	
Size L. 11cm (4½in), H. 4.5cm (2in)	
Milk Ewe	
Classification Aged fresh	
Producer M. Froideveaux	

Buchette Pont d'Yeu

This log-shaped goat's cheese takes its name from the island of Yeu in the Vendée region of France. It has a natural rind that is sprinkled with wood ash.

TASTING NOTES The flavour of the thick paste varies depending on the level of maturation of the cheese. When it is young (at about three weeks), it is nutty, but as it ages, it develops a peppery taste.

HOW TO ENJOY Serve on a cheeseboard alongside crusty bread, berries, and jam. The Buchette is best enjoyed with a fruity white wine, such as Lillet.

FRANCE Pays de la Loire	
Age 3–8 weeks	
Weight and Shape 200g (7oz), log	
Size L. 10cm (4in), H. 5cm (2in)	
Milk Goat	
Classification Aged fresh	
Producer Various	

Cabri Ariégeois

The passionate farmers in Ariège have created this modern French cheese, which has become one of the best goat's cheeses on the market. Based on the famous Mont d'Or cheese, Cabri Ariégeois is bound up in a strip of spruce bark.

TASTING NOTES Very smooth and creamy, this washed cheese has a pronounced, sharp flavour and a hint of pine that comes from the bark.

HOW TO ENJOY This cheese is best appreciated alongside a full-bodied and structured red wine with a strong berry flavour, such as a Côtes du Roussillon.

FRANCE Ariège, Midi-Pyrénées
Age From 4–6 weeks
Weight and Shape 500g (11lb 2oz), round
Size D. 11cm (4⅓in), H. 6cm (2⅓in)
Milk Goat
Classification Semi-soft
Producer Fromagerie Fermier Cabrioulet

Camembert au Calvados

Some believe an iconic cheese like Camembert should be left well alone. But Androuet, the retailer named after France's legendary cheese maker Pierre Androuët, and Isigny, one of the biggest producers in France, soak this cheese in Calvados and cover it in breadcrumbs.

TASTING NOTES With the rind scrapped off, the breadcrumbs absorb the aroma of alcohol and apples from the apple brandy or Calvados. The creamy interior has a gamey taste with hints of mushrooms.

HOW TO ENJOY Enjoy this cheese with Calvados de Normandy or cider with perhaps walnuts rather than bread.

FRANCE Normandy, France
Age 6–8 weeks
Weight and Shape 250 gm (9oz), round
Size D. 10cm (4in), H. 3 cm (1in)
Milk Cow
Classification Soft white
Producer Various

Camembert de Normandie AOC

This, one of the most famous French cheeses, is said to have been created in 1791 by Marie Harel, a farmer's wife in Camembert. The most important invention, though, was its wooden box, which enabled it to be shipped around the world. The AOC granted in 1983 states it must be made with raw milk.

TASTING NOTES Its flavour is fruity, with a slight aroma of mushrooms and mould. Locals prefer Camembert when the heart is white and not yet creamy.

HOW TO ENJOY Serve with fruity, elegant red wines of Burgundy and Côtes-du-Rhône, or a traditional Normandy cider.

FRANCE Basse-Normandie
Age Best around 1 month
Weight and Shape 250g (9oz), round
Size D. 11cm (4⅓in), H. 3.5cm (1⅓in)
Milk Cow
Classification Soft white
Producer Various

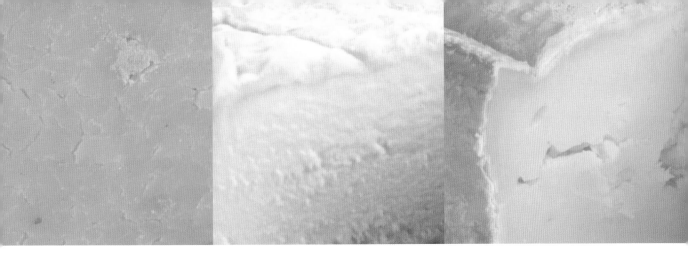

Cantal AOC

AOC protected since 1956, Cantal is the forefather of all cheeses from the Auvergne region. It is made using the cheddaring process typical of many English traditional hard cheeses, and is unique in being the only French cheese produced this way.

TASTING NOTES The flavour differs depending on the age of the cheese: a well-ripened Cantal is strong in taste, while a young cheese has a mild, nutty and milky flavour.

HOW TO ENJOY Pair Cantal with a light fruity wine, such as a Côtes d'Auvergne, Côtes Roannaises, or Beaujolais.

FRANCE Auvergne	
Age Best around 3–6 months	
Weight and Shape 35–45kg (77–99lb), cylinder	
Size D. 35–46cm (14–18in), H. 35–39cm (14–16in)	
Milk Cow	
Classification Hard	
Producer Various	

Capri Lezeen

These farmhouse goat's cheeses are produced by the GAEC du Capri Lezéen in the marshy part of Poitou. They have quite a sticky yellow rind with traces of light blue mould and are sold wrapped in a signature chestnut leaf, packaged up in a wooden box.

TASTING NOTES The creamy, runny paste and soft rind has a slightly nutty taste and only a subtle goaty flavour.

HOW TO ENJOY Pair Capri Lezeen with a dry white wine, such as a Sancerre or Viognier. It tastes delicious served alongside fresh figs or berries.

FRANCE Lezay, Poitou-Charentes	
Age 2–3 weeks	
Weight and Shape 175g (6oz), round	
Size D. 8cm (3¼in), H. 1.5cm (½in)	
Milk Goat	
Classification Aged fresh	
Producer GAEC du Capri Lezéen Patrick Cantet	

Carré de l'Est

As its name suggests (it means "square of the east"), this co-operative or industrial washed-rind cheese is square in shape and is most famous in the eastern regions of France (Lorraine, the Ardennes, and Champagne).

TASTING NOTES Soft and grainy when young, this cheese becomes almost liquid when mature. It has a salty flavour and the orange sticky rind gives it a smokey bacon tang. Those covered with white mould are milder.

HOW TO ENJOY Spread this semi-soft cheese on bread for a delicious snack and team with light fruity wines, such as Châteauneuf-du-Pâpe or Gigondas.

FRANCE Champagne-Ardenne and Lorraine	
Age About 3 weeks	
Weight and Shape 125–250g (4½–9oz), square	
Size L. 10cm (4in), H. 3.5cm (1½in)	
Milk Cow	
Classification Semi-soft	
Producer Various	

Brie de Meaux AOC

Made just 50km (31 miles) east of Paris in the region of Ile-de-France, Brie de Meaux can trace its history back to Emperor Charlemagne who, in 774ce, extolled the virtues of Brie in his Chronicles.

At the Congress of Vienna, *1814, Brie de Meaux was declared the "King of Cheeses".*

The worldwide reputation of Brie de Meaux was established in 1814, when it was declared *Le Roi des Fromages,* "The King of Cheeses", at a culinary tournament during the Congress of Vienna. The close proximity of Ile-de-France to the markets of Paris and the charming wooden box in which it is sold have also contributed to its rise to fame.

Brie de Meaux is one of only 46 French cheeses protected by the AOC label, which guarantees the quality of a cheese as well as where and how it is made (see p8). To qualify, Brie must be made in specific areas with calf rennet and 25 litres (6.6 gallons) of unpasteurized milk. The curd must be ladled by hand into the moulds and each cheese must be dry salted then ripened slowly at a specific temperature and humidity.

Brie de Meaux and Camembert de Normandie (see p44) are often considered similar, but in fact they each have their own distinct character influenced by size, microflora, unique climate, and grazing.

TASTING NOTES Brie de Meaux is probably the strongest of all the soft white cheeses. The aroma should be of mould, damp leaves, and mushrooms; becoming more intense with age. At its peak, it has a glossy pale straw to butter-yellow coloured soft interior that oozes irresistibly towards you, and a characteristic rich taste like wild, smoky mushroom soup made with beef consommé. If it smells strongly of ammonia, then it will deliver a vicious bite. However, one man's meat is another man's poison.

If you prefer Brie that is runny rather than with a chalky band of immature curd through the centre, buy it near its "best by" date. Don't be alarmed by any white mould that grows down the cut surface – this just tells you the cheese is alive and well, and merely trying to protect its soft interior from drying out. It's best kept in its original paper or wax paper. Plastic wrap prevents the cheese from breathing and the ammonia, released during ripening, will be trapped and, within a day or so, the cheese will start to sweat.

HOW TO ENJOY It would almost be a crime to do anything with Brie de Meaux except allow it to reach room temperature and enjoy it with a red Côte-du-Rhône, Bordeaux, or Burgundy or, as befits the King of Cheeses, a glass of vintage Champagne.

FRANCE Ile-de-France	
Age 6–8 weeks	
Weight and Shape 3kg (6½lb), wheel	
Size D. 25cm (10in), H. 8cm (3¼in)	
Milk Cow	
Classification Soft white	
Producer Various	

A CLOSER LOOK

From Paris to Peru, Brie de Meaux is enjoyed the world over. Surprisingly, there are only a handful of producers, and most cheeses are then matured and aged by special *affineurs*, each creating their own unique style.

THE LADLE To achieve the smooth, voluptuous custard-like interior and to prevent the fat and protein being lost in the whey, cheesemakers must handle the fragile, floppy curd by hand, using a perforated ladle known as a *pelle à brie*, first used in the 12th century.

RIND The cheese is softest under the rind where the mould is working to ripen the curd.

FRANCE

SALTING The cheeses are dry salted by hand. This helps to seal the cheese as well as helping to draw out the moisture.

RIPENING The cheeses spend a minimum of four weeks in a special cellar where they are turned regularly. First, a sprinkling of red or brown streaks or spots known as *ferment du rouge* start to appear, then the more virulent white moulds, *penicillium candidum* and *penicillium camemberti* gradually cover the rind in a fine coat of white velvet.

The fat content is around 26 per cent, significantly less than hard cheeses such as Cheddar (see pp178–179).

Whole cheese, slice removed

Cendré de Niort

Cendré traditionally refers to the method of maturing cheese in a box of wood ash to form the rind, rather than simply sprinkling the coat with ash. Most of these cheeses originate in wine-growing regions; they were made when milk was abundant, preserved in wood ash until harvest time, and then served to the hungry grape pickers.

TASTING NOTES This *fermier* cheese has a real countryside aroma and a fairly milky flavour. The chestnut leaf it is wrapped in imparts a vegetal hint.

HOW TO ENJOY Open a fruity and light red wine with Cendré de Niort, such as a Chinon or an Alsace Pinot Noir.

FRANCE La Fragnée, Poitou-Charentes		
Age 6 weeks		
Weight and Shape (125g) 4½oz, round		
Size D. 8cm (4in), H. 2.5cm (1in)		
Milk Goat		
Classification Aged fresh		
Producer Patrick Cantet		

Chabichou du Poitou AOC

This natural-rinded cheese comes from the Loire, home to the majority of French goat's cheeses. It has been protected by the AOC label since 1990, and its production can be *fermier*, cooperative, or industrial.

TASTING NOTES The thin, white rind, with its yellow and blue mould, conceals a cheese with a distinct aroma and a pronounced sharp flavour, compared to other goat's cheeses.

HOW TO ENJOY It tastes delicious with the lively, fruity red wines of the Neuville-de-Poitou, Dissay, and Saint-martin-la-rivière regions.

FRANCE Poitou-Charentes		
Age 3 weeks		
Weight and Shape 100g (3½oz), cylinder		
Size D. 6cm (2½in), H. 5cm (2½in)		
Milk Goat		
Classification Aged fresh		
Producer Various		

Chaource AOC

Said to have been created by the monks of Pontigny, the name of this white-rinded cheese comes from the town that is the centre of that region. Originally sold fresh, now it is preferred as a more mature cheese. AOC protected since 1970.

TASTING NOTES Its white, crusty and downy rind becomes pigmented with brown as it ages. It has a creamy texture and a milky, fruity flavour with a faint aroma of mushrooms, becoming sharper and salty as it matures.

HOW TO ENJOY Team with fruity white wines such as Saint-Bris-le-Vineux, Chablis, and Irancy, or fruity reds and rosés.

FRANCE Saligny, Bourgogne		
Age 2 weeks–2 months		
Weight and Shape 600g (1lb 5oz), small cylinder		
Size D. 12cm (5in), H. 6cm (2½in)		
Milk Cow		
Classification Soft white		
Producer Lincet		

Charolais AOC

This *fermier* cheese made from goat's milk hails from the Bourgogne region. A distinctive-looking cheese, Charolais is shaped like a small barrel and often displays a characteristic bluish rind.

TASTING NOTES Charolais has a firm and compact paste and a natural rind. Faintly sour, it holds a distinct flavour of milk and almonds.

HOW TO ENJOY Serve with chestnuts and walnuts or a loaf of sourdough bread. Fruity wines, such as Fleurie, are most appropriate for drinking alongside this cheese.

FRANCE Bourgogne	
Age 2–6 weeks	
Weight and Shape 120g (4oz), barrel	
Size D. 4.5cm (2in), H. 7.5cm (3in)	
Milk Goat	
Classification Aged fresh	
Producer Various	

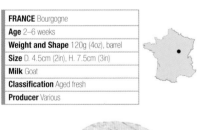

Chevrotin des Aravis AOC

One of the few washed-rind goat's cheeses, Chevrotin des Aravis is named after the type of milk used and the place Vallée des Aravis, where it is made. It is similar in appearance and texture to Reblochon; a moist, yellowish-orange rind is covered with a fine white mould. It was granted an AOC in 2002 as the 40th member.

TASTING NOTES This cheese has a mild, slightly goaty flavour. The fine-textured paste melts slightly at the edges.

HOW TO ENJOY It is best paired with a sharp-tasting red wine, such as a Mondeuse or Chignin-Bergeron.

FRANCE Rhône-Alpes	
Age 2 months	
Weight and Shape 600–675g (1lb 5oz–1lb 8oz), round	
Size D. 9–12cm (3½–5in), H. 4cm (2in)	
Milk Goat	
Classification Semi-soft	
Producer Various	

Cœur de Neufchâtel AOC

Neufchâtel, a cow's milk cheese produced in Haute-Normandie, has benefited from the AOC label since 1969. As its name suggests, this version is heart-shaped, but it can also be found as a small cylinder or brick, when it is simply called Neufchâtel.

TASTING NOTES The white rind is dry, velvety and crumbly with a mushroomy aroma. The paste is firm but slightly grainy, with a subtle milk taste and salty tang.

HOW TO ENJOY Its flavour works well with good crusty bread; locals like to melt it on warm bread and eat it for breakfast.

FRANCE Haute-Normandie	
Age 8–10 weeks	
Weight and Shape 200g (7oz), heart	
Size L. 10cm (4in), H. 2.5cm (1in)	
Milk Cow	
Classification Soft white	
Producer Various	

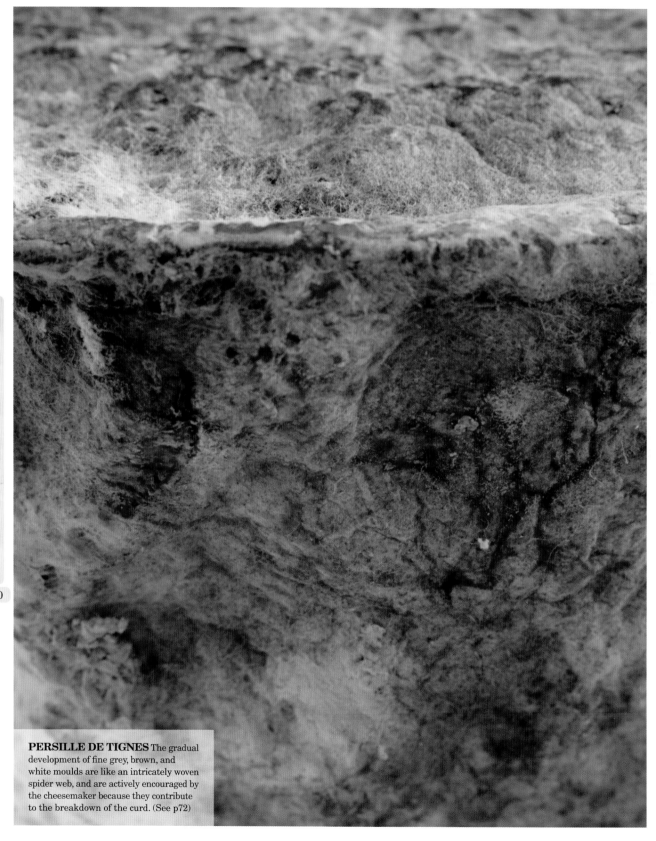

PERSILLE DE TIGNES The gradual
development of fine grey, brown, and
white moulds are like an intricately woven
spider web, and are actively encouraged by
the cheesemaker because they contribute
to the breakdown of the curd. (See p72)

Chevrotin des Bauges AOC

This *fermier* cheese is produced in the mountain region of Savoie, known for its magnificent scenery and colourful, diverse natural pastures. This area is home to many of France's best-loved cheeses, including Reblochon, which Chevrotin resembles except that it is made with goat's milk.

TASTING NOTES A thick, rustic rind covers a smooth, supple, melting paste with small irregular eyes. The creamy, sweet flavour has a hint of goat.

HOW TO ENJOY Pair this cheese with a fruity, dry white Savoie wine, such as the Roussette.

FRANCE Rhône-Alpes	
Age 21 days	
Weight and Shape 300g (10½oz), round	
Size D. 9–11.5cm (3½–4⅓in), H. 4cm (1½in)	
Milk Goat	
Classification Semi-soft	
Producer Various	

Ch'ti Roux

The deep tangerine-orange colour of this cheese is the result of roucou or annatto being added to the milk, and the rind being washed with a mix of dark beer and annatto. Ch'ti Roux is one of many cheeses made by the family of Bernard-Wierre Effroy in the Nord-Pas-de-Calais, from its own cows.

TASTING NOTES This firm-textured cheese has a powerful, spicy, and salty flavour with a long, slightly peppery finish.

HOW TO ENJOY A dark beer or a wine from Bourgogne, such as Côte de Baune or Beaujolais, will complement this flavoursome cheese.

FRANCE Nord-Pas-de-Calais	
Age 4 months	
Weight and Shape 400g (14oz), brick	
Size L. 11cm (4⅓in), W. 2.5cm (1in), H. 4.5cm (2in)	
Milk Cow	
Classification Semi-soft	
Producer Saint Godeleine Farm (M. Bernard)	

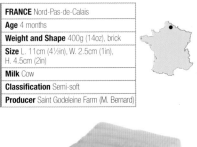

Clochette

This name of this goat's cheese reflects its dramatic-looking shape – *clochette* translates as "little bell". It is produced in the Poitou-Charentes region, which is also home to another well-known goat's cheese, Chabichou. Clochette has a dry and crusty rind of natural mould, but a firm and tender paste.

TASTING NOTES The pleasant aroma of dried hay and goats derives from its mould and from the cellar in which it was ripened. It has a smooth texture and a warm, powerful flavour.

HOW TO ENJOY Eat it warm with olives or nuts and serve alongside full-bodied Burgundy wines.

FRANCE Roullet-Sainte-Estéphe, Poitou-Charentes	
Age 2–3 weeks	
Weight and Shape 225g (8oz), bell	
Size D. 7.5cm (3in), H. 10cm (4in)	
Milk Goat	
Classification Aged fresh	
Producer GAEC Jouseaume	

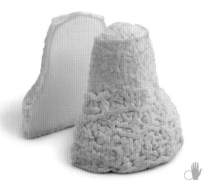

Cœur de Touraine

The Loire is famous not only for its great chateaux, but also for its goat's cheeses. This heart-shaped cheese (reflecting its name – the 'heart' of Touraine) with its ash-covered rind is very popular.

TASTING NOTES Like all traditional Loire goat's cheese, the inside is a bit sticky on the palate and the rind is edible – including the mould, which is very savoury. The overall taste is mild; a little salty yet mouth-watering.

HOW TO ENJOY Cœur de Touraine is a real delight with nut bread or raisin bread and a white wine, such as a Montlouis.

FRANCE Centre	
Age 3 weeks at least	
Weight and Shape 150g (5½oz), heart	
Size W. 9cm (3½in), H 4cm (1½in)	
Milk Goat	
Classification Aged fresh	
Producer Various	

Coulommiers

A more petite member of the Brie family, Coulommiers is produced in the Ile-de-France region, near Paris. A *fermier* or industrially-produced cheese, it has a downy white rind that is dotted with reddish ferments and a supple texture.

TASTING NOTES Coulommiers has a rather pronounced tang and leaves a long aftertaste. The pale yellow paste is smooth and melts in the mouth.

HOW TO ENJOY Delicious eaten as part of a cheeseboard at the end of the meal, or for lunch. It is best served with lively and fruity red wines, such as a Côtes de Beaune.

FRANCE Seine-et-Marne, Ile-de-France	
Age 4–8 weeks	
Weight and Shape 500g (1lb 2oz), round	
Size D. 12cm (5in), H 2.5cm (1in)	
Milk Cow	
Classification Soft white	
Producer Nugier, Dongé dairies	

Crayeux de Roncq

The farmer and cheesemaker Marie-Therese Couvreur teamed up with cheese *affineur* Philippe Olivier to create this cheese, which is named *crayeux* after its chalky centre. Washed regularly with salt water and beer, its distinct aroma belies a mild and creamy taste under an orange-coloured crust. Produced in very small volume, it is rarely seen outside the region.

TASTING NOTES It has a subtle, nutty flavour between sweet and acid, which leaves a pleasing, unusual aftertaste.

HOW TO ENJOY The best match for this cheese is a structured red wine, such as a Médoc or Graves.

FRANCE Roncq, Nord-Pas-de-Calais	
Age 2 months	
Weight and Shape 425g (15oz), square	
Size L. 10cm (4in), W. 10cm (4in), H. 4.5cm (2in)	
Milk Cow	
Classification Semi-soft	
Producer Marie-Therese Couvreur	

Crémeux du Puy

This soft cheese is injected with blue mould and is produced in the Auvergne region, which is renowned for its excellent cheeses. It has a thick blue rind, which is overlaid by a delicate layer of white mould.

TASTING NOTES It has a creamy, delicate taste, with a hint of mushrooms and flavours of the cave in which it was left to mature.

HOW TO ENJOY Extremely flavoursome, with a texture not unlike Reblochon, Crémeux du Puy makes a popular addition to any cheeseboard. Serve this delicious cheese with some fresh, crusty bread and a glass of Côtes-du-Rhône.

FRANCE Auvergne	
Age 6–8 weeks	
Weight and Shape 50g (1¾oz), disc	
Size D. 8cm (3in), H. 5cm (2in)	
Milk Cow	
Classification Blue	
Producer Various	

Crottin de Chavignol AOC

AOC protected since 1976, this cheese has an unfortunate name because, *crottin* literally means horse dung, but this is actually a reference to the shape and colour of when at full maturity. However, most are sold much younger, when the rind is pale brown-white.

TASTING NOTES Known for its piquant taste, it can be eaten at various stages; when young it is tender in texture, becoming harder, dry, crumbly, and sharp as it ages.

HOW TO ENJOY Best paired with the most vigorous full-bodied wines to enjoy the flavour of both wine and cheese.

FRANCE Centre	
Age Best around 2 months	
Weight and Shape 60g (2oz), small drum	
Size D. 5cm (2in), H. 2cm (¾in)	
Milk Goat	
Classification Aged fresh	
Producer Various	

Curé Nantais

This cheese is believed to have been introduced to the Pays de la Loire region by a Vendéen monk who was enduring the food shortage of the French Revolution. Now it is produced by a dairy that respects the traditional methods of making it. It is also known as Fromage du Pays Nantais dit du Curé.

TASTING NOTES A strong-tasting cheese with a soft and slightly elastic golden paste, featuring a few small holes.

HOW TO ENJOY It tastes delicious served with crusty bread and onion relish. Accompany it with a fruity Muscadet, such as a Melon Blanc.

FRANCE Pays de la Loire	
Age 1 month	
Weight and Shape 400g (14oz), round	
Size D. 10cm (4in), H. 5cm (2in)	
Milk Cow	
Classification Semi-soft	
Producer Curé Nantais dairy	

Dauphin

It is said that when Louis XIV was travelling through the Hainaut (in modern Belgium) with the Dauphin, his son and heir, he liked this cheese so much that he asked local cheesemakers to name the cheese in his son's honour. This distinctive cheese's washed, reddish rind encases a semi-soft paste.

TASTING NOTES A member of the Maroilles family, this is a strong, spicy, and aromatic cheese flavoured with tarragon, parsley, pepper, and cloves.

HOW TO ENJOY This full-flavoured cheese makes an interesting addition to any cheeseboard and is best paired with a robust wine, such as Côtes-du-Rhône.

FRANCE Nord-Pas-de-Calais	
Age 2–3 months	
Weight and Shape 400g (14oz), dolphin	
Size L. 12.5cm (5in), H. 3.5cm (1½in)	
Milk Cow	
Classification Flavour-added	
Producer Various	

Deauville

This modern French cheese combines attributes from two of Normandie's most famous washed-rind cheeses: Pont l'Evêque and Livarot. In spite of that, Deauville also has its own unique character and style.

TASTING NOTES The rich and flowery qualities of the cows' grazing pastures comes through in the flavour of this slightly milky semi-soft cheese, which has a sticky and supple texture.

HOW TO ENJOY Some apple marmalade and a glass of fresh cider make for perfect accompaniments to this tasty cheese.

FRANCE Normandiy	
Age 7 weeks	
Weight and Shape 225g (8oz), round	
Size D. 12cm (5in), H. 4cm (1½in)	
Milk Cow	
Classification Semi-soft	
Producer Fromagerie Thebault	

Dôme de Vézelay

This is a raw-milk *fermier* cheese that is produced in very small volume and therefore rarely found outside the Yonne region. It is distinctive in its unusual shape, which is, as indicated by its name, that of a dome.

TASTING NOTES Vézelay has a natural rind and a fine, mellow paste. It has a subtle flavour that is later echoed by a spicier aftertaste.

HOW TO ENJOY This cheese combines well with sweet flavours such as honey or fig jam and with fruity and aromatic white wines such as a Chablis, a Mâcon blanc or a Meursault.

FRANCE Bourgogne	
Age 10 days at least	
Weight and Shape 120g (4oz), dome	
Size D. 7.5cm (3in), H. 4.5cm (2in)	
Milk Goat	
Classification Fresh	
Producer Various	

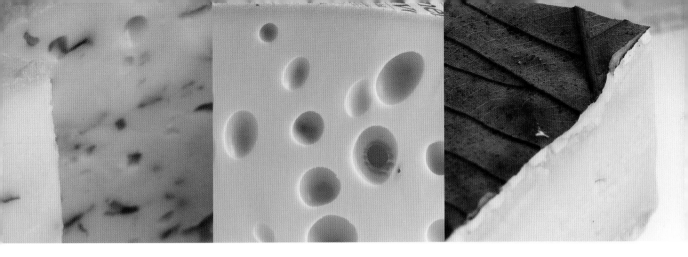

Embruns aux Algues

This cheese will certainly impress dinner guests. Embruns aux Algues is made in the same way as Curé Nantais, but it is round in shape and the curd is mixed with seaweed. This encourages the rind to develop a coral, pink-orange colour and sticky texture.

TASTING NOTES A taste sensation, the special salt spray gives this cheese a salty and powerful flavour, coupled with a distinctive aroma of the sea.

HOW TO ENJOY It is delicious eaten with fresh bread and onion relish. Team it with a fruity Muscadet, such as a Melon Blanc.

FRANCE Pays de la Loire
Age 1 month
Weight and Shape 200g (7oz), round
Size D. 8.5cm (4in), H. 3.5cm (1½in)
Milk Cow
Classification Flavour-added
Producer Curé Nantais dairy

Emmental de Savoie

Production of this now-popular hard cheese began in France in the 19th century, thanks to the imagination of German-Swiss cheesemakers. It is a distinctive-looking cheese, with a firm, ivory to pale paste punctuated with holes of about 1.5–3cm (½–1in).

TASTING NOTES Emmental has a smooth texture and a mild, pleasant flavour – it is fruity but also has a sweet and slightly nutty taste.

HOW TO ENJOY This popular choice for any cheeseboard can also be grated into recipes or simply served in chunks as a canapé. It goes well with all light and fruity wines.

FRANCE Savoie, Rhône-Alpes
Age 6 months
Weight and Shape 80–99kg (176lb–220lb), wheel
Size Various, D. 87cm (34in), H. 25cm (10in) (pictured)
Milk Cow
Classification Hard
Producer Various

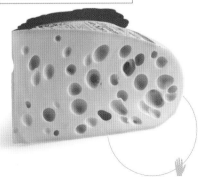

Feuille de Dreux

This very distinctive, ancient artisan cheese was historically eaten by workers in the fields as a snack and is still enjoyed by local farmers today. The decorative addition of a chestnut leaf on the top also has a practical purpose – it stops the cheeses sticking to each other when stacked.

TASTING NOTES This soft white cheese has a fruity, mushroomy flavour, and the faint smell of the chestnut leaf mingles with a pleasant, mouldy aroma.

HOW TO ENJOY Excellent on a formal cheeseboard or as a simple snack with crackers or bread. Serve with a fruity, lively red wine, such as a Chinon.

FRANCE Centre
Age Around 2 months
Weight and Shape 500g (1lb 2oz), round
Size D. 18cm (7in), H. 2.5cm (1in)
Milk Cow
Classification Soft white
Producer Various

Comté AOC

This ancient French cheese has been made in small village-based cooperative dairies or, *fruitière*, for over eight centuries. This system has created a sense of solidarity and pride, and has preserved the traditions and the small-scale production techniques that have helped ensure Comté continues to be one of France's most popular cheeses.

It takes about 530 litres (120 gallons) of milk to make just one 35kg (80lb) Comté wheel – the daily yield of 30 cows. On average, each *fruitière* has 19 members or local dairy farms, located within an eight-mile radius.

The method, and the area in which Comté is made, has not changed for centuries, and it is now defined by Appellation d'Origine Contrôlée (AOC) regulations as the rugged mountains and wide plateaux of the Massif du Jura, a region that spans the Jura, the Doubs (both of which are in the Franche-Comté), and the Ain (in the Rhône-Alpes).

It is the richness and diversity of its mountain pastures and markedly different seasons that give Comté its unique flavour along with the two native breeds of cow that must be used: the native Montbéliarde cow, known for its sweet milk, makes up around 95 per cent of the herds, the rest are French Simmental cows.

During spring, the meadows, a blaze of colourful flowers, echo with the clanging bells as the cows return from winter in the valleys. During the winter the cows are fed on a diet of hay cut from the summer pastures.

TASTING NOTES Each *fruitière* has its own distinct profile that reflects the soil, climate, and flora where the cows graze – from melted butter, milk chocolate, hazelnuts, and fudge to aromas of toast, plum jam, leather, pepper, and dark chocolate. Others are more reminiscent of butterscotch and hazelnuts and even sweet oranges.

HOW TO ENJOY The French enjoy Comté at virtually any time of day. As it melts well, it can be found in numerous French dishes from quiches, soups, tarts, and gratins to fondue, sauces, and salads. Its creamy texture and fruity tang marries well with fish and white meat and the local Jura wines – Chardonnay, Chenin Blanc, or Viognier.

The milk of *the Montbéliarde cow is known for its sweetness.*

FRANCE	Franche-Comté and Rhône-Alpes
Age	4–18 months
Weight and Shape	35–40kg (77–88lb), wheel
Size	D. 60–70cm (24–28in), H. 10cm (4in)
Milk	Cow
Classification	Hard
Producer	Various

A CLOSER LOOK

Local *affineurs* take the young cheeses from the *fruitière* and, with a love of their craft and centuries of knowledge, coax the very best from each cheese.

RIND Comté is recognized by its thin, beige rind.

GRADING When the affinage is complete, each batch is graded out of 20 based on its taste, texture, and appearance. Cheeses with a grading of at least 15 get a green Comté Extra label; those between 12 and 14 are awarded a brown label reading Comté; but those with a rating below 12 do not qualify for the AOC Comté label.

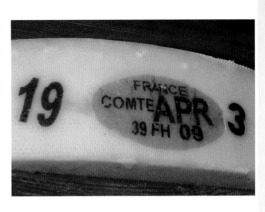

THE AFFINAGE The *affineur* must decide on the time and conditions that suit the potential of each wheel. Regular turning, brushing, and rubbing with salty brine are vital to the process.

The texture is firm, dry, slightly grainy, and more dense than Cheddar.

Interior

The green Extra label indicates a score by the grader of at least 15 out of 20.

Exterior

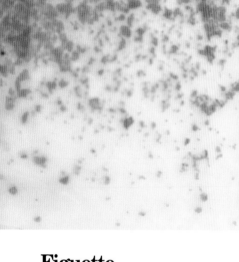
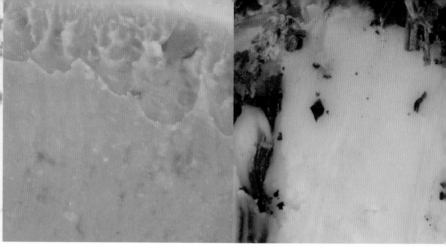

Figuette

This small and charming fig-shaped goat's cheese from the Pyrénées is sometimes covered with dried grasses, ash, or, as shown here, paprika in order to make it even more decorative and appealing to the tastebuds.

TASTING NOTES Figuette is sweet and has a lactic flavour. The delicious aromas come from the various coatings that it is given.

HOW TO ENJOY Eat it with a little honey to enhance its sweetness and tone down its goaty flavour. Bergerac wines are light and therefore most appropriate with this cheese.

FRANCE Midi-Pyrénées	
Age 1–3 weeks	
Weight and Shape 175g (6oz), fig	
Size H. 4.5cm (2in), D. 8cm (3in)	
Milk Goat	
Classification Fresh	
Producer Various	

Fium'Orbu

The sticky-rinded artisanal cheese Fium'Orbu is named after a small river in a little-known unspoilt part of Corse. As with other cheeses made on this mountainous Mediterranean island, its complex flavours and unique qualities can be partially attributed to the warm climate, the robust local breeds and the wild, diverse grazing.

TASTING NOTES Soft, tender and buttery, the complex herbaceous flavours originate from the ewe's fragrant grazing. Washing endows this semi-soft cheese with a lingering meaty tang.

HOW TO ENJOY Corsicans eat it with fig jam accompanied by a fruity red wine.

FRANCE Corse	
Age 8–12 weeks	
Weight and Shape 450g (16oz), block	
Size L. 8.5cm (3½in), W. 8cm (3in), H. 3cm (1in)	
Milk Ewe	
Classification Semi-soft	
Producer Various	

Fleur du Maquis

Covered with herbs and chillies, this unusual artisan cheese is called the "flower of the maquis" – the maquis being the Corsican landscape. Not only does it look better than other cheeses, it also smells pretty good. It is also known as Brindamour.

TASTING NOTES The combination of herbs and spicy chillies does not overwhelm the flavour, thanks to the proportions being cleverly thought out; the cheese itself is quite tender, and the overall taste is rather honeyed.

HOW TO ENJOY This is a full-flavoured cheese, so serve it alone, at the end of a meal, with a local red like Cap Corse.

FRANCE Corse	
Age 3 months	
Weight and Shape 750g (1lb 10oz), round	
Size D. 12cm (5in), H. 4.5cm (2in)	
Milk Ewe	
Classification Aged fresh	
Producer Various	

Forme d'Antoine

This recently created, semi-soft cow's milk cheese is produced in the Nord Pas-de-Calais region. It is formed into an unusual but attractive dome shape, encased in an orange crusty rind which is formed over six weeks through the process of regular washings.

TASTING NOTES It has a quite strong flavour balanced with a milky and spicy taste. The semi-soft paste has a milky aroma.

HOW TO ENJOY Pair this cheese with a full-bodied wine, such as a Côte de Beaune or Beaujolais, or with a sweet wine, such as Gewürztraminer.

FRANCE Nord-Pas-de-Calais	
Age 4 months	
Weight and Shape 400g (14oz), dome	
Size D. 12cm (5in), H. 4.5cm (2in)	
Milk Cow	
Classification Semi-soft	
Producer M. Bernard	

Fouchtra

The rind is similar to that of Cantal and St Nectaire, and is dusted with a colourful mix of white, red, and sulphur-yellow moulds. It has a subtle, mild taste and its flavour reflects the flora found in the volcanic mountains where it is produced. It is also made using cow's milk.

TASTING NOTES This cheese has a surprisingly soft and silky texture. The distinctive and memorable flavour has a lingering almondy aftertaste.

HOW TO ENJOY A full-bodied, structured red wine, such as Saint Joseph or Vacqueyras, is the best match for this flavorsome cheese.

FRANCE Cantal, Auvergne	
Age 3 months	
Weight and Shape 6kg (13lb 4oz), wheel	
Size D. 36cm (14in), H. 7cm (3in)	
Milk Goat or cow	
Classification Semi-soft	
Producer Various	

Fougerus

An artisan cheese that was originally made for family consumption, Fougerus has been commercially produced since the beginning of the 20th century. In size it is slightly bigger than its Brie relative, Coulommier.

TASTING NOTES The fern leaves used to decorate the cheese give it a "forest" aroma, and the rind has a mouldy, mushroomy scent. Soft in texture, it melts in the mouth with a rather pronounced tang.

HOW TO ENJOY This decorative cheese brightens up a cheeseboard. Try pairing it with a lively fruity red wine, such as a Côte de Beaune.

FRANCE Ile-de-France	
Age 3–4 weeks	
Weight and Shape 500g (1lb 2oz), round	
Size D. 15cm (6in), H. 4cm (1½in)	
Milk Cow	
Classification Soft white	
Producer Various	

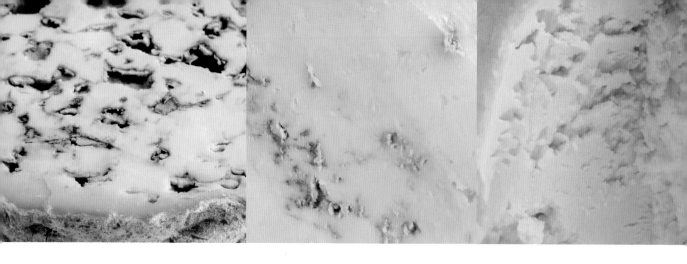

Fourme d'Ambert AOC

One of the oldest cheeses in France, this blue cheese dates from the Roman period. The AOC was granted in 1972 along with Forme de Montbrison. In 2002, in recognition of their differences in style and terroir, Forme de Montbrison received its own AOC.

TASTING NOTES It has a quite pronounced flavour, with some bitterness. The texture is creamy, bold, and rich, while the aroma gives a hint of the cellar in which it is aged.

HOW TO ENJOY Serve with wines such as Coteaux d'Auvergne, Côtes Roannaises, and a full-bodied Beaujolais, or try it with a sweet Sauternes or Banyuls.

FRANCE Auvergne	
Age 3 months	
Weight and Shape 1.5kg (3lb 5oz), cylinder	
Size D. 12cm (5in), L. 17cm (7in)	
Milk Cow	
Classification Blue	
Producer Various	

Fourme de Montbrison AOC

Fourme d'Ambert and Fourme de Montbrison are made in their two different namesake towns. Till 2002, both shared an AOC, but now have separate AOC requirements. *Fourme* comes from the Latin *forma*, meaning form or shape.

TASTING NOTES Less creamy, slightly stronger and more complex than Fourme d'Ambert, with a long, spicy finish. The yellow interior has uneven blotches and broken lines of blue.

HOW TO ENJOY Team with local wines like Coteaux d'Auvergne or Côtes Roannaises or a sweet wine.

FRANCE Rhône-Alpes	
Age 3 months	
Weight and Shape 1.5kg (3lb 5oz), cylinder	
Size D. 12cm (5in), H. 21cm (8in)	
Milk Cow	
Classification Blue	
Producer Various	

Gaperon

In the past, the number of these cheeses hanging in the kitchen was an indication of a farmer's wealth and therefore his daughter's dowry. This speciality of Auvergne was originally made by mixing buttermilk with fresh milk; buttermilk is no longer used, but it is still ripened by airing.

TASTING NOTES Beneath the dry, hard rind is an elastic paste containing garlic and pepper, which gives it a pronounced flavour. As it is hung and cured by the fire, it has a smoky tang.

HOW TO ENJOY It is a delicious cheese for snacking. Partner with robust, full-bodied wines, such as Côtes-du-Rhône.

FRANCE Auvergne	
Age 1–2 months	
Weight and Shape 350g–500g (12½oz–1lb 2oz), flattened ball	
Size D. 9cm (3½in), H. 6cm–7.5cm (2½–3in)	
Milk Cow	
Classification Semi-soft	
Producer Various	

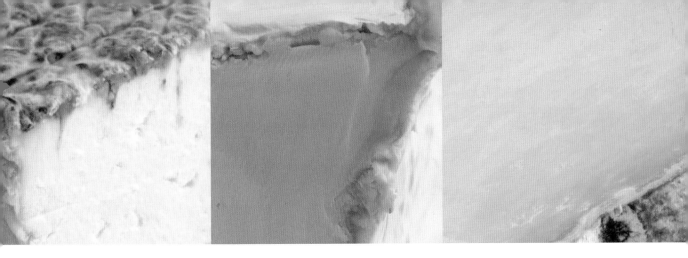

Gour Noir

This delicious artisan cheese, made from goat's milk and sprinkled with wood ash, is the product of farmers of the Auvergne who are passionate about cheesemaking and their products. These same cheesemakers also make Gour Blanc, a variety without ash.

TASTING NOTES Beneath the soft, wrinkly rind, the taste changes according to its age. It can be very sweet or spicy, but it is always full of subtle flavours and has a delicate hint of goat's milk.

HOW TO ENJOY Serve Gour Noir with a slice of simple country bread. It is complemented well by a light Loire wine, such as a Chateaumeillant.

FRANCE Auvergne	
Age 2–6 weeks	
Weight and Shape 200g (7oz), oval	
Size L. 10cm (4in), H. 3.5cm (1in)	
Milk Goat	
Classification Aged fresh	
Producer La Fromagerie Corbreche	

Gratte-Paille

This white-rinded cheese, created in the 1970s, is a real treat for those who are not put off by a high fat content. Made with triple cream (70 per cent cream for every 100g of cheese), the rind bears the imprint of the straw mats on which it is ripened.

TASTING NOTES The triple cream gives Gratte-Paille a rich, very milky taste while the almost buttery paste has an oily texture and sometimes a mushroomy flavour.

HOW TO ENJOY Grate on vegetables and chicken dishes. It is delicious served with strawberries. Drink with a red wine, such as a Sancerre Rouge or Champagne.

FRANCE Seine-et-Marne, Ile-de-France	
Age About 4 weeks	
Weight and Shape 300g (10½oz), brick	
Size H. 7.5cm (3½in), W. 6cm (2½in)	
Milk Cow	
Classification Soft white	
Producer Rouzaire dairy	

Laguiole AOC

Also known as Fourme de Laguiole, this is a very old cheese that dates back centuries, first produced by monks in their monastery in the Aubrac mountains. Laguiole has benefited from the AOC label since 1961.

TASTING NOTES Laguiole has a firm, smooth texture; a strong smell with a penetrating bouquet; and a spicy tang but a mild, milky flavour. As the cheese ages, it becomes more delicious.

HOW TO ENJOY It is excellent for snacks or served on a cheeseboard at the end of a meal. You can serve it with all fruity wines of Marcillac, du Fel, Costières de Nîmes.

FRANCE Laguiole, Midi-Pyrénées	
Age 4–6 months	
Weight and Shape 30–40kg (66–88lb), cylinder	
Size D. 40cm (16in), H. 35cm–40cm (14–16in)	
Milk Cow	
Classification Hard	
Producer Jeune Montagne cooperative	

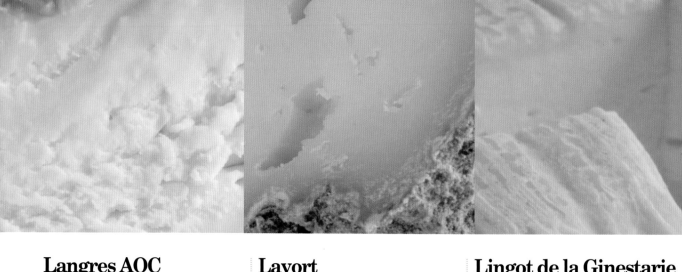

Langres AOC

With its orange-coloured rind, Langres resembles Epoisses de Bourgogne, while its name comes from the plateau of Langres in Champagne, where it was traditionally sold. The annatto used in the wash gives the rind its colour. AOC protected since 1991.

TASTING NOTES This strong-smelling cheese has a penetrating bouquet, and it tastes a little spicy when young. The texture changes with age, starting grainy and becoming very creamy, sticky and melt-in-the-mouth.

HOW TO ENJOY Pair it with any of the full-bodied red wines of the Bourgogne region to match its strong flavour.

FRANCE Langres, Champagne Ardenne
Age 2–3 months
Weight and Shape 300g (10oz), cylinder with sunken top
Size D. 10cm (4in), H. 5cm (2in)
Milk Cow
Classification Semi-soft
Producer Schertenleib Dairy and Reumillet

Lavort

Shaped like a crater as a tribute to the Auvergne volcanoes, this ewe's cheese was created in the late 20th century. The five bands of rush leaves were originally positioned around it to prevent the cheese from collapsing as it matured.

TASTING NOTES It is creamy and delicate paste has numerous holes and differs in texture depending on the level of maturity. On the finish it has a subtle taste of hazelnuts.

HOW TO ENJOY It is excellent in a crunchy salad, so much so that it features in several local salad-based specialities.

FRANCE Puy Guillaume, Auvergne
Age 3–6 months
Weight and Shape 500g (1lb 2oz), drum
Size D. 15cm (6in), H. 11cm (4½in)
Milk Ewe
Classification Hard
Producer Fromagerie de Terre-Dieu

Lingot de la Ginestarie

This small, fresh ewe's milk cheese is produced in the Pyrénées by M. Teosky, a passionate farmer who is originally from Poland and grazes both sheep and goats on his pastures.

TASTING NOTES A farmhouse cheese, Lingot de la Ginestarie is soft, becoming almost runny with age, and tastes sweet with a fresh and pleasant countryside aroma.

HOW TO ENJOY Its brick shape makes it distinctive-looking on a cheeseboard, and its fresh, delicate taste is best paired with a light red wine such as a Chinon.

FRANCE Tarn, Midi-Pyrénées
Age 2 weeks
Weight and Shape 140g (5oz), brick
Size L. 10cm (4in), W. 5cm (2in), H. 5cm (2in)
Milk Ewe
Classification Aged fresh
Producer M. Teosky

FRANCE

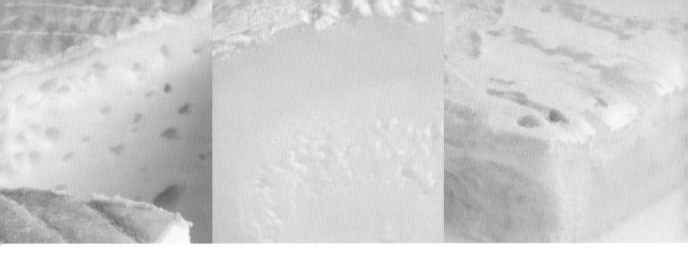

Livarot AOC

One of the most ancient cheeses of Normandie, Livarot was probably invented by local monks. Its nickname, "the Colonel", comes from the five stripes of sedge grass that encircle the cheese's washed rind and resemble the stripes used on military uniforms to denote an officer's rank.

TASTING NOTES A good Livarot should have a firm, orange-brown, slightly sticky rind and a strong spicy flavour.

HOW TO ENJOY Team a perfectly ripe cheese with any well-knit red wine, but it is equally good with a cider, such as one from Normandy, or a sweet late-harvest Alsace wine.

FRANCE Basse-Normandie	
Age 3 months	
Weight and Shape 500g (1lb 2oz), drum	
Size D. 12cm (5in), H. 5cm (2in)	
Milk Cow	
Classification Semi-soft	
Producer Fromagerie E Graindorge; Fromagerie Thebault	

Lou Rocaillou

Lou Rocaillou means "the craggy cheese" in local dialect, referring to the causse Méjean, a large limestone plateau where the ewes whose milk creates this cheese enjoy grazing.

TASTING NOTES Rocaillou has a white moulded rind and a smooth, supple and fine paste that almost melts in the mouth. Whether it is eaten young or kept until it is more mature, it is always a very sweet cheese.

HOW TO ENJOY It makes a delicious snack whether eaten on its own or spread on fresh bread. As part of a cheeseboard, it offers an interesting alternative to sharper cheeses.

FRANCE Aveyron, Midi-Pyrénées	
Age 2 weeks	
Weight and Shape 85g (3oz), round	
Size D. 5cm (2in), H. 3.5cm (1½in)	
Milk Ewe	
Classification Aged fresh	
Producer M. Dombres	

Lou Sotch

Lou Sotch is a small, oval ewe's milk cheese from the Grands Causses Nature Park in the Aveyron area. With its thin wrinkly rind dusted with white mould it looks a little like Rocamadour, a small goat's milk cheese, but this cheese is more flavoursome.

TASTING NOTES A smooth paste, tender rind and nutty powerful taste makes Lou Sotch a delightful alternative for all lovers of goat's cheese.

HOW TO ENJOY Eat with savoury chutneys and serve with a chilled dry white wine as an aperitif.

FRANCE Aveyron, Midi-Pyrénées	
Age 12–20 weeks	
Weight and Shape 30g (1oz), oval	
Size L. 15cm (6in), H. 1.5cm (½in)	
Milk Ewe	
Classification Aged fresh	
Producer M. Dombres	

Epoisses de Bourgogne AOC

According to legend, this cheese was created in the 16th century in the village of Epoisses, by the local monks. It was based on the first washed-rind cheese created at Maroilles Abbey in Thierache, Northern France around 960CE.

The monks were forbidden meat on fast days, and with over a hundred of these (not to mention compulsory fish on Friday), cheese was an essential part of their diet. The washed-rind cheeses with their strong, pungent meaty taste must have seemed like a gift from above. When the monastery closed, the monks left behind the recipe, which was then passed from mother to daughter. However, it was all but lost until Robert and Simone Berthaut decided to revive the old recipe in 1956. Other producers have since joined the revival and, in 1991, Epoisses was awarded an AOC Protected Designation Origin.

To qualify for AOC status it must be made in the departments of the Côte d'Or, the Yvonne, or the Haute Marne, and a small area west of the famous town of Dijon. Despite being made by only four producers, it is found in cheese shops as far afield as the United States, China, and Australia.

TASTING NOTES Epoisses *Frais*, at 30 days, is firm, moist, slightly grainy with a softening around the thin, pale orange rind and is mild and lactic with a subtle savoury, yeasty tang. At 40 days, Epoisses *Affinée* has a sticky, wrinkled, terracotta rind and pungent spicy aroma and a smooth velvety texture. When the outer edges are near to collapsing, the inside is not far behind and the aroma, described by some as reminiscent of smelly socks, is matched by the wickedly strong, strangely meaty taste.

HOW TO ENJOY No cheeseboard is complete without a washed-rind cheese, and Epoisses is among the greatest. Smear it on nut and raisin bread or, if you love strong cheese, bake and serve it with crusty bread or dollop some on sliced potatoes and bake. Cooking brings out its sweeter side, but its intense flavour and aroma means it should be used sparingly. The smooth velvety texture and strong aromatic flavour demands a fine red Burgundy Pinot Noir or a rich buttery Chardonnay, but a spicy aromatic Riesling or Marc de Bourgogne are equally good companions.

The milk for Epoisses *comes from Brune, French Simmental, and Montbéliarde cows.*

FRANCE Bourgogne and Champagne Ardenne	
Age 4–6 weeks	
Weight and Shape 250g (9oz), round	
Size D. 16.5 (6in), H. 3cm (1in)	
Milk Cow	
Classification Semi-soft	
Producer Various	

A CLOSER LOOK

The unique colour of Epoisses is caused by the regular hand washing of the cheeses in brandy and brine, which also make it one of the most pungent of the washed-rind cheeses.

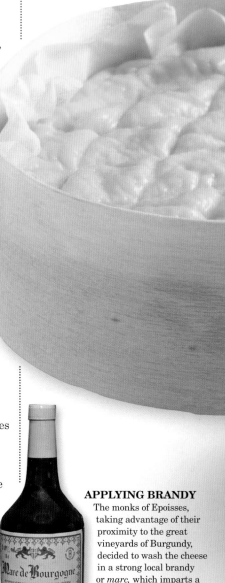

APPLYING BRANDY

The monks of Epoisses, taking advantage of their proximity to the great vineyards of Burgundy, decided to wash the cheese in a strong local brandy or *marc*, which imparts a distinct alcoholic whiff and creates an intense, sticky, orange rind.

SMEAR-RIPENING Every day for 4–6 weeks, the young cheeses are washed in a mix of brine and a special bacteria called *brevibacterium linens*, a process often referred to as smear-ripening.

PACKAGING The cheeses are packed in small round wooden boxes made with wood from the Jura mountains. Traditionally, they were lined with chestnut leaves, but these are now banned due to health regulations. Now, attractive brown paper leaves are used instead. The perforated micro film stretched over the box in which the cheese is sold prevents the buyer from feeling if the cheese is ripe. Instead you judge its maturity by the intensity of its colour.

YELLOWING Smear-ripening causes the rind to gradually change from pale yellow-orange to an increasingly sticky, glistening tangerine-orange with a fine dusting of white flora or yeast.

The washed rind is orange to terracotta in colour, and pungent in flavour.

The interior is moist and creamy-coloured.

Round, portion removed

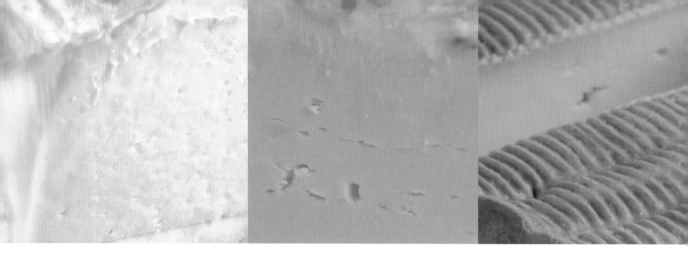

Lucullus

This soft white cheese is produced in Normandy and named after a famous Roman general and gourmet. It is made by adding generous quantities of cream to the milk before it is coagulated. The high cream content means it is more stable than other soft white cheeses, so keeps for longer in the fridge.

TASTING NOTES It develops a soft white rind with a mushroomy aroma. It has a wickedly rich, luxurious feel in the mouth and a nutty flavour. Forget the fat content; just enjoy the taste!

HOW TO ENJOY Eat on crackers or crusty bread and team with a light fruity wine with bouquet, such as red Bouzy.

FRANCE Ile-de-France and Normandie	
Age 3–4 weeks	
Weight and Shape 225g (8oz), drum	
Size D. 7.5cm (3in), H. 5cm (2in)	
Milk Cow	
Classification Soft white	
Producer Various	

Mâconnais AOC

The Mâconnais is made from pure goat's milk or from a combination of goat's and cow's milk, which is available all year round. It is produced in the Bourgogne region and was given the AOC label in 2005.

TASTING NOTES It has a unique taste: a faint goaty and slightly nutty flavour, and a delicate aroma of spring herbs. Eaten fresh, it is white and creamy; left to mature it becomes harder and slightly salty.

HOW TO ENJOY It is best served with the dry and fruity whites of the Mâconnais region, such as Beaujolais and Mâcon.

FRANCE Bourgogne	
Age 1–2 weeks	
Weight and Shape 60g (2oz), truncated cone	
Size D. 5cm (2in) at base, 3.5cm (1.5in) at top, H. 3.5cm (1.5in)	
Milk Goat and cow	
Classification Aged fresh	
Producer Various	

Maroilles AOC

The most famous cheese in the north of France, Maroilles was invented by monks in 962CE. Regular turning and washing eliminates the natural white mould and promotes the development of the bacteria that gives the rind its distinctive orange-red colour.

TASTING NOTES Maroilles' paste is golden-yellow, soft, and oily, and it has a strong flavour and aroma with a sweet, lingering aftertaste.

HOW TO ENJOY A local favourite involves using Maroilles in a sauce for chicken dishes. Eat it alongside all very strong, vigorous red wines, such as Châteauneuf-du-Pâpe.

FRANCE Nord-Pas-de-Calais	
Age 4 months	
Weight and Shape 800g (1¾lb), square	
Size L. 13cm (5in), W. 13cm (5in), H. 4cm (1½in)	
Milk Cow	
Classification Semi-soft	
Producer Various	

Mimolette

This hard cheese originated in the Netherlands, but since the 17th century it has also been made in northern France. It is produced using the same methods as Edam, but is coloured with annatto and aged for a minimum of three months.

TASTING NOTES As it ripens, the paste of this colourful cheese changes from bright orange to orange-brown and the texture becomes brittle. The flavour is mild but becomes stronger with age.

HOW TO ENJOY Eat as an appetizer. Serve with all light and fruity wines, such as Côte de Beaune, but it is commonly served with beers, port or Madeira.

FRANCE Nord-Pas-De-Calais	
Age 3–24 months	
Weight and Shape 2.5kg–2.7kg (5½lb–6lb), ball	
Size D. 16cm (6in), H. 13cm (5in)	
Milk Cow	
Classification Hard	
Producer Various	

Mont d'Or AOC

The Mont d'Or mountains lie on the French–Swiss border, and it is there that this cheese is made between the end of August and the middle of March. It has been produced in both countries for centuries, however it is the French who have been granted an AOC label (in 1981).

TASTING NOTES This creamy cheese has a delicate taste with a hint of the spruce band that binds it and helps it to keep its shape while maturing.

HOW TO ENJOY Scoop it out with a spoon at the end of the meal or melt it in the oven and eat it like a fondue.

FRANCE Franche-Comté	
Age 1 month	
Weight and Shape 115g (4oz), round	
Size D. 7.5cm (3in), H. 1cm (½in)	
Milk Cow	
Classification Semi-soft	
Producer Various	

Morbier AOC

This washed-rind cheese is made by the cheesemakers of Comté in the Jura mountains. It is characterised by a horizontal dark line in the centre of the cheese. Traditionally, the producers sprinkled soot from wood fires over the morning curd, then covered it with curd from the evening milking. Today, wood ash is used to recreate the look.

TASTING NOTES It has a soft and delicate paste, a rather pronounced flavour and a mild, milky aroma. The more it ages, the sweeter and stronger the taste.

HOW TO ENJOY Serve with a local Arbois wine or light and fruity wines like Beaujolais or Jura.

FRANCE Franche-Comté	
Age 2–3 months	
Weight and Shape 5–9kg (11lb–19lb 13oz), wheel	
Size D. 36–41cm (14–16in), H. 7.5–10cm (3–4in)	
Milk Cow	
Classification Semi-soft	
Producer Various	

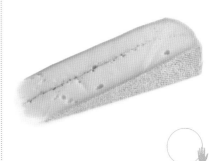

Morvan

This is a soft cheese that is typically eaten during spring and summer. It is a *fermier* cheese that is produced in Bourgogne and named after the Regional Nature Park of Morvan, a beautiful nature preserve of woods, forests, and mountains.

TASTING NOTES This cheese is best eaten fresh. It is slightly nutty and has a faint goaty flavour.

HOW TO ENJOY Eat it with fresh seasonal berries. Team with a light white wine such as Mâconnais, Beaujolais, or Mâcon.

FRANCE Bourgogne	
Age 3 weeks	
Weight and Shape 115g (3½oz), drum	
Size D. 7cm (3in). H. 4cm (1½in)	
Milk Goat	
Classification Aged fresh	
Producer Various	

Mothais-sur-Feuille

Goats were introduced to the Poitou by the Moors during the 15th century and now play a significant role in the local economy. This farmhouse cheese undergoes an unusual production method for a goat's cheese; it is placed on a chestnut leaf and ripened at a high humidity, rather than in dry conditions, so it retains more moisture.

TASTING NOTES With a soft, sticky white rind and creamy texture, the Mothais-sur-Feuille has a light, mouldy aroma and a long-lasting, delicate aftertaste.

HOW TO ENJOY Partner this melt-in-the-mouth cheese with a full-bodied red wine of Poitou.

FRANCE Poitou-Charentes	
Age 2 weeks	
Weight and Shape 225–250g (8–9oz), round	
Size D. 10cm (4in), H. 2.5cm (1in)	
Milk Goat	
Classification Aged fresh	
Producer Various	

Munster AOC

Munster is an ancient, washed-rind cheese of monastic origin that dates back to the Middle Ages. It is also known as Géromé when made in the Lorraine region. Its AOC status was established in 1969.

TASTING NOTES When properly matured, it has a strong penetrating smell and the flavour of rich milk. There is also a version available that comes ready flavoured with cumin.

HOW TO ENJOY Eat this like a local: serve it with cumin on boiled potatoes. Pair a young cheese with Gewürztraminer, and an older one with very full-bodied reds like Côte-Rôtie or Haut-Médoc.

FRANCE Alsace and Lorraine	
Age 2–3 months	
Weight and Shape 280g–1.5kg (10oz–3lb 3oz), round	
Size D. 13–19cm (5–7in), H. 2.5–8cm (1–3in)	
Milk Cow	
Classification Semi-soft	
Producer Various	

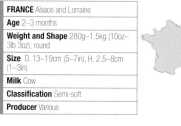

Olivet

Named after the town on the Loire River in which it was first made, Olivet is produced in a variety of forms. Cendré (shown here), matured in ashes, has a rather gritty, ash-grey rind; au Foin has a white rind covered with a few strands of dry grass; and Poivre is covered in crushed pepper.

TASTING NOTES Olivet has a subtle taste of salt and mushrooms, tinged with a slight scent of mould.

HOW TO ENJOY Serve with rosé wines from the region, such as a Pinot Meunier from Orléanais or any fruity red, such as a Borgueil.

FRANCE Centre	
Age 1 month	
Weight and Shape 300g (10½) oz, round	
Size D. 12cm (5in), H. 2.5cm (1in)	
Milk Cow	
Classification Soft white	
Producer Various	

Ossau-Iraty AOC

The name of this hard cheese refers to the valley of Ossau, in Béarn, and the forests of Iraty, in the Basque Country, and encompasses a number of wonderful cheeses made using the milk of the Manech ewes that graze in this breathtakingly beautiful region.

TASTING NOTES Ossau-Iraty has a sharp and somewhat nutty taste, and the rind is pretty firm, especially after a long maturation. If you have a strong palate, try the Espelette pepper variety.

HOW TO ENJOY Eat in traditional fashion with itxassou (a local black cherry jam) which counterbalances its sharpness. It also features in numerous local dishes.

FRANCE Pays Basques	
Age 3 months minimum	
Weight and Shape 2–7kg (4½lb–15lb 7oz), round	
Size D. 18–28cm (7–11in), H. 7–15cm (3–4½in)	
Milk Ewe	
Classification Hard	
Producer Various	

Palet de Bourgogne

This is a 20th-century creation of the well-known Burgundian cheesemaker, Raymond Gaugry. This cheese is based on Epoisse and is washed every two days with brine and Marc de Bourgogne so that it becomes wet and a reddish colour.

TASTING NOTES The paste of this strongly scented cheese is fine and creamy, and has a powerful and penetrating flavour that is not unlike the Epoisses and the Ami du Chambertin, but not as strong.

HOW TO ENJOY This full-flavoured cheese is best eaten alongside a light red wine, such as a Savigny-les-Beaune.

FRANCE Gevrey-Chambertin, Bourgogne	
Age 4 weeks	
Weight and Shape 125g (4½oz), round	
Size D. 9cm (3½in), H. 3.5cm (1in)	
Milk Cow	
Classification Semi-soft	
Producer Fromagerie Gaugry	

Pavé d'Auge

An old variation of Pont-L'Evêque, this semi-soft cheese is nowadays a generic name for several square, washed-rind cheeses produced in the Auge area. These include Pavé de Moyaux (the name of an area), Pavé du Plessis (the name of a dairy), and Trouville (named after a small seaside town). *Pavé* is the French for the rough paving stones found in most old local towns.

TASTING NOTES Pavé d'Auge has a spicy flavour and strong tang that can be a little bitter.

HOW TO ENJOY Pair this with a strong, full-bodied red wine with some bouquet: Bourgueil, Fleurie, or Pomerol.

FRANCE Basse-Normandie	
Age 2 months	
Weight and Shape 750g (1lb 10oz), square	
Size L. 11cm (4½in), W. 11cm (4½in), H. 5cm (2in)	
Milk Cow	
Classification Semi-soft	
Producer Various	

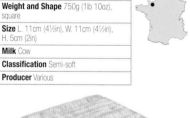

Pavé Blésois

This artisan cheese is produced in both a square and a rectangle shape, and its dry surface is covered in an elegant and interesting silvery blue mould. It is made in the Blesois region of France, near the River Loire.

TASTING NOTES It has an aroma of goat's milk. The paste is clean and smooth, with a hazelnut note and a tongue-tingling aftertaste.

HOW TO ENJOY An excellent country cheese, Pavé Blésois makes a great addition to a simple salad and is best served with a dry and simple light white wine, such as a Chinon.

FRANCE Centre	
Age 6 weeks	
Weight and Shape 250g (9oz) square, 300g (10oz) rectangle	
Size Square: L. 8cm (3in), W. 8cm (3in) H. 4cm (1½in); Rectangle: L. 12cm (5in), W. 7cm (3in), H. 3.5cm (1½in)	
Milk Goat	
Classification Aged fresh	
Producer Various	

Pavé de la Ginestarie

A unique cheese, Pavé de la Ginestarie is produced from the milk of goats that live in the Pyrénées mountains, but exactly how it is made is a well-kept secret. What is known is that there are traces of straw in the rind and that its bacteria form part of the ripening process.

TASTING NOTES This organic, white-rinded cheese has a pale paste with a hint of straw in the flavour. It has a subtle taste but a long-lasting finish.

HOW TO ENJOY For a delicious combination, pair this delicate cheese with fresh blackberries or currants to give it a real sweetness.

FRANCE Tarn, Midi-Pyrénées	
Age 3 weeks	
Weight and Shape 30g (1oz), square	
Size L. 9cm (3½in), W. 9cm (3½in), H. 2cm (¾in)	
Milk Goat	
Classification Aged fresh	
Producer M. Teosky	

Pavé du Nord

This cheese is also known as Pavé de Roubaix, named after the textile city of Roubaix located in the north of France. Historically, the cheese could always be found on the weavers' tables. Its attractive, carrot-orange interior, like Mimolette, derives from the use of annatto in its production.

TASTING NOTES It has a rock-hard, orange to brown rind and a very hard, compact texture with a few small holes, and an intense, mouth-tingling, tangy finish.

HOW TO ENJOY Shave or thinly slice as an appetizer with a beer, or use to add character and flavour to cheese sauces.

FRANCE Nord-Pas-de-Calais		
Age 6–24 months		
Weight and Shape 4kg (8lb 13oz), brick		
Size L. 27cm (11in), W. 13cm (5in), H. 8cm (3in)		
Milk Cow		
Classification Hard		
Producer Various		

Pavin

Produced in the mountains of Forez using a similar method to that for Saint-Nectaire, this semi-soft cheese is named after a Lake in the Auvergne. Pavin is washed with a mix of brine and annatto to create a sticky orange rind that is dusted with a fine white mould.

TASTING NOTES The paste is light yellow in colour and is tinged with the scent of mushrooms, and it has the flavour of hazelnuts.

HOW TO ENJOY Serve it with a full-bodied wine from the Bourgogne, such as a Pommard or Mercurey.

FRANCE Auvergne		
Age About 8 weeks		
Weight and Shape 450g (1lb), round		
Size D. 13cm (5in), H. 4cm (1½in)		
Milk Cow		
Classification Semi-soft		
Producer Various		

Pechegos

This cheese derives its name from a plateau in the Tarn region. It is here that the goats whose raw milk is used in the production of Pechegos graze. The finished washed cheese has a distinctive-looking copper-coloured rind and is bound with spruce bark.

TASTING NOTES Pechegos has a very creamy texture, similar to the famous Mont d'Or on which the recipe is based. It is a real taste sensation, with many different mushroomy and truffle flavours.

HOW TO ENJOY Serve it alongside potatoes or eggs, with a full-bodied white such as Jurancon, or a red, such as Madiran.

FRANCE Tarn, Midi-Pyrénées		
Age 8 weeks		
Weight and Shape 300g (10oz), round		
Size D. 10cm (4in), H. 4cm (1½in)		
Milk Goat		
Classification Semi-soft		
Producer Le Pic Cooperative		

Pélardon AOC

Pélardon is a generic name for small goat cheeses produced in the Cévennes region of France, near the Alps. These include Pélardon des Cévennes (shown here), Pélardon d'Anduze, and Pélardon d'Altier.

TASTING NOTES Pélardon cheeses have a creamy and dense texture; a full, rich milky and nutty flavour; and a lingering aftertaste. The rind is barely formed, thin, soft and wrinkled, and as it matures it develops a natural mould.

HOW TO ENJOY Lightly grill or bake and accompany with a red Costières de Nîmes or a full-bodied Côtes-du-Rhône, such as Gigondas or Vacqueyras.

FRANCE Languedoc-Roussillon	
Age 2–3 weeks	
Weight and Shape 85–125g (3–4½oz), disc	
Size D. 6–7.5cm (2½–3in), H. 2.5cm (1in)	
Milk Goat	
Classification Aged fresh	
Producer Various	

Pérail

Although it has existed for centuries, this small cheese used to be made only as a way to prevent wastage, using up small quantities of milk when there was not enough left to make Roquefort. Nowadays it is considered to be a renowned speciality.

TASTING NOTES Pérail has a less pronounced flavour than most ewe's milk cheeses, probably because of its rather short ageing period. With its smooth paste and tender rind, it has a soft yet distinguishable nutty taste.

HOW TO ENJOY Serve it with rose hip jam. It pairs well with all lively wines from the South of France.

FRANCE Aveyron, Midi-Pyrénées	
Age Best around 2 weeks	
Weight and Shape 85–140g (3–5oz), disc	
Size D. 8–10cm (3–4in), H. 2cm (1in),	
Milk Ewe	
Classification Aged fresh	
Producer M. Dombres	

Persillé de Tignes

Although *persillé* translates as "parsley", it in fact refers to the fine blue-green mould that appears naturally inside the cheese rather than as a result of piercing to encourage the blue. The mustard-coloured pigment on the rind is thought to be linked to the fact that the goats whose milk is used graze on sulphurous soil.

TASTING NOTES It is lactic and herbaceous with richer flavours in summer and autumn. As it ripens, it becomes dry, spicy, and intense, and it breaks easily.

HOW TO ENJOY Persillé can be enjoyed with all fruity and light red wines, such as a Crépy or Saumure.

FRANCE Rhône-Alpes	
Age 2–6 months	
Weight and Shape 900g (2lb), cylinder	
Size D. 11cm (4½in), H. 9cm (3½in)	
Milk Goat	
Classification Hard	
Producer Various	

Petit Fiancé des Pyrénées

First created in 1989, this unpasteurized goat's cheese is made from the milk of an alpine breed of goats. After the whey is drained from the curds, the cheese is circled with a band of ash wood and washed repeatedly for six weeks as it matures.

TASTING NOTES The washing process gives the cheese a moist texture, and the ash binding infuses it with a woody aroma. The finished cheese has a supple melting interior.

HOW TO ENJOY Petit Fiancé des Pyrénées is best paired with a fruity white wine, such as a Condrieux.

FRANCE Midi-Pyrénées	
Age 6 weeks	
Weight and Shape 300g (10oz), round	
Size D. 12cm (5in), H. 3.5cm (1in)	
Milk Goat	
Classification Semi-soft	
Producer Fromagerie Fermier Cabrioulet	

Picodon AOC

This cheese is made from the milk of the goats that graze on the mountain grass and shrubs of the Ardèche and Drome regions. These pastures are filled with strong aromas and flavours, which in turn produce milk of the highest quality. Picodon has been AOC protected since 1983.

TASTING NOTES The goats' diet gives Picodon its spicy flavour; however, the paste is so dry that the flavour is best obtained by sucking the cheese.

HOW TO ENJOY Picodon tastes delicious when added to salads or paired with lively, full-bodied red and white wines from the Côtes-du-Rhône.

FRANCE Rhône-Alpes	
Age 1 month	
Weight and Shape 115g (4oz), round	
Size D. 7.5cm (3in), H. 2.5cm (1in)	
Milk Goat	
Classification Aged fresh	
Producer Various	

Pierre-Robert

Pierre-Robert originally owes its name to Robert Rouzaire, the producer, and his friend Pierre. This soft white cheese is now made by Rouzaire's son. It is not a cheese for anyone watching their calorie intake; this triple-cream cheese has extra cream added to the milk to give it a fat content of 75 per cent for every 100g and a luxurious, rich taste.

TASTING NOTES This very creamy, buttery and slightly sour cream tang melts in the mouth when young. Over time, it becomes richer and tangy.

HOW TO ENJOY It is delicious with pears, or with a full-bodied Bourgogne, such as Pommard or Mercurey.

FRANCE Seine-et-Marne, Ile-de-France	
Age 1 month	
Weight and shape 450g (1lb), round	
Size D. 12cm (5in), H. 5cm (2in)	
Milk Cow	
Classification Soft white	
Producer Fromagerie Rouzaire	

Reblochon de Savoie AOC

Although Reblochon has been made in the summer Alpine pastures since the 13th century, it was unheard of until after the French revolution. The reason for secrecy was the introduction of a tax. In the 14th century, farmers who grazed their cattle in the magnificent Haute-Savoie pastures overlooking Lake Annecy were forced to pay a tax based on the milk yield of their cattle.

To avoid payment of the tax, the farmer would only partially milk his cows in the presence of the tax man, then, once he departed, the cows were re-milked. This additional "tax-free" milk was then made into Reblochon – from the old Savoie word *reblocher*, to "re-milk" or "pinch the cow's udder again", and was kept for family consumption only.

After the French revolution, the tax was removed and the farmers were free to sell all their cheese. Reblochon has been protected by the AOC regulations since 1976, which states that the milk can only come from the indigenous Abondance, Tarine, and Montbéliarde cows that graze the Alpine pastures in summer and dine on hay cut from those rich summer pastures in winter. The feeding of silage or concentrates is banned, as it can taint the sweetness of the milk, and the stipulation that it can only be made from unpasteurized milk ensures production is always near the source of the raw material.

Reblochon must be made and matured in the Haute-Savoie and north-eastern parts of the Savoie by individual farmers (*fermier*), cooperatives (*fruitière*), or commercial dairies (*industriel*), who receive their milk from local farms.

TASTING NOTES When young, the cheese has the sweetness of stolen fruit. As it matures it is no longer sweet but tastes of freshly pickled, crunchy walnuts and a hint of the mountain flowers. Its supple, creamy texture flows over and caresses the palate like warm, English custard. The *fermier* cheese has a more intense, complex flavour and a farmyard aroma, but do not be deterred.

The interior captures the aroma of the wild flowers and herbs of the Haute-Savoie pastures.

HOW TO ENJOY Traditionally served with crusty *pain de campagne* (a sourdough bread), a few slices of sweet *jambon de pays* (air-dried ham), and pickled gherkins. However, it melts like a river of cheese and is amazing grilled on bread or vegetables, as a toppings for soups, or baked with potatoes and cream or on ratatouille.

Apremont, a crisp local white wine, light beer, or sweet cider make perfect companions, or enjoy with a soft red with low tannin, such as Merlot.

The Haute-Savoie pastures *and Lake Annecy.*

FRANCE Rhône-Alpes	
Age 4–12 weeks	
Weight and Shape 240–550g (9oz–1¼lb), round	
Size D. 9–12cm (3½–5in), H. 3cm (1in)	
Milk Cow	
Classification Semi soft	
Producer Various	

A CLOSER LOOK

Reblochon is a piece of history and a reflection of the unique geology of the region, the indigenous breed of cows, and the people who make it.

THE CASEIN LABEL A round green casein stamp on the rind means it's a *fermier,* "farmhouse", cheese, made in an Alpine chalet or farms in the Thones area. A red stamp means it has been made in a factory, or from the milk of more than one herd within a wider defined area.

Round of Reblochon

The supple interior oozes beneath the rind.

PRESSING A large piece of white cloth is stretched over a tray of cheese moulds. The curd is then ladled into each mould and a small wooden disc placed over the top to lightly press the curd.

FORMING THE RIND In cool cellars, often carved into the hillside under mountain chalets, the rind grows a mix of grey and white moulds, which are discouraged by regular brushing and washes in brine. The rind should be dry not damp, smooth not cracked or split, and feel supple.

The rind ranges from pinkish-yellow when young to a pale terracotta-red, usually covered with whitish flora.

PACKAGING Reblochon is wrapped with a little wooden disc on the base and sometimes on top so you need to rely on your cheese merchant to tell you if it is ripe.

The wrinkles and irregularities in the rind are formed when the cloth is trapped in the curd during pressing.

SELLES-SUR-CHER Over the fine
ash coating, a fine, velvet-like white
Penicillium candidum mould is overlaid by
splodges of blue-grey *Penicillium glaucum*.
As the cheese dries out, the original skin
shrinks and wrinkles. (See p87)

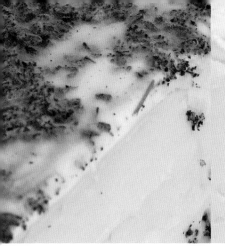

Pithiviers

Produced in Bondaroy, near Orléans, Pithiviers used to be made in summer when milk was plentiful and then stored in hay until the autumn. Now it is produced all year round, but it is still covered in fine strands of dried grasses, herbs and meadow flowers.

TASTING NOTES The white rind is sprinkled with hay, and the paste is soft with a slight fragrance of mould and mushrooms, giving a tangy flavour.

HOW TO ENJOY Team Pithiviers with the pale red Pinots of Orléanais and the fruity, lively light red wines of Orléans and Touraine (Chinon and Bourgeuil).

FRANCE Centre		
Age 4–5 weeks		
Weight and Shape 300g (10½oz), round		
Size D. 12cm (5in), H. 2.5cm (1in)		
Milk Cow		
Classification Soft white		
Producer Various		

Pont-l'Evêque AOC

Originally called Angelot, this washed-rind cheese is probably one of the oldest French cheeses – even being mentioned by Guillaume de Lorris in his 13th century allegorical poem "Roman de la Rose". Pont-L'Evêque was granted an AOC in 1976.

TASTING NOTES The creamy, yellow, smooth paste develops small holes as it ripens and has a lingering, sweet taste. Older cheeses have a stronger flavour.

HOW TO ENJOY Try eating this cheese alongside a glass of stout, or with a glass of full-bodied red wine, from Bordeaux, Burgundy, or Côtes-du-Rhône.

FRANCE Pont-l'Evêque, Basse Normandie		
Age 5–6 weeks		
Weight and Shape 350g (12oz), square		
Size L. 10cm (4in), W. 10cm (4in) H. 2.5cm (1in)		
Milk Cow		
Classification Semi-soft		
Producer Fromagerie E Graindorge, Fromagerie Thebault		

Port Salut

Created in 1816 by the monks at Abbaye du Port du Salut in the Loire, by 1873 it was so popular a flag was raised in the Paris markets announcing its arrival. It is now made by master craftsmen at the Bel creamery in the classic round and commercial styles.

TASTING NOTES Wedges are mild, squishy, velvety smooth, and taste like your best-ever cheese sauce. Traditional rounds have an elastic texture and farmyardy notes of trappist style cheeses.

HOW TO ENJOY An integral part of a French cheeseboard for over 100 years, it is perfect grilled or squished on a fresh baguette, served with a Trappiste beer.

FRANCE Loire Sable		
Age 8–12 weeks		
Weight and Shape 320g (11oz), round		
Size D. 10cm (4in), H. 4.4cm (1½in)		
Milk Cow		
Classification Semi-soft		
Producer Bel Group		

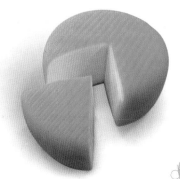

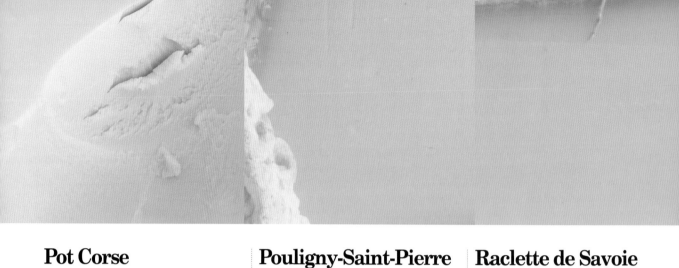

Pot Corse

Pot Corse is a *fromage fort*, a recipe developed by the French as a means of using leftover cheese. The remnants of ewe's milk cheeses are gathered together and combined with a little white wine, garlic, spices, and perhaps some herbs, then spread on bread like butter. This Corsican variation is presented in a small pot.

TASTING NOTES The strong, powerful and buttery flavour has vegetal overtones.

HOW TO ENJOY Do as the Corsicans do and match it with spicy food and a full-bodied red wine. Its pretty presentation is a bonus.

FRANCE Corse	
Age 20 weeks	
Weight and Shape 300g (10oz), jar	
Size No size	
Milk Ewe	
Classification Fresh	
Producer Various	

Pouligny-Saint-Pierre AOC

This goat's cheese, AOC protected since 1972, is nicknamed "the Pyramid" or "the Eiffel Tower" because of its shape. It has a dry, vaguely nobbly, pale cream to reddish rind which is dusted with a blue-grey mould.

TASTING NOTES With a moist, soft, and crumbly paste, the flavour changes from sour to salty to sweet. It has an aroma of the straw and of the milk of the Alpine goats used to produce it.

HOW TO ENJOY It is superb for a cheeseboard or grilled. Team it with a fruity Chenin or Sauvignon wine from the Touraine and Berry regions.

FRANCE Centre	
Age 3–5 weeks	
Weight and Shape 200g (7oz), pyramid	
Size D. 7.5cm (3in), H. 8cm (3½in)	
Milk Goat	
Classification Aged fresh	
Producer Various	

Raclette de Savoie

The name derives from the French verb *racler*, meaning to scrape, as this cheese was traditionally placed in front of an open fire and, as it melted, scraped on to hot potatoes or bread. Some are made with added flavours, such as Raclette fumée, which is smoked over beech wood; au vin blanc, rubbed with a white wine; and la moutarde, made with mustard seeds.

TASTING NOTES The supple, elastic texture melts superbly and has a sweet taste that is stronger when melted.

HOW TO ENJOY Slice and grill over potatoes and serve with cooked meats and fruity red or white Savoie wines.

FRANCE Rhône-Alpes	
Age Minimum 2 months	
Weight and Shape 4.5–7kg (8¾lb–15lb 7oz), wheel	
Size D. 28–36cm (11–14in), H. 5.5–7.5cm (2in–3in)	
Milk Cow	
Classification Semi-soft	
Producer Various	

Racotin

During the production process, the curd of this goat's cheese is drained, and it is the natural flora in the milk that brings a yellow tinge to the blue-white crinkled rind of the finished product. Similar to Charolais, but smaller, it is aged by Bernard Sivignon, a renowned affineur based in Bourgogne.

TASTING NOTES Racotin has a dense, firm, slightly grainy texture and a goaty flavour with a peppery, buttery tang.

HOW TO ENJOY Fresh raspberries and nutty bread are good accompaniments to this goat's cheese, along with a crisp white wine.

FRANCE Bourgogne	
Age 3–4 weeks	
Weight and Shape 100g (3½oz), cylinder	
Size D. 5cm (2in), H. 6cm (2½in)	
Milk Goat	
Classification Aged fresh	
Producer Various	

Rigotte de Condrieu AOC

This farmhouse cheese is quite rare, since it is made with goat's milk unlike most rigottes, which are made with cow's milk. It is a very old cheese and has been AOC protected since 2008.

TASTING NOTES Rigotte de Condrieu tastes milky but does not have a very pronounced flavour. It has a natural rind, a robust paste, and a honey and acacia aroma.

HOW TO ENJOY It goes perfectly with the light and fruity wines of Côtes du Lyonnais, Beaujolais, and Côtes- du-Rhône.

FRANCE Rhône-Alpes	
Age 2 weeks	
Weight and Shape 60g (2oz), round	
Size D. 4cm (1½in), H. 3cm (1in)	
Milk Goat	
Classification Aged fresh	
Producer Various	

Rocamadour AOC

This goat's cheese was once known as Cabécou de Rocamadour, but since it gained its AOC status in 1996 it has been renamed simply Rocamadour, after the best-known market in the region. This change in name sets it apart from other Cabécou cheeses that are not made in the Rocamadour area, and so cannot carry the AOC label.

TASTING NOTES With a tender and creamy paste, Rocamadour tastes mild and slightly milky, but has a delicious sweet and nutty aftertaste.

HOW TO ENJOY Serve with figs and pair and a fruity, robust red wine, preferably of the Cahor region.

FRANCE Lot, Midi-Pyrénées	
Age 1–3 weeks	
Weight and Shape 30g (1oz), disc	
Size D. 4.5cm (2in), H. 1.5cm (½in)	
Milk Goat	
Classification Aged fresh	
Producer Various	

Rollot

This semi-soft washed-rind cheese used to be exclusively round, but in recent times a factory version has been produced, called Cœur de Rollot, which has been moulded into a heart shape.

TASTING NOTES This powerful cheese is similar in taste to a Maroilles (see p66) and has a spicy tang. The paste has a soft, sticky texture.

HOW TO ENJOY The heart-shaped version looks decorative on an after-dinner cheeseboard. You can serve it with all lively and fruity wines, such as Saint-Emilion, Côte Rôtie, and Savigny-les-Beaune.

FRANCE Picardie	
Age 6–8 weeks	
Weight and Shape 200–300g (7–10oz), round or heart	
Size D. 7.5cm (3in), H. 4cm (1½in)	
Milk Cow	
Classification Semi-soft	
Producer Various	

Rouelle du Tarn

This creamy goat's cheese was created by a farmer from the Tarn region in 1984. Its unusual and distinctive shape is achieved by ladling the curd into a mould with a hole in the middle. It is then sprinkled with ash to create a white-grey rind. The combination of these techniques makes it an aesthetically-pleasing addition to any cheeseboard.

TASTING NOTES Rouelle du Tarn has a milky, deliciously creamy flavour and a hazelnut note.

HOW TO ENJOY Ideal with all fruity and light red wines, particularly a Saumur or Chinon.

FRANCE Midi-Pyrénées	
Age 1 month	
Weight and Shape 250g (9oz), round	
Size D. 10cm (4in), H. 1cm (½in)	
Milk Goat	
Classification Aged fresh	
Producer Various	

Rove Cendré

Generously sprinkled with ash, the Rove Cendré comes from a farm that has around 200 Rove goats with their distinct long horns and red coats. It is made only from March to December, although the hardy goats remain outdoors, grazing on the wild fragrant pastures, berries, and small bushes.

TASTING NOTES The texture is smooth and creamy, and the flavour is aromatic and herbaceous.

HOW TO ENJOY The ash coating and fresh lemony tang make Rove Cendré an attractive apéritif. Serve with fresh fig and berries, and a glass of Provençal rosé.

FRANCE Provence-Alpes-Côte D'Azur	
Age 2 weeks	
Weight and Shape 75g (2½oz), oval	
Size D. 5cm (2in), H. 3cm (1in)	
Milk Goat	
Classification Aged fresh	
Producer Various	

80

Rove des Garrigues

This fresh cheese is named after the Rove breed of goat that is native to the Mediterranean and now very rare. Rove goats produce very little milk each day (about 2 litres compared with an average of 5 litres in other breeds), but what it does produce is extremely dense and flavoursome.

TASTING NOTES The paste is pure white with a soft melt-in-the-mouth sensation and a fresh lemony tang that is overlaid with a hint of thyme and wild herbs.

HOW TO ENJOY Excellent served with a quince paste and washed down with a glass of red Côtes du Ventoux.

FRANCE Provence-Alpes-Côte D'Azur	
Age 1–2 weeks	
Weight and Shape 75g (2½oz), round	
Size D. 5cm (2in), H. 4cm (1½in)	
Milk Goat	
Classification Fresh	
Producer Various	

Sablé de Wissant

A recent creation made in Wissant, on France's northern coast, this semi-soft cheese is rolled in breadcrumbs to give it a rough, sandy (or *sablé*) rind that absorbs the pale local beer in which it is washed.

TASTING NOTES Supple with small holes, this cheese feels rich and creamy in the mouth. It has the aroma and taste of beer – yeasty and slightly sweet with a pungent farmyard finish.

HOW TO ENJOY Great on a cheeseboard because of its unusual appearance, but like all washed-rind cheeses it should be use sparingly in cooking. Serve with a light ale or a glass of Champagne.

FRANCE Wissant, Nord-Pas-de-Calais	
Age 7 weeks	
Weight and Shape 350g (13oz), square	
Size L. 12cm (5in), H. 5cm (2in)	
Milk Cow	
Classification Semi-soft	
Producer Bernard Brothers	

Saint-Christophe

Although this goat's cheese is made in the same way as Saint-Maure de Touraine (see pp92–93), it is made outside the area designated by the AOC regulations so the cheesemaker must use another name. It is available plain or with ash, as seen here.

TASTING NOTES Since it is matured in a very moist environment, it develops a soft, sticky, wrinkled rind and creamy texture. It is distinctly goaty with a nutty taste and a light, mouldy aroma.

HOW TO ENJOY It is excellent with any of the crisp white wines of the Loire or a light red wine of the Chinon.

FRANCE Saint-Christophe-Vallon, Midi-Pyrénées	
Age 2–3 weeks	
Weight and Shape 280g (10oz), log	
Size L. 14cm (5½in), W. 5.5cm (2in), H. 4.5cm (1½in)	
Milk Goat	
Classification Aged fresh	
Producer Pavé Jacquin	

Roquefort AOC

Folklore has it that Roquefort was created some 2000 years ago when a love-struck shepherd, distracted by his young love from tending his sheep, left his lunch, a piece of bread and cheese, in the cave where he had been sheltering. A few days later, he remembered the cheese and found it had developed a greenish mould through the centre.

Since then, shepherds have been maturing their cheese in the deep limestone caves of Cambalou. No chemicals, unwanted moulds, or stainless steel shelves are used to disturb the delicate balance that has for centuries produced one of the world's finest cheeses. The natural caves are about 300m (984ft) wide, and go down four to five levels.

The often harsh climate with its hot, dry summers and cold winters, and the rugged, rocky geography has for centuries been home to a local breed of hardy indigenous sheep. Lactation lasts from December to July, and each sheep, grazing on the tussock grasses and wild herbs, produces around 2–3 litres (3½–5pt)

of rich, flavoursome milk. It takes milk from 6–8 ewes to make one 3kg (6lb 6oz) cheese.

Roquefort has been protected since 1411 when Charles VI signed a charter granting the people of Roquefort-sur-Soulzon the right to make it, and in 1926 it was the first cheese to be granted Appellation d'Origine Contrôlée (AOC) status. Only those ignorant of the process would compare other ewe's milk cheese with Roquefort.

TASTING NOTES When fully aged, the mould will have fanned out to the edges of the buttery mass in streaks and pockets and the flavour is spicy, strong, and mouth-watering. Sadly, some Roquefort is consumed too young when there is barely a hint of blue and the texture is crumbly rather than cohesive and the bite has no backbone.

HOW TO ENJOY Roquefort is sublime when eaten in chunks with sourdough bread, and spectacular in sauces, or when crumbled on top of salads or pasta. Traditionally it is paired with Port or Sauternes, but it is fantastic with just about any dessert wine as the sweetness of the wine cuts though the salty tang and highlights the sweetness of the milk.

Penicillium roqueforti, *the fungus responsible for Roquefort's blue-grey mould.*

France Midi-Pyrénées	
Age 3 months	
Weight and Shape 2.5–2.9kg (5½–6¼lb), drum	
Size D. 20cm (8in), H. 8.5–10.5cm (3–4in)	
Milk Ewe	
Classification Blue	
Producer Various	

A CLOSER LOOK

There are only seven producers of Roquefort in the world, each using the same basic process and yet each achieving their own distinct and individual character. The biggest is the Roquefort Société.

Pockets of mould

THE CAVES The numerous cracks and fissures of the limestone caves allow the cool air and indigenous moulds to circulate. To encourage the growth of the blue *penicillium roqueforti* moulds, large loaves of locally grown rye bread are placed in the caves and, over three months, grow a fine fury grey coat which, when dried and powdered, is sprinkled over the newly formed cheeses.

Once pierced, the spore-laden air quickly penetrates the nooks and crannies of the loosely packed curd, developing pockets of delicious blue-green mould.

FOIL WRAPPING The cheeses are wrapped in foil four weeks after their arrival in the caves. This prevents any further mould growth on the rind.

The rind is very open and porous.

Drum, quarter removed

Saint-Domnin

This is an Alpine goat's cheese that has a character all of its own. Made in the Alpes-de-Haute-Provence, near ancient Sisteron, it is decorated with sprigs of the lavender that thrives on the region's rocky plateaus. It is also known as Carré Saint-Domnin.

TASTING NOTES The smooth texture melts in the mouth and is imbued with the scent of lavender and the subtle flavours associated with this sun-drenched land.

HOW TO ENJOY It makes the perfect ending to a hearty lunch; serve with a Provençal rosé or a sweet Muscat de Beaumes-de-Venise.

FRANCE Provence-Alpes-Côte-D'Azur	
Age 2 weeks	
Weight and Shape 150g (5½oz), bar	
Size L. 10cm (4in), W. 10cm (4in), H. 3cm (1in)	
Milk Goat	
Classification Aged fresh	
Producer Various	

84

Saint-Félicien

A natural-rinded cheese, Saint-Félicien was originally produced using goat's milk but now it is made with cow's milk. Made in the Rhône-Alpes area, it is similar to, but slightly larger than, Saint-Marcellin.

TASTING NOTES The rind is very soft, wrinkly and creamy; the interior varies from firm to almost runny and very creamy, with a delicate nutty flavour.

HOW TO ENJOY Accompany it with a sharp, strong-tasting red wine such as Saint Amour or a white Vin de Paille from Jura.

FRANCE Saint-Félicien, Rhône-Alpes	
Age 2 weeks	
Weight and Shape 200g (7oz), round	
Size D. 12cm (5in), H. 1cm (½in)	
Milk Cow	
Classification Aged fresh	
Producer Etoile du Vercors Dairy	

Saint-Florentin

Saint-Florentin, a town near the famous wine area of Chablis, is also located in the heart of one of France's great dairy regions. The traditional-style cheeses, with their reddish-brown crusts, are now quite rare, having been replaced by paler, factory-made cheeses that are sold when very young.

TASTING NOTES The smooth, shiny rind has a strong penetrating aroma, while the supple interior has a fresh, slightly salty flavour and can be quite spicy.

HOW TO ENJOY It makes a delicious addition to a fresh salad, and is best served with a robust Burgundy.

FRANCE Bourgogne	
Age 2 months	
Weight and Shape 450g (1lb), round	
Size D. 12cm (5in), H. 2.5cm (1in)	
Milk Cow	
Classification Semi-soft	
Producer Fromagerie Lincet	

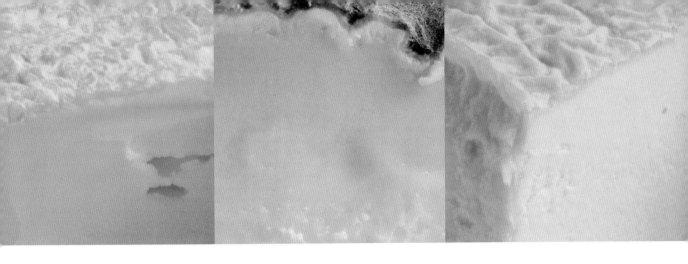

Saint-Marcellin

This pale and creamy cheese has been made in homes and small farms in the Dauphine region for centuries. It is traditionally produced from goat's milk, but today, all but a handful are made from cow's milk.

TASTING NOTES The taste, texture and appearance vary according to how the cheese is ripened, but the best have an orange-tinged rind and are soft inside. Saint-Marcellin can be firm to creamy, almost liquid, with a light, subtle lemony freshness and a nutty aroma.

HOW TO ENJOY It is superb when baked; serve with a light and fruity Beaujolais or fruity Côtes du Rhône.

FRANCE Rhône-Alpes	
Age 2–6 weeks	
Weight and Shape 85g (3oz), round	
Size D. 7.5cm (3in), H. 2.5cm (1in)	
Milk Cow or goat	
Classification Aged fresh	
Producer Various	

Saint-Nectaire AOC

One of the great cheeses of France, Saint-Nectaire is made with milk from Salers cows that graze the rich and perfumed volcanic pastures of the uplands of the Auvergne region. The traditional methods of production have been AOC protected since 1955.

TASTING NOTES At maturity, the thick rind gives off a subtle, slightly pungent aroma of straw and mushrooms, while the paste should have a pronounced taste of nut, milk and lush pastures.

HOW TO ENJOY Eat on its own with crusty bread and any light fruity wines, especially Côteaux d'Auvergne and Côtes Roannaises.

FRANCE Auvergne	
Age 8–10 weeks	
Weight and Shape 1.5kg (3lb 5oz), wheel	
Size D. 20cm (8in), H. 4cm (1½in)	
Milk Cow	
Classification Semi-soft	
Producer Various	

Saint-Nicolas-de-la-Dalmerie

At the monastery of St Nicholas, founded in 1965, the monks live off the land and keep goats. Using raw milk from the herd, they create an aromatic cheese, redolent with the flavour of thyme. As the rind develops, it turns from gentle orange to chestnut in colour. The interior is stark white.

TASTING NOTES Tangy, fruity, deep flavours typical of only the best goat's cheeses characterise this fine example, which is firm to the touch but melts in the mouth

HOW TO ENJOY Serve accompanied by a glass of fruity dry white wine.

FRANCE Languedoc, Languedoc-Roussillon	
Age 3 weeks	
Weight and Shape 100g (3½oz), bar	
Size L. 8.5cm (3⅓in), W. 4cm (1½in), H. 3cm (1in)	
Milk Goat	
Classification Aged fresh	
Producer Le Monastère Orthodoxe Saint-Nicolas	

LANGRES The cheese has been rubbed frequently with a mix of the natural dye annatto and brine, giving it a gorgeous tangerine-orange sticky rind that attracts white *Penicillium candidum* mould once the washing stops. (See p62)

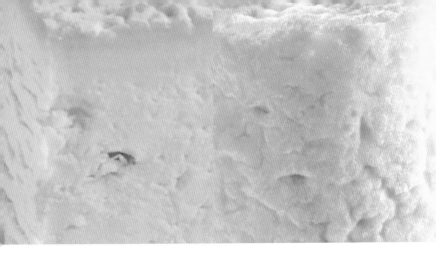

Sancerrois

Since the 16th century, the Sancerre region has been successfully breeding goats, which has led to the production of a range of superb goat's cheeses like Sancerrois, a big brother to Crottin de Chavignol.

TASTING NOTES As it ages, the rind becomes more wrinkled and dusted with grey and blue moulds. The texture also changes from firm and grainy to dense and compact, with a pronounced tang and a light goaty aroma.

HOW TO ENJOY It is excellent paired with local dry white wines, such as Sauvignon or fruity Pinot.

FRANCE Centre	
Age 3–5 weeks	
Weight and Shape 100g (3½oz), round	
Size D. 6cm (2½in), H. 6cm (2½in)	
Milk Goat	
Classification Aged fresh	
Producer Various	

Sarments d'Amour

For centuries, the vineyards around Lyon have been home to herds of goats that produce the milk for these charming cheeses. These vineyards are the inspiration behind the "branch of love" that decorates this modern French cheese; the protruding vine stem lends it an attractive air.

TASTING NOTES Sarments d'Amour has a dense white paste that feels luscious in the mouth and a subtle, but distinct, goat flavour.

HOW TO ENJOY Its charming appearance and small size makes it perfect for an appetizer; serve it with a crisp rosé or even a sparkling wine.

FRANCE Rhône-Alpes	
Age 1 week	
Weight and Shape 30g (1oz), cylinder	
Size Various	
Milk Goat	
Classification Aged fresh	
Producer Various	

Selles-sur-Cher AOC

This popular goat's cheese has been AOC protected since 1975 to maintain its traditional artisan methods of production. About 1.3 litres of milk are needed to make a single Selles-Sur-Cher; it is then coated with ash on which a bluish-grey mould develops.

TASTING NOTES It has a firm texture but melts in the mouth. The taste is a combination of sour, salty, and sweet. The locals eat the rind because they believe it gives the true taste.

HOW TO ENJOY Team Selles-Sur-Cher with all dry whites and rosés of Blésois, and light and fruity reds of Touraine, such as Chinon and Bourgeuil.

FRANCE Centre	
Age 10–21 days	
Weight and Shape 125–140g (4½–5oz), round	
Size Various. D. 7.5cm (3in), H. 2.5cm (1in) (pictured)	
Milk Goat	
Classification Aged fresh	
Producer Various	

Signal

This seasonal cheese is only made from March to November using the milk of goats that graze near Lac d'Aiguebellette in Savoie. This is France's third-largest lake, and it is set against a stunning backdrop of meadows, forests and the mountains of Epine, which were crossed in 218BCE by Hannibal, his army, and 37 elephants.

TASTING NOTES The very dense and rich paste is quite similar to that of Charolais (see p49), while the flavour has a hint of mountain flowers.

HOW TO ENJOY Eat this flavoursome cheese with ripe, fresh fruit, such as pears and mountain berries.

FRANCE Savoie, Rhône-Alpes	
Age 3 weeks	
Weight and Shape 150g (5½oz), round	
Size Various	
Milk Goat	
Classification Aged fresh	
Producer La Chèvrerie du Signal	

Soumaintrain

This brine-washed cheese is a member of the Epoisses family, but Soumaintrain is larger and tends to be eaten when much younger when it has a very thin orangey rind. The summer cheese is creamy and fresh, but it can be left to mature until winter, when it has a slightly harder rind.

TASTING NOTES The rind is barely formed, moist, and orange in colour, while the paste is soft but grainy, becoming smoother with age. It has a spicy tang and a penetrating aroma.

HOW TO ENJOY Team this young cheese with full-bodied Burgundies, such as Nuits and Beaune.

FRANCE Bourgogne	
Age 6 weeks	
Weight and Shape 350g (12oz), round	
Size D. 12cm (5in), H. 2.5cm (1in)	
Milk Cow	
Classification Semi-soft	
Producer Fromagerie Berthault; Fromagerie Gaugry	

Tarentais

This authentic *fermier*, or farmhouse, cheese originates in the Tarentaise Valley in the mountains that border Italy. It is washed with a regional white wine. The best cheeses are those aged by *affineur* Denis Provent in Chambery.

TASTING NOTES Tarentais has buttery and flowery flavours and a long finish. Although it is usually eaten fresh, it can be allowed to mature to take on a more piquant flavour.

HOW TO ENJOY It is superb grilled or served on its own with bread or quince paste, and it goes with a salad or roast vegetables.

FRANCE Rhône-Alpes	
Age 15 days–3 months	
Weight and Shape 240g (8½oz), cylinder	
Size D. 15cm (6in), H. 8.5cm (3½in)	
Milk Goat	
Classification Aged fresh	
Producer Various	

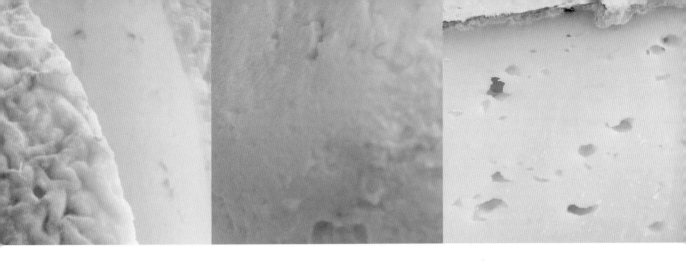

Taupinette Charentaise

This cheese is at its best in spring. The curd of Taupinette is ladled into dome-shaped moulds to mature. The crinkled, grey-white rind of the finished product closely resembles sphere-shaped coral.

TASTING NOTES Taupinette has a mild, sometimes nutty flavour that becomes more robust and stronger as it ages and the mould spreads. It has a smooth texture when young.

HOW TO ENJOY Serve this attractive cheese with a red wine such as Pinot Noir or Saint Joseph.

FRANCE Poitou-Charentes	
Age 3 weeks	
Weight and Shape 250g (9oz), sphere	
Size D. 7.5cm (3in), H. 5cm (2in)	
Milk Goat	
Classification Aged fresh	
Producer Various	

Tétoun de Santa Agata

The name of this recently created goat's cheese translates to "Santa Agata's nipple" because of the peppercorn on its peak. The cheese sits on a bed of sweet, herbaceous Provençal olive oil and finely chopped herbs, giving it an original taste and appearance.

TASTING NOTES The contrast of smooth, white creamy paste with olive oil and fresh herbs gives this delicately flavoured cheese an aromatic quality.

HOW TO ENJOY For full effect, serve it alone, spread on bread, or lightly grilled. It is excellent with a light rosé de Provence wine.

FRANCE Provence-Alpes-Côte D'Azur	
Age 1–2 weeks	
Weight and Shape 125g (4½oz), cone	
Size D. 6cm (2½in) base, H. 6cm (2½in)	
Milk Goat	
Classification Fresh	
Producer Various	

Tomme des Bauges AOC

The milk for this semi-soft cheese comes from the cows that graze on the Alpine pastures of the Natural Park of Bauges. The meadows of wild flowers provide a rich diet, which is reflected in the sweet, complex flavours of the cheese.

TASTING NOTES This is one of the tastiest of the Tomme de Savoie cheeses, since it is made with full milk and lightly pressed to give it a supple texture with tiny holes. The rind becomes thick, wrinkled and grey with age.

HOW TO ENJOY Combine it with hazelnuts and prunes, or add to omelettes, soups or a salad with fennel and endive.

FRANCE Rhône-Alpes	
Age Around 5 weeks	
Weight and Shape 75g (2½oz), round	
Size D. 18cm (7in), H. 4cm (1½in)	
Milk Cow	
Classification Semi-soft	
Producer Various	

Tomme à l'Ancienne

Invented by a couple living near the town of Banon, Tomme à l'Ancienne is made with pure goat's milk and is ladled by hand into disc-shaped moulds to create delicate soft texture.

TASTING NOTES This cheese is marinated in a strong local brandy – the *eau de vie* (the water of life) – along with some pepper, cloves, thyme, and bay leaves. This combination gives it a wonderful complexity of flavours.

HOW TO ENJOY It is delicious served with fresh figs and nuts and either a glass of *eau de vie* or a local rosé wine.

FRANCE Provence-Alpes-Côte D'Azur	
Age 2 weeks–2 months	
Weight and Shape 100g (3½oz), disc	
Size D. 8cm (3in), H. 3cm (1in)	
Milk Goat	
Classification Semi-soft	
Producer Various	

Tomme de Brebis Corse

This typical Corsican hard cheese has a rustic, brown wrinkled crust and is made with ewes milk. It is similar to the Basque cheese Ossau-Iraty.

TASTING NOTES This cheese contains a wonderful mix of various delicate Corsican aromas, including pepper and the native aromatic scrub or "maquis".

HOW TO ENJOY Fig jam makes a very tasty accompaniment. Serve with a good Corsican wine, a Chinon, a Menetou Salon, or a Faugères.

FRANCE Corse	
Age 3 months	
Weight and Shape 2.5kg (5½lb), cylinder	
Size D. 19cm (7½in), H. 9cm (3½in)	
Milk Ewe	
Classification Hard	
Producer Various	

Tomme Caprine des Pyrénées

This *fermier* goat's cheese is produced in the Pyrénées, a region better known for its excellent ewe's milk cheese. This hard cheese is at its best when made during the spring and summer months, which is when the mountainside pastures are at their most verdant.

TASTING NOTES The taste is rich and buttery, and it has a melt-in-the-mouth texture. The pleasant aroma is flowery and exotic.

HOW TO ENJOY Team this rustic goat's cheese with a sweet Jurançon wine.

FRANCE Midi-Pyrénées	
Age 6–8 weeks	
Weight and Shape 2.7kg (6lb), wheel	
Size D. 18cm (7in), H. 7.5cm (3in)	
Milk Goat	
Classification Hard	
Producer Various	

Tomme de Chartreux

Chartreux is a member of the Tomme de Savoie family, which is a generic name for Savoie cheeses that differ from producer to producer. This cheese, with its flavouring of mountain herbs, has characteristics reminiscent of the Swiss Raclette (see p239), but with a bite. This similarity is not surprising because the family makers of this cheese originate from Switzerland.

TASTING NOTES It varies from mild and milky to nutty with a rich savoury tang and a pleasant farmyard aroma.

HOW TO ENJOY Try with fresh fruit and a light, fruity Savoie wine or richer regional wines, such as Mondeuse.

FRANCE Alex, Rhône-Alpes
Age 8–16 weeks
Weight and Shape Various
Size Various
Milk Cow
Classification Semi-soft
Producer Schmidhauser Dairy

Tomme de Chèvre des Charentes

It is produced by just one farmer on the small Island of Ré, near La Rochelle. This goat's cheese is washed twice a week with a mix of brine and local white wine to develop the complexity of aromas and flavours for which it is renowned.

TASTING NOTES The flavour is rich, with a sea breeze tang that derives from the Atlantic Ocean that surrounds the island. The rind is hard and compact.

HOW TO ENJOY Serve lightly grilled on crusty bread with apples, walnuts or with a mellow white wine, such as a Muscat.

FRANCE Ile de Ré, Poitou-Charentes
Age Minimum 3 months
Weight and Shape 3.6kg (8lbs), wheel
Size D. 30cm (12in), H. 6cm (2½in)
Milk Goat
Classification Semi-soft
Producer M. Barthélémy

Tomme de Savoie

Tomme de Savoie, the generic name for the cheeses or "tommes" of Savoie, vary from producer to producer, village to village, and season to season. Some might be flavoured with herbs or spices such as cumin, or aged under a thick layer of *marc*, which is the residue left after wine pressing.

TASTING NOTES The flavour ranges from mild and milky to nutty with a savoury tang. It has a herbaceous or farmyard aroma. A label showing four red hearts is a guarantee of quality.

HOW TO ENJOY Excellent baked or grilled. Try with light, fruity Savoie wines or a lively Mondeuse or les Abymes.

FRANCE Rhône-Alpes
Age 1–2 months
Weight and Shape 1.35–2.7kg (3–6lbs), round
Size D. 18–30cm (7–12in), H. 5–8cm (2–3in)
Milk Cow
Classification Semi-soft
Producer Various

Sainte-Maure de Touraine AOC

Goats were introduced to the Loire in the 8th century by the Saracens who also left behind a lasting legacy of cheesemaking. Today, the *chèvre*, "goat's cheeses", of the Loire are considered by cheese lovers around the world as the benchmark against which all aged fresh goat's cheeses should be measured.

They include six AOC cheeses – Chabichou du Poitou (p49), Crottin de Chavignol (p54), Pouligny-Saint-Pierre (p78), Selle-sur-Cher (p88), Valençay (p97), and Sainte-Maure de Touraine. They are made in every conceivable shape, from tiny buttons, bells, and pears to bricks, rounds, cylinders, logs, and pyramids. They are all undeniable classics, but Sainte-Maure de Touraine, until modern times referred to simply as *le long chèvre*, is one of the most popular. The rind is dusted with ash and covered with tufted blue moulds, patches of grey, and mottled with pinks and yellow. The high rainfall, warm summers, lush pastures, woodlands, wide rivers, and rolling hills of the Loire provide the perfect environment for the goats to produce a high yield of excellent, aromatic milk. The best are made between Easter and All Saints Day at the beginning of November.

TASTING NOTES The wood ash provides a stark contrast against the pure white, slightly grainy interior. As the moulds develop, it becomes more dense and the lemony fresh, slightly nutty flavour intensifies to a more aromatic, herbaceous taste typical of Loire goat's cheeses. It should not, however, develop the musky goat taste that many people find distasteful until the surface becomes deeply wrinkled and covered with dark grey and reddish moulds.

HOW TO ENJOY Its unusual shape makes it an attractive addition to a cheeseboard, like all the Loire *chèvre*. It is also an integral part of Chèvre Salad, France's ubiquitous salad, with thick rings grilled on slices of crusty bread – bringing out its rich, aromatic, nutty side. Sadly, chefs across the world have assumed that any goat's cheese can be used in Chèvre Salad but in fact *chèvre* refers solely to the Loire-style goat's cheeses. Crisp whites, light Rosés, or fruity red wines of the Loire make the best drink companions.

Alpine and Saanen *goats provide the milk used to make Sainte-Maure.*

A CLOSER LOOK

Like most aged fresh cheeses, Sainte-Maure is best when allowed to age gracefully in the hands of an *affineur*, who will sell them at varying stages of ripeness depending on the tastes of the clientèle.

As the cheese matures, the wrinkles will become deeper and more pronounced.

FRANCE	Centre and Poitou Charentes
Age	10–28 days
Weight and Shape	250g (9oz), log
Size	D. 4cm (1½in), L. 18cm (7in)
Milk	Goat
Classification	Aged fresh
Producer	Various

SHAPING The soft, wet, fragile curds achieved by coagulation are ladled into log-shaped moulds to drain and take shape.

THE STRAW The use of the straw, *paille*, indicates the cheese has been made by an artisan producer. You can also use it to pick the cheese up, but it will usually collapse into large indelicate chunks.

The surface is encased with a dusty blue-grey mould.

Halved log

The cheese's texture is firm, almost brittle.

The straw inside is placed there by hand and shows that the cheese has been made by an artisan producer.

THE ASH The logs are sprinkled with a mix of salt and wood ash. Initially, only the ash covers the bright, white, moist young curd. It must be at least 10 days old when sold, to comply with the AOC rules.

AGEING Gradually, the cheese starts to lose moisture, a soft thin wrinkly rind develops and the surface attracts a variety of microflora. First, the familiar white velvet of *penicillium candidum*, then, within 12 days, a delicate blue powder puff-like mould appears that will take over from the white mould.

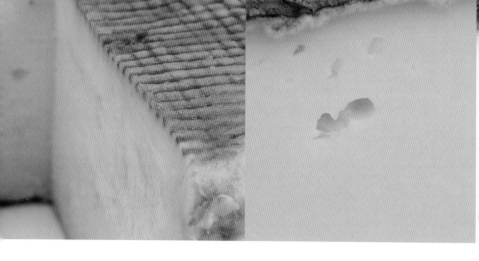

Tommette Brebis des Alpes

The high altitudes of this region produce glorious pastureland, which influences the wonderful flavours of cheeses produced here. This particular example is made in small quantities and is distinguished by its brown rind. The "Brebis" of its name signifies the use of ewe's milk.

TASTING NOTES This cheese has a mix of delicate aromas and herbaceous flavours, evocative of Alpine meadows.

HOW TO ENJOY Gooseberry jam makes a tasty accompaniment. Serve with a fruity and full-bodied red wine, such as Chinon or Menetou Salon.

FRANCE Rhône-Alpes		
Age 2–4 months		
Weight and Shape 1.35kg (3lb), round		
Size D. 11.5cm (5in), H. 4cm (1½in)		
Milk Ewe		
Classification Semi-soft		
Producer Various		

Tommette de Chèvre des Bauges

This rarely produced, authentic goat's cheese originates in the Bauges mountains in Savoie. *Tommette* refers to a small tommes – a French term that simply means a small cheese that is usually made on small farm in mountain regions. It has a hard, dry, grey-brown crust.

TASTING NOTES The slightly moist, soft and sticky paste fills the mouth with mountain flavours. It has subtle and structured aromas.

HOW TO ENJOY Team this goat's cheese with a fruity, full bodied white wine of Condrieux.

FRANCE Rhône-Alpes		
Age 2 months		
Weight and Shape 675g (1½lb), round		
Size D. 11cm (4½in), H. 7.5cm (3in)		
Milk Goat		
Classification Semi-soft		
Producer Various		

Trappe d'Echourgnac

Since 1868, the nuns at the Abbaye d'Echourgnac have been using milk from neighbouring farms to make and ripen this artisan cheese. Produced only in small quantities, it is well worth seeking out.

TASTING NOTES Washing with walnut liquor gives the rind an attractive dark brown colour, and the supple paste has a smokier taste and a simple, balanced flavour.

HOW TO ENJOY It becomes runny and slightly stringy when cooked and is especially good for stuffing into homemade ravioli. Serve with cider or a red or rosé from Cahors.

FRANCE Dordogne, Aquitaine		
Age 2 months		
Weight and Shape 300g (10½oz), round		
Size D. 10cm (4in), H. 5cm (2in)		
Milk Cow		
Classification Semi-soft		
Producer Abbaye d'Echourgnac		

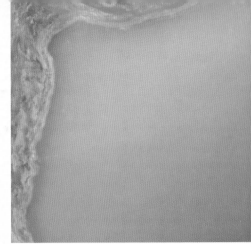

Trois Cornes de Vendée

After a halt of several years, production of this fresh goat's cheese, with its distinctive triangular shape, was resumed in the 1980s near the sea-side city of Marans. The curious name comes from the shape of the famous goat's horn that belong to Monsieur Seguin, a character in the tales of the French writer Alphonse Daudet.

TASTING NOTES The paste is bold and rich with a bittersweet flavour. It is best eaten fresh, but can be stored for one or two weeks.

HOW TO ENJOY Try with dry white Loire wines such as Sancerre or Chinon.

FRANCE Poitou-Charentes	
Age 1 month	
Weight and Shape 225g (8oz), triangular	
Size W. 9cm (3½in), H 2.5cm (1in)	
Milk Goat	
Classification Aged fresh	
Producer Various	

Truffe de Valensole

The area around the village of Valensole, in the Haute-Provence region, is renowned for its truffles. This hand-shaped cheese reflects its origins because it is covered with a fine layer of black charcoal to resemble highly scented and much-prized mushrooms.

TASTING NOTES It is soft and almost mousse-like with a delicate lemony freshness and a hint of herbs on the finish.

HOW TO ENJOY For pure luxury, try it stirred into pasta with a fine shaving of fresh truffles. Serve with a light white wine, such as Coteaux Varois, or with a light fruity red, such as Beaujolais.

FRANCE Provence-Alpes-Côte D'Azur	
Age Around 2 weeks	
Weight and Shape 100g (3½oz), ball	
Size Various	
Milk Goat	
Classification Aged fresh	
Producer Various	

U Bel Fiuritu

This washed-rind cheese has a thick, slightly sticky, orange-coloured rind that is dusted with white and grey mould and exudes a pungent farmyard aroma. It is one of the few Corsican ewe's milk cheeses made with pasteurized milk.

TASTING NOTES It is supple, smooth and creamy with small holes scattered through the pale yellow paste. Its sweet aromatic flavour reflects the Corsican landscape and the wild herbs and grasses on which the ewes graze.

HOW TO ENJOY U Bel Fiuritu can be enjoyed with full-bodied, structured red wines, such as a Muscat du cap Corse or a 12-year-old Frontignan.

FRANCE Venaco, Corse	
Age 4–10 weeks	
Weight and Shape 400g (14oz), round	
Size D. 11cm (4⅓in), H. 4cm (1⅓in)	
Milk Ewe	
Classification Semi-soft	
Producer Pierucci Dairy	

U Pecurinu

U Pecurinu is a dense washed-rind cheese from Corse, an island renowned for its unique and flavoursome cheeses, thanks to its warm climate, robust local breeds and wild and diverse grazing.

TASTING NOTES This semi-soft cheese is tender and buttery and has a complex herbaceous flavour with vegetal overtones. The repeated washing leaves a lingering meaty tang and pungent farmyard aroma.

HOW TO ENJOY Corsicans often eat this cheese with fig jam; a fruity red wine makes the perfect accompaniment.

FRANCE Corse		
Age 2–16 weeks		
Weight and Shape 400g (14oz), round		
Size D. 11cm (4½in), H. 4cm (1½in)		
Milk Ewe		
Classification Semi-soft		
Producer Various		

Valençay AOC

It is said that this cheese was once made in the shape of a pyramid, but on seeing it, Napoleon became angry because it reminded him of his Egyptian defeat. He angrily chopped off the top with his sword, creating a truncated shape. Valençay has been AOC protected since 1998.

TASTING NOTES This natural-rinded cheese is covered in salted charcoal ashes. It has a soft, moist paste and a mild and slightly nutty flavour.

HOW TO ENJOY Valençay is delicious paired with all fruity and lively white wines of the Berry and Touraine regions of France, especially Sancerre.

FRANCE Centre		
Age 5 weeks		
Weight and Shape 200–250g (7–9oz), truncated pyramid		
Size D. 6–7cm (2½–3in) base, 3.5–4cm (1–1½in) top, H. 6–7cm (2½–3in)		
Milk Goat		
Classification Aged fresh		
Producer Various		

Venaco

Named after a small picturesque village in central Corse where it was once made, this is one of the best known Corsican cheeses. It is a washed-rind *fermier* cheese and is best produced between spring and autumn, when the milk benefits from the ewes grazing lush pastures.

TASTING NOTES Beneath its thin and sticky orange rind, the paste is dense yet soft and sticky, with a full-bodied and very spicy taste.

HOW TO ENJOY Spread sparingly on bread with herbs, garlic or olive oil for an excellent snack. Sharp and tasty, it is best with big reds like Gigondas.

FRANCE Corse		
Age 3–4 months		
Weight and Shape 500g (1lb 2oz), round		
Size D. 10cm (4in), H. 4cm (1½in)		
Milk Ewe		
Classification Semi-soft		
Producer Various		

Ventadour

Ventadour originates from Corrèze, a part of the Limousin, which lays claim to 5000km (3106mi) of river, including the Corrèze itself. The unadulterated countryside of this real rural idyll allows famers such as Xavier Cornet to indulge a passion for cheesemaking; he established his well-respected dairy in 1977.

TASTING NOTES The taste of this goat's cheese changes according to its age: it can be very sweet or spicy but is always full of subtle flavours, with a delicate hint of goat.

HOW TO ENJOY Eat with a white Loire wine, such as Sancerre.

FRANCE Corrèze, Limousin	
Age 3–6 weeks	
Weight and Shape 140g (5oz), round	
Size D. 8cm (3in), H. 6cm (2½in)	
Milk Goat	
Classification Aged fresh	
Producer Xavier Cornet	

Vieux-Boulogne

Considered to be one of the most odorous cheese in the world, Vieux-Boulogne is washed with beer several times during the production process. Despite its strong aroma, the taste is not aggressive or overpowering.

TASTING NOTES The rind is orange and the paste rubbery with small holes. Surprisingly enough, Vieux-Boulogne is not sharp; instead having a rich and mellow flavour.

HOW TO ENJOY It is too strong for most dishes and is best enjoyed with crusty bread and a variety of drinks – from a good-quality beer to Champagne or full-bodied red wines.

FRANCE Nord-Pas-de-Calais	
Age 7–9 weeks	
Weight and Shape 600g (1lb 5oz), square	
Size L. 10.5cm (4in),W. 10.5cm (4in), H. 4cm (1½in)	
Milk Cow	
Classification Semi-soft	
Producer Various	

Vieux-Lille

Once eaten down in the pits by miners, the nickname of this cheese is "*Puant de Lille*", or "the smelly cheese of Lille", because of its strong farmyard aroma. It is similar to Maroilles but is soaked, rather than washed, in brine and aged for longer.

TASTING NOTES It has a very powerful, sometimes piquant, salty taste with a thin, barely formed, slightly sticky pale orange-coloured rind and a supple, dense, and slightly dry texture.

HOW TO ENJOY Serve with juniper berries and a variety of drinks, such as beer, black coffee or even light wines. The taste is not as pungent as the scent.

FRANCE Nord-Pas-de-Calais	
Age 3–4 months	
Weight and Shape 675g (1½lb), square	
Size L. 12cm (5in), W. 12cm (5in), H. 5cm (2in)	
Milk Cow	
Classification Semi-soft	
Producer Various	

More Cheeses of France

The following cheeses are rare – either because they are only available seasonally or because they are produced in very remote areas. As a result, it has proved impossible to photograph them, but as they are important and interesting examples of French cheese we are including them.
So, read, savour, and seek out.

98

Abbaye de Troisvaux

This is one of several cheeses that are produced at the Abbaye de Troisvaux. This semi-soft, washed-rind cheese is based on Trappist-style cheeses like Trappe de Beval. Another of these cheeses is Losange de Saint-Paul, which is also a washed-rind cheese but it is moulded into a lozenger shape.

TASTING NOTES The elastic rind is a yellow-orange colour from being washed with beer during maturation. The paste is smooth and creamy, without any bitterness, and has a mild aroma.

HOW TO ENJOY Team this cheese with a light and fruity red wine, such as a Beaujolais or a Bourgogne.

FRANCE Nord-Pas-de-Calais	
Age 5–6 weeks	
Weight and Shape 480g (17oz), round	
Size D. 25cm (10in), H. 4cm (1½in)	
Milk Cow	
Classification Semi-soft	
Producer Abbaye de Troisvaux	

Bastelicaccia

Originating in the south of Corse, Bastelicaccia is a ewe's milk cheese with a thin and fragile rind. It is made using a little rennet; this addition makes the curdling last longer and creates a creamy, smooth paste.

TASTING NOTES Old-school Bastelicaccia, made during the winter months, is fine, fragile, and very creamy. The fresher and younger it is, the more character it has. Most producers, however, age Bastelicaccia longer, resulting in a more robust flavour.

HOW TO ENJOY As this is a rare cheese, it is an impressive addition to any cheeseboard. Serve it with light red wine, such as a Chinon.

FRANCE Corse	
Age 2–8 weeks	
Weight and Shape 400g (14oz), drum	
Size D. 13cm (5in), H. 4cm (1½in)	
Milk Ewe	
Classification Semi-soft	
Producer Various	

Boulette de Papleux

A variation on Boulette d'Avesnes, Boulette de Papleux is made from young, imperfect Maroilles cheeses rather than from fresh curd. It is then mashed with pepper, cloves, tarragon, and parsley.

TASTING NOTES Its deep red, beer-washed rind is covered with paprika, while the paste is ivory white and flecked with herbs. It is a very strong, hot, spicy cheese in both flavour and aroma.

HOW TO ENJOY A hearty winter cheese, because it is strong. It goes well with beer, very full-bodied wines, such as Cahors or Brouilly, or a shot of gin.

FRANCE Nord-Pas-de-Calais	
Age 2–3 months	
Weight and Shape 200g (7oz)	
Size D. 7.5cm (3in), H. 10cm (4in)	
Milk Cow	
Classification Flavour-added	
Producer Various	

Crabotin

This is an unfairly little-known goat's milk cheese. The name is derived from the Occitan language; *crabot* simply means *caprine*, which translates as relating to goats. The cheese is washed with brine during maturation, producing a distinctive looking orange-coloured rind.

TASTING NOTES This delicious cheese has a soft paste, a mild and quite creamy, fruity flavour, and a very goaty aroma.

HOW TO ENJOY Crabotin is excellent eaten with fresh crusty bread and fruit preserves. It is very well paired with Madiran wine.

FRANCE Aquitaine and Midi-Pyrénées	
Age 6 weeks	
Weight and Shape 500g (1lb 2oz), round	
Size D. 15cm (6in), H. 2.5cm (1in)	
Milk Goat	
Classification Semi-soft	
Producer Various	

Crémet du Cap Blanc-Nez

A beautiful and rare double-cream, white-rinded farmhouse cheese that takes its name from the white clay cliffs of the Cap Blanc-Nez, between Boulogne-sur-Mer and Calais.

TASTING NOTES The high cream content gives it a very rich taste that leaves a long finish in the mouth. The salty flavour is reminiscent of the breezes coming off the sea.

HOW TO ENJOY This is delicious eaten with bread and honey. Team it with a Champagne or a fruity white wine, such as Mont Louis from the Loire valley.

FRANCE Wiere Effroy, Nord-Pas-de-Calais	
Age 3 weeks	
Weight and Shape 450g (1lb), dome	
Size Various	
Milk Cow	
Classification Soft white	
Producer Saint Godeleine Farm	

Fort de Béthune

Cheeses of the Nord-Pas-de-Calais are known for their strong flavours – and one of strongest of them all is Fort de Béthune. This cow's milk cheese was once a favourite of the mining community, who would team it with local beer. It is made by soaking the pungent local Maroilles cheese in brine for three months.

TASTING NOTES The fermentation process used for this cheese gives it a very creamy, silky texture, but with an almost eye-wateringly strong flavour.

HOW TO ENJOY Eat this spread on bread alongside a glass of a full-bodied red wine, such as a Faugères from Languedoc, or an *eau de vie*.

FRANCE Nord-Pas-de-Calais	
Age 3 months	
Weight and Shape Various	
Size Various	
Milk type Cow	
Classification Various	
Producer Various	

Mascare

This goat's milk cheese originates in the 'provençales' Alps, in Banon. It has a thin, natural rind that is wrapped in a decorative chestnut leaf. It is a seasonal cheese and is only made by one producer, so it is rarely found outside its local area.

TASTING NOTES Beneath its soft, creamy rind, Mascare has a mild lactic to nutty flavour and a soft, almost runny paste around the edge as it ripens.

HOW TO ENJOY At its best when served simply with fresh crusty bread from the local market along with a fruity, lively red, white, or rosé wine, preferably from the Mont Ventoux or Durance area.

FRANCE Provence-Alpes-Côte D'Azur	
Age 3 weeks	
Weight and Shape 100g (3½oz), square	
Size D. 7.5cm (3in), H. 2.5cm (1in)	
Milk Goat	
Classification Aged fresh	
Producer Fromagerie de Banon – M Greggo	

Mont Ventoux

This goat's cheese is unique for its very unusual shape. It is moulded into a cone shape to represent Mount Ventoux, the famous mountain that dominates the skyline in the Luberon area. The top half of the cheese is white, representing the limestone part of the mountain, the lower half is black (with ash), representing the forest.

TASTING NOTES This is a tender and smooth cheese with real farmland flavours and aromas.

HOW TO ENJOY Add this distinctive cheese to your cheeseboard and serve alongside a local full-bodied red wine of Vaucluse, such as a Gigondas or Mont Ventoux.

FRANCE Provence-Alpes-Côte D'Azur	
Age 10 days	
Weight and Shape 30g (1oz), cone	
Size Various	
Milk Goat	
Classification Aged fresh	
Producer Various	

Nîmois

An interesting addition to a cheeseboard, this newly developed goat's cheese is washed with the local red wine of Costières de Nîmes as part of the production process, giving the rind a distinctive dark red colour.

TASTING NOTES Nîmois has a pronounced and powerful flavour. Because of this, it should be eaten without accompaniments.

HOW TO ENJOY Best enjoyed on its own with a red wine of Costières de Nîmes or Pic St Loup.

FRANCE Languedoc-Roussillon	
Age 3 weeks	
Weight and Shape 50g (1¾oz), round	
Size D. 5cm (2in), H. 5cm (2in)	
Milk Goat	
Classification Aged fresh	
Producer Various	

Persillé des Aravis

The name comes from the irregular dark green veining that looks like parsley, or *persille* in French. This goat's milk cheese is produced in the Aravis Valley in the Haute-Savoie. Two similar cheeses are made in nearby valleys: Persillé des Grand-Bornand and Persillé des Thônes.

TASTING NOTES It has a very savoury and sharp, spicy flavour with a strong aftertaste. It has a texture similar to aged Cheddar and is best when made in summer and autumn.

HOW TO ENJOY Good with all full-bodied red wines, such as Mondeuse, Beaujolais-Village, and Chinon.

FRANCE Rhône-Alpes	
Age 2 months	
Weight and Shape 1kg (2¼lb), cylinder	
Size D. 10cm (4in), H. 15cm (6in)	
Milk Goat	
Classification Hard	
Producer Various	

Tomme de Bargkas

Tomme de Bargkas comes from the Vosges mountains in Lorraine; *Barg* means mountain and *kass* means cheese in the local dialect. It is here that farmers also produce Munster cheese.

TASTING NOTES The paste is soft, elastic and has a few holes. It gives off a light, soft aroma and has a flavour of hazelnut with a slightly acidic aftertaste.

HOW TO ENJOY Locals often eat this cheese with black sourdough bread. Team it with a Bourgogne, such as Pommard, or a Rhône wine, such as Châteauneuf-du-pape.

FRANCE Vosges, Alsace-Lorraine	
Age 6 months	
Weight and Shape 1.4kg (3lb), round	
Size D. 30cm (12in), H. 6cm (2⅓in)	
Milk Cow	
Classification Hard	
Producer M. Minoux	

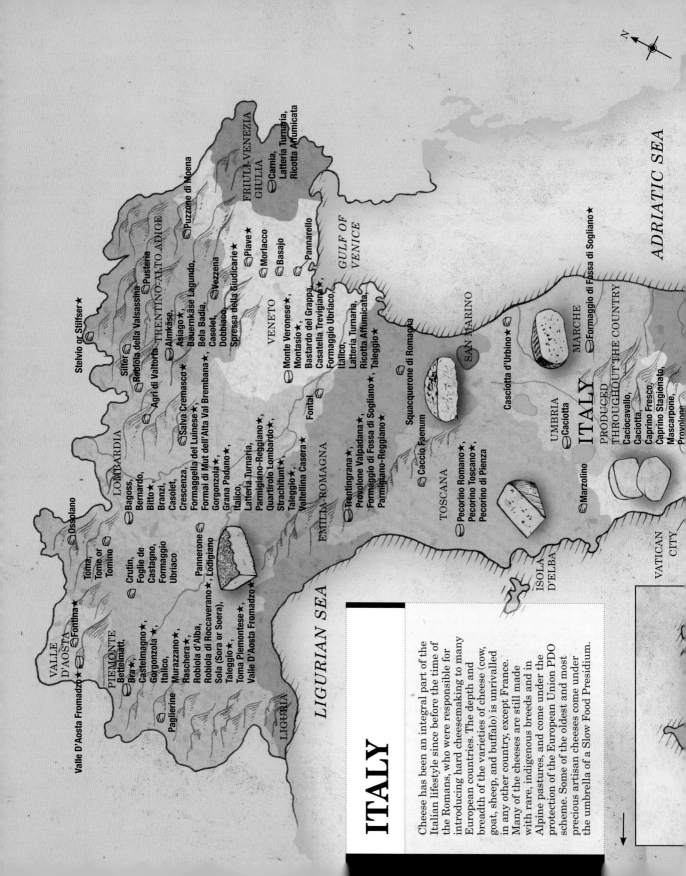

ITALY

Cheese has been an integral part of the Italian lifestyle since before the time of the Romans, who were responsible for introducing hard cheesemaking to many European countries. The depth and breadth of the varieties of cheese (cow, goat, sheep, and buffalo) is unrivalled in any other country, except France. Many of the cheeses are still made with rare, indigenous breeds and in Alpine pastures, and come under the protection of the European Union PDO scheme. Some of the oldest and most precious artisan cheeses come under the umbrella of a Slow Food Presidium.

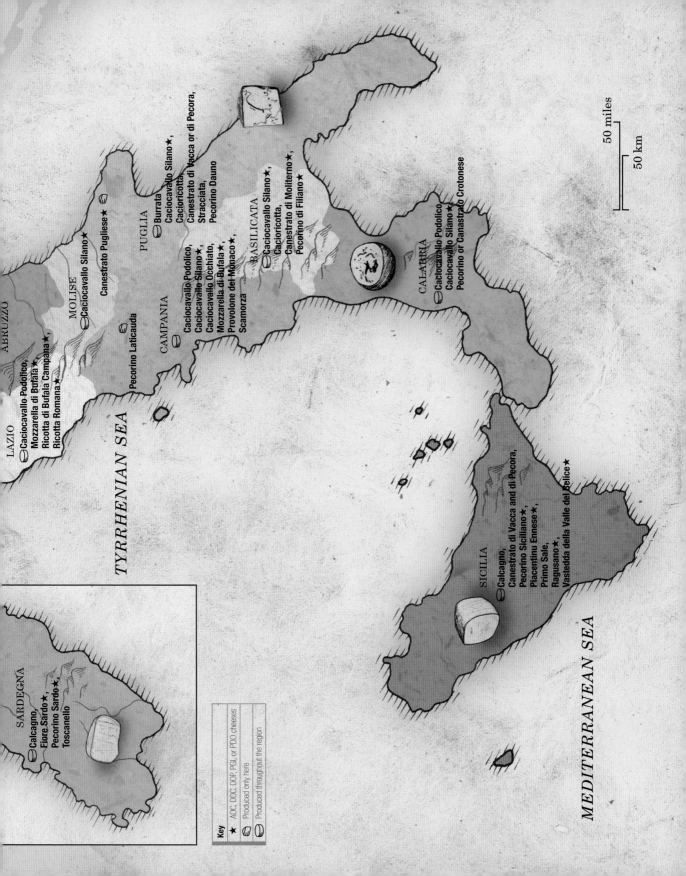

TYRRHENIAN SEA

MEDITERRANEAN SEA

LAZIO
🧀 **Caciocavallo Podolico,**
Mozzarella di Bufala ★,
Ricotta di Bufala Campana ★,
Ricotta Romana ★

ABRUZZO

MOLISE
🧀 **Caciocavallo Silano ★**

Canestrato Pugliese ★

PUGLIA
🧀 **Burrata**
Caciocavallo Silano ★,
Cacioricotta,
Canestrato di Vacca or di Pecora,
Stracciata,
Pecorino Dauno

Pecorino Laticauda

CAMPANIA
🧀 **Caciocavallo Podolico,**
Caciocavallo Silano ★,
Caciocavallo Occhiato,
Mozzarella di Bufala ★,
Provolone del Monaco ★,
Scamorza

BASILICATA
🧀 **Caciocavallo Silano ★,**
Cacioricotta,
Canestrato di Moliterno ★,
Pecorino di Filiano ★

CALABRIA
🧀 **Caciocavallo Podolico,**
Caciocavallo Silano ★,
Pecorino or Canastrato Crotonese

SICILIA
🧀 **Calcagno,**
Canestrato di Vacca and di Pecora,
Pecorino Siciliano ★,
Piacentinu Ennese ★,
Primo Sale,
Ragusano ★,
Vastedda della Valle del Belice ★

SARDEGNA
🧀 **Calcagno,**
Fiore Sardo ★,
Pecorino Sardo ★,
Toscanello

Key
★ AOC, DOC, DOP, PGI, or PDO cheeses
🧀 Produced only here
🧀 Produced throughout the region

50 miles

50 km

Almkäse PDO

Deriving its name from the German *Alm*, meaning "Alpine pasture", this part full-cream, part skimmed raw milk cheese is one of the oldest in Bolzano. The cheeses are turned, scraped, and brushed every day for three months until they are an ivory-white to deep straw-yellow and dotted with small holes or "eyes".

TASTING NOTES Firm with sweet rather than sharp high notes, it has a floral aroma reminiscent of Alpine meadows.

HOW TO ENJOY It grates and melts well. Wrap in thin slices of sautéed aubergine and serve with olive bread and a white Schiava Grigia.

ITALY Trentino-Alto Adige	
Age 6–8 months	
Weight and Shape 7–14kg (15lb 7oz–31lb), flat wheel	
Size D. 35–40cm (14–15½in), H. 8–10cm (3–4in)	
Milk Cow	
Classification Hard	
Producer Various	

Asiago PDO

Made only within officially recognised production areas, this cheese takes its name from its homonym plateau. It is available as two types: Asiago Pressato is made in low-lying pastures and is semi-soft with irregular-shaped holes; Asiago d'Allevo is hard and made using milk from mountain pastures.

TASTING NOTES Springy and moist in texture, Asiago Pressato is aromatic, fairly salty, and slightly piquant. Asiago d'Allevo is drier, crumbly to the bite, and has a savoury, spiced flavour.

HOW TO ENJOY Perfect with a Cabernet Sauvignon from Friuli's Colli Orientali, or Torcolato Maculan.

ITALY Trentino-Alto Adige	
Age 20–40 days	
Weight and Shape 11–15kg (24¼–33lb), round	
Size D. 30–40cm (12–16in), H. 11–15cm (4½–6in)	
Milk Cow	
Classification Semi-soft	
Producer Various	

Bagòss

Bagòss is the local nickname for the residents of Bagolino. Made with raw milk from cattle grazing on mountain pastures, this hard cheese must be matured for at least 12 months, but on average is at least 24–36 months old. During ageing, the cheeses are brushed with raw linseed oil, which gives the rind an ochre brown colour.

TASTING NOTES Has strong aromas of saffron, then floral pastures and hay. Early fresh green notes combine with a slight almond taste and a tangy finish.

HOW TO ENJOY Use as a table cheese, or grated over pasta. Try with a robust red wine like Amarone.

ITALY Lombardia	
Age Over 12 months	
Weight and Shape 14–22kg (30–48½lb), flat wheel	
Size D. 40–50cm (16–20in), H. 12–14cm (5–5½in)	
Milk Cow	
Classification Hard	
Producer Various	

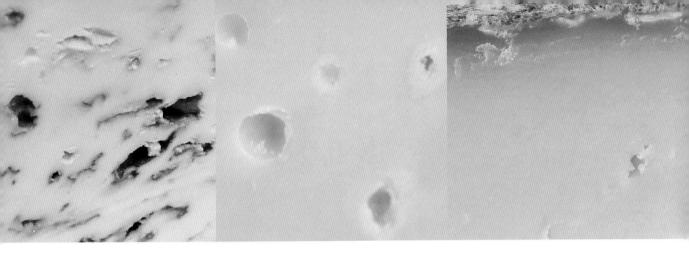

Basajo

La Casearia Carpenedo, best known for their innovative cheeses like Umbriaco, have created this blue, ewes' milk cheese. Adorned with luscious, gold raisins it spends 3 weeks soaking in *Passito di Pantelleria*, a sweet Sicilian wine.

TASTING NOTES The wild honey aroma and sweetness of the wine seeps into the open textured, blue streaked cheese making it crumbly and soggy, softening the peppery bite of the blue.

HOW TO ENJOY Enjoy with a glass of Passito di Pantelleria or late harvest Riesling and fresh figs to absorb the lush flavours.

ITALY Forli, Treviso	
Age 5–6 months	
Weight and Shape 2kg (4½lb), drum	
Size D. 20cm (8in), H. 8cm (3in)	
Milk Ewe	
Classification Flavour-added	
Producer La Caseraia Carpenedo	

Bastardo del Grappa

Made in mountain dairy huts around Grappa during the summer months, this cheese gained the name "Bastardo" from being made using a mix of sheep's, goat's, and cow's milk, depending on availability. It has a dark mustard-yellow rind with burnt brown blotches.

TASTING NOTES The light, straw-coloured paste darkens with age and has small eyes throughout. It has a floral aroma and a full flavour with notes of wild herbs, which intensifies as it matures.

HOW TO ENJOY Eat with semolina, or potato gnocchi, along with a Cabernet Franc or a sparkling Chardonnay.

ITALY Veneto	
Age 6 months	
Weight and Shape 2.5–5kg (5½–11lb), wheel	
Size D. 25–30cm (10–12in), H. 2–8cm (¾–3in)	
Milk Cow, goat, and ewe	
Classification Semi-soft or hard	
Producer Various	

Bettelmatt

Legend has it that the flavour of this red-rinded cheese comes from a herb known as *mottolina*, found only in the high pastures of Val d'Ossola, but it could be just the quality of grazing that creates this unique taste. Bettelmatt is made in summer from the raw milk of Brown Mountain cattle, using similar methods to those for making Gruyère.

TASTING NOTES Sometimes dotted with irregular medium eyes, it has a strong, buttery, herby aroma and tastes sweet yet salty with an earthy finish.

HOW TO ENJOY Used traditionally as a table cheese; it is good with polenta and for filling for *agnolotti* pasta.

ITALY Piemonte	
Age 2–6 months	
Weight and Shape 8–10kg (17lb 10oz–22lb), flat wheel	
Size D. 45–55cm (18–21½in), H. 8cm (3in)	
Milk Cow	
Classification Semi-soft and hard	
Producer Various	

103

CANESTRATO di MOLITERNO PGI
The curd is pressed by hand into rush
baskets then removed and rubbed with
olive oil and sometimes vinegar to create
this waxy, smooth rind with a dusting of
brown and white moulds. (See p110)

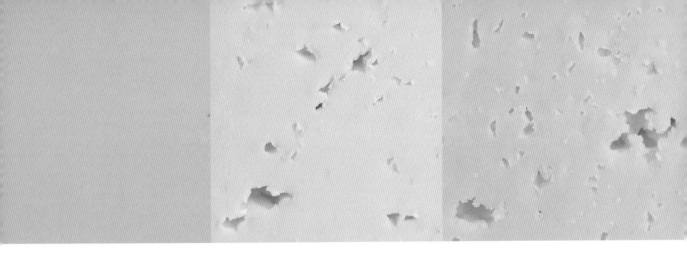

Bitto PDO

Named after the fast-flowing River Bitto, this cheese is made in the summer months in mountain dairies or *calecc*, unroofed stone refuges that are covered with canvas when in use. This is where the maturation process begins, but it is then completed in the valley cheese stores and can last for ten years.

TASTING NOTES When young, this cheese has a mild fragrant flavour, which develops into unmistakable nutty notes and caramel hints after at least six months maturation.

HOW TO ENJOY Use in local dishes such as *pizzoccheri*, a flat pasta, and *sciatt*, small buckwheat fritters.

ITALY Lombardia	
Age 70 days–1 year	
Weight and Shape 8–25kg (17lb 10oz –55lb), flat wheel with concave edge	
Size D. 50cm (20in), H. 9–12cm (3½–5in)	
Milk Cow and goat	
Classification Hard	
Producer Various	

Bra PDO

Named after the town of Bra, famous for the cheese festival held by the Slow Food organisation. Generic Bra is made from cow's milk from lowland dairies and can contain small amounts of ewe's or goat's milk. Bra Tenero is a semi-soft cheese aged for 45–60 days; Bra Duro is ripened for at least 180 days.

TASTING NOTES Bra Tenero (pictured) is soft, mild, and aromatic, while Bra Duro has a delicious tang that stings the tongue with its intensity.

HOW TO ENJOY Eat Bra Tenero as a main dish, use Bra Duro shredded over pasta. Serve with red Bricco dell'Uccellone or white Gavi dei Gavi.

ITALY Piemonte	
Age 1–2 months; 8–9 months	
Weight and Shape 5–9 kg (11–19lb 13oz), flat wheel	
Size D. 30–40cm (12–16in), H. 7–9cm (3–3½in)	
Milk Cow	
Classification Semi-soft	
Producer Various	

Branzi

Originating in the village of the same name, Branzi cheese uses the milk of Brown Mountain cattle. In the past it was made only in Alpine huts in the summer, but now it is produced all year. A variety of *formai de mut,* it has a pale yellow paste laced with holes and encased in a yellow-brown crust.

TASTING NOTES When young it has a sweet and milky flavour with a slight aroma of grass. When aged it can be grated and tastes stronger, tangy, and nutty.

HOW TO ENJOY Used in *polenta taragna*, polenta with cheese and butter, and with gnocchi made from chestnut flour. Serve with Valcalepio Rosso.

ITALY Lombardia	
Age 1–7 months	
Weight and Shape 5–15kg (11–33lb), flat wheel	
Size D. 40–45cm (16–18in), H. 9cm (3½in)	
Milk Cow	
Classification Hard	
Producer Various	

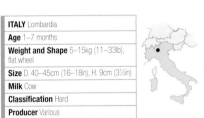

Burrata

A *pasta filata* cheese very similar to mozzarella, differing only in the stretching technique employed to produce it and the fact that Burrata contains a filling made from fresh pieces of Mozzarella soaked in heavy cream. *Burrata* means "buttery" in Italian, and this cheese certainly lives up to its name.

TASTING NOTES Eat it fresh at room temperature. It has a full buttery aroma and tastes mild and sweet with the consistency of very soft mozzarella.

HOW TO ENJOY Toss with avocado, tomatoes, and olive oil, or eat with a salty cured ham. Serve with Primitivo di Manduria or Moscato di Trani.

ITALY Puglia	
Age 24–48 hours	
Weight and Shape 250–500g (9oz–1lb 2oz), sphere	
Size Various	
Milk Cow	
Classification Fresh	
Producer Various	

Caccio Faenum

L'Antiqua Cascina are best known for their Formaggio di Fossa Sogliano PDO. However, the discovery of dozens of ancient wine barrels in the cellars of Villa Corte lead to the revival of an old local recipe. The result was this ewe's cheese, wrapped in hay and aged in the barrels.

TASTING NOTES The young cheese is wrapped in spring hay which imbues the nutty sweetness of the cheese with the aroma and taste of the wild flowers, and grasses of the alpine meadows.

HOW TO ENJOY Grate over your favourite pasta dish or serve with pears, green figs, and a Pinot Grigio or Ribolla.

ITALY Castellina, Emilia-Romagna	
Age 2–4 months	
Weight and Shape 1.5–2kg (3lb3oz–4½lb), round	
Size various	
Milk Ewe	
Classification Hard	
Producer L'Antica Cascina	

Caciocavallo

This semi-soft cheese is an archetype of the Italian cheese-making technology *pasta filata,* or "stretched-curd". Mainly made in southern Italy, there are many regional variations; it is produced using sheep's, goat's, cow's, or buffalo milk. It can also be smoked.

TASTING NOTES During the first 30 days of maturation it is sweet, milky, and buttery. After 90 days it becomes pungent with oily and gamey flavours.

HOW TO ENJOY Serve with rustic bread and a sparkling white wine.

ITALY All over	
Age From a few days until one year	
Weight and Shape 1–10kg (2¼–22lb), sphere	
Size D. 11–20cm (4½–8in), H. 23cm (9in)	
Milk Cow, buffalo, goat, and ewe	
Classification Semi-soft or hard	
Producer Various	

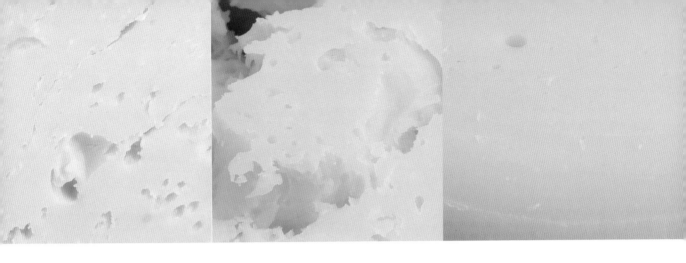

Caciocavallo Occhiato

This classic *pasta filata* cheese has plenty of round "eyes", as the *occhio* in the name suggests. It is produced using milk from cattle that naturally graze on the mountain pastures in Campania.

TASTING NOTES Typically generous with propionic aroma, it is elastic when young, and friable when aged. More sweet than tangy, citrusy and floral hints are also present.

HOW TO ENJOY Eat on its own, in a salad, or with vegetables. Pair it with Aglianico Sorrentino wine or, for those who like sweet tastes, try a Lacryma Christi del Vesuvio.

ITALY Campania	
Age 3–6 months	
Weight and Shape 8–12kg (17lb 10oz–26½lb), oval or sphere	
Size D. 30cm (12in), H. 33cm (13in)	
Milk Cow	
Classification Semi-soft or hard	
Producer Various	

Caciocavallo Podolico

Semi-hard when young, this full-fat cheese hardens after four months of ageing. It is a typical Caciocavallo cheese, made using the milk of Podolian cattle that graze on Appenine mountain pastures.

TASTING NOTES Extremely aromatic with vegetal cues of mountain herbs and flowers. Basically sweet, it has a very high solubility with persistent nutty and spicy hints.

HOW TO ENJOY When the cheese is well aged, simply serve dressed with olive oil. It is great alongside Aglianico del Volture di Paternoster or Moscato di Saracena.

ITALY Lazio, Campania, and Calabria	
Age 1 month–1 year	
Weight and Shape 2–3kg (4½–6½lb), oval or sphere	
Size D. 15cm (6in)	
Milk Cow	
Classification Hard	
Producer Various	

Caciocavallo Silano PDO

Originating in the Middle Ages, this semi-soft cow's milk cheese was already well known during the 14th century and continues to be popular now. It appears light-straw coloured when young and brown when aged.

TASTING NOTES A typical stirred paste with small and sparse eyes. Its taste is aromatic and sharply sweet with milky and buttery cues when young, becoming pungent as it matures.

HOW TO ENJOY Traditionally used as a main dish or in filled pasta, it is happily balanced with Greco Bianco di Melissa or Rosato di Scavigna.

ITALY Basilicata, Calabria, Campania, Molise, and Puglia	
Age 1 month–1 year	
Weight and Shape 1–2.5kg (2¼–5½lb), various shapes (oval pictured)	
Size D. 19cm (7½in), H. 9cm (3½in)	
Milk Cow	
Classification Semi-soft	
Producer Various	

Gorgonzola PDO

Everything about Gorgonzola is sexy – its rustic yet elegant appearance, its voluptuous, melt-in-the-mouth texture, its musky aroma, and its sweet, spicy tang. Even its name is seductive. It is thought to be the first blue cheese, and its origin is steeped in folklore and legend.

The most charming version of the story is the tale of a careless youth who, distracted by his young love, left a bundle of moist curd hanging overnight on a hook in a damp cellar. The following day, hoping to disguise his mistake, he added the curd to the morning batch. Weeks later, he found the cheese had a greenish mould through the centre. Curious, he sampled it and found it so good he repeated the procedure and the rest, as they say, is history.

Gorgonzola's first name was Stracchino di Gorgonzola, derived from the Italian word *stracca* meaning "tired", as it was made in the autumn when the exhausted cows returned from the mountain pastures to the watery meadows of Lombardia where Gorgonzola was the main trading town for centuries.

Today, Gorgonzola is made under strict regulations by around 40 small family dairies and large factories. A few artisan cheesemakers still use unpasteurized milk and follow the traditional "two day curd" method, allowing the curd to become naturally inoculated by mould, then mixing it with the curd from the morning milking. Since the mid 1900s, however, most Gorgonzola has been made in factories using pasteurized milk and the "one day curd" method with the blue mould added to the milk, producing even more blueing than the traditional cheese, though not that strong a flavour.

Gorgonzola is made in large drums and, when ripe, the sides bulge like a riverbank ready to collapse. Around the edges, it can be slightly greyish – but it should never be brown, as this indicates excessive drying and poor handling.

TASTING NOTES The uneven and erratically spread streaks and patches of blue mould impart a sharp, spicy flavour to the rich, creamy cheese. It tastes creamier and sweeter than Stilton but is similar in strength, whereas Roquefort is stronger, sharper, and slightly more salty.

HOW TO ENJOY Dollop it onto thick wedges of walnut loaf or stir it into steaming pasta with a little cream or mascarpone and toasted pinenuts. Toss into salads with sun-blushed tomatoes, flageolet beans, and a honey dressing, or add to sauces and dips. It is exquisite drizzled with a little honey, and with most sweet wines including Marsala, a robust red, and even a rosé.

The moulds, *each bears the number of the individual producer, which is imprinted on the cheese.*

ITALY Lombardia and Piemonte	
Age 3–6 months	
Weight and Shape 6–13kg (13lb 4oz–28½lb), drum	
Size D. 25–30cm (10–12in), H. 15–20cm (6–8in)	
Milk Cow	
Classification Blue	
Producer Various	

A CLOSER LOOK

In 1970, a Consortium was created to ensure Gorgonzola was only made with milk from designated areas, by approved producers. Only those that meet the tough standards are stamped with the Consortium "G".

WOODEN BELT Once firm, the cheese is removed from the mould, rubbed and rolled in salt, or in brine baths to save labour costs, then encased in a wide belt made of thin, slatted wood, and left to mature.

MATURING Traditionally ripened in *casere*, "natural caves", with ideal conditions for natural mould formation, now they are ripened in purpose-built store rooms to ensure they attain the consistency and high quality demanded by today's market.

PIERCING AND GRADING At four weeks, each cheese is pierced with thick needles, encouraging the spread of the blue-green mould. This is carried out in a place called Purgatory and the cheese is kept at around 22°C (71°F) and up to 95 per cent humidity. A grader takes a sample of cheese to check for the even distribution of the blue mould.

FOIL WRAPPING To slow the further development of mould and prevent the cheese from drying out, each one is wrapped in foil.

The ivory white interior is paler than other blue vein cheeses and almost translucent.

Once exposed to air, the blue mould grows along the tunnels made by the piercing rods.

Drum, quarter

The sticky white rind is overlaid with a medley of orange, brown, red, grey, and blue moulds.

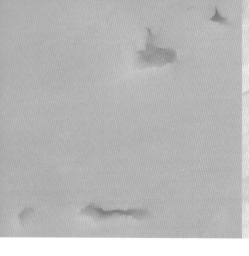
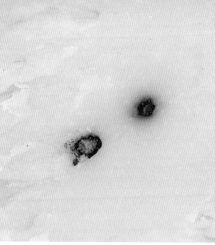

Caciotta

A generic name for a host of popular cheeses mainly from Umbria made with cow, goat or ewes' milk. Typically sold young and often combined with flavours like peppercorns or shavings of black truffles, Caciotta al Tartufo.

TASTING NOTES Typically mild and sweet with a doughy, soft texture. Milky when made with cow's milk; they can be buttery, and nutty when made with ewe's or goat's milk, or a mix.

HOW TO ENJOY Eat as a snack. Unites nicely with many Italian Spumante Classico, or pair with young red wine like Rosso di Franciacorta, or, when available, Vino Novello.

ITALY Umbria	
Age From a few days to 2–3 months	
Weight and Shape 1kg (2¼lb), cylinder	
Size D. 20cm (8in), H. 5cm (2in)	
Milk Cow, Ewe, or Goat	
Classification Hard or Flavour-added	
Producer Various	

Calcagno

This traditional sheep's cheese is made by simply adding black peppercorns to fresh curd, draining the cheeses in hand-woven rush baskets and, once salted, ageing them for at least three months. The baskets leave behind a pattern on the brownish-yellow rind.

TASTING NOTES Calcagno becomes grainy with age, and as it matures the taste becomes saltier, pungent, and spicy, and the sheep flavour more distinct.

HOW TO ENJOY Serve a younger cheese with roasted peppers and use an older cheese for grating over pasta or vegetable dishes. Team with Torgiano Rosso, or a late-harvested white wine.

ITALY Sardegna and Sicilia	
Age 3–10 months	
Weight and Shape 10–15kg (22lb–33lb), cylinder	
Size D. 26–40cm (10–15½), H. 16cm (6in)	
Milk Ewe	
Classification Flavour-added	
Producer Various	

Canestrato di Moliterno PGI

Clotted using kid goat's rennet, this hard cheese is moulded and drained in rush baskets, *canestri*, then ripened in stores called *fondachi* that are located at a minimum of 700m above sea level.

TASTING NOTES *Primitivo* is less than six months old and is sweet and salty; *stagionato*, aged for 6–12 months, is pungent and salty, while *extra*, over 12 months, is very hard, brittle, pungent, and salty.

HOW TO ENJOY Delicious with slices of apple when young. More mature cheeses are ideal for grating. Perfect with a glass of Aglianico del Volture Riserva.

ITALY Basilicata	
Age 2–18 months	
Weight and Shape 2–3kg (4½–6lb), cylinder	
Size D. 20–25cm (8–10in), H. 10–15cm (4–6in)	
Milk Ewe or Goat	
Classification Hard	
Producer Various	

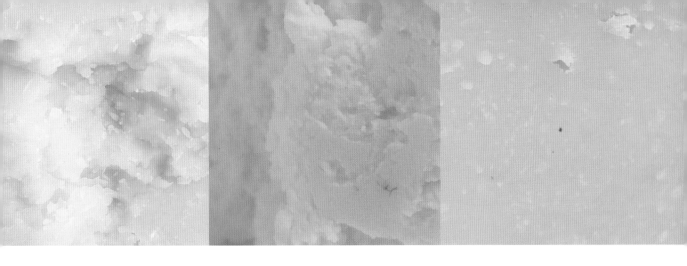

Canestrato Pugliese PDO

Like all Canestrato cheeses, this ewe's milk cheese derives its name from the reed baskets used to drain it. The rind is rubbed with olive oil and wine vinegar as the cheese matures to give a golden colour.

TASTING NOTES Firm and straw-coloured paste with small eyes. Its milky taste has sweet notes, becoming salty and pungent with a hint of roast lamb.

HOW TO ENJOY Grate it on pasta, in regional artichoke dishes, or over stuffed lamb and veal cutlets. Pair with a red like Nero d'Avola or a sweet Primitivo di Manduria Dolce Naturale.

ITALY Corato, Puglia	
Age 2–12 months	
Weight and Shape 7kg (15½lb), cylinder	
Size D. 25cm (10in), H. 10cm (4in)	
Milk Ewe	
Classification Hard	
Producer Caseificio Pugliese, Corato	

Caprino Fresco

The name of this cheese concisely describes it: *capra* means "goat" and *fresco* means "fresh". Caprino Fresco is produced by the ancient method of allowing the curd to coagulate over 24 hours using only a small quantity of rennet. At least ten varieties of this cheese are produced all over Italy.

TASTING NOTES This crumbly cheese is fragrant with a delicate, lemony fresh acidity, and it has a nutty, slightly goaty aroma.

HOW TO ENJOY Typically it is served with bread or crackers, but it can be used for filling pasta or bresaola. Pair it with a glass of Franciacorta Millesimato.

ITALY All over	
Age 2–5 days	
Weight and Shape 50–150g (1¾–5½oz), small logs	
Size D. 3–5cm (1–2in), L. 10–15cm (4–6in)	
Milk Goat	
Classification Fresh	
Producer Various	

Caprino Stagionato

Caprino Stagionato is made throughout Italy, and in particular in areas where the grazing is poor because, unlike cows and sheep, goats are browsers and are happy to feed on rough, rocky pastures.

TASTING NOTES It has a fine dusting of white mould overlaid with grey and blue; the paste is ivory and tastes better as it matures, when it develops a nutty and more distinctive goaty aroma and taste.

HOW TO ENJOY Caprino Stagionato is perfect as a table cheese and delicious grated over pasta dishes. Team it with a glass of Merlot di Torre Rosazza.

ITALY All over	
Age 1–6 months	
Weight and Shape 2–3kg (4½–6lb), cylinder	
Size D. 20–25cm (8–10in), H. 10–15cm (4–6in)	
Milk Goat	
Classification Hard	
Producer Various	

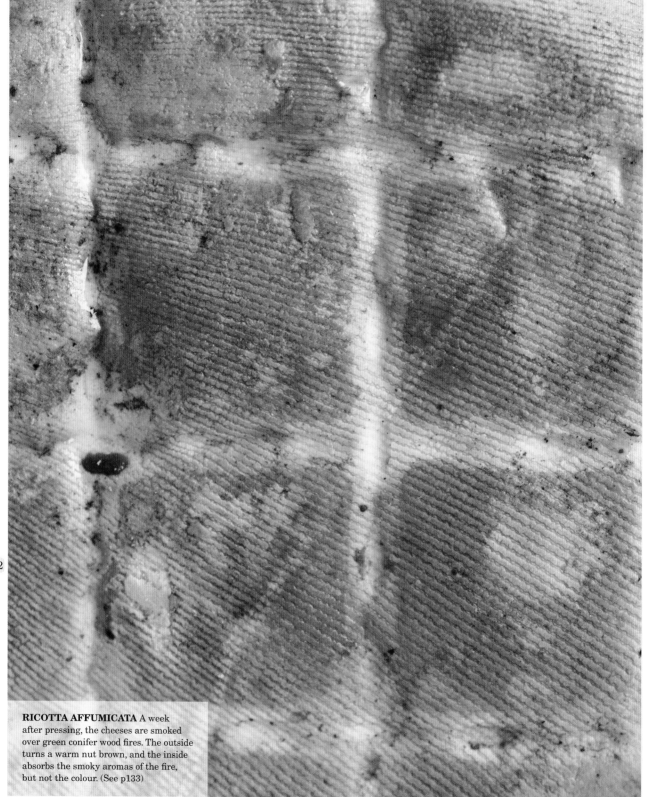

RICOTTA AFFUMICATA A week
after pressing, the cheeses are smoked
over green conifer wood fires. The outside
turns a warm nut brown, and the inside
absorbs the smoky aromas of the fire,
but not the colour. (See p133)

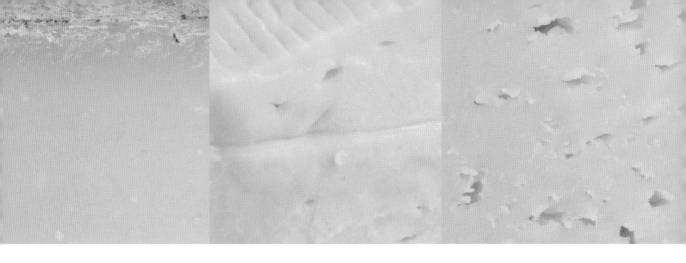

Carnia

This hard cheese is made from the milk of the Bruna Alpina cattle that graze the Alps. The best ones are made with raw milk and aged for over a year, but to ensure a regular income most producers sell it at around six months.

TASTING NOTES Sweet when young, becoming more aromatic as it matures. However, as the pastures change, so does the aroma and flavour of the cheese; at times herbaceous or fruity.

HOW TO ENJOY Carnia is typically used in *frico*, a local omelette-type dish, and is best served with a local wine like Refosco Isonzo del Friuli or Verduzzo Friulano Passito.

ITALY Friuli-Venezia Giulia	
Age 6–12 months or more	
Weight and Shape 8kg (17lb 10oz), wheel	
Size D. 30cm (12in), H. 6cm (2½in)	
Milk Cow	
Classification Hard	
Producer Various	

Casatella Trevigiana PDO

The inclusion of *casa*, meaning "home", in this fresh cheese's name hints at its original use. It was produced in homes for the family's consumption rather than for sale. Now, though, it is made commercially throughout the area in small co-operatives.

TASTING NOTES A soft, tender, shiny creamy cheese with milky and buttery notes and a melt-in-the-mouth texture. Small irregular eyes can be present.

HOW TO ENJOY Traditionally used to stuff Bresaola rosettes as part of a winter Italian dish. It goes well with Prosecco Millesimato Bisol, a sparkling wine.

ITALY Veneto	
Age 5–10 days	
Weight and Shape 400g–2.2kg (14oz–5lb), wheel	
Size D. 8–22cm (3–9in), H. 4–6cm (1½–2½in)	
Milk Cow	
Classification Fresh	
Producer Various	

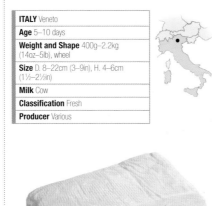

Casciotta d'Urbino PDO

This historic cheese dates back to 1545, when it was mentioned in the writings of the Montefeltro Duke; it is also said to have been a favourite of Michelangelo. A semi-soft cheese, Casciotta is made from a combination of ewe's milk and some cow's milk.

TASTING NOTES A white or slightly yellow cheese with an elastic texture and an aroma and taste that is sweet with vegetal notes.

HOW TO ENJOY Conventionally a table cheese, it complements Verdicchio dei Castelli di Jesi Casal Serra or Malvasia delle Lipari.

ITALY Montemaggiore al Matauro, Marche	
Age 20–30 days	
Weight and Shape 800g–1.2kg (1¾lb–2¾lb), small cylinder	
Size D. 12–16cm (5–6in), H. 5–7cm (2–3in)	
Milk Ewe and cow	
Classification Semi-soft	
Producer Fattorie Marchigiane Cons. Coop	

Casolet

Produced in the Adamello mountains, by a number of dairies from raw and pasteurised milk, Casolet means "small cheese"and is easily recognised as it is stamped with the *Rosa Camuna*, an ancient drawing of a rose found in the rock carvings of Capo di Ponte.

TASTING NOTES The thin orange rind is dusted with white and grey moulds. The straw-yellow paste is supple with an aroma of fermented fruits, while the herbaceous flavours change with the pastures.

HOW TO ENJOY Eat with dried fig conserve along with Vendemmia Tardiva Cavit or Franciacorta Millesimato Bellavista.

ITALY Lombardia and Trentino-Alto Adige	
Age 2–12 months	
Weight and Shape 1.3–2kg (3–4¾lb), triangle	
Size W. 20–25cm (8–10in), H. 5–8cm (2–3in)	
Milk Cow	
Classification Semi-soft	
Producer Various	

Castelmagno PDO

An ancient cheese, made from the milk of Piedmontese cows, Castelmagno was traditionally encouraged to develop some internal blueing through cracks in the rind and the fine curd. Nowadays, most is sold before the natural blueing has developed.

TASTING NOTES The crust is wrinkled, the interior is white-yellow and very friable or crumbly in the centre, and it is delicate when young, becoming strong and very savoury when ripe.

HOW TO ENJOY Traditionally eaten on its own and married with Barolo or used in fondues or *Veloutés* (creamy cheese sauces). It is also delicious with honey.

ITALY Piemonte	
Age 2–6 months	
Weight and Shape 2–7kg (4½–15½lb), drum	
Size D. 15–25cm (6–10in), H. 12–20cm (5–8in)	
Milk Cow	
Classification Hard	
Producer Various	

Crescenza

This fresh cheese derives its name from the Latin *carsenza*, meaning "flat bread", because when it is kept in a warm place the cheese ferments, swelling up like rising bread and bursting through its thin rind.

TASTING NOTES Crescenza is a fresh and delicate cheese with a balanced sweet taste and pleasant, lemony, milky, and creamy aroma. The paste is moist and sticky.

HOW TO ENJOY In Italy, Crescenza is sometimes used for preparing a delicate sauce with chestnuts, or in puff-pastry dishes. It goes well with Pinot Nero or Valcalepio Rosso.

ITALY Lombardia	
Age 5–10 days	
Weight and Shape 1.8–2kg (4lb–4½lb), rectangle	
Size L. 16–20cm (6–8in), H. 4–5cm (1½–2in)	
Milk Cow	
Classification Fresh	
Producer Various	

ITALY

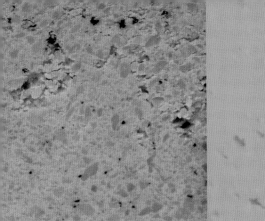
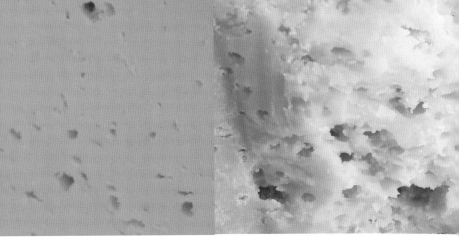

Crutin

Since 1986, Beppino Occelli has been in the dairy industry, first producing one of the best butters in the world, then creating this original cheese. Crutin is named after a small cellar excavated from stone, originally used for storage by Langhe farmers.

TASTING NOTES Made from local cow's milk it is pale yellow, and crumbly. The fine, black truffle shavings scattered throughout give this slightly citrusy cheese the intense aroma and flavour of truffle, and a hint of the stone cellars.

HOW TO ENJOY It flakes or crumbles easily so try it over pasta, carpaccio or eggs, along with an Italian red.

ITALY Langhe, Piemonte	
Age 1–2 months	
Weight and Shape 300g and 1kg (10 oz and 2¼lb)	
Size D. 6–11cm (2½–4in), H. 8–12cm (3–5in)	
Milk Cow	
Classification Flavour-added	
Producer Beppino Occelli	

Dobbiaco

Unlike most Italian cheeses, this is a rectangular or large brick-shaped cheese, so is easy for cutting. It is made from cow's milk in the mountain town of Dobbiaco in the attractive region of Val Pusteria.

TASTING NOTES The rind is reddish or brownish-red and slightly sticky. The paste is supple and straw-yellow with a few irregular small eyes. Fresh and lemony, it becomes sweet at the end with a buttery, vegetal, and nutty aroma.

HOW TO ENJOY Great on a cheeseboard with black rye bread and a generous aromatic wine, or served with polenta.

ITALY Trentino-Alto Adige	
Age 3–5 months	
Weight and Shape 5kg (11lb), long brick	
Size H. 10cm (4in) W. 10cm (4in) L. 40cm (15½in)	
Milk Cow	
Classification Semi-soft	
Producer Latteria di Dobbiaco	

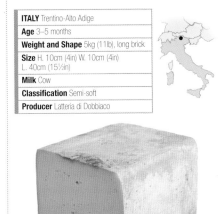

Fiore Sardo PDO

Fiore Sardo possibly dates back to the Bronze Age, and some cheeses are still made by shepherds in mountain huts over open fires, then stored in the rafters to imbue them with smoky overtones.

TASTING NOTES The brown rind, rubbed with olive oil, has a distinctive aroma and appearance. The texture is hard and crumbly with the distinct sweet taste of sheep's milk and a long-lasting, smoky, salty, pungent finish.

HOW TO ENJOY Serve as an hors d'oeuvres with fresh broad beans, or when aged it can be grated over numerous pasta or vegetable dishes.

ITALY Sardegna	
Age 3–6 months	
Weight and Shape 1.5–4kg (3⅓–8lb 13oz), drum	
Size D. 15–25cm (6–10in), H. 10–15cm (4–6in)	
Milk Ewe	
Classification Hard	
Producer Various	

ITALY

115

Foglie de Castagno

The Occelli goats, sheep and cows graze in the meadows and woods at the foot of the Maritime Alps and produce milk with extraordinary complexity, giving the cheese an exceptional flavour. It is aged in deep brown chestnut leaves, that look elegant but are very bitter.

TASTING NOTES Hard, flaky and dense, it packs a serious mouth-watering, lip-puckering punch, which is both sweet and savoury, like raw onions leaving the taste buds waiting for more. Strong salty finish in the end.

HOW TO ENJOY As the last cheese on the board with a big red wine or a dark craft beer.

ITALY Langhe, Piemonte
Age 3–4 months
Weight and Shape 3.5kg (7½lb), cylinder
Size D 22cm (8½in), H 7cm (2½in)
Milk Cow and Goat
Classification Flavour-added
Producer Beppino Occelli

Fontal

Fontal is a combination of two great cheeses: the famous Fontina, and Emmental. It is produced industrially in much of Northern Italy all year round, rather than only in summers.

TASTING NOTES The rind is reddish-brown while the paste is dense, straw-yellow, smooth, and slightly elastic. It is an aromatic cheese, with milky, buttery notes and a hint of almonds.

HOW TO ENJOY It melts superbly so it is ideal in fondues or grilled, especially with wild mushrooms. Pair it with Pignolo di Filiputti and Terre d'Agata di Salaparuta.

ITALY Gottolengo, Lombardia
Age 45–60 days
Weight and Shape 8–10kg (17lb 10oz–22lb), wheel
Size D. 30–40cm (12–15½in), H. 7–10cm (3–4in)
Milk Cow
Classification Semi-soft
Producer Scuola Casearia Pandino, Caseificio Foresti, Gottolengo

Fontina PDO

An exceptional cheese, Fontina is made twice a day from the milk of the Valdostana cows that graze at the foot of Mont Blanc. Dating back to the Middle Ages, this semi-soft cheese is thought to take its name from a local family, "Fontin".

TASTING NOTES The washed rind is reddish and sticky while the supple paste has small holes and a mild, nutty flavour that hints of the herbaceous pastures on which the cows graze.

HOW TO ENJOY Famously used in a *fonduta*, a dish in which the cheese is whipped with eggs and cream. It goes well with full-flavoured red wines.

ITALY Saint-Cristophe, Valle D'Aosta
Age 3 months
Weight and Shape 8–12kg (17lb 10oz–26½lb), flat wheel
Size D. 30–40cm (12–15½in), H. 7–10cm (3–4in)
Milk Cow
Classification Semi-soft
Producer Cooperativa Produttori Latte e Fontina, Saint-Cristhophe, Aosta

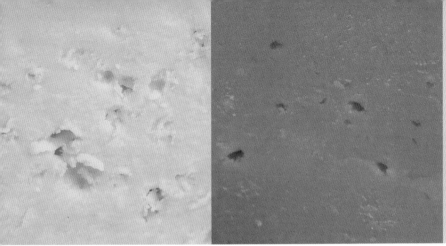

Formaggella del Luinese PDO

Dating back to the 17th century it is produced from the milk of the goats that graze on Alpine pastures and cuttings from the spring hedgerows. Unlike most goat's cheeses, the milk is held in vats for around 30 hours at 4°C/39°F before being coagulated. The curd is cut small to give it a soft, compact texture.

TASTING NOTES Wrinkled and white with a goaty aroma, moist, crumbly texture, and a herbaceous taste, with sweet almond notes to finish.

HOW TO ENJOY It is excellent with Cabernet Sauvignon di Walch or Moscato Strevi Passito.

ITALY Lombardia	
Age 20–30 days	
Weight and Shape 700–900g (1¼–2lb), flat cylinder	
Size D. 13–15cm (5–6in), H. 8–12cm (3–5in)	
Milk Goat	
Classification Aged fresh	
Producer Various	

Formaggio di Fossa di Sogliano PDO

Fossa, or "hole", refers to the technique by which cheeses are stored in holes carved into the walls of caves in Sagliano, which are then sealed with chalk paste to ensure a constant temperature as the cheeses ripen.

TASTING NOTES Covered in green, yellowish, and white mould, the taste is variable, but typically it has a pungent smell and a sharp bitterish taste.

HOW TO ENJOY Grate over regional pasta, such as passatelli or tortelloni, and minestrone soup. Impressive when served with Cagnina di Romagna, or even better with Albana Passito.

ITALY Emilia Romagna, and Marche	
Age 3–4 months	
Weight and Shape Various	
Size Various	
Milk Ewe, cow, or both	
Classification Semi-soft	
Producer Various	

Formaggio Ubriaco

Ubriaco, or "drunken", refers to the technique of placing young cheeses in barrels of crushed grape skins and seeds left over from wine-making. Over two to three days they are sprinkled with wine then left to mature and harden for a week or more.

TASTING NOTES The creamy richness of the cheese marries well with the distinct flavour and aroma of the wine, which varies according to the preferences of the cheesemaker.

HOW TO ENJOY Superb when served with a baked potato or partnered with polenta and mushrooms. Try with an aromatic wine.

ITALY Veneto and Langhe	
Age 2–12 months	
Weight and Shape 2.5–5kg (5½–11lb), drum	
Size D. 20–25cm (8–10in), H. 5–8cm (2–3in)	
Milk Cow, or cow and goat	
Classification Flavour-added	
Producer Latteria di Soligo, La Casara di Roncolato Romano, Beppiano Ocelli	

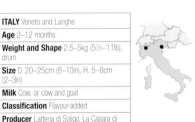

Mozzarella di Bufala PDO

Mozzarella is made around the world and varies from lush, juicy pure white balls to yellow, rubbery blocks of cow's milk, suitable for family pizzas. But none can match Mozzarella di Bufala, made with milk from the handsome water buffalo of Campania.

The buffalo was introduced to Italy in the 7th century as a working beast to plough the marshes south of Naples, but as the Roman Empire disintegrated, the drainage systems and rivers silted up. The buffalo and the land were eventually abandoned as malaria became rife. It was not until the 12th century that records show cheese was made from its milk.

In the 18th century, the marshes were drained, malaria was all but eradicated, and the once wild Buffalo was domesticated, and production of Mozzarella became widespread throughout Campania in southern Italy. The recipe was introduced from the Eastern Mediterranean and Middle East where you can find other stretched curd or *pasta filata* cheeses in Israel and Cyprus.

Rich in calcium, high in protein, and with a high vitamin and mineral salt content, it is highly nutritious and easily digested, plus, at 21 per cent fat (270kcal per 100g), Mozzarella is surprisingly low in fat. Protected under Italian and European law, it is strictly monitored to ensure the quality and provenance of the product. In fact, authentic Mozzarella di Bufala can only be made in seven provinces in Central-South Italy: Caserta and Salerno, and part of Benevento, Naples, Frosinone, Latina, and Rome.

The water buffalo *of Campania.*

TASTING NOTES When cut, it has a grainy texture composed of many layers, like cooked chicken – pearls of milky whey should seep out. It is very sweet and mild, like aged (but not sour) milk, with an earthy, mossy aroma and a taste reminiscent of new leather. Springy at first, it becomes softer, but never crinkled, slippery or salty, and is bitter and sour only when over ripe.

HOW TO ENJOY Its role is primarily to give texture rather than taste to a dish, and to trap, absorb, and intensify the juices and ingredients between its luscious layers of curd, producing some of the most memorable culinary combinations. Perfect on pizza; salads of olive oil, balsamic vinegar, sun-ripened tomatoes, and basil; Melanzane alla Parmigiana made with layers of aubergine and Mozzarella in "a tomato sauce; or in a *carrozza* (carriage), sandwiched between two slices of bread, battered, and fried. When using fresh Mozzarella to top a pizza or fill a calzone, it is best to slice it and allow it to drain for several hours in a colander so that the crust doesn't become soggy.

A CLOSER LOOK

The extraordinarily versatile and irresistibly stretchy texture of Mozzarella di Bufala make it loved the world over. However, with its short shelf life and premium price, it is not readily available outside of Europe, so cow's milk alternatives are more widely available. If authentically made, their texture may be similar but they lack the earthy, mossy, and new-leather notes of buffalo's milk.

THE CURD the freshly made curd is allowed to ferment for a few hours before being cut into blocks then put through a mill that shreds it into small pieces. The rubbery pieces are covered with boiling water.

Whole ball

ITALY	Campania and Lazio
Age	From 1 day
Weight and Shape	Various
Size	Various
Milk	Water buffalo
Classification	Fresh
Producer	Various

STRETCHING In a process known as *pasta filata*, the curds are spun and stretched into balls, small balls (*bocconcini*), or plaits of varying sizes. This creates layers of curd with droplets of whey trapped within the concentric circles that resemble cooked chicken breast.

THE TEXTURE To achieve the desired texture, the rubbery curd and boiling water is stirred until the lumps turn into a smooth, plastic-looking mass.

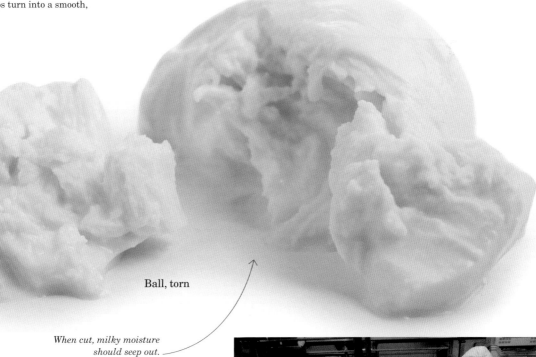

Ball, torn

When cut, milky moisture should seep out.

It must not be soft or mushy when cut, but fibrous and elastic, so that, if poked, it springs back to its original shape.

BRINING The balls are put into cold brine to soak and absorb a small amount of salt which heightens the flavour and helps to preserve it.

Formai de Mut dell'Alta Valle Brembana PDO

Mut, or "mountain cheese" refers to the Alpine grazing of the cows that make this cheese. This hard cheese is produced in summer in 40 *casere* or "mountain dairies", and in winter 2,500 wheels are made in the valley.

TASTING NOTES Beneath the thin, straw-tinged, ivory rind the paste is compact and springy with widely scattered holes. The delicate taste has an aroma of forage fragrances.

HOW TO ENJOY Use in *polenta taragna*, a local dish. Try with Dolcetto d'Ovada.

ITALY Lombardia	
Age 7 weeks–6 months	
Weight and Shape 8kg (17lb 10oz), wheel	
Size D. 30cm (12in), H. 8cm (3in)	
Milk Cow	
Classification Hard	
Producer Various	

Grana Padano PDO

Created in the 12th century by the Cistercian monks of Chiaravalle Abbey, this hard cheese is now made in numerous dairies in the Padana Valley and is the biggest of all PDO cheeses.

TASTING NOTES The reddish-yellow or yellow rind is very thick while the paste is hard, white, or straw-yellow and brittle. It has a sweet fruity taste, and a fragrant, buttery aroma with hints of dried fruits.

HOW TO ENJOY Classically used on *pastasciutta al dente*, in ravioli, and in hundreds of other recipes. Goes well with bold whites, reds, and sparkling wines.

ITALY Lombardia	
Age 1–2 years	
Weight and Shape 24–40kg (53–88lb), drum	
Size D. 35–45cm (14–17½in), H. 18–25cm (1–10in)	
Milk Cow	
Classification Hard	
Producer Various	

Latteria Turnaria

This cheese was created in Latteria Turnaria, where the shareholders are the cheesemakers, who use the facilities to make their own individual-style cheeses. Now the production has come under the protection of the Slow Food presidium scheme.

TASTING NOTES When it is young, the aroma hints of milk and cream; flowers and hay, when aged. It has a sweet-salty taste and an elastic texture which turns compact and floury after 2–3 months.

HOW TO ENJOY Pair with bread, olive oil, oregano, and a glass of red wine: either I Balzini di Filiputti, or Amarone di Valpolicella.

ITALY Lombardia, Veneto, and Friuli	
Age 1–12 months	
Weight and Shape 6–8kg (13–17lb 10oz), wheel	
Size D. 25–35cm (10–14in), H. 5–8cm (2–3in)	
Milk Cow	
Classification Semi-soft, or hard	
Producer Various	

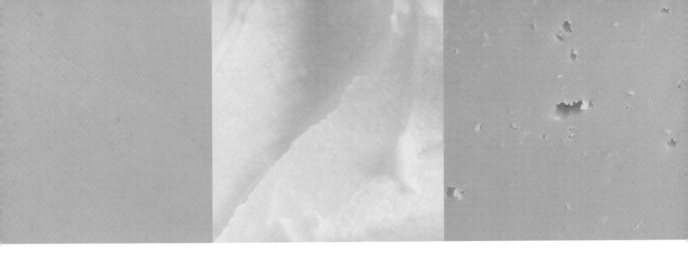

Marzolino

Marzolino means "little March", as traditionally this ewe's cheese was only produced at the beginning of lactation in March. When 14-year-old Catherine De Medici became Queen Consort of King Henry II, in 1533, this cheese was supplied to the Court of France in order to alleviate her homesickness.

TASTING NOTES It has a straw-yellow or white paste with irregular eyes, and is full of sweet flavours and floral and vegetal hints.

HOW TO ENJOY *Bomboloni* ("doughnuts") are made with Marzolino, bread, oil, and pepper. Good with Ansonica Costa dell'Argentario or Sagrantino Passito.

ITALY Roccalbegna Grosseto, Toscana	
Age 15–90 days, best at 30 days	
Weight and Shape 500g–1.5kg (1lb 2oz–3lb 3oz), oval	
Size D. 15–22cm (6–8¾in), H. 9–13cm (3½–5in)	
Milk Ewe	
Classification Semi-soft	
Producer Caseificio "Il Fiorino", Roccalbegna Grosseto	

Mascarpone

This fresh cheese is made by heating cream and allowing the natural acidity to gradually separate or curdle it, before draining off the whey. It dates back to the 12th century and was known to be a favourite of Napoleon.

TASTING NOTES Milky coloured and velvety smooth, like rich double cream, it has a marked sweet and lemony taste and a full, persistent, and buttery aroma.

HOW TO ENJOY Essential for making tiramisù and Charlottes and fantastic served with apple slices with sugar and lemon. For a wonderful combination, pair it with a classic dessert wine.

ITALY All over	
Age Ready after 1 day	
Weight and Shape 100–200g (3½–7oz), Pots	
Size No size	
Milk Cow	
Classification Fresh	
Producer Various	

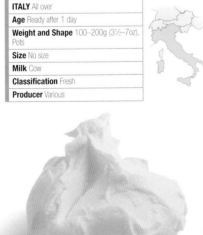

Montasio PDO

Created by an unknown monk from the Moggio Abbey during the 13th century, the production of this hard cheese has been protected by the Montasio consortium since 1987 and is now also covered by the PDO scheme.

TASTING NOTES The taste depends on the age: fresh, semi-aged, or very old. It can be milky and buttery when young, and savoury and aromatic when aged. Small eyes can be present.

HOW TO ENJOY Try Montasio with large ravioli and asparagus. Pair it with a glass of Sassò di Felluga, with its intense spiciness, or the sweet Picolit del Collio.

ITALY Veneto	
Age 2–12 months	
Weight and Shape 6–8kg (13lb 4oz–17lb 10lb), wheel	
Size D. 30–35cm (12–14in), H. 8cm (3in)	
Milk Cow	
Classification Hard	
Producer Consorzio per la Tutela del Formaggio Montasio	

Monte Veronese PDO

This was created in 1273 when Bishop Bartholomeus della Scala authorized the Cimbri shepherds to live in the Lessinia Alps. Even today, pastures and grazing cows are the basic elements of this traditional product.

TASTING NOTES With a brown-yellow rind (sometimes treated with oil), it is compact and elastic, with a sweet herbaceous taste when young, which becomes crumbly and floral in middle age; spicy and fruity when old.

HOW TO ENJOY Great with fruit and nuts. Team with a full-bodied red, such as Recioto della Valpolicella; when very old, pair it with a sweet Torcolato Maculan.

ITALY Veneto	
Age 2, 4 or 8 months	
Weight and Shape 6–9kg (13lb 4oz–19lb 3oz), wheel	
Size D. 25–35cm (10–14in), H. 7–11cm (3–4½in)	
Milk Cow	
Classification Hard	
Producer Various	

Morlacco

Named after the Morlachs nomadic people, who arrived in Italy as shepherds from the Balkans and the river Grappa, this prized cheese was originally made with skimmed milk as the cream was sold for butter. Today it is made with semi-skimmed milk.

TASTING NOTES The thin rind bears the imprint of the basket mould, while the ivory paste is soft, yet crumbly, with delicate floral and fruity notes.

HOW TO ENJOY Simply serve it with pepper and olive oil, or cook with gnocchi. It is delightfully matched with Merlot dei Colli Trevigiani: a ruby red, full-bodied, tannic and balanced wine.

ITALY Cesiomaggiore, Veneto	
Age 3–5 months, better at 3	
Weight and Shape 4–8kg (9lb–17lb 10oz), round	
Size D. 20–30cm (8–12in), H. 7–12cm (3–5in)	
Milk Cow	
Classification Semi-soft	
Producer Caseificio Montegrappa, Pove del Grappa, Formaggio di Spelonca	

Murazzano PDO

One of the Robiolas family of cheeses, it was documented by Pliny the Elder during the Roman Empire. Today it is still an authentic farmhouse cheese, and is produced by many small dairies.

TASTING NOTES The rind is white-yellow, the texture smooth, fine, and elastic, and the flavour is a careful balance of sweet and acid with a creamy aroma and vegetal hints.

HOW TO ENJOY It is used in the famous Murazzano's timbale, and for preparing Bruss (a cream with spices and Grappa, or other spirits). It matches perfectly with Langhe Freisa di Cozzo, or the rich, red Verduno Pelaverga.

ITALY Piemonte	
Age 4–10 days	
Weight and Shape 300–400g (10–14oz), round	
Size D. 10–15cm (4–6in), H. 3–4cm (1–1½in)	
Milk Ewe, Cow	
Classification Semi-soft	
Producer Various	

ITALY

122

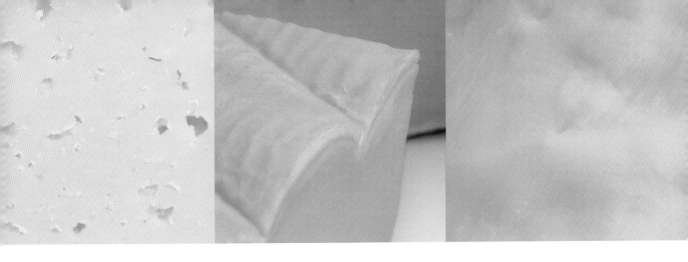

Ossolano

This traditional cheese is made in summer in mountain huts from the milk of the Bruna Alpina cattle that graze the Ossola Alps. The secret of the cheese's flavour lies in the mottolina herbs, which only grow in that region.

TASTING NOTES The rind is brown and the paste creamy or straw-yellow, sometimes with small eyes. With a sweet taste, it has an intense, herby aroma, and is slightly bitter.

HOW TO ENJOY An impressive way to serve this cheese is melted over turkey breasts. It pairs well with a red Sizzano di Zanetta, where the bouquet has a hint of violets, and Ghemme.

ITALY Corato, Piemonte	
Age 2–6 months	
Weight and Shape 5–7kg (11–15lb 7oz), wheel	
Size D. 30–40cm (12–16in), H. 6–8cm (2½–3in)	
Milk Cow	
Classification Semi-soft	
Producer Latteria Sociale Antigoriana	

Paglierina

Also called Braculina or Paglietta, this cheese takes its name from the *paglia* ("straw") on which it was traditionally placed to allow excess whey to drain off. Created in 1891 by Signor Quaglia, in San Francesco al Campo, near Turin.

TASTING NOTES The white, bloomy rind covers a soft, delicate, creamy paste that melts in the mouth and has a fresh, mushroomy aroma and taste.

HOW TO ENJOY Fill Paglierina with nuts, raisins, white pepper, and chillies, Italian-style, or serve with sesame and speck (juniper-flavoured raw ham). Pair with a balanced red such as Dolcetto d'Asti, or an intense white Roero.

ITALY Rifreddo, Piemonte	
Age 15–20 days	
Weight and Shape 300–500g (10oz–1lb 2oz), small cylinder	
Size D. 10–15cm (4–6in), H. 3–4cm (1½–2in)	
Milk Cow	
Classification Soft white	
Producer Caseificio Oreglia	

Pannarello

One of only a handful of Italian cheeses that are made by adding extra cream to the milk before it is curdled. This technique is reflected in its name: *panna,* which means "cream".

TASTING NOTES Very delicate in the mouth and very creamy, Pannarello has a scalded milk aroma and taste, and when eaten it feels almost elastic, but pleasantly so.

HOW TO ENJOY Pannarello is perfect for fondues or paired with mixed-berry jams. Try serving it with the sparkling and fruity white Prosecco Cartizze Bisol, or the fresh and grassy white Roero Arneis.

ITALY Giavera del Montello, Veneto	
Age 1–2 days	
Weight and Shape 5–9kg (11–19lb 2oz), cylindrical	
Size D. 25–30cm (10–12in), H. 6–8cm (2½–3in)	
Milk Cow	
Classification Fresh	
Producer Latteria Montello, Latteria Modolo Dino	

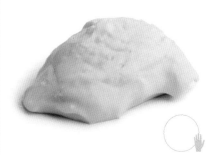

PRIMO SALE Many ancient Italian cheeses were drained in woven or plaited rush baskets, creating intricate and attractive patterns on the cheese, which also identified the producer. (See p130)

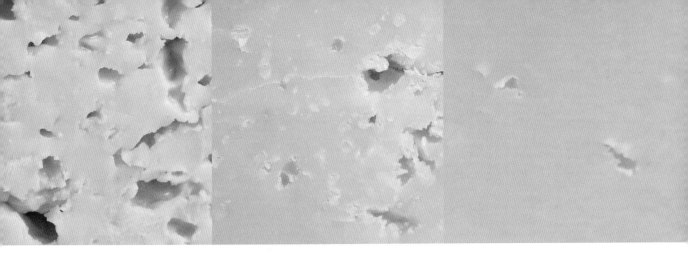

Pannerone Lodigiano

Unlike most cheeses, Pannerone is made without salt, so the flavour is instead derived from the action of the natural bacteria. The Slow Food organisation hope to expand production of this cow's milk cheese.

TASTING NOTES Soft, with myriad small holes and a persistent alcoholic aroma, it is at first quite mild but the finish has a distinct almondy taste and bitter tang, which has led to its near demise.

HOW TO ENJOY A must-have cheese on Christmas Eve, stirred into steamed vegetables. Serve with aromatic Pelago Umani Ronchi, or the intense, slightly bitter, Refosco dal Peduncolo Rosso.

ITALY Pandino, Lombardia	
Age 15–20 days	
Weight and Shape 10–13kg (22–29lb), cylindrical	
Size D. 28–30cm (11–12in), H. 20cm (8in)	
Milk Cow	
Classification Semi-soft	
Producer Caseificio Uberti 1896, Pandino Carena, Caselle Lurani	

Pecorino or Canastrato Crotonese

The art of making Pecorino Crotonese is described in a book written in 1759. This hard cheese takes its name from the city of Crotone and is made from the milk of sheep and goats. The brownish-yellow rind bears the imprint of the rush basket used to drain it.

TASTING NOTES The straw yellow paste is firm, friable, and sometimes has small eyes. The taste is pungent and sweet, with a vegetal aroma.

HOW TO ENJOY Delicious grated on macaroni, and grilled with mince and aubergines. Team it with a full-bodied Cirò or fruity Bivongi Bianco.

ITALY Calabria	
Age 2–12 months	
Weight and Shape 1.5–2.5kg (3lb 3oz–5½lb), cylindrical	
Size D. 15–20cm (6–8in), H. 12–15cm (5in–6in)	
Milk Ewe and Goat	
Classification Hard	
Producer Various	

Pecorino di Pienza

This ancient cheese is also called *Pecorino delle crete senesi* ("*creta*" is a sort of clay). Sadly, the cheese is now mostly made with pasteurized ewe's milk. The rind varies in colour as it is rubbed during maturation with a mixture of oil and tomato or clay.

TASTING NOTES It is very sweet and has an elastic texture that becomes firm and crunchy with age. The flavour is fruity and floral, and when well matured has hints of toasted hazelnuts.

HOW TO ENJOY Often used for filling stuffed peppers and artichokes, or grated over grilled lamb. It goes perfectly with Chianti dei Colli Senesi.

ITALY Toscana	
Age 1–4 months	
Weight and Shape 1–2kg (2¼lb–4½lb), round	
Size D. 15–20cm (6–8in), H. 6–8cm (2½–3in)	
Milk Ewe	
Classification Hard	
Producer Various	

Pecorino Romano PDO

In 100BC, Pecorino Romano was described by Marcus Terentius Varro as essential for the rations of the Roman legions, as it provided fat, protein, and salt and could survive the rigours of soldiers on the move. Lamb's rennet is still used for coagulation.

TASTING NOTES The firm, compact paste is crumbly and crunchy and has the sweetness typical of ewe's milk, with a salty tang and hints of lanolin.

HOW TO ENJOY Grate over pasta and risottos, and serve with Carasau bread (dry bread), and a glass of Montesodi Chianti Rùfina or Vernaccia Sarda.

ITALY Toscana	
Age 5–12 months	
Weight and Shape 20–35kg (44–77lb), cylinder	
Size D. 25–35cm (10–14in), H. 25–40cm (10–15½)	
Milk Ewe	
Classification Hard	
Producer Various	

126

Pecorino Sardo PDO

Pecorino Sardo Dolce is made from calf's rennet, while Maturo is made using lamb's rennet. Both are made from the milk of sheep that are free grazing, rather than housed in barns.

TASTING NOTES Dolce is a young, elastic, white cheese with buttery and floral notes. Maturo is more intense, and full of pleasant pungent and salty flavours. Meat broth notes may also be present.

HOW TO ENJOY Excellent with onion soup and lamb dishes. It is also a basic ingredient in the local dish *culingiones*, a sort of ravioli with ricotta and herbs. Pair with Dolcetto di Dogliani and Nuragus di Cagliari.

ITALY Sardegna	
Age Dolce 1–2 months, Maturo 8 months	
Weight and Shape 1–2.3kg (2¼–4¾lb), drum	
Size D. 15–20cm (6–8in), H. 8–13cm (3–5in)	
Milk Ewe	
Classification Hard	
Producer Various	

Pecorino Siciliano PDO

This cheese is documented as far back as 900BC, when Odysseus meets the Cyclops Polyphemus in Homer's *Odyssey*. As in ancient times, this cheese is still hand-made using lamb's rennet. The brown-yellow rind is imprinted with a rush basket design.

TASTING NOTES Yellow and sometimes studded with whole black peppercorns, it is firm and friable with a pungent, salty, full, and long-lasting flavour.

HOW TO ENJOY Serve young cheeses with vegetables; aged ones with bread and olives or grated over pasta. Team with Anthìlia Donnafugata or sweet Zibibbo.

ITALY Sicilia	
Age 4–12 months	
Weight and Shape 4–12kg (9–26½lb), wheel	
Size D. 14–38cm (5½–15in), H. 10–18cm (4–7in)	
Milk Ewe	
Classification Hard	
Producer Various	

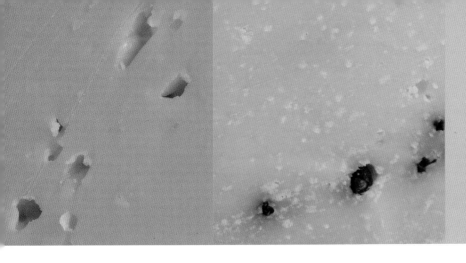

Pecorino Toscano PDO

A historic cheese, during the Roman Empire it was referred to by Pliny the Elder as *Caseus Lunensis*; and in 1832 Ignazio Malenotti, in his book *Manuale del Pecoraio*, wrote about its use of vegetable rennet from *Cynara cardunculus* flowers.

TASTING NOTES The oil-rubbed rind is yellow or brownish-yellow. The paste is yellow or white with a sweet taste and milky aroma. Aged, it becomes crumbly and savoury with dry, fruity notes.

HOW TO ENJOY Eat with a lettuce or chicory salad, along with Morellino di Scansano or Moscadello di Montalcino.

ITALY Toscana	
Age 1–6 months	
Weight and Shape 1–3.5kg (2¼–7lb 11oz), drum	
Size D. 15–22cm (6–9in), H. 7–12cm (21/2–5in)	
Milk Ewe	
Classification Hard	
Producer Various	

Piacentinu Ennese PDO

First recorded in the days of the Roman Empire, this cheese is also known as Maiorchino. It is flavoured with saffron and black pepper and is shaped in traditional reed baskets.

TASTING NOTES The outside and inside are marked yellow-orange from the addition of saffron. It tastes lightly sweet, but is also pungent and astringent with saffron and black pepper notes.

HOW TO ENJOY Fantastic for grilling, it is often used for Bucatini pasta. Match it with Etna Rosso or Cerasuolo di Vittoria.

ITALY Sicilia	
Age 2–4 months	
Weight and Shape 4.5kg (9lb 9oz), cylinder	
Size D. 20cm (8in), H. 14cm (5in)	
Milk Ewe	
Classification Flavour-added	
Producer Various	

Piave PDO

Made throughout the area around the Piave river, this hard cheese is produced in *Latteria* – small co-operatives where cheesemakers share facilities but each makes their own individual cheeses.

TASTING NOTES The rind is straw-yellow becoming brown-yellow with age. The texture ranges from elastic to firm, compact and friable. It has a rich, intense fruity sweetness, becoming more aromatic when aged.

HOW TO ENJOY Delicious for snacking, cheeseboards, or grating. Serve with full-bodied fruity reds like Pinot Noir.

ITALY Belluno, Veneto	
Age Fresco 1–2 months, Mezzano 2–6 months, Vecchio over 6 months	
Weight and Shape 6–7kg (13lb 4oz–15lb 7oz), wheel	
Size D. 30–34cm (12–13½in), H. 8cm (3in)	
Milk Cow	
Classification Hard	
Producer Lattebusche, Busche-Cesiomaggiore	

Parmigiano-Reggiano PDO

To taste a piece of Parmigiano-Reggiano, also known as Parmesan, is to taste a piece of Italian geological, culinary, and cultural history. This cheese is influenced by the soil, the grazing, the climate, the cows, and the Consortium who rigidly control its production according to a recipe barely changed since the 12th century.

The official stamp *of the Consorzio.*

In 1955, the Consorzio del Formaggio Parmigiano-Reggiano protected the name "Parmigiano-Reggiano", and latterly "Parmesan", and specified it could only be made in the provinces of Modena, Parma, Reggio Emilia, and Bologna in the region of Emilia-Romagna and Mantova in Lombardia. It also stipulated that the cows whose milk is used to produce it could be fed no silage, only fresh grass, hay, or alfalfa. As a result, the cheeses change subtly with the seasons.

Parmigiano-Reggiano is made with skimmed milk, which reduces the fat content; however, it is also very hard when mature, with significantly lower moisture content than Cheddar.

In Italy it is sold in large rough, grainy chunks chiselled to order from the magnificent shiny drum.

TASTING NOTES Parmigiano-Reggiano should never taste sour or dull, but fresh, fruity, and sweet like fresh pineapple; strong and rich but not overpoweringly salty; and certainly not vicious or bitter, nor should it ever smell acrid. Spring cheeses are a soft yellow with a delicate flavour and herbal scent attributed to the wildflowers on which the cows graze. Newly formed wheels of summer-made cheese exude butterfat so they are drier and more pungent while those made in autumn are noted for their higher casein content. The diet of hay in winter produces a paler cheese but is richer tasting. Brittle and crumbly, not plastic or supple, and pale yellow, a chunk will last for weeks and a little goes a very long way.

HOW TO ENJOY Superb simply eaten in chunks, and probably the most versatile cheese in the world for cooking, as it dissolves when heated, leaving behind a sweet, fruity, tangy flavour in virtually any savoury dish you choose to make – from bread to sauces, soups, salads, and pasta.

Parmigiano-Reggiano will keep for weeks in the fridge but the rough surface may grow some mould, which can be scraped off. Or, if you have bought a large chunk, or use it infrequently (an unthinkable possibility), keep it in, and grate it straight from, the freezer. It will quickly defrost on a hot dish. The full-bodied flavour lends itself to crisp white wines, robust reds, and even dessert wines.

A CLOSER LOOK

Parmigiano-Reggiano is made in 383 dairies, producing around 10 million cheeses per year. A staggering 120 gallons (550 litres) of milk are required to make one 38kg (84lb) drum, and each must adhere to the Consorzio's strict regulations.

DRAINING Large, copper cauldrons are used to make the cheese. After the curd is broken up, an enormous mass forms at the bottom of the cauldron, requiring two men to raise it, using a very strong piece of cloth, knotted and slung around a length of wood. This huge mass is then cut into two quantities, which are left to hang for 24 hours to drain off excess whey.

BRANDING Cheeses that pass the rigorous tests are branded with "Parmigiano-Reggiano" to indicate they can be aged for a further two years or more; the addition of *"Mezzano"* means they are suitable for immediate consumption. Later, some will be branded with "Extra" to indicate they have passed an additional test, or "Export" if they are of first-class quality. Those that do not meet the requirements have their brand polished off and are sold as *Grana*, which simply means "hard cheese" in Italian.

ITALY Emilia-Romagna and Lombardia	
Age 18–36 months	
Weight and Shape 38kg (83lb), drum	
Size D. 50cm (20in), H. 45cm (18in)	
Milk Cow	
Classification Hard	
Producer Various	

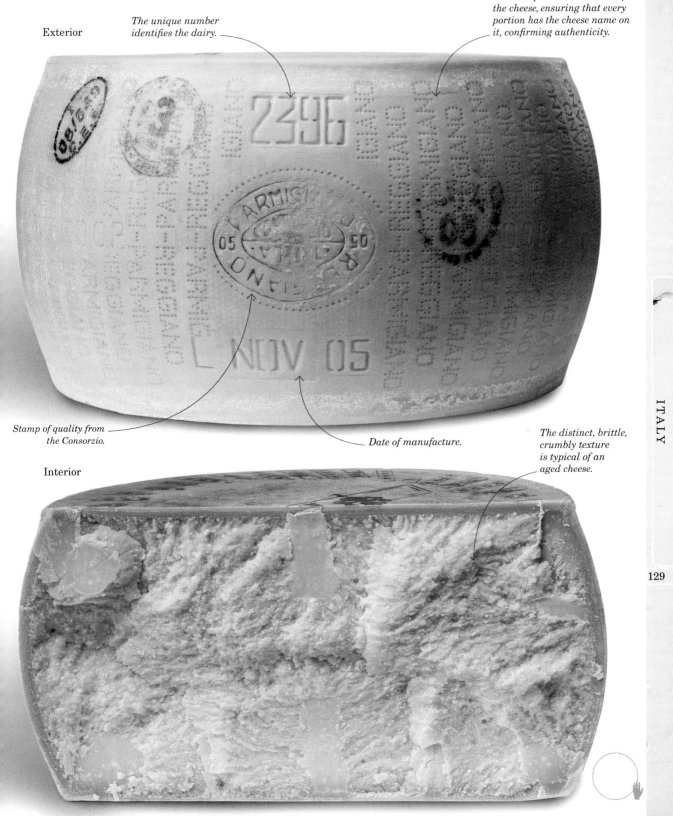

Exterior

The unique number identifies the dairy.

The stamp circles the width of the cheese, ensuring that every portion has the cheese name on it, confirming authenticity.

2396

NOV 05

Stamp of quality from the Consorzio.

Date of manufacture.

Interior

The distinct, brittle, crumbly texture is typical of an aged cheese.

Primo Sale

Primarily produced on small farms on Sicily and Sardinia using lamb rennet, the name means "first salt", a reference to the fact that it is sold a few days after it has been salted. Some are flavoured with black or red peppercorns.

TASTING NOTES It has a sharp, refreshing acidity, but with sweet notes. The texture is crunchy, with irregular eyes that exude whey. The pungent aroma has herbal hints.

HOW TO ENJOY Serve it sliced into thin layers and dressed with olive oil, salt, black pepper, and chopped mint leaf. It is used in fish dishes too. It goes well with local wines, as well as Pinot Grigio.

ITALY Sicilia	
Age 7–10 days	
Weight and Shape Various	
Size Various	
Milk Ewe	
Classification Fresh	
Producer Various	

Provolone PDO

A *pasta filata* cheese, like Caciocavallo, Provolone was traditionally the cheese of the poor because just a little piece gave a lot of flavour. Originally from southern Italy, it was brought to the North at the end of the 19th century by the Margiotta and Auricchio families.

TASTING NOTES It can be mild, sweet, and milky when clotted with calf rennet, but has a stronger flavour when the milk is coagulated with kid rennet.

HOW TO ENJOY The Dolce variety can be grilled when young; use Piccante or aged in risotto. Pair with Gutturnio di Poggiarello, or Collio Rosso di Russiz.

ITALY All over	
Age 1–12 months	
Weight and Shape 2–10kg (4½–22lb), various	
Size Various	
Milk Cow	
Classification Semi-soft	
Producer Various	

Provolone del Monaco PDO

Legend has it this cheese was created by a visiting monk, while the milk is linked to a race of dairy cattle, named Agerolese, that was bred by the House of Bourbon in the 18th century. It is aged in *tufa*, natural caves that are formed near mineral springs.

TASTING NOTES The aromatic herbs of the Lattari mountain pastures, such as thyme, oregano, and marjoram, give the milk, and cheese, a delicious flavour.

HOW TO ENJOY Simply serve it with olive oil and fresh aromatic herbs, such as wild fennel, parsley, and basil. Pair with a robust red or a sweet Marsala.

ITALY Campania	
Age 1–2 months, or 2 years in caves	
Weight and Shape 1.5–3kg (3lb 3oz–6lb 6oz), pear or sausage-shaped	
Size Various	
Milk Cow	
Classification Hard	
Producer Various	

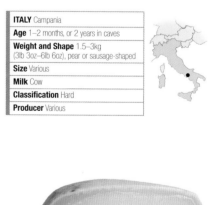

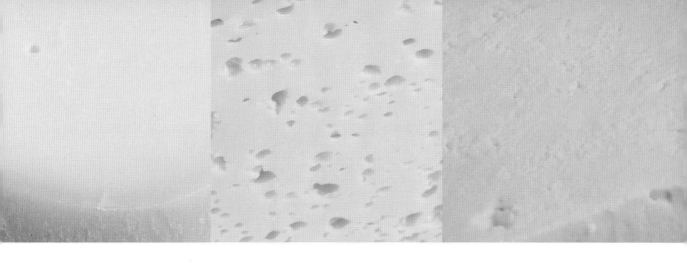

Provolone Valpadana PDO

This *pasta filata* cheese is produced in two varieties: it is Dolce when made using calf liquid rennet, and Piccante when produced using the paste rennet from young goats.

TASTING NOTES Dolce is elastic, smooth, and velvety, and has a sweet, lightly salty, milky, and buttery flavour. Piccante is dense and compact, grainy, pungent, and salty with nutmeg hints.

HOW TO ENJOY Try it with nuts and pears. Use the Dolce variety in mild dishes; Piccante in stronger flavoured ones. Serve with Freisa d'Asti, or Lambrusco Secco di Sorbara (sparkling red wine).

ITALY Emilia-Romagna	
Age 1–12 months	
Weight and Shape 1–100kg (2¼–220lb), flask, salamino, pancetta, pear, melon, and mandarino	
Size Various	
Milk Cow	
Classification Semi-soft	
Producer Various	

Puzzone di Moena PDO

Puzzone means "stinking", in reference to the very strong odour of this cheese. It is a singularly hard cheese and the rind is washed weekly with salty tepid water. Locally, it is called *Spretz Tzaorì*, meaning "savoury cheese".

TASTING NOTES It has an orange sticky rind and an elastic, white interior that melts in the mouth. The flavour is a balance of sweet, sour, and bitter tastes with a hint of citrus fruit on the finish.

HOW TO ENJOY Locals eat it with boiled potatoes, olive oil, salt, vinegar, and chopped chives. Good with Teroldego Rotaliano Rosso, or Pinot Noir.

ITALY Fassa Valley, Trentino-Alto Adige	
Age 5–10 months	
Weight and Shape 9kg (19lb 13oz), wheel	
Size D. 35–45cm (14–17½in), H. 10–25cm (4–10in)	
Milk Cow	
Classification Semi-soft	
Producer Caseificio Sociale Predazzo e Moena, Predazzo, Trento	

Quartirolo Lombardo PDO

Traditionally this cheese was made using milk from cattle that had grazed the sweet, aromatic hay harvested at the beginning of autumn – the fourth (*quartirola*) and final cut before winter. Today it is produced all year round.

TASTING NOTES Ivory-white outside and inside, with a friable, grainy texture. Both sour and a little sweet, it is very refreshing, having an aroma of yogurt and a suggestion of wild herbs.

HOW TO ENJOY Put in the speciality dish of Quartirolo pie, or serve with celery and parsley. Try with Valbissera di san Colombano, or Malvasia delle Lipari.

ITALY Lombardia	
Age 5–10 days	
Weight and Shape 1.5–3.5kg (3lb 3oz–7lb 11oz), flat square	
Size L. 18–22cm (7–8½in), W. 4–8cm (1½in–3in), H. 4–8cm (1½in–3in)	
Milk Cow	
Classification Semi-soft	
Producer Various	

THE ROSA CAMUNA The famous Rosa Camuna imprint derives from an ancient drawing of a rose found in rock carvings in Capo di Ponte, Lombardy. This version is found on the cheese Rosa Camuna, a petal-shaped version of Casolet. (See p114)

Ragusano PDO

Ragusano is a *pasta filata* cheese and the symbol of the Sicilian dairy industry. The unusual dumbbell shape was created to make it easy to transport by mule from the mountains to the villages, and gave it the name *Quattrofacce* ("four faces"). This is not a compliment, as a man with four faces is considered unreliable.

TASTING NOTES The yellow paste has small eyes and a taste that is sweet-sour-salty, pungent, and astringent, with vegetal and animal hints.

HOW TO ENJOY Marinate in olive oil and garlic, then dress with white vinegar and oregano. Match with Grecanico.

ITALY Sicilia		
Age 3–12 months		
Weight and Shape 10–16kg (22–35lb), dumbbell		
Size L. 43–55cm (17–21½in), W. 15–18cm (6–7in), H. 15–18cm (6–7in)		
Milk Cow		
Classification Hard		
Producer Various		

Raschera PDO

A classic mountain cheese that is quoted in the *Summa lacticiniorum* by Pantaleone da Confienza in 1477, where he describes how strips of lamb's stomach are soaked in water to remove the natural rennet.

TASTING NOTES It has a thin, leathery, brown rind dusted with white and an elastic, pale white, velvety interior with a few irregular eyes or holes. A Mild and sweet-sour taste with marked vegetal notes like grass, hay, and cauliflower.

HOW TO ENJOY Very good for fondues and a great vol-au-vent filling. It tastes delicious alongside a glass of Nebiolo d'Alba, or Sciacchetrà.

ITALY Piemonte		
Age 1–3 months		
Weight and Shape 5–8kg (11lb–17lb 10oz), square with rounded edges		
Size D. 30–40cm (12–16in), 6–9cm (2½–3½in)		
Milk Cow		
Classification Hard		
Producer Various		

Ricotta Affumicata

Ricotta is typically made from whey left over from making large, hard cheeses. Once drained, the tiny white lumps of curd are lightly pressed and dry-salted, then smoked over green conifer-wood fires for about a week, when they are ready to be eaten. Cheese aged for a month can be grated.

TASTING NOTES The relatively high moisture content turns the outside a warm nut-brown. The texture is soft, very fine, and crumbly with a light, fresh, delicate taste and hints of pine.

HOW TO ENJOY At its best with blueberry jam, acacia honey, and black rye bread. Pair it with crisp, light white wines.

ITALY Friuli-Venezia Giulia and Veneto		
Age 15–30 days		
Weight and Shape 0.2–0.5kg (7oz–1lb 2oz), money bag		
Size Various		
Milk Cow		
Classification Flavour added		
Producer Various		

Ricotta Romana PDO

In 2CE, Cato the Elder made reference to this delicate ewe's milk whey cheese, and the recipe was recorded by Columella in 1CE and Galen of Pergamum in 2CE. Today, it has been granted the European Union's Protected Designation of Origin.

TASTING NOTES This refreshing cheese has a smooth, fine, grainy texture, with a taste more sweet than sour and a citrus aroma. The flavour changes depending on the pastures on which the sheep graze.

HOW TO ENJOY Ricotta Romana is a major ingredient in the dessert "Fingers of Apostle". Pair with Frascati Superiore.

ITALY Lazio	
Age 1 day	
Weight and Shape 500g–2kg (1lb 2oz–4½lb), truncated cone	
Size Various	
Milk Ewe	
Classification Fresh	
Producer Various	

Robiola d'Alba

It is believed that this fresh cheese took its name from Robbio Lomellina, an area where it has been made for centuries, or possibly from *rubeola* (red), the colour of the bacteria that develops on the rind.

TASTING NOTES Rubiola d'Alba is smooth, mild, and delicate, with a taste that is more sweet than sour. It has a creamy and buttery aroma, with vegetal and floral hints.

HOW TO ENJOY A traditional Italian dish is an omelette made with Robiola d'Alba. The cheese is best served with a dry red wine such as Alabarda Barbera d'Alba, or Dolcetto d'Alba.

ITALY Piemonte	
Age 6–7 days	
Weight and Shape 300–500g (10oz–1lb 2oz), round	
Size D. 10–12cm (4–5in), H. 3–4cm (1½–2in)	
Milk Cow, ewe, or goat	
Classification Fresh	
Producer Various	

Robiola di Roccaverano PDO

Thought to have been introduced by the Celts, who settled in Liguria around 1000CE, and named after the village of Roccaverano. The Roccaverano goat is now rare, replaced by high-yielding breeds.

TASTING NOTES The rind is white to pale brown with a fine grey mould, while the paste is creamy and smooth, having a balance of sweet-sour-salt with a hint of lanolin from the ewe's milk.

HOW TO ENJOY Eat as it is, or dress with olive oil and aromatic herbs. Match it with generous reds, such as Barbaresco.

ITALY Piemonte	
Age 7–10 days	
Weight and Shape 250–400g (9–14oz), round	
Size D. 10–14cm (4–5½in), H. 4–5cm (1½–2in)	
Milk Goat and cow and/or ewe	
Classification Semi-soft	
Producer Various	

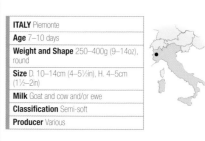

ITALY

134

Salva Cremasco PDO

The name Salva comes from *salvare*, "to save", and refers to the fact that the cheese was made in May from excess milk when the yield from the cows was too great, creating another vital source of income.

TASTING NOTES It has a grey, green or reddish washed rind but is white inside. The texture is friable and grainy, and the taste equally sweet and sour. It has a milk-yogurt aroma with citrus fruits notes.

HOW TO ENJOY Eat in risotto with porcini. Team it with Cabernet Sauvignon La Stoppa or a sweet Malvasia di Candia.

ITALY	Trescore Cremasco, Lombardia
Age	2 months, better after 1 year
Weight and Shape	3–4kg (6½–9lb 9oz), square
Size	L. 17–19cm (6½–7½in), W. 17–19cm (6½–7½in), H. 9–15cm (3½–6in)
Milk	Cow
Classification	Semi-soft
Producer	Caseificio San Carlo, Coccaglio, Brescia Az. Agr. Eredi Carioni

Scamorza

Also called *Mozzarella Passita* ("withered mozzarella") Scamorza is a *pasta filata* that is made all year round in southern Italy. It is shaped by hand into two balls, one slightly smaller than the other. Scamorza Affumicata is a version smoked over wood or straw.

TASTING NOTES It is white to straw yellow outside, and the paste has an elastic texture, sweet taste, and milky aroma. Scamorza Affumicata is brown on the outside, brown-yellow inside and the smoky aroma enhances the sweet taste.

HOW TO ENJOY Eat fresh or grill it. Team with Pomino Rosso Frescobaldi, or Spumante Classico Italiano.

ITALY	Campania
Age	2–10 days
Weight and Shape	200–500g (7oz–1lb 2oz), balls or large pears
Size	Various
Milk	Cow
Classification	Semi-soft
Producer	Various

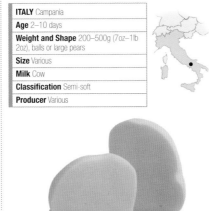

Sola (Sora or Soera)

Known as the "witch's cheese", as it is said to have been first made by a "witch cheesemaker". However, the name means "shoe" in local dialect, due to its flattened shape, brown shape and the imprint of the cloth in which it is pressed, making it resemble the sole of a shoe.

TASTING NOTES Soft, dense, and smooth with some eyes, it has a bold, complex taste of the milk used to make it, with floral, fruity, or citrusy notes. It is especially good in summer.

HOW TO ENJOY Have it in slices of speck or use it in fondues and sauces. Pair with any dry, white, local Cortese wine.

ITALY	Piemonte
Age	1–3 months
Weight and Shape	1.8–2kg (4–4½lb), flat square
Size	D. 15–20cm (6–8in), W. 15–20cm (6–8in), H. 4–5cm (1½–2in)
Milk	Ewe, cow, or goat
Classification	Semi-soft
Producer	Various

Taleggio PDO

Mention of Taleggio dates back to the 10th and 11th centuries, when there is evidence of it being traded. However, the name has only been used since the 20th century and refers to the Val Taleggio in the province of Bergamo where it is made – an area also famous for its great cheeses such as Grana Padano (see p120) and Gorgonzola (see pp108–109).

The dramatic landscape *of the Alpine valley of Val Taleggio in Italy's northern Bergamo province, Lombardia.*

Taleggio was created to preserve the local milk, and the natural caves of Valsassina, in Lecco, Lombardia, provide the perfect ripening room. Their deep crevices and fissures provide natural air-conditioning and soft breezes to spread the moulds that grow in the rind. With increasing awareness and popularity, Taleggio is now made from both pasteurized and raw milk in many small dairies, as well as larger factories where the recipe has been adapted to modern technology while still remaining true to the traditional methods, essential to retain its unique character.

The best, however, are undoubtedly those made with raw milk from the summer Alpine pastures and matured in the caves.

The surface of every cheese is imprinted with the distinctive four-leafed brand of the Consorzio Tutela Taleggio. The imprint is visible even if the cheese is sold in portions. It is a guarantee of quality and origin, and even the paper that wraps the cheese when it is retailed must be of a certain type and carry the Taleggio brand.

TASTING NOTES The moulds and yeasts of the rind speed up the breakdown of the curd, ripening it from the outside towards the centre. It exudes a gentle but insistent herbaceous fragrance of fermenting fruit, hay, and mountain flowers like rich Cream of Broccoli soup. It is not necessary to remove the crust before eating or cooking with it, but it is a little gritty so it is best to gently scrape it.

Sadly, Taleggio is often sold and eaten under-ripe, or before it comes to room temperature, when it is dull, rubbery, and grainy and the true character has either been killed off with excessive refrigeration or remains hidden.

HOW TO ENJOY An excellent table cheese, it can be eaten as is or used in various recipes because it melts so readily. Typically served at the end of the meal with apples, pears, or figs, or in pastas, risottos, soups, omelettes, and salads as well as some types of pizza and crêpes. Best with a local wine from Franciacorta, like Terre di Franciacorta DOC, a sturdy red from Cabernet, Barbera, and Nebbiolo grapes, or the outstanding bottle-fermented sparkling wines that qualify as Franciacorta DOCG.

A CLOSER LOOK

Taleggio is aged by the producer or an *affineur* in the local caves or specially controlled rooms where the temperature, humidity, and native microflora play a vital role.

The enzymes produced from the microflora on the crust break down the curd by working from the outside, a process known as "mould-ripening".

The interior is soft, almost liquid, under the rind.

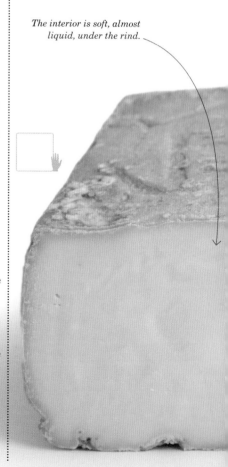

ITALY Lombardia, Piemonte, and Veneto	
Age 25–40 days	
Weight and Shape 1.7–2kg (3½–4½lb), square	
Size D. 40cm (16in) and 70cm (28in), H. 10cm (4in)	
Milk Cow	
Classification Semi-soft	
Producer Various	

ITALY

136

DRAINING The cheeses are drained on special tables called *spersori*, and then placed in moulds with rounded edges. The consortium brand, along with the maker's number, is pressed into the soft cheese.

SALTING Each cheese is rubbed in dry salt or soaked in brine for 8–12 hours. The cheeses are then put in wooden boxes each holding eight cheeses.

THE IMPRINT The four-leaf brand from the Consorzio becomes more distinct as the cheese ages and the brand is outlined by the fine grey and white moulds that dust the rind.

The orange-pink colour of the rind becomes more pronounced with age.

Half square

SOLA The streaks and splashes of colour resemble a piece of modern Italian art, but instead are the work of the wild yeasts, bacteria, and moulds that proliferate in the raw milk, mountain pastures, and special rooms where Sora is ripened. (See p135)

Spressa delle Giudicarie PDO

An ancient, mountain cheese, which was traditionally made with milk that was skimmed several times, as the farmers could sell butter for a higher price than cheese. Today it is made with partially skimmed milk.

TASTING NOTES It has a straw-yellow or brown rind and a crunchy texture when low in fat, being yellower, sweeter, and more buttery when higher in fat. The strong aroma comes from the pastures on which the cows graze.

HOW TO ENJOY Enjoy this on its own, or with barley soup. Team it with fruity red wines.

ITALY Trentino-Alto Adige	
Age 4–12 months	
Weight and Shape 8–10kg (17lb 10oz–22lb), wheel	
Size D. 30–35cm (12–14in), H. 10–11cm (4–4½in)	
Milk Cow	
Classification Hard	
Producer Various	

Strachìtunt PDO

Made using the milk from Bruna Alpina cows since the late 1800s, and combining two batches of curd. Strachìtunt has recently been revived by a small consortium of producers who are now making around 50 cheeses a week.

TASTING NOTES Unlike most Italian blues, it has a dense, compact texture, very fine, erratic blueing and a dry, wrinkled crusty rind. The taste is sweet with a hint of spiced mushrooms.

HOW TO ENJOY For an authentic flavour, try this with gnocchi and polenta. Match it with an austere red, such as the velvety Valtellina Superiore, or a sweet, late-harvest white wine.

ITALY Lombardia	
Age 3–5 months	
Weight and Shape 4–5kg (9–11lb), wheel	
Size D. 24–28cm (9½–11in), H. 15–18cm (6–7in)	
Milk Cow	
Classification Blue	
Producer Arrigoni Valtaleggio	

Toma Piemontese PDO

Made since the Roman Empire, Toma could be the Italian version of the French cheese Tomme, which is made in the nearby Savoy region. It is a gourmet, versatile cheese.

TASTING NOTES Toma Piemontese has a hundred tastes, depending on its weight, ripening time, and art of the cheesemaking. It is sweet and melts easily, with vegetal and woody notes.

HOW TO ENJOY Use grated in Bruss or Pastasciutta, or melted in many recipes. Team it with a dry Magnus Langhe Chardonnay, or a light and dry sparkling red Barbera del Monferrato.

ITALY Piemonte	
Age 1–4 months	
Weight and Shape 2–8kg (4½–17lb 10oz), wheel	
Size D. 15–35cm (6–14in), H. 6–12cm (2½–5in)	
Milk Cow	
Classification Semi-soft	
Producer Various	

Toma, Tome or Tomino

There are over 30 different Tome and Tomino; small cheeses, each with their own unique character. One of the best known is Tomino di Melle, made with full-fat milk and invented in 1889 by a cheesemaker and her nephew.

TASTING NOTES This supple, springy cheese is mild with a sweet acidity. It has a creamy taste and sometimes vegetal, nutty, or woody hints.

HOW TO ENJOY Typically used to make Bagnet – a parsley, garlic, minced anchovies, and tomato sauce. It is a perfect match for lively reds – Rocca Giovino Dolcetto d'Alba, or the striking Diano d'Alba Superiore.

ITALY Arona, Piemonte		
Age 1–3 days, sometimes 10 days		
Weight and Shape 50–500g (1¾–1lb 2oz), round or cylinder		
Size Various		
Milk Cow, or mixed		
Classification Soft white		
Producer Luigi Guffanti 1876, Arona, Novara		

Trentingrana PDO

In 1926, a dairyman from Trentino married a dairywomen from Mirandola, home of Parmigiano Reggiano, who brought to the Non Valley the art of making *grana* cheese. They created Trentingrana; today the production and sales of this cheese are controlled by the Trentingrana Cheese Consortium.

TASTING NOTES Under a thick yellow rind is a hard, brittle interior with a sweet, fruity taste and hints of cooked butter and spiced meat broth.

HOW TO ENJOY Shave into salads and grate over pasta or vegetables. Team it with a sparkling white Ferrari Riserva or a sweet Vin Santo di Nosiola.

ITALY Emilia-Romagna		
Age 1–2 years		
Weight and Shape 35kg (77lb), drum		
Size D. 35–38cm (14–15in), H. 20–22cm (8–8½in)		
Milk Cow		
Classification Hard		
Producer Various		

Vezzena

During the Austro–Hungarian Empire, this was the preferred cheese of the House of Habsburg, and Franz Joseph I wanted it on his table at all times. Even today, the milk used comes from cows grazing at 1,000–1,500m (3,300–4,900 ft) above sea level and is much sought after.

TASTING NOTES A brown-yellow rind protects the straw-yellow, hard inside, with its small holes. Sweet and pleasant-tasting, it has a strong aroma, mainly of green and fermented grass and toasted seeds.

HOW TO ENJOY Serve aged Vezzena on its own or with fruit. Try it with a white Nosiola Spagnolli or Refrontolo Passito.

ITALY Lavarone, Trentino-Alto Adige		
Age 4–12 months		
Weight and Shape 8–12kg (17lb 10oz–26½lb), round		
Size D. 30–40cm (12–16in), H. 9–12cm (3½–5in)		
Milk Cow		
Classification Hard		
Producer Caseificio degli Altipiani del Vezzena di Lavarone		

More Cheeses of Italy

The following cheeses are rare – either because they are only available seasonally or because they are produced in very remote areas. As a result, it has proved impossible to photograph them, but as they are important and interesting examples of Italian cheese, we are including them. So, read, savour, and seek out.

Agrì di Valtorta

Though rarely found outside the small valley where it has been made for centuries, it now comes under the protection of the Slow Food Presidium. Soured whey is used to curdle the milk, then the curds are put into small ricotta moulds and left to stand before being salted by hand.

TASTING NOTES Soft in texture, with a milky aroma. It is creamy with a slightly sour, savoury taste.

HOW TO ENJOY Eat on its own with vegetables or spread on fresh bread. Good with aromatic Bianco Valcalepio.

ITALY Valtorta, Lombardia	
Age From 3 days	
Weight and Shape 50–100g (1¾–3½oz), squat cone	
Size D. 3–4cm (1½–2in), H. 8–10cm (3–4in)	
Milk Cow, goat, raw	
Classification Fresh	
Producer Latteria Sociale, Monaci Sebastiano	

Bauernkäse or Lagundo

This cheese ranges from semi-soft to firm in consistency, depending on the ripening time. Made from cow's milk, it develops a marked brown rind from being washed. Lagundo is the village in which it first originated, but is known as *Bauernkäse*, which is German for farmhouse cheese.

TASTING NOTES With irregular eyes thoughout the white or straw-coloured paste, it is flavoured with a sweet, buttery aroma and a tangy taste.

HOW TO ENJOY Eat with rye bread or melt onto potatoes. Try with Pinot Bianco (Weissburgunder) or Moscato Giallo (Goldenmuskateller).

ITALY Trentino-Alto Adige	
Age 2 months, better after 6 months	
Weight and Shape 8kg (17lb 10oz), brick	
Size Various	
Milk Cow	
Classification Semi-soft and hard	
Producer Various	

Bela Badia

This soft cheese with a smooth, dry crust is a recent addition to the ranks of Italian cheeses. It takes its name from the Badia valley in which it was created, and is appreciated for its high lactic bacteria content.

TASTING NOTES The light, straw-coloured paste of Bela Badia becomes intense with time and has a fresh, creamy, and sweet taste. As the cheese is chewed, its flavour is enhanced by generous milky and grass hints.

HOW TO ENJOY Eat this cheese grilled and accompany it with a glass of Riesling Renano or sparkling Brut Hausmannhof Riserva.

ITALY Trentino-Alto Adige	
Age 2 months	
Weight and Shape 2 kg (4½lb), flat wheel	
Size D. 7cm (3in), H. 8–10cm (3–4in)	
Milk Cow	
Classification Fresh or semi-soft	
Producer Various	

Bernardo

A classic, fresh, summer cheese made only with milk from cows grazing on high Alpine pastures. It is virtually rindless and is reddish-yellow in colour, due to a little saffron powder being added to the curds during production. It can be matured, during which time it will develop a brownish-yellow rind and an intense aromatic flavour.

TASTING NOTES The added saffron gives a floral aroma and a sweet, slightly bitter taste to this delicate cheese.

HOW TO ENJOY Eaten fresh with crusty bread, it pairs well with a red or a white Valcalepio wine.

ITALY Lombardia	
Age 10–15 days	
Weight and Shape 0.5–1kg (1lb 2oz–2¼oz), flat wheel	
Size D. 15cm (6in), H. 5cm (2in)	
Milk Cow	
Classification Fresh	
Producer Various	

Cacioricotta

Affectionately known in southern Italy as the "hockey puck" for its flat and round shape, this cheese comes from a strong tradition of Italian farmhouse types. Its name reflects the blended nature of this cheese; it is a mixture of ricotta and fresh cheese, made from a combination of ewe's and goat's milk.

TASTING NOTES It has a mild aroma of sweet milk when fresh, and is citrusy, tangy, and pungent when aged.

HOW TO ENJOY Used fresh in salads, or grated over pasta when aged. Pair with Messapia of Leone de Castris, or Marsala Vergine di Terre Arse.

ITALY Puglia and Basilicata	
Age From 2–3 weeks, until 2–3 months	
Weight and Shape 0.4–1kg (14oz–2lb ¼oz), cylinder or truncated cone	
Size D. 13–24cm (5½–9½in), H. 4–7cm (1½–3in)	
Milk Goat and ewe	
Classification Fresh, hard when ripened	
Producer Various	

Canestrato di Vacca and di Pecora

Named after the rush basket (*canestro*) in which it is made, this cheese is coagulated or curdled with kid rennet. The curd is still manipulated by hand in the traditional way that dates back to the days of the Roman Empire.

TASTING NOTES Cow's milk Canestrato is sweet, becoming salty and nutty when mature, while the Pecora (ewe's milk) is more aromatic and has a nutty aroma at around six months.

HOW TO ENJOY Use in salads, grated over pasta, in béchamel sauce or stuffed vegetables. It goes well with Greco di Tufo, or light and fruity red wines.

ITALY Puglia and Sicilia	
Age 2–10 months	
Weight and Shape 1.5–8kg (3lb 3oz–17lb 10oz), cylinder	
Size D. 20–35cm (8–14in), H. 6–10cm (2½–4in)	
Milk Cow	
Classification Hard	
Producer Various	

Pecorino di Filiano PDO

An ancient cheese that is made in the Basilicata region using milk from the native sheep, *gentile di puglia*. The cheeses are ripened in local caves.

TASTING NOTES It has a golden-yellow or brown-yellow rind imprinted with the pattern of the basket moulds. The firm, crunchy paste is light yellow with very small eyes. Sweet and buttery when young, it becomes pungent, salty, and strongly aromatic when mature.

HOW TO ENJOY Use in the dish *Pecorino maritato*, or grated over boiled broad beans. Pair with local red wines.

ITALY Basilicata	
Age 6 months or more	
Weight and Shape 2.5–5kg (5½–11lb), drum	
Size D. 15–25cm (6–10in), H. 8–18cm (3–7in)	
Milk Ewe	
Classification Hard	
Producer Various	

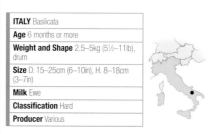

Pecorino di Laticauda

This hard cheese is named after the Laticauda breed of sheep that was introduced from Africa in the 18th century, then crossed with the local Pagliarola race.

TASTING NOTES The thin, waxy rind is yellow-orange over an ivory white, grainy, and friable paste. With a sweet and salty taste, it has an aroma of cut grass, wild flowers, and citrus fruit.

HOW TO ENJOY Serve fresh as a table cheese, or use to stuff and fill artichokes and in delicious local cheese pies. Try with Vino Bianco Avignonesi and Vino Nobile di Montepulciano.

ITALY Faicchio, Campania	
Age 3–6 months	
Weight and Shape 2kg (4½lb), drum	
Size D. 20cm (8in), H. 12cm (5in)	
Milk Ewe	
Classification Hard	
Producer Azienda Torre Vecchia	

Pusteria

Its Italian name is Pusteria, but as it is produced in a bi-lingual area, it also has German names of *Pustertaler*, *Bergkäse*, or *Hocpustertaler*. It is produced in the Puster Valley mainly from Pustertaler Sprinzen cattle. Until 1800 it was made only in summer.

TASTING NOTES Under the yellow-orange rind is a white paste with irregular eyes and an elastic texture. The taste is sweet, becoming bitter and pungent. It has mild vegetal and floral aromas.

HOW TO ENJOY It is used in Spätzle con Pustertalerspecial noodles, grilled with butter. Try with Müller-Thurgau.

ITALY Bolzano, Trentino-Alto Adige	
Age 60–70 days	
Weight and Shape 9kg (20lb), wheel	
Size D. 35cm (14in), H. 9cm (3½in)	
Milk Cow	
Classification Semi-soft	
Producer Milkon Alto Adige, Bolzano	

Ricotta di Bufala Campana PDO

In some Italian regions, buffaloes are used to produce milk instead of cows, as they are better adapted to the humid climate and poor grazing. This cheese uses whey left over from making Mozzarella di Bufala Campana.

TASTING NOTES Refreshing with a sweet, slightly acidic flavour and a delicate grainy texture.

HOW TO ENJOY Use in many Italian recipes. Try it with white Falanghina Spumante, or red Palummo Passito.

ITALY Lazio	
Age 1–2 days	
Weight and Shape 500g–2.5kg (1lb 2oz–5½lb), basket mould	
Size Various	
Milk Buffalo	
Classification Fresh	
Producer Various	

Silter

This Celtic-named cheese dates back to the 17th century. Silter comes in two types: those made in the high mountain pastures, and those made in the valley.

TASTING NOTES Under a brownish-yellow rind is a straw-yellow paste that has a friable, crumbly texture when aged. The mountain cheese has more vegetal and floral aromas, while the valley cheese has hints of hay and dry fruits.

HOW TO ENJOY It is a delicious ingredient in *Cannelloni alla zucca* (pasta rolls filled with pumpkin and Silter). Pair it with sparkling white Franciacorta Millesimato or Sagrantino Passito.

ITALY High Camonica and Sebino Valley, Lombardia	
Age 4–12 months	
Weight and Shape 10–20kg (22–44lb), wheel	
Size D. 35–40cm (14–15½in), H. 10–15cm (4–6in)	
Milk Cow	
Classification Hard	
Producer Romelli Giacomo, Pedena-Breno	

Squacquarone di Romagna PDO

Gaius Petronius Arbiter, the author of *Satyricon,* called this cheese *Caseum mollem.* In the local dialect the name means "without consistency", because it is mousse-like and easily melts in the mouth.

TASTING NOTES A shining white cheese, it has a very soft, high-moisture texture, a creamy, buttery aroma, and a balance of sweet and sour with citrus hints.

HOW TO ENJOY Traditionally it is used to fill pasta, along with beef marrow, but try it simply in a fresh salad. Pair it with a dry white Albana di Romagna, or a red such as Sangiovese Superiore.

ITALY Bologna, Emilia-Romagna	
Age 1–4 days	
Weight and Shape 1–3kg (2¼–6½lb)	
Size Various	
Milk Cow	
Classification Fresh	
Producer Caseificio Pascoli, Savignano sul Rubiconde (FC) Granarolo, Bologna	

Stelvio or Stilfser PDO

This washed-rind cheese takes its name from the highest Alps pass, and has been traded in the Tirol since Medieval times. As it is made in a bi-lingual area, Stelvio is also known as Stilfser.

TASTING NOTES It has a yellow-orange to orange-brown rind and straw-yellow paste with irregular holes, and a compact, supple, texture. Its sweet-sour flavour is sometimes pleasantly bitter, with hints of hay and boiled vegetables.

HOW TO ENJOY Often melted on polenta or used in barley or lentil soups. Pair with Merlot Kretzer, or Lagrein Dunkel.

ITALY Stelvio National Park, Lombardia	
Age 2–4 months	
Weight and Shape 8–10kg (17lb 10oz–22lb), cylindrical	
Size D. 36–38cm (14½–15in), H. 8–10cm (3–4in)	
Milk Cow	
Classification Semi-soft	
Producer Milkon Alto Adige, Bolzano	

Stracciata

This artisan cheese is produced by cutting or tearing the curd, which is then stretched into ribbons that are folded and shaped. The result is a sweet, fresh, fatty paste which is sold as it is or used to fill Burrata cheese.

TASTING NOTES A shining, white, creamy cheese, Stracciata is mild and sweet with fresh lactic notes. It easily melts in the mouth, leaving a taste like warm melted butter.

HOW TO ENJOY Serve this refreshing summer cheese as a main dish with fresh salad and tomatoes, and a glass of Locorotondo Spumante, or Aleatico di Puglia Liquoroso.

ITALY Puglia	
Age 1–2 days	
Weight and Shape 200–500g (7oz–1lb 2oz), long cylinder, or balls	
Size Various	
Milk Cow	
Classification Fresh	
Producer Various	

Valle D'Aosta Fromadzo PDO

Well known in the 15th century, this hard cheese is made using morning and evening milk, then left to stand before the cream is skimmed off. Some cheeses contain up to 10 per cent goat's milk.

TASTING NOTES Often flavoured with juniper, cumin, or wild fennel, it is supple with tiny holes and has a slightly sweet taste that becomes stronger and more aromatic when aged.

HOW TO ENJOY Grate onto toast or into soups, such as spinach or cabbage. Pair it with a dry red wine such as Enfer d'Arvier, or Vallée d'Aosta Donnas.

ITALY Valle D'Aosta	
Age 2–10 months	
Weight and Shape 1–7kg (2¼–15½in), wheel	
Size D. 15–30cm (6–12in), H. 5–20cm (2–8in)	
Milk Cow	
Classification Hard	
Producer Various	

Valtellina Casera PDO

This is made in Valtellina, an isolated valley in the Alps, using milk from the Bruna Alpina cows, known for their excellent, sweet-flavoured milk.

TASTING NOTES The thin, yellow rind covers a dense but creamy interior with small, irregular eyes. Its sweet-and-sour flavour becomes salty when aged. The aromatic flavour has honey and floral notes, sometimes with a bitter finish.

HOW TO ENJOY It is the basic ingredient of Pizzoccheri, and is used to fill Sciatt, stuffed buckwheat pancakes. Best teamed with a red Sassella Negri.

ITALY Lombardia	
Age 2–4 months	
Weight and Shape 7–12kg (15lb 7oz–26½lb), wheel	
Size D. 30–45cm (12–17½in), H. 8–10cm (3–4in)	
Milk Cow	
Classification Hard	
Producer Various	

Vastedda della Valle del Belice PDO

Unlike other Italian *pasta filata* cheeses, this is made with ewe's milk, in particular from the local Belice breed. Vastedda derives from *vasta,* the base of the cheese-shaping dish.

TASTING NOTES The fine white rind covers a shiny, straw-yellow, very moist, soft paste. The flavour is sour and sweet and becomes aromatic after a few days, with hints of herbs and flowers.

HOW TO ENJOY Eat as an appetizer with a glass of Regaleali Tasca d'Almerita.

ITALY Sicilia	
Age 2–3 days	
Weight and Shape 500–700g (1lb 2oz–1lb 7oz), cylindrical	
Size D. 15–17cm (6–6½in), H. 3–4cm (1–1½in)	
Milk Ewe	
Classification Fresh	
Producer Various	

BAY OF BISCAY

La Peral

ASTURIAS
Cebreiro ★
Afuega'l Pitu ★,
Ahumado de Pría,
Cabrales ★,
Casín ★,
Gamonedo ★,
Taramundi

CANTABRIA
Cantabria ★
Liébana ★,
Picón Bejes Tresviso ★

Pasiego de
las Garmillas

PAÍS
VASCO

GALICIA
Arúza-Ulloa ★,
San Simón da Costa ★,
Tetilla ★

Valdeón ★

NAVARRA
Idiazábal ★,
Roncal ★

Castellano,
Ibérico,
Pata de Mulo,
Zamorano ★

LA RIOJA

Camerano ★

CASTILLA-LEÓN

VIANA DO
CASTELO

VILA
REAL

Beato de Tábara

Cañarejal

ARAGÓN
Tronchón

BRAGA

Cabra Transmontano ★

BRAGANÇA

PORTO

Cabra Transmontano ★

Zamorano ★

AVEIRO

Serra da Estrela ★

VISEU

GUARDA

PORTUGAL

Monte Enebro

SPAIN

MADRID

COIMBRA

LEIRIA

CASTELO
BRANCO
Castelo Branco ★

Los Montes de Toledo

SANTARÉM

CASTILLA-LA MANCHA
Ibérico,
Manchego ★

PORTALEGRE
Nisa ★

LISBOA

EXTREMADURA
Ibores ★,
Tortas Extremeñas

ÉVORA
Évora ★

SETÚBAL
Azeitão ★

Cabra Rufino

← Azores

BEJA
Serpa ★

Murcia al Vino ★

Payoyo

MURCIA

ANDALUCÍA

FARO

GOLFO DE
CÁDIZ

ATLANTIC OCEAN

COSTA DEL SOL

↓ Madeira   ↓ Islas Canarias   COSTA DE LA LUZ

GIBRALTAR

MEDITERRANEAN SEA

N

SPAIN AND PORTUGAL

SPAIN During the 9th century, when many rural folk and their livestock took refuge with the monasteries, monks became the principal producers of cheese. When livestock populations grew, the monasteries needed more pastures, which saw the beginning of transhumance, or the migration of shepherds. This movement of animals and shepherds helped spread the sc ience of cheesemaking across the country. Many of the cheese shapes or patterns originated from whatever local materials were available: ceramic bowls of the Levante, sycamore leaves, carved wood, and even grass belts. During the last 40 years, transhumance almost disappeared, but in the late 1900s, cheese experienced a well-deserved resurgence, although artisan chees emaking was almost entirely replaced by large cooperatives.

PORTUGAL With the Atlantic Ocean to the west and high mountains to the east, Portugal received protection from the invasion of Goths, Vandals, and Moors. That protection and the harsh climate led to cheese playing a very minor role in Portuguese cuisine. Those that were made, however, were exceptional, and most used (and still do) the thistle or cardoons to curdle the rich milk of the hardy sheep.

With the boom of the economy and the tourist industry since the 1960s, Portugal has seen a revival of artisan cheeses and cheesemaking, as well as the introduction of bigger manufacturing plants. It can now boast around 15 cheeses that qualify for PDO and PGI status.

Map

100 miles

100 km

ANDORRA

Tou del Til•Iers

Benasque   Benabarre

Bauma Carrat

L'Alt Urgell y La Cerdanya ★

CATALUÑA

Garrotxa, Tupí

MEDITERRANEAN SEA

Mahón ★

Peña Blanca de Corrales

ILLES BALEARS

GOLFO DE VALENCIA

PAÍS VALENCIANO

Key

Key	
★	AOC, DOC, DOP, PGI, or PDO cheeses
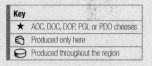	Produced only here
	Produced throughout the region

ISLAS CANARIAS

LANZAROTE

Palmero ★   TENERIFE

LA PALMA

Majorero ★

GOMERA   Flor de Guía   FUERTEVENTURA

Herreño

HIERRO   GRAN CANARIA

ATLANTIC OCEAN

MOROCCO

MADEIRA

PORTO SANTO

São Jorge ★

MADEIRA

DESERTA GRANDE

ATLANTIC OCEAN

BUGIO

AZORES

CORVO

FLORES   GRACIOSA

Ilha Graciosa

TERCEIRA

FAIAL   SÃO JORGE

SÃO MIGUE

ATLANTIC OCEAN

SANTA MARIA

Afuega'l Pitu DOP

A small, wrinkled cheese with a sticky exterior shaped into a cone or like a pumpkin, Afuega'l Pitu is moulded by hand in a cloth. The most striking version has its curd seasoned by hot pimentón (Spanish smoked paprika) and is matured for two months.

TASTING NOTES Afuega'l Pitu, named "stick in the throat" after its tart, creamy texture, is made from acidified white curd. The dusty red pimentón variety has a seriously fiery finish.

HOW TO ENJOY Fresh white Afuega'l Pitu has a thick, yogurty consistency and is excellent with jam or honey; the hot variety needs a dry sherry.

SPAIN Asturias	
Age Fresh 7 days; with pimentón 2 months	
Weight and Shape 200–600g (7oz–1lb 5oz), cone or pumpkin	
Size D. 8–14cm (3–5½in), H. 8–12cm (3–5in)	
Milk Cow	
Classification Flavour-added	
Producer Various	

Ahumado de Pría

This lightly smoked, creamy northern cheese with an orange rind was originally made in smoky shepherd's huts in high summer pasturelands that are also famous for their sweet butter.

TASTING NOTES It is matured for two months before being gently smoked over beech and oak, allowing the fragrance of added ewe cream to complement the heady aromas of cow's milk produced on mountain pastures.

HOW TO ENJOY Ideal with an apéritif, it is delicious with the fruity white wines of Galicia, or try it dipped in cinnamon, cumin, and breadcrumbs, then fried and served with muscatel grape jelly.

SPAIN Asturias	
Age 2–6 months	
Weight and Shape 600g (1lb 5oz), cylinder	
Size D. 12cm (5in), H. 10cm (4in)	
Milk Cow with ewe's cream	
Classification Flavour-added	
Producer Various	

L'Alt Urgell y La Cerdanya DOP

This tender and approachable cheese hails from the high Catalan Pyrenees, and is the initiative of a cooperative dairy that is famous for its Cadí butter. Washed in brine, the cheese develops a thin leathery orange-red rind and small holes in the pale interior.

TASTING NOTES The aroma is reminiscent of grassy meadows, the paste is springy, and the initial impression its mild and buttery, but with unexpected depth.

HOW TO ENJOY Melts well in gratins and sauces for vegetable and fish dishes, and pairs extremely well with a chilled dry cava or fruity or sweet white wines.

SPAIN La Seu d'Urgell, Cataluña	
Age 6–12 weeks	
Weight and Shape 2–2½kg (4½–5½ lb), round	
Size D. 19.5cm–20cm (7½–8in)	
Milk Cow	
Classification Semi-soft	
Producer La Cooperativa del Cadi	

Arzúa-Ulloa DOP

This elegant round cheese with a waxy clean yellow-coloured rind and soft almost squishy, smooth interior, remains the most popular within Galicia. Various artisan producers near the river Ulla make it, hence its name.

TASTING NOTES Although the paste is unexpectedly mild, more like butter than cheese, it is deeply aromatic, and its sweet, milky flavours develop with quiet confidence on the palate.

HOW TO ENJOY Relish its gentle flavours simply on breadsticks, or spread the cheese like butter onto wholemeal, sourdough, or pumpernickel bread. Pairs well with a white Ribeiro wine.

SPAIN Galicia		
Age 15–30 days		
Weight and Shape 500g–3.5kg (1lb 2oz–7lb 11oz), round		
Size D. 10–26cm (4–10in), H. 5–12cm (2–5in)		
Milk Cow		
Classification Semi-soft		
Producer Various		

Bauma Carrat

Toni Chueca, with Rose Heras, began making cheese using milk from their own herds in 1980, but they now focus on making the cheeses and acquiring excellent milk from a single farmer.

TASTING NOTES Fragile and striking, the deep black ash rind protects the bright white, smooth and moist interior. The paste is fresh yet luxuriously creamy, with a distinct but not strong goaty taste.

HOW TO ENJOY Ripe tomatoes alone are excellent partners to Carrat, and its perfect Catalan partner would be *escalivada* (grilled aubergines, green peppers, and Aragón olives) with a fruity white wine such as Alella.

SPAIN Borreda, Cataluña		
Age 15–21 days		
Weight and Shape 400g (14oz), square		
Size L. 10cm (4in), W. 10cm (4in), H. 3cm (1in)		
Milk Goat		
Classification Aged fresh		
Producer Formatge Bauma SL		

Beato de Tábara

Santiago Lucas Leon and his sons shepherd their own flock in the Sierra de la Culebra and make this artisan cheese, inspired by the illustrated manuscripts of the monastery at San Martín de Tábara.

TASTING NOTES Cool on the palate, its stone-grey rind and aroma of cellars take you to dark underground spaces, while the bright white paste brings you back to the meadows. This is an elegant and exceptional cheese.

HOW TO ENJOY To be true to the monastic purity of the cheese's inspiration, it is best appreciated on its own or after dinner with a refreshing Riesling.

SPAIN San Martin de Tábara, Castilla-León		
Age 60–100 days		
Weight and Shape 500g–1kg (1lb 2oz–2¼lb), cylinder		
Size D. 10–15cm (4–6in), H. 6–7cm (2½–3in)		
Milk Goat		
Classification Hard		
Producer Santiago Leon Lucas		

Benabarre

Blessed with an absolutely stunning setting, this dairy sits in the foothills of the Pyrenees facing the valleys of Aran, where herds of Granadina goats pasture. The cheese is shaped like a pumpkin and possesses the size and weight of a small rock.

TASTING NOTES Matured in cellars ventilated by clean mountain air, the natural moulds on the rind develop an aroma of fresh mushrooms. The paste is compact, revealing flavours of hazelnuts, acorns, and wild herbs.

HOW TO ENJOY Serve simply, accompanied by a good red Somontano wine and a bowl of dark Aragón olives.

SPAIN Benabarre, Aragón	
Age 14–60 days	
Weight and Shape 500g (1lb 2oz) or 3kg (6½lb). square	
Size L. 11–23cm (4½–9in), W. 11–23cm (4½–9in), H. 5–8cm (2–3in)	
Milk Goat	
Classification Semi-soft	
Producer Quesos Benabarre	

Benasque

Produced on a family-run farm in the stunning Benasque valley in the heart of the Pyrenees, also known as the *Valle Escondido,* or hidden valley. The cattle graze on natural mountain pastures, supplemented with a diet of dry food, ensuring that milk quality remains consistent year-round.

TASTING NOTES Hand-moulded and slowly matured in underground cellars, it is moist yet crumbly, with a hint of salt and a full-bodied strong, tangy finish.

HOW TO ENJOY This well-rounded cheese is best served, simply with fresh crusty white bread and a glass of the local Somontano wine.

SPAIN Huesca, Aragón	
Age 3–6 months	
Weight and Shape 1kg (2¼lb), round	
Size D. 12cm (5in), H. 5–7cm (2–3in)	
Milk Cow	
Classification Hard	
Producer Quesería el Benasques	

Cabrales DOP

This notorious strictly artisan blue cheese is matured in the mould-rich caves of the isolated Picos de Europa mountains, where mixed herds pasture. Its original maple-leaf covering has now been replaced by green foil.

TASTING NOTES The thin soft grey rind envelops a creamy paste that is heavily streaked with blue veins and punctuated with irregular cavities. Although the cheese's aroma is a touch fetid, a keen creaminess comes through.

HOW TO ENJOY This very strong cheese is best sampled at the end of a meal with a dry Asturian cider. Even a young Cabrales will overwhelm most pairings.

SPAIN Asturias	
Age 3 months minimum	
Weight and Shape 600g–4kg (1lb 5oz–8lb 13oz), drum	
Size D. 15–22cm (6–8½in), H. 7–10cm (3–4in)	
Milk Cow, ewe, and goat	
Classification Blue	
Producer Various	

Cabra Rufino

For 40 years the Rufino family has been ageing these five-day-old *tortas*. Each piece is methodically turned, washed, and checked daily. The best are made in autumn, when the goats enjoy the local acorns, making the cheese particularly creamy. Its full name is Queso de Cabra Rufino.

TASTING NOTES Seasonality and ageing affect the cheese, which varies from dense and compact with a crumbly yet moist paste and a strong, genuine spicy bite to unctuous in the autumn.

HOW TO ENJOY Ideally, enjoy while in the local Bar Rufino, with country-style bread and a strong wine or beer.

SPAIN Oliva de la Frontera, Extremadura	
Age 60–120 days	
Weight and Shape 600g (1lb 5oz), round	
Size Various	
Milk Goat	
Classification Semi-soft	
Producer Quesos Artesanos Rufino	

Camerano DOP

Also known as La Aulaga Camerano, this is the brainchild of Monica Figuerola. Shaped in traditional wicker moulds and aged for up to two months, this is a resolutely artisan cheese made only in spring and summer.

TASTING NOTES The natural mould has a powerful aroma of mushrooms. The texture of the cheese itself is close and dissolves on the palate into subtle flavours of goat and mountain herbs.

HOW TO ENJOY Eat as a pudding with honey, grapes, or quince when young, or serve simply with toasted pistachios, country bread, and a young Rioja wine.

SPAIN Munilla, La Rioja	
Age 7 days fresh; 60 days cured	
Weight and Shape 500g–1kg (1lb 2oz–2¼lb), drum	
Size D. 11.5–15cm (4½–6in), H. 5.5–10cm (2–4in)	
Milk Goat	
Classification Semi-soft	
Producer Quesería la Aulaga	

Cañarejal

This artisan torta, a contemporary northern version of the more famous Torta La Serena, was an initiative of the local ewe-farming Santos family. It is produced using milk from the Santos' flock of robust Awassi ewes, which graze the local grasslands.

TASTING NOTES Made with thistle rennet, this is the creamiest of all the Spanish tortas. Very aromatic, with soft, earthy flavours, it has a typical bitter finish.

HOW TO ENJOY Open the thin rind to expose the silky interior, and scoop out with a teaspoon or breadsticks. It is also delicious melted on a rare fillet steak served with caramelized onions.

SPAIN Pollos, Castilla-León	
Age 2–3 months	
Weight and Shape 250–500g (9oz–1lb 2oz), round	
Size D. 10–12cm (4–5in), H. 5–6cm (2–2½in)	
Milk Ewe	
Classification Semi-soft	
Producer Cañarejal SL	

Cantabria DOP

Also known as Queso Nata de Cantabria, this was originally made in the Cóbreces Cistercian monastery but is now produced by numerous small and medium-sized family dairies using milk from the abundant dairy cattle found pasturing in sheltered green valleys.

TASTING NOTES Its smooth, waxy rind hides a pale interior that has a dense, springy texture and a mellow, sweet, and buttery flavour, sometimes with a tart finish.

HOW TO ENJOY Eat on crusty toast with chestnut honey, quince, or apple jelly. It's ideal picnic fare with a salad and a dry white or young red wine.

SPAIN Cantabria	
Age Minimum 15 days	
Weight and Shape 5kg (11lb), round	
Size D. 20cm (8in), H.10cm (4in)	
Milk Cow	
Classification Semi-soft	
Producer Various	

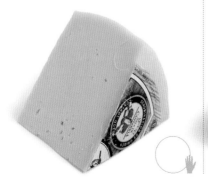

Casín DOP

Casina cattle feed on lush, mountain meadows to provide milk for one of the oldest cheeses in Asturias. The unique recipe involves repeated rolling of the curds during the first week before they are kneaded into shape to produce Casín's peculiar grainy paste.

TASTING NOTES With a strong smell that suggests rancid butter, the taste is very fiery and oily on the palate. The dense, creamy-looking paste is oddly grainy.

HOW TO ENJOY Producers imprint their name on the cheese with a wooden stamp, making Casín a very attractive option to serve whole on a cheeseboard. It is best enjoyed with beer or cider.

SPAIN Asturias	
Age 60 days	
Weight and Shape Various. 2.5kg (5½lb), round (pictured)	
Size D. 10–20cm (4–8in), H. 4–7cm (1½–3in)	
Milk Cow	
Classification Semi-soft	
Producer Various	

Castellano

Little known and understood mainly by its brand name, Castellano cheese can actually be of outstanding character when made well, because the Castilla-León region produces the best, creamiest ewe's milk in Spain.

TASTING NOTES When aged for six months and made with raw milk, it gains piquancy and a smooth texture that reveals a distinct caramelized onion flavour of sheep and an intense finish.

HOW TO ENJOY This apéritif cheese is ideal with a bold red wine such as Somontano, and is also excellent with unsalted nuts and dried fruit, quince jelly or paste, or fresh pears and apples.

SPAIN Castilla-León	
Age 2–6 months	
Weight and Shape 2–3kg (4½–6½lb), drum	
Size D. 11–19cm (4½-7½in), H. 8–10cm (3–4in)	
Milk Ewe	
Classification Hard	
Producer Various	

Cebreiro DOP

Reminiscent of a chef's hat or stout mushroom in shape, Cebreiro is rarely found away from its mountain home in Galicia. The characteristic shape is achieved when the curd is put in a bag and a hoop slipped over the top to hold it in position; as the hoop is not tall enough, the curd spills over the top.

TASTING NOTES The fresh white paste is moist and close-textured but granular. It has a fresh, lightly acidic yogurt tang, with an aroma of warm butter.

HOW TO ENJOY Serve with honey and fruit jams and preserves, or use in gratins and béchamel sauce. Cebreiro happily pairs with chilled young Albariño wine.

SPAIN Lugo, Galicia
Age 3–7 days
Weight and Shape 300g–2kg (10oz–4½lb), chef's hat
Size D. 9–15cm (3½–6in), H. 7cm (3in)
Milk Cow
Classification Fresh
Producer Queixerías Castelo de Branas; Carmen Arrojo Valcarcel Xan Busto

Flor de Guîa

This exceptional and very rare cheese, curiously only ever made by women, is named Flor de Guîa (thistle flower) after the local thistle used to coagulate the milk. Shaped with a grass belt, the cheese develops gently rounded sides.

TASTING NOTES Creamiest of all Canarian cheeses, Flor de Guîa has an unctuous, rich texture that melts in the mouth, releasing its mildly acidic, aromatic flavour and the typical bitterness of thistle rennet on the finish.

HOW TO ENJOY This rare treat complements fruity white wines from Galicia, tropical fruit such as bananas, and fruit jams such as those made from berries.

SPAIN Gran Canaria, Islas Canarias
Age 2–3 weeks
Weight and Shape 2–5kg (4½–11lb), wheel
Size D. 22–30cm (8½–12in), H. 4–6cm (1½–2⅓in)
Milk Ewe and cow
Classification Semi-soft
Producer Various

Gamonedo DOP

Although this blue mountain cheese is overshadowed by its neighbour Cabrales (see p148), it still has quite an individual character because it is lightly smoked before it is placed in the natural caves and it has a harder, pressed, elegant-looking rind and less blue veining.

TASTING NOTES This cheese blues lightly in patches nearer to the hard dry rind and has a gentle spikiness, revealing hints of damp mushroom, salt, and a nutty aftertaste of hazelnuts.

HOW TO ENJOY Relish in the rustic flavour of this cheese from the Picos de Europa mountains. Gamonedo del Valle is a milder, more accomplished cheese.

SPAIN Asturias
Age 3–5 months
Weight and Shape 500g–7kg (1lb 2oz–15lb 7oz), drum
Size D. 10–30cm (4–12in), H. 6–15cm (2½–6in)
Milk Cow, with some ewe or goat
Classification Blue
Producer Various

Mahón DO

Granted Denomination of Origin status in 1985, Mahón comes from the Balearic Island of Menorca. The tiny island has a colourful history, with invasions by the Carthegians, Romans, Arabs, French, and lastly the British in the 18th century, who introduced the Friesian cow.

Port of Mahón, *Menorca, from which the cheese takes its name.*

Records show that Mahón was traded around the Mediterranean since the 13th century. However, it owes its international reputation to the local merchants who, in the late 1800s, started taking the farmers' cheese in exchange for goods. Known as *recogedor-afinador*, gatherer-ripeners, they ripened the young cheeses in underground caves where the airflow, temperature, and humidity provided the cheese with a unique microclimate. This practice continues, with about 300 family-owned dairy farms selling their milk to the big cooperatives. Today, the best-known *afinador* is Nicolas Cardona.

152

TASTING NOTES At 20–60 days it is supple, buttery, and mild; semi-cured at 2–5 months – the flavour increases and the texture becomes firmer; cured, or *añejo*, at 5–10 months. It is hard and slightly granular, not unlike Parmigiano-Reggiano (see pp128–129), and has an aroma and taste of peaches with a sea-salt finish. Green-labelled Mahón is made by hand from raw milk on small farms and finished by an *afinador*, who brings out the best in each cheese. The harder, more piquant style with its red label and bright orange rind is made in cooperatives and has an unexpectedly sharp, mouth-puckering bite.

HOW TO ENJOY It is traditionally served as an appetizer, drizzled with olive oil and topped with a sprig of fresh rosemary. Serve it alongside a glass of sherry, which brings out the personality of the cheese. However, like all hard cheeses, it is extremely versatile and is used in many recipes from the Spanish omelette to tapas and pastries. The more matured or cured Mahón pairs well with beer or even *sake* (Japanese rice wine).

SPAIN Menorca	
Age 20 days–10 months	
Weight and Shape 1.5kg (3lb 4oz), square "cushion"	
Size L. 20cm (8in), W. 20cm (8in) H. 5cm (2in)	
Milk Cow	
Classification Hard	
Producer Various	

A CLOSER LOOK

Mahón is lovingly nurtured and matured by the skilful *afinadores* who buy the generic young cheeses and age them according to their own individual methods.

Interior

THE RACKS The cheeses are stored on wooden racks in underground caves where the *afinador* carefully controls the temperature, humidity, and flow of fresh air.

All aged Mahón is speckled with small, irregular holes, caused by the fermentation that occurs as the cheese ripens.

CLOTH PRESSING The young artisanal cheese is wrapped in cloth (*fogasser*) and tied by its corners. This is pressed manually, forcing out excess whey and forming the cheese into its distinct "cushion" shape.

The upper surface of matured artisanal Mahón bears the pattern of the creases and folds of the fogasser.

Exterior

The ochre-yellow colour of the rind is created by rubbing butter, paprika, and olive oil into the rind to enhance its appearance and prevent mould.

Garrotxa

Garrotxa is one of the new generation of Spanish artisan cheeses to come to prominence in recent years and is notable for its subtle goaty flavour and dark grey velveteen rind, or *pell florida*. First produced in 1981 by a single maker, Garrotxa is now made by other artisan cheesemakers in the region.

TASTING NOTES A fresh slice, unusually chalky for Spanish cheese, invokes memories of mountain herbs, walnuts, and mushrooms; the lingering finish has distinct creamy overtones of goat.

HOW TO ENJOY It is ideal for tapas or at the end of a meal, served with almonds, walnuts, and a robust white Priorat.

SPAIN Cataluña	
Age 2–4 months	
Weight and Shape 1kg (2¼lb), round	
Size D. 15cm (6in), H. 7cm (3in)	
Milk Goat	
Classification Semi-soft	
Producer Various	

Herreño

Similar cheeses are produced all over these rugged islands under the various island names, but this has the most interesting texture and flavour. When smoked, there are beautiful burnished lines on the rind from the racking.

TASTING NOTES It is bright white and refreshingly acidic when young, while smoked Herreño balances its light smoke, usually fig or prickly pear branches, with delicate flavour.

HOW TO ENJOY When young, it pairs well with white and rosé wines; aged, it is better with red wines. It is excellent lightly grilled and served with red or green *mojo* sauces or in cheesecake.

SPAIN El Hierro, Islas Canarias	
Age 10–60 days	
Weight and Shape 350g–4kg (12oz–8lb 13oz), cylinder	
Size D. 8.5–25.5cm (3½–10in), H. 6–8.5cm (2½–3⅓in)	
Milk Goat, cow, and ewe	
Classification Semi-soft	
Producer Sociedad Cooperativa Ganaderos de El Hierro; Valverde	

Ibérico

Imprinted with the marks of the woven-basket mould, Ibérico is a blend of cow's, goat's, and ewe's milk, typical of many traditional Spanish cheeses, and makes up more than 50 per cent of the nation's consumption of cheese.

TASTING NOTES The rind is often coloured to indicate age, and the blend of different milks brings the best of each one together: creamy and mellow from the cow, sweet and nutty from the ewe, and herbaceous notes from the goat.

HOW TO ENJOY The flavour changes subtly with the seasons, but Ibérico is always delicious in a toasted sandwich or used for a gratin, whatever time of year.

SPAIN Castilla-La Mancha and Castilla-León	
Age 1 month minimum	
Weight and Shape 1–3½kg (2¼–7lb 11oz), drum	
Size D. 9–22cm (3½–8½in), H. 7–12cm (3–5in)	
Milk Cow, goat, and ewe	
Classification Hard	
Producer Various	

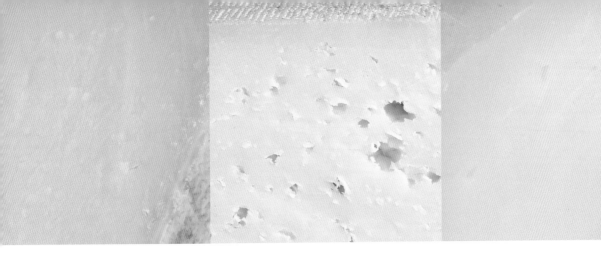

Ibores DOP

This rustic cheese, whose roots lie in the migrating herds of native Verata and Retinta goats and the wild vegetation and oak forests of the area, is found either plain or brushed with olive oil and pimentón (smoked paprika).

TASTING NOTES The firm white paste is rich with aromas of broom, lavender, and thyme, while the copper-coloured pimentón rind imparts a warmth to the cheese's tangy finish.

HOW TO ENJOY Sprinkle a slice with some pimentón, lightly toast it, and serve with an apéritif or as a light supper with salad. It is ideal with a crisp dry white wine and unsalted nuts.

SPAIN Caceres, Extremadura	
Age 2 months minimum	
Weight and Shape 650g–1.2kg (1lb 7oz–2½lb), drum	
Size D. 11–15cm (4½–6in), H. 5–9cm (2–3½in)	
Milk Goat	
Classification Semi-soft	
Producer Queserías de las Villuercas; Berrocales Trujillanos	

Idiazábal DOP

This ancient cheese comes from the Basque mountains, where shepherds spent summers in the high pastures before returning with their cheeses in the autumn. Stored in the rafters of the shepherds' huts over the summer, the cheese took on a wood-smoke flavour.

TASTING NOTES Hard and chewy, with tiny holes and a coppery rind, Idiázabal is smoked with beech wood, adding a light smokiness to the distinctive caramel sweetness of the ewe's milk. Artisan varieties are a rare treat.

HOW TO ENJOY Try a Basque recipe, such as squid and Idiazábal risotto, or serve simply with Txacoli or a Basque cider.

SPAIN Navarra	
Age 3–6 months	
Weight and Shape 1–3kg (2¼–6½lb), drum	
Size D. 10–30cm (4–12in), H. 8–12cm (3–5in)	
Milk Ewe	
Classification Flavour-added	
Producer Various	

Liébana DOP

Small cheeses are made in each village in the foothills of the Picos de Europa. Mainly fresh or semi-soft, but sometimes smoked, they are made with cow's or sometimes either ewe's or goat's milk.

TASTING NOTES It is lemony when fresh, but most are supple, buttery, and aromatic, with a hint of caramel when made with ewe's milk. The rinds are typically thin, rough, and straw-coloured, or bright white if fresh. Smoking adds piquancy.

HOW TO ENJOY Serve on a cheeseboard alongside dried fruits and nuts, with a selection of young wines. Young cheeses are delicious with mountain honey.

SPAIN Cantabria	
Age 2 weeks minimum	
Weight and Shape 400g–500g (14oz–1lb 2oz), round	
Size D. 8–12cm (3–5in), H. 3–10cm (1–4in)	
Milk Cow and occasionally ewe and goat	
Classification Fresh or semi-soft	
Producer Various	

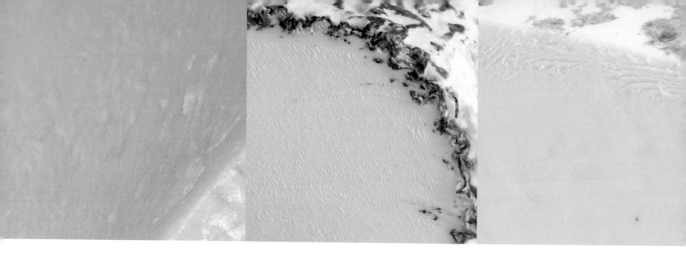

Majorero DOP

The scrubby desert landscape of Fuerteventura nourishes the Majorero goats that produce this exceptional cheese. The rind, rubbed with olive oil, bears the imprint pattern of a palm frond belt. Some are rubbed with either paprika or *gofio* (roasted corn flour).

TASTING NOTES Supple to firm, Majorero varies from creamy fresh with a subtle goaty flavour to a more robust nutty, almondy sweetness.

HOW TO ENJOY It is traditionally grated into vegetable soups or summer salads, and served with a minerally white local wine. Young Majorero makes a superb fondue flavoured with orange zest.

SPAIN Fuerteventura, Islas Canarias	
Age 20 days minimum	
Weight and Shape 1–6kg (2¼lb–13lb 4oz), round	
Size D. 15–35cm (6–14in), H. 6-9cm (2½–3½in)	
Milk Goat	
Classification Hard	
Producer SAT Ganaderos de Fuerteventura	

Monte Enebro

When most would be retiring, Rafael Báez chose to create this *pata de mulo*, or mule's-hoof shaped goat's cheese, with its distinctive rind covered in grey and black moulds. It was the first modern artisan cheese in Spain to gain international recognition.

TASTING NOTES Dense curds are gently compressed, and the flavour matures over time from a light citric creaminess to an assertive, pungent bite.

HOW TO ENJOY Savour with muscatel dessert wine, add to a beetroot salad, or fry in tempura batter and serve with orange blossom honey, accompanied by a light, white La Mancha wine.

SPAIN Avila, Castilla-León	
Age 6–8 weeks	
Weight and Shape 1.4kg (3lb), mule's hoof	
Size L. 23cm (9in), W. 12cm (5in), H. 6.5cm (2½in)	
Milk Goat	
Classification Aged fresh	
Producer Queserias del Tietar	

Los Montes de Toledo

This is the innovation of a spirited individual, Anna Maria Rubio. The Toledo Mountains neighbour Ibores, where goats dominate, so local goat farmers joined the cooperative to provide milk for this soft, unique torta.

TASTING NOTES It has a clean aroma and silky texture, with flavours that vary with the seasons from more acidic with a touch of salt to sweeter during the spring. It is a mild cheese.

HOW TO ENJOY It is sublime on crusty white bread with fruits and nuts such as pistachios, apples, and quince paste. Pair with fruity white wine or chilled dry fino.

SPAIN Navalmorales, Castilla-La Mancha	
Age 2–3 months	
Weight and Shape 1kg (2¼lb), round	
Size D. 17cm (6½in), H. 4cm (1½in)	
Milk Goat	
Classification Semi-soft	
Producer La Merendera Sociedad Cooperativa	

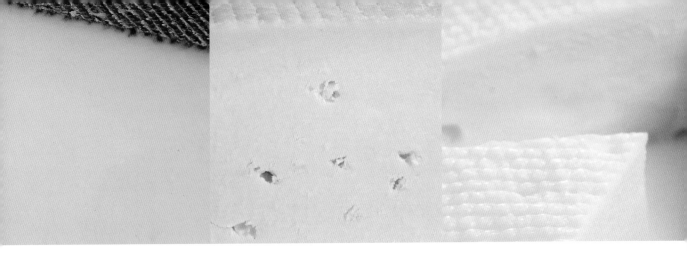

Murcia al Vino DOP

Spain's Murcia region has a growing cheese industry based on the native goats, Murciano-Granadinas, that have been honed by genetic selection for generations. This cheese is washed with local Jumilla and Yecla red wines and also comes in an unwashed version.

TASTING NOTES This washed-curd cheese has a slightly elastic texture and distinct, aromatic flavour, with hints of almonds from the rich milk and a slightly winey, fermented fruit finish.

HOW TO ENJOY Try the cheese in salads, lightly fried, or grilled on toast and served with the young white or rosé wines from Jumilla and Yecla.

SPAIN Murcia	
Age 3 weeks minimum	
Weight and Shape 300g–2 kg (10oz–4½lb), drum	
Size D. 7–18cm (3–7in), H. 6–9cm (2½–3½in)	
Milk Goat	
Classification Semi-soft	
Producer Various	

Palmero DOP

Spain's largest cheese comes from the greenest of the Canary Islands, where the Palmero goat feeds on rich pastures, moving steadily up the slopes as the weather warms.

TASTING NOTES Diverse and lush grazing gives this lightly smoked cheese a rich flavour. Palmero is pleasantly crumbly, salty, earthy, and lightly acidic, with a toasted aroma.

HOW TO ENJOY Palmero breaks up easily, so it is commonly used in local cuisine, grated into the mojo sauces or sliced alongside fish, vegetable, and potatoes. It is also good on its own with the local mineral Malvasia wines.

SPAIN La Palma, Islas Canarias	
Age 1–3 months	
Weight and Shape 7–15kg (15lb 7oz–33lb), wheel	
Size D. 12–60cm (5–23½in), H. 6–15cm (2½–6in)	
Milk Goat	
Classification Semi-soft	
Producer Various	

Pasiego de las Garmillas

This fragile primitive cheese made without a mould was originally from the valley of Pas. It is now made to more contemporary standards and available at the weekly market in the town of Ampuero.

TASTING NOTES So fresh that the pale rind has barely formed, its interior is soft and fatty, with an aroma of fresh yogurt and mountain streams.

HOW TO ENJOY Its delicate, sweet flavours work well with crusty bread, salted anchovies, and piquillo peppers, accompanied by a cold dry cider. Used for the local dessert "quesada pasiega".

SPAIN Ampuero, Cantabria	
Age 15–20 days	
Weight and Shape 500g (1lb 2oz), flat disc	
Size D. 14cm (5½in), H. 2cm (¾in)	
Milk Cow	
Classification Fresh	
Producer Queso Las Garmillas	

Pata de Mulo

Named "mule's hoof" because of its shape, this was traditionally moulded by hand in cheesecloth, then rolled on a table until the typical shape was achieved. Thankfully, since the late 1990s, production of this disappearing cheese has been reinvigorated.

TASTING NOTES A rounded flavour, grainy texture, nutty nose, light oil on the palate, and persistent finish are typical of this very Castilian aged ewe's cheese, with its straw-coloured wrinkled rind.

HOW TO ENJOY Attractive for slicing into salads or displayed on a cheeseboard, it pairs beautifully with young red or rosé wines of Ribera del Duero or Navarra.

SPAIN Castilla-León	
Age 2–6 months	
Weight and Shape 2kg (4½lb), flattened oval log	
Size L. 23cm (9in), W. 13cm (5in), H. 8cm (3in)	
Milk Ewe	
Classification Hard	
Producer Various	

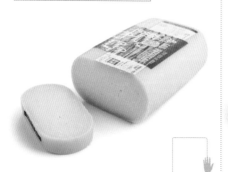

Payoyo Cabra Curado

Queso Payoyo was established in 1995 by Andrés Peña and Carlos Rios. They have a wide range of cheeses.They use milk from the Payoyo goats and Grazalemeña ewes that roam the pastures of the Sierra de Grazalema, 900m (2,750ft) above sea level.

TASTING NOTES The strictly artisan methods used mean that even the rennet derives from the Payoyo goat. The plain rind can be coated with lard or paprika, and it has a firm texture that reveals a nutty taste, with hints of toffee.

HOW TO ENJOY It is ideal with an apéritif. Serve with almonds and a Manzanilla dry sherry or a cold refreshing beer.

SPAIN Sierra de Grazalema, Andalucia	
Age 3–6 months	
Weight and Shape 2.5kg (5½lb), drum	
Size D. 17cm (6½in), H. 10cm (4in)	
Milk Goat	
Classification Hard	
Producer Quesos Artesanales de Villaluenga	

Peña Blanca de Corrales

This assertive ewe's milk cheese with a rind of red and ochre moulds is an original recipe that uses lactic coagulation. Its makers successfully capture the terroir of the Sierra de Espadas where it is made.

TASTING NOTES The aroma is reminiscent of a Cabrales (see p148), but the dense paste has the texture of fresh curds, with hints of leather, caramelized onions, and wool.

HOW TO ENJOY Its restrained piquancy works well with fino or palo cortado sherry, black olives, extra virgin olive oil, and fresh crusty bread.

SPAIN Almedíjar, Valencia	
Age 90 days	
Weight and Shape 2.2kg (5lb), cylinder	
Size D. 19cm (7½in), H. 8cm (3in)	
Milk Ewe	
Classification Hard	
Producer Quesería Los Corrales	

La Peral

This relatively modern foil-wrapped blue cheese from Asturias is made by the third generation of creator Antonio León's family. Production remains small scale and consistent, resulting in an accessibly priced, very pleasant cheese.

TASTING NOTES This sticky yellow rind with a pale yellow interior lightly inked with blue veins emits a gentle buttery smell. The shiny curd-like cheese has a creamy salty flavour that gradually develops into a clean, fresh mild blue.

HOW TO ENJOY Savour this cheese with blackberries and walnuts, accompanied by either an Asturian cider or a Pedro Ximenez sherry.

SPAIN Illas, Asturias	
Age 60–150 days	
Weight and Shape 2kg (4½lb), tall cylinder	
Size D. 18cm (7in), H. 9cm (3½in)	
Milk Cow with ewe's cream	
Classification Blue	
Producer Herederos de Antonio León	

Picón Bejes Tresviso DOP

From the villages of Bejes and Tresviso in the Picos de Europa, this ancient blue cheese has the hallmark sharp flavour characteristic of cheeses made in these high peaks. Abandoned mines and natural caves provide excellent damp space for curing.

TASTING NOTES The light grey rind with orange overtones conceals an interior veined with dense blue streaks. This pungent blue cheese has a distinctive balance of bite, butter, and salt.

HOW TO ENJOY Sprinkle with ground hazelnuts or serve with prunes; pair with muscatel or a sweet red Priorat.

SPAIN Cantabria	
Age 3–6 months	
Weight and Shape 500g–3kg (1lb 2oz–6½lb), drum	
Size D. 10–21cm (4–8in), H. 6–13cm (2½–5in)	
Milk Cow, goat, and ewe	
Classification Blue	
Producer Various	

Roncal DOP

Records for this Pyrenean ewe's cheese date back to 13th century and detail movement of the herds as they moved between summer and winter pastures, in routes up and down the Roncal valley. The cheese is pressed, then aged in cloth.

TASTING NOTES It is dense, with a rind that goes from smooth straw colour to grey and bears the imprint of the cloth. With age, there can be hints of dried fruit, a growing piquancy, and a lingering aftertaste.

HOW TO ENJOY Serve simply with crusty white bread and a good Navarran red wine or cider. Artichoke gratin with Roncal is a popular local dish.

SPAIN Navarra	
Age 4 months minimum	
Weight and Shape 1–3kg (2¼–6½lb), drum	
Size D. 15–20cm (6–8in), H. 10–11cm (4–4½in)	
Milk Ewe	
Classification Hard	
Producer Various	

Manchego DOP

Manchego takes its name from the dry plateau of La Mancha, south of Madrid and not far from Toledo. Baptised by the Arabs, *Al Mansha* (land without water), La Mancha is a vast, dry, flat region with few trees, scorched by temperatures of up to 50°C and minimal rainfall. It is a magnificent part of Spain with a sense of timelessness and history, dotted with old ruins, scrawny sheep, and the windmills made famous by Don Quixote.

Modern irrigation has meant vast acres of vines, olive groves, sunflowers, and crops have replaced much of the indigenous shrubs, acorns, blackthorn, vetch, and wild grasses of the *dehesa,* "uncultivated land". However, sufficient natural, uncultivated land still exists in the mountains, woodlands, around riverbanks, and on the plains to provide summer grazing for the hardy sheep, whose thick, aromatic milk gives Manchego its character. In autumn and winter their diet is supplemented with sweet tendrils from vines and the stubble from crops and hay.

Most Manchego is made in factories but milking is still largely done by hand. It is an awesome sight to see the shepherds as they work methodically through the herds, often upwards of 700 at a time. Each sheep is lifted off its back legs so their milk-swollen udder collects in the bucket, yielding but a few litres of milk each a day. Yet every drop is imbued with the essence of the wild thyme, aromatic herbs, and withered acorns that form their diet. The resulting thick, sweet, aromatic milk is what makes Manchego unique.

TASTING NOTES The depth and complexity of flavour depends on age, but all Manchego has an unmistakable richness reminiscent of Brazil nuts and caramel, with a distinct aroma of lanolin and roast lamb, and a slightly salty finish. The texture is dry yet creamy. It can be slightly oily on the surface and may feel a little greasy in the mouth, but that just makes it taste better. Each mouthful is a taste of Spanish culture, history, and gastronomy.

Manchego that reach a great age have a peppery bite to the finish. Once cut into thin wedges and marinated in the strong aromatic local green olive oil, the flavour is intensified.

HOW TO ENJOY Like all hard cheeses, Manchego keeps well and is gorgeous eaten just as it is, however, like any hard cheese, it is extremely versatile and, when cooked, lends a nutty sweetness to the dish.

Manchego will absorb tannin so enjoy it with a robust or young rough red, crisp white, or perhaps the best combination is with sherry, either dry or sweet.

A CLOSER LOOK

Most Manchego is now made with pasteurized milk in modern factories that comply with EU regulations, however, great care is taken to ensure the finished cheese is as close to the traditional handmade cheeses as possible.

PRESSING AND AGEING Once the curd is in the moulds, they are placed on a horizontal press to expel excess whey. Artisan cheeses are then aged in stone barns, sometimes dug into the sides of the limestone hills. Factory cheeses are aged in large, airy barns.

The vast, *dry plains of La Mancha.*

SPAIN Castilla La Mancha	
Age 6–18 months	
Weight and Shape 3kg (6½lb), drum	
Size D. 20cm (8in), H. 10cm (4in)	
Milk Ewe	
Classification Hard	
Producer Various	

MARKING To qualify for the DOP label, the cheese must bear the distinct zigzag markings along the sides and the "flor" (flower) design on the top and bottom. Originally, the zigzag marks were made by encircling the fresh curd with plaited esparto grass and placing it on hand-carved wooden boards to drain. Regrettably, the boards and grass have been replaced with plastic moulds, imprinted with the zigzag pattern.

ESPAÑA
Denominación de Origen
MANCHEGO
74979
FO

The texture of the ivory-coloured interior is firm and dry, yet rich and creamy.

Interior

The distinctive yellow to brownish beige rind gathers a multitude of moulds that must be washed and scrubbed and sometimes waxed before being sold.

Exterior

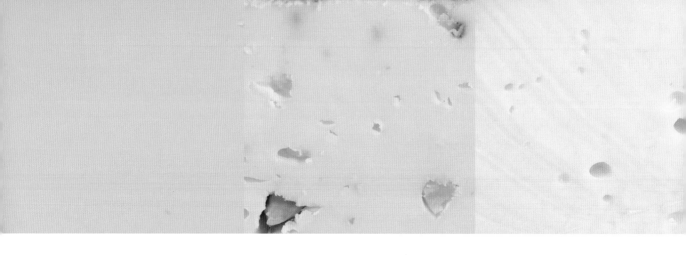

San Simón da Costa DOP

Shaped as a large teardrop with a small 'nipple' on top, it is thought to have its origins in Celtic culture. Its distinctive smooth copper-coloured rind is the result of gentle smoking over birch wood.

TASTING NOTES The smoky taste blends with the buttery aroma and taste, while the overall flavour is mild with some salt that gives a pleasant balance of acidity and sweetness in the aftertaste.

HOW TO ENJOY This good melting cheese, works well in rice, pasta, and vegetable dishes, or added to salads. It is delicious with a glass of a young red Valdeorras wine and some peanuts.

SPAIN Galicia	
Age 3 weeks	
Weight and Shape 800g–1.5kg (1¾lb–3lb 3oz), large cone	
Size D. 12–15cm (5–6in), H. 13–18cm (5–7in)	
Milk Cow	
Classification Flavour-added	
Producer Various	

Taramundi

Taramundi, the creation of a splinter cooperative who wanted to respond to the growth in popularity of local cheese and take advantage of the rich mountain milk, is inspired by the sweeter, more elastic cheeses of Switzerland.

TASTING NOTES Made plain or with walnuts or hazelnuts, this cheese has an unusual but pleasant flavour – a mix of toast, butter, and sweetness – and a springy texture.

HOW TO ENJOY This cheese makes an excellent hors d'oeuvre alongside crudités, and also has the same superb melting qualities as raclette. It is perfect when combined with young, fruity white wines or cider.

SPAIN Asturias	
Age 2–3 months	
Weight and Shape 500g–1kg (1lb 2oz–2¼lb), wheel	
Size D. 10–20cm (4–8in), H. 4–6cm (1½–2½in)	
Milk Cow and goat	
Classification Flavour-added	
Producer Various	

Tetilla DO

This popular cheese from northwestern Spain is well known beyond its borders due to its mellow taste and distinctive shape. The name Tetilla means "small breast". Original farmhouse production has been almost totally replaced by a strong dairy industry.

TASTING NOTES It is ready to eat after only seven days, when the deep bright yellow interior is sweet, clean, buttery, and unctuous; with maturity, Tetilla becomes firmer and more resilient, with a slight acidity on the finish.

HOW TO ENJOY Delicious when served at the end of a meal, with either quince paste or a sharp apple purée.

SPAIN Galicia	
Age 7 days minimum	
Weight and Shape 500g–1.5kg (1lb 2oz–3lb 3oz), flattened cone	
Size D. 9–15cm (3½–6in), H. 9–15cm (3½in–6in)	
Milk Cow	
Classification Semi-soft	
Producer Various	

Tortas Extremeñas

Once considered fit only for peasants, these lush cheeses have taken Europe by storm with their near-liquid interiors. There are three versions, including Torta de Barros (pictured), Torta del Casar and Torta La Serena.

TASTING NOTES Thistle rennet gives these cheeses a distinctive earthy flavour and a gentle bitterness on the finish; the paste is very soft and rich, with aromas reminiscent of dry hay.

HOW TO ENJOY Heat in the oven until warmed right through, cut a hole in the top of the cheese, and scoop out the soft interior with a teaspoon or breadsticks.

SPAIN Extremadura	
Age From 8 weeks	
Weight and Shape 500g–1.3kg (1lb 2oz–3lb), round	
Size D. 11–16cm (4½–6in), H. 5–6cm (2–2½in)	
Milk Ewe	
Classification Semi-soft	
Producer Various	

Tou del Til·lers

This tender soft cheese, with its white mould rind, is a thoroughly modern cheese created at a dairy founded in 1995. It is situated in the heart of the Pyrenees, in Pallars Sobirà, where varied high pasture enriches the quality of the milk.

TASTING NOTES The rind reveals notes of ammonia and, although there are hints of fresh mushroom and rich cream, the pungent, gluey, and assertive flavour of this cheese is hard to deny.

HOW TO ENJOY Full of character, it is best enjoyed with a dense white country-style loaf and a strong red wine, such as a Terra Alta or Somontano.

SPAIN Sort, Lleida	
Age 6–12 weeks	
Weight and Shape 450–500g (1lb–1lb 2oz) and 1kg (2¼lb), round	
Size D. 13 and 22cm (5in and 8½in), H. 3 and 4cm (1 and 1½in)	
Milk Cow	
Classification Soft white	
Producer Tros de Sort	

Tronchón

This delightful volcano-shaped cheese is imprinted with original carved wooden moulds made by the shepherds. The tradition of taking mixed herds of goats and ewes into the Sierra del Maestrazgo extends its spread throughout the provinces of Tarragona, Teruel, and Castellón.

TASTING NOTES Mountain pastures endow this soft, buttery cheese, available either fresh or cured, with hints of lavender and oregano.

HOW TO ENJOY Serve fresh ewe's milk Tronchón with crusty bread and green olives; the cured goat's milk variety is sharper and pairs well with young reds.

SPAIN Aragón and Pais Valenciano	
Age From 45 days	
Weight and Shape 500g–2kg (1lb 2oz–4⅓lb), round with a crater	
Size D. 10–15cm (4–6in), H. 7–10cm (3–4in)	
Milk Ewe or goat, or a blend	
Classification Hard	
Producer Various	

Tupí

This spread, which is a very ancient shepherd's recipe that is firmly back on the modern-day Catalan cheese menu, is made from the second fermentation of fresh and cured cheeses, blended with olive oil and brandy or liqueur.

TASTING NOTES Matured in small ceramic clay pots, this is a strangely compulsive cheese. It has the texture of porridge, a strong piquant flavour, and a slightly fetid aroma, but develops a surprisingly satisfying finish.

HOW TO ENJOY Its soft texture makes it perfect for canapés on dry bread, but it is not a cheese for the faint-hearted. It pairs well with cold beers and ciders.

SPAIN Cataluña		
Age A few weeks		
Weight and Shape 160g (5½oz) and 200g (7oz), pots		
Size No size		
Milk Cow		
Classification Aged fresh		
Producer Various		

Valdeón DO

The innovative Alonso brothers, Tomás and Javier, produce this on the León side of the Picos de Europa, where the climate of Valdéon is less humid than that of Picón. The resulting less-virulent mould produces a less intense flavour than similar blues. Valdeón is often marketed as Picos de Europa.

TASTING NOTES The rind is rough, sticky, speckled with moulds, and wrapped in sycamore leaves. Distinctly spicy, but not strong, and flavoured with a touch of salt, it leaves an elegant aftertaste.

HOW TO ENJOY Serve with hazelnuts, walnuts, prunes, and port or cider. It also makes an excellent sauce.

SPAIN León, Castilla-León		
Age 2–3 months		
Weight and Shape 2.5kg (5½lb), drum		
Size D. 19cm (7½in), H. 9cm (3½in)		
Milk Cow, occassionally with goat		
Classification Blue		
Producer Queserías Picos de Europa		

Zamorano DO

The dry pastures of northern Castilla contribute to Zamorano's complex character. Shepherding and moving herds between summer and winter pasture have a strong heritage here, and the dramatic landscape offers a great variety of vegetation and climate.

TASTING NOTES The quality and character of the ewe's milk allow the cheese to be matured for long periods. It develops an intense, slightly tart, nutty complexity with a distinct sheepy aroma.

HOW TO ENJOY Select a Gran Reserva, aged for 12 months, and serve alone at the end of a meal, or perhaps with quince paste, and the local wine Toro.

SPAIN Zamora, Castilla y León		
Age 100 days minimum		
Weight and Shape 2–4kg (4½lb–8lb 13oz), drum		
Size D. 20–24cm (8–9½in), H. 9–14cm (3½–5½in)		
Milk Ewe		
Classification Hard		
Producer Various		

Azeitão DOP

This rustic-looking cheese wrapped in gauze hails from the lush foothills of the Arrabida mountains, where the flora and local soil conditions strongly influence the quality of the milk.

TASTING NOTES The curds are moulded in cloth, the rind is washed in brine, and the paste is pale yellow. It has a sweet, slightly acidic, and very delicate taste, with fatty spice on the finish.

HOW TO ENJOY Cut open the top, scoop out the runny paste, dollop into mini cooked pastry shells, and sprinkle with oregano to serve with an apéritif, or eat with nutty bread and wash down with Tempranillo or Albarinho wine.

PORTUGAL Setúbal	
Age 20–30 days	
Weight and Shape 100–250g (3½–9oz), soft round	
Size D. 5–11cm (2–4½in), H. 2–6cm (¾–2⅓in)	
Milk Ewe	
Classification Semi-soft	
Producer Various	

Cabra Transmontano DOP

This cheese, which comes from the area famous for Port, is made from the hardy and resilient Serrana goat. The herds are moved from high to low altitudes as the weather moves into winter, and spring brings the opportunity for milking and, of course, cheesemaking.

TASTING NOTES Rich in butterfat and protein, the paste is firm with a slightly unctuous texture. The flavour is lemony and zesty, with earthy undertones.

HOW TO ENJOY It is excellent for grating or crumbling over a summer salad and can be served as a table cheese, paired with a tawny Port or fruity white wine.

PORTUGAL Bragança and Vila Real	
Age 60 days	
Weight and Shape 600g–900g (1lb 5oz–2lb), round	
Size D. 12–19cm (5–7½in), H. 3–6cm (1–2½in))	
Milk Goat	
Classification Semi-soft	
Producer Various	

Castelo Branco DOP

This DOP, which is also called Beira Baixa, describes three cheeses made with thistle rennet. Castelo Branco, which is a white ewe's milk cheese, is the most common, but there is also a yellow version blended with goat's milk and a hotter, more mature recipe.

TASTING NOTES It is tangy with a slightly bitter finish, becoming more spicy as it is matured for up to 60 days. Young cheeses have a soft texture that gets firmer and chewier with age.

HOW TO ENJOY In all its variations, this cheese adds interest to a cheeseboard alongside dried fruit and nuts. Serve with reds such as Pinot Noir.

PORTUGAL Castelo Branco	
Age 45–60 days	
Weight and Shape 750g–1kg (1lb 10oz–2¼lb), tall round	
Size D. 12–16cm (5–6in), H. 6–7cm (2½–3in)	
Milk Ewe	
Classification Semi-soft	
Producer Various	

165

Évora DOP

The home of this washed-rind cheese shaped by the hand, is the famous walled town of Évora, where it was once traded as currency. Merino ewe's milk and cardoon thistle rennet combine to create one of the best cheeses of its kind.

TASTING NOTES This is a delicious, light-yellow cheese with a crumbly texture, light acidity, spicy fruity flavour, and salty finish. Spring pastures create a creamier, fruitier, and stronger version.

HOW TO ENJOY It is traditionally thinly sliced and accompanied by olives, cured meats, and sourdough bread dowsed in olive oil. It is also an excellent salad cheese. Pair it with Sangiovese wines.

PORTUGAL Évora	
Age 30–90 days	
Weight and Shape 120–300g (4–10oz), wheel	
Size D. 7–10cm (3–4in), H. 3–3.5cm (1in)	
Milk Ewe	
Classification Semi-soft	
Producer Various	

Ilha Graciosa

The cheesemaking technique used to produce Ilha Graciosa has been handed down by settlers of the Azores' most northern island for many centuries. It is similar to São Jorge, but is matured for a shorter period.

TASTING NOTES The island's fertile volcanic soil and damp climate provide the lush pastures that characterize this firm straw-yellow cheese, with its strong, clean, spicy taste and aroma.

HOW TO ENJOY Graciosa cheese is well-suited to eating before or after meals with the local minerally white wines or sugarcane rum. Very mature versions are ideal for grating over gratin dishes.

PORTUGAL Ilha Graciosa, Azores	
Age 90 days	
Weight and Shape 10kg (22lb), cylinder	
Size D. 30cm (12in), H. 15cm (6in)	
Milk Cow	
Classification Hard	
Producer Various	

Nisa DOP

Merina Branca, the local breed of ewes, produce the rich milk for this traditional cheese, which farmers and locals have enjoyed for years. Local thistle rennet coagulates the milk, and the cheese can be preserved in terra-cotta pots of olive oil called *talhas*.

TASTING NOTES The texture of this yellow-white cheese with a well-formed crust is dense, with small eyes in the paste. Nisa has a slightly sweet taste and is very rich and creamy.

HOW TO ENJOY As one of Portugal's most popular cheeses, it is perfect on a cheeseboard with fruits such as plums or apricots, and a crisp white wine.

PORTUGAL Portalegre	
Age 3–4 months	
Weight and Shape 200g–1.3kg (7oz–3lb), round	
Size D. 10–13cm (4–5in), H. 12–16cm (5–6in)	
Milk Ewe	
Classification Semi-soft	
Producer Various	

São Jorge DOP

This cheese dates back to the 15th century when a group of Flemish sailors who made Madeira their home created this Gouda-type recipe.

TASTING NOTES The abundant grass and salty pastures allow the cheese to gain a strong spicy flavour, a clean bouquet, and a hard but crumbly texture. It is akin to a cross between Cheddar and Gouda, with some small holes.

HOW TO ENJOY Ideal for fondues, São Jorge also makes a fine addition to a traditional cheeseboard with fresh fruit such as pears and muscatel grapes.

PORTUGAL São Jorge, Madeira
Age 4–6 months
Weight and Shape 10–11kg (22lb–24¼lb), cylinder
Size D. 30cm (12in), H. 12.5cm (5in)
Milk Cow
Classification Hard
Producer Various

Serpa DOP

Serpa is similar to Serra, but is made with the milk of the Lacaune ewes rather than the Bordeleira. The hot dry climate and sparse aromatic grazing gives the cheese a rich and fruity taste.

TASTING NOTES This full, creamy cheese, is soft, clean, and slightly salty on the palate, with a distinctly tangy finish. The cardoon or thistle rennet used to make it adds a lightly acidic aftertaste and a slight bitterness.

HOW TO ENJOY It is perfect paired with red wine as an apéritif. Scoop out the middle with breadsticks, then fill the shell with mild onions and potatoes, and bake for complete enjoyment.

PORTUGAL Beja
Age 30 days
Weight and Shape 200g–1.5kg (7oz–3lb 3oz), round
Size D. 10–18cm (4–7in), H. 12–20cm (5–8in)
Milk Ewe
Classification Semi-soft
Producers Various

Serra da Estrela DOP

Made from milk of the Bordeleira da Serra da Estrela ewes, Serra has a long history dating back to the time of the Romans. The flocks are moved to different pastures within the northern mountains, and they feed on wild herbs, flowers, and grasses.

TASTING NOTES The supple and luscious yellow paste, coagulated with thistle rennet, possesses a mild acidity with the sweetness of toffee and a hint of strawberries and thyme.

HOW TO ENJOY Bring the cheese to room temperature, cut off the top like a lid, and eat with breadsticks or a spoon along with marmalade or quince paste.

PORTUGAL Guarda
Age 45 days
Weight and Shape 500g and 1kg (1lb 2oz–2¼lb), round
Size D. 10–18cm (4–7in), H. 12–20cm (5–8in)
Milk Ewe
Classification Semi-soft
Producer Various

GREAT BRITAIN AND IRELAND

SCOTLAND Harsh, unpredictable weather, long, dark, unforgiving winters, and brief summers meant that cheeses were originally made mainly by the old clan folk and crofters for their own consumption. Inspiration for cheeses came from various sources, including the Vikings and the Irish.

Today there are around 20 Scottish artisan cheesemakers producing both traditional and unique cheeses from cow's, goat's, and ewe's milk.

IRELAND Irish cheesemaking dates back centuries thanks to high rainfall levels, lush pastures, proximity to Europe, and the influence of itinerant monks. In recent decades, the industry has seen a major revival of farmhouse-based productions, beginning in 1976 when Veronica Steele created Milleens, Ireland's first modern farmhouse cheese.

Raw and pasteurized milk from goats, cows, and sheep is now used here for a wide variety of styles and flavours, including superb soft fresh cheeses, blues, hard Cheddar, and Dutch and Swiss styles. Today there are around 70 farmhouse cheesemakers in the country.

Key
★ AOC, DOC, DOP, PGI, or PDO cheeses
◐ Produced only here
◑ Produced throughout the region

ATLANTIC OCEAN

NORTH SEA

N

100 miles
100 km

Orkney

Blue Murder, Caboc, Crowdie, Strathdon Blue

Clava Brie

SCOTLAND

Anster

Dunlop

Lanark Blue

Isle of Mull Cheddar

GREAT BRITAIN

Doddington

Cairnsmore
Ewes
Northumberland

Cairnsmore
Ewes
Kebbuck

Cairnsmore
Ewes

Allerdale

NORTHERN IRELAND

WALES Wales is primarily a pastoral country boasting beautiful and varied landscapes with high mountain ranges, luscious lowlands, and a mild variable climate. The grasses, wild herbs, and flowers give a unique character to the milk of the goats, cows, and sheep that graze there.

Simple cheese has been made in Wales for centuries and was an essential part of the local economy, but the best known is Caerphilly, initially made on lowland farms for the mining community.

The past 25 years brought an extraordinary revival of on-farm cheesemaking. Welsh cheese producers now make a variety of traditional and modern cheeses, from mild creamy goat's to robust blues.

ENGLAND A great wedge of the geology and history of England can be told through its iconic cheeses, such as Cheddar, Lancashire, and Red Leicester. However the last 30 years has seen a significant increase in small, English artisan cheeses, not only resulting in an increase in complex and flavourful cheeses, but also ensuring a future for some of the rare native breeds that give cheese the subtleties, nuances and quality so essential for these handmade products. Cheese is a reflection of the cheesemaker, his craft, and his passion. As a result, the cheeses of England are a reflection of the very landscape, its people, and the animals that graze it.

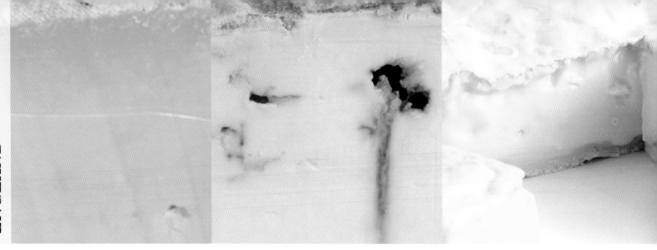

Allerdale

Carolyn Fairbairn's first cheese was created when she began her dairy career in the basement of the family home in 1979, using milk from her herd of goats. Nowadays she works alongside her daughter Leonie, translating the flavours of Cumbria's lush green grazing into delicious cheese.

TASTING NOTES Sweet and moist, with a clean hint of almond and a texture similar to Cheshire, its maturation in cloth over several months allows different layers of flavours to permeate.

HOW TO ENJOY Oven-bake or grill it, then serve it on a bed of baby spinach with a drizzle of oil and a full-bodied white.

ENGLAND Thursby, Cumbria	
Age 3–5 months	
Weight and Shape 2.5kg (5½lb), truckle	
Size D. 14cm (5½in), H. 14cm (5½in)	
Milk Goat	
Classification Hard	
Producer Thornby Moor Dairy	

Barkham Blue

The buttery consistency of Channel Island milk, which colours the interior deep yellow, characterizes this excellent cheese that looks as good as it tastes. Ammonite-shaped with an attractive rustic mould-covered rind, it has blue-green veining from the *Penicillium roqueforti* mould.

TASTING NOTES Rich and creamy, this blue melts in the mouth, and while it admirably avoids harshness, it achieves a satisfying and spicy depth. It is a blue for anyone who usually avoids blue.

HOW TO ENJOY Serve it on its own, in a soup, or on a salad with Conference pears, mixed leaves, and dressing.

ENGLAND Barkham, Berkshire	
Age 6–8 weeks	
Weight and Shape 1.3kg (3lb), ammonite	
Size D. 18cm (7in), H. 7.5cm (3in)	
Milk Cow	
Classification Blue	
Producer Two Hoots Cheese	

Bath Soft Cheese

Graham Padfield, a third-generation farmer, began making cheese in 1993, but the recipe for Bath Soft dates back to the time of Admiral Lord Nelson, who, in 1801, was sent some by his father as a gift. Today's organic version of this cheese is packed in parchment bearing a distinctive red wax seal.

TASTING NOTES Reminiscent of a mellow Brie, this mild cheese begins with a fresh hint of spring onion and matures to a creamier, more mushroomy taste.

HOW TO ENJOY Remove from the refrigerator an hour beforehand, and enjoy as part of a cheeseboard with Bath Oliver Biscuits and wheat beer.

ENGLAND Bath, Somerset	
Age 4–6 weeks	
Weight and Shape 225g (8oz), square	
Size L. 10cm (4in), W. 10cm (4in), H. 3cm (1¼in)	
Milk Cow	
Classification Soft white	
Producer Bath Soft Cheese Company	

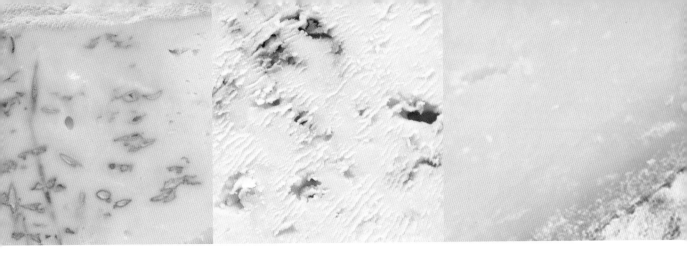

Beauvale

Cropwell Bishop, an old creamery dating back to 1847, is owned by the Skailes family and best known for their award winning Stilton and Shropshire Blue with their crusty rinds and buttery texture. However in 2012 this impressive European style blue appeared.

TASTINGS NOTES It exudes aromas of stone walls, has an amazingly goopy texture and a soft, silky feel with blue clumpy streaks yet is mellow with a sweetness of caramel and a spicy kick.

HOW TO ENJOY Worth seeking out, it is so runny you need to spread it on crusty bread and serve with a big juicy red wine like Barolo or a pink Prosecco.

ENGLAND Nottinghamshire	
Age 12 weeks	
Weight and Shape 12kg, wheel	
Size D. 36cm (14in), H. 12cm (5in)	
Milk Cow	
Classification Blue	
Producer Cropwell Bishop Creamery	

Beenleigh Blue

Created by Robin Congdon, a skilled blue-cheese aficionado whose dairy skirts the banks of the river Dart, this cheese is one of the very few British blue cheeses made from ewe's milk. It is only available from August to January.

TASTING NOTES Rich, sweet, and slightly crumbly, with a blue-green mould running through it, this cheese has hints of burnt caramel that show what an excellent ewe's milk cheese it really is. The rough exterior has a slight stickiness.

HOW TO ENJOY Use in a salad or serve on its own, complemented with a sweet Devon cider.

ENGLAND Sharpham Barton, Devon	
Age 5-plus months	
Weight and Shape 3–3.5kg (6½–7½lb), drum	
Size D. 20cm (8in), H. 10–13cm (4–5in)	
Milk Ewe	
Classification Blue	
Producer Ticklemore Cheese	

Berkswell

This consistent award winner at the British Cheese Awards was created by Stephen Fletcher and his mother, Sheila, on their 16th-century farm near the village of Berkswell. It is now made by their cheesemaker Linda Dutch, who uses milk from their flock of East Friesland sheep.

TASTING NOTES Originating from a traditional recipe, this full of character cheese provides a satisfying mouthful: firm texture; sweet, nutty, and caramel hints; and a surprisingly tangy finale.

HOW TO ENJOY Its texture makes it ideal for dishes that call for grated cheese; when cooked, it forms a delicious crust.

ENGLAND Berkswell, West Midlands	
Age 4–6 months	
Weight and Shape 3kg (6½lb), flying saucer	
Size D. 20cm (8in), H. 9cm (3½in)	
Milk Ewe	
Classification Hard	
Producer Ram Hall Dairy Sheep	

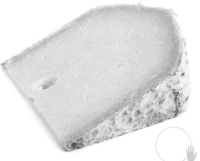

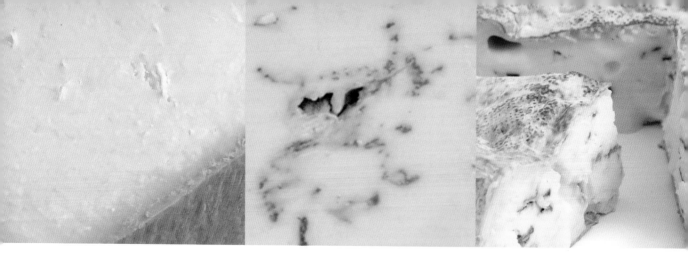

Billy's Smokey Goat

Ford Farm, near the magnificent Dorset Jurassic coast, make excellent cheddars including the popular crunchy Coastal cheddar and Wookey Hole cheddar, aged in the Cheddar caves. But they also make a small amount of this delicious hard goat cheese and some of it is sent off for smoking.

TASTINGS NOTES Natural smoking gives the rind a deep russet red colour and imbues the dense, flaky, yet creamy interior with a delicate smoky taste.

HOW TO ENJOY The almondy and smoky notes make it hard to match, but a light rosé or a dry riesling brings out the best in both the smoked and unsmoked kinds.

ENGLAND Dorset	
Age 3–4 months	
Weight and Shape 1 kg (2¼lb), block	
Size L .19.5cm (8in), W. 9cm (3.5in), H. 6.0cm (2⅓in)	
Milk Goat	
Classification Flavour-added	
Producer Ford Farm	

Blacksticks Blue

Named after a group of chestnut trees that resemble a collection of black sticks in winter, the Blacksticks range was originally developed for the restaurant trade. By popular request, it has made it into the shops. Blacksticks Blue is a contemporary soft blue-veined cheese, milder and creamier than other British blues such as Stilton (see pp192–93).

TASTING NOTES Blacksticks Blue starts by delighting the nose, then strokes the tongue, and finally lingers delightfully on the palate with a mild spicy tang.

HOW TO ENJOY Pair with hot buttered Irish soda bread, or use in a rich blue sauce for grilled steak or pasta.

ENGLAND Inglewhite, Lancashire	
Age 9–12 weeks	
Weight and Shape 2.5kg (5½lb), drum	
Size D. 21cm (8¼in), H. 6cm (2⅓in)	
Milk Cow	
Classification Blue	
Producer Butlers Farmhouse Cheese	

Blue Heaven

Jonathan and Melissa Ravenhill's herd of Dairy Shorthorns, graze on the unimproved limestone grassland of Minchinhampton Common and provide the milk to create a range of organic cheeses. This range includes this blue, which is made by adding *Penicillium roqueforti* to the sweet, organic milk.

TASTING NOTES The creamy, soft paste, streaked with patches of blue and encased in a natural moulded crust, is pleasantly piquant.

HOW TO ENJOY Perfect for canapés or on a cheeseboard with crusty bread and a drizzle of extra virgin olive oil. Serve with a Cotswold Brewery wheat beer.

ENGLAND Minchinhampton, Gloucestershire	
Age 6–8 weeks	
Weight and Shape 400g (14oz) and 1.5kg (3lb 3oz), flat round	
Size D. 5cm (2in) and 20cm (8in), H. 5cm (2in) and 15cm (6in)	
Milk Cow	
Classification Blue	
Producer Woefuldane Organic Dairy	

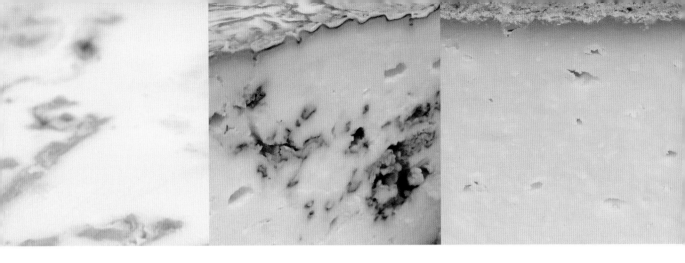

Buffalo Blue

From the only maker of buffalo blue cheese in Yorkshire, this is handmade from the milk of local water buffalo. One of Judy Bell's aims in using milk from sheep and buffalo was to help people with dairy allergies. She created something rather special in the process.

TASTING NOTES It looks light – soft and creamy – and it is light, although there is, of course, a reminder that it is a "blue" in its nutty, slightly salty taste.

HOW TO ENJOY Stir a healthy portion of cheese and a dollop of double cream into a potato soup before liquidizing to produce a deliciously rich and creamy broth.

ENGLAND Newsham, North Yorkshire	
Age 8–10 weeks	
Weight and Shape 3kg (6½lb), drum	
Size D. 20cm (8in), H. 20cm (8in)	
Milk Buffalo	
Classification Blue	
Producer Shepherds Purse Cheeses	

Burt's Blue

Claire Burt started out analysing cheese and researching the best cheeses for grating, grilling, and melting. As cheesemaking took over her life, she decided to turn "professional" in 2010. All her cheeses are handmade in small batches using milk from a few local farms and Burt's Blue was the first.

TASTINGS NOTES The thin sticky rind attracts white, blue, and grey moulds that help ripen the creamy interior with its blotchy blue chunks to an almost runny consistency that hints of yeast and distinct, spicy blue tang.

HOW TO ENJOY A perfect partner would be a tawny port or surprisingly, Samos Anthemis, a Greek Muscat Wine.

ENGLAND Cheshire	
Age 6–8 weeks	
Weight and Shape 1kg (2¼lb), round	
Size D. 18cm (7in), H. 6cm (2½in)	
Milk Cow	
Classification Blue	
Producer Burt's Cheese	

Canterbury Cobble

Jane Bowyer has been in the dairy industry for over 30 years but only started cheesemaking in 2007. Since then she has extended the range to include both hard and soft raw cow and goat milk cheeses.

TASTINGS NOTES The crusty, ridged rind dusted with grey and brown moulds hides the chewy yet creamy interior with its tiny uneven holes. There is a slight sharpness on the tongue, a hint of green grass, and a tingly acidity on the finish.

HOW TO ENJOY In Kent, the only thing to drink with cheese is Kentish Ale made from the world famous hops.

ENGLAND Kent	
Age 2–3 months	
Weight and Shape 1kg (2¼lb), wheel	
Size D. 17cm (6.5in), H. 6cm (2½in)	
Milk Cow	
Classification Hard	
Producer Cheesemakers of Canterbury	

Capra Nouveau

The Hamptons farm in the Shropshire hills is home to around 100 goats, whose raw milk is used in a wide range of cheeses that reflect their passion and commitment to their land and animals. The quality of their cheese is inspired by the artisan cheesemakers of France.

TASTINGS NOTES The orange-pink sticky cheese is bound with spruce bark which permeates the thick, almost liquid, interior. Pale ivory with tiny holes, it has hints of almonds with meaty overtones.

HOW TO ENJOY Like all washed rind cheeses, it goes best with an Alsace style white wine or a Shropshire cider.

ENGLAND Shropshire	
Age 6–8 weeks	
Weight and Shape 900g (2lb), wheel	
Size D. 16cm (6in), H. 5cm (2in)	
Milk Goat	
Classification Semi-soft, washed	
Producer Brock Hall Farm	

Capricorn Goat

Lubborn Creamery, which is nestled in a green Somerset valley, specializes in making continental style cheeses. Ripened for seven weeks, this cheese develops a thin, delicate white rind.

TASTING NOTES Like the goats themselves, this cheese changes character with age. Eaten young, it has a slight nutty flavour; however, as it ripens, it develops a salty-sweetness, and the paste is softer and creamier.

HOW TO ENJOY Crumble the young cheese into salads, or grill. Savour the mature cheese simply as it comes, with a glass of Sauvignon Blanc.

ENGLAND Cricket St Thomas, Somerset	
Age 7 weeks	
Weight and Shape 120g (4¼oz), cylinder	
Size D. 6cm (2½in), H. 4cm (1½in)	
Milk Goat	
Classification Soft white	
Producer Lubborn Creamery	

Cerney Pyramid

Handsome and fresh, this eye-catching cheese is made by hand from a recipe developed by Lady Angus of Cerney. It is a full-fat Valençay-type cheese, made using a unique starter culture. It is coated with oak ash and a sea salt mix, and shaped into a truncated pyramid.

TASTING NOTES Luxuriously smooth, with a creamy texture, it exudes a fresh, clean taste with floral notes. It is far milder than expected from a goat's cheese, but develops as it matures.

HOW TO ENJOY A striking addition to the cheeseboard, this black-and-white truncated pyramid is heavenly with biscuits and a dry white wine.

ENGLAND South Cerney, Gloucestershire	
Age 1 month	
Weight and Shape 250g (9oz), pyramid	
Size D. 6cm (2½in), H. 4cm (1½in)	
Milk Goat	
Classification Fresh	
Producer Cerney Cheese	

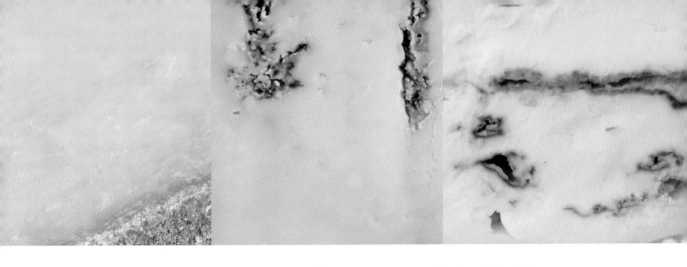

Cheshire

A cheese woven into the fabric of English history, Cheshire was mentioned in the Domesday Book. Since the cattle were grazed on salt marshes, the salt content caused the cheese to ripen slowly and gave it a crumbly texture. It is available in white, but most are coloured with annatto.

TASTING NOTES Dense, slightly dry with a very fine crumbly texture and a mild fresh acidity, Cheshire has a savoury, salty tang that lingers in the mouth.

HOW TO ENJOY Grill it (as in traditional Welsh Rarebit), bake it, crumble it in soups and salads, or marry it with a glass of real ale.

ENGLAND Cheshire, Shropshire, and Wales	
Age 2–6 months	
Weight and Shape 22kg (48½lb), cylinder	
Size D. 30cm (12in), H. 26cm (10½in)	
Milk Cow	
Classification Hard	
Producer Various	

Cornish Blue

In 2001 Philip and Carol Stansfield, looking for a way to diversify their dairy farm, spotted the gap in the market for a young blue cheese that could compete with imported blue cheese. This mild blue was the result, and the Stansfields have since won many awards.

TASTING NOTES With a creamy texture like Gorgonzola (see pp108–09) and thick streaks of blue, it is surprisingly mild and sweet, becoming spicier and tangier as it ages.

HOW TO ENJOY Perfect for pepping up – but not overpowering – risotto, sauces, appetizers, and more; it goes beautifully with fruit and a glass of Champagne.

ENGLAND Liskeard, Cornwall	
Age 14 weeks	
Weight and Shape 6kg (13¼lb), round	
Size D. 28cm (11in), H. 18cm (7in)	
Milk Cow	
Classification Blue	
Producer Cornish Cheese Company	

Cote Hill Blue

Michael and Mary Davenport started making cheese in October 2005, using milk produced by their herd of 70 Friesian, Holstein, and Red Poll cows. They make award-winning raw milk cheeses with an individuality that is unique to Cote Hill Farm.

TASTINGS NOTES Under the grey and white moulds, the interior is dense and creamy with horizontal blue streaks. It is mild, spicy with a subtle crescendo of cocoa, peppery dandelions, and salt.

HOW TO ENJOY Mary's friends have persuaded her to put her recipe for Cote Hill Blue and spring onion scones on their website–they are the best.

ENGLAND Lincolnshire	
Age 8–10 weeks	
Weight and Shape 1.2 kg (2¾lb), round	
Size D. 19.5cm (8in), H. 4.5cm (2in)	
Milk Cow	
Classification Blue	
Producer Cote Hill Farm	

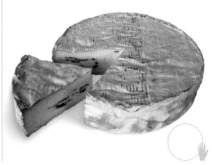

Cotherstone

Cotherstone and similar cheeses were once common in the wild and beautiful Pennines, but today, at Quarry Farm on the banks of the river Tees, Joan Cross is the only remaining producer of this cheese, thanks to a recipe handed down to her by her mother.

TASTING NOTES Cotherstone's interior is pale yellow, moist, crumbly, and fatty, and it luxuriates in a buttery richness of flavour that is edged with a fruity tang on the finish.

HOW TO ENJOY The signature tanginess goes well with a variety of wines, but in the Dales they favour a glass of dark stout as the requisite accompaniment.

ENGLAND Teesdale, Durham
Age 1–3 months
Weight and Shape 500g–3kg (1lb 2oz–6⅗lb), millstone
Size D. 7.5–22cm (3–8½in), H. 7.5cm (3in)
Milk Cow
Classification Hard
Producer Cotherstone Cheese

Curworthy

With its own natural rind or, more strikingly, a black wax coating, the traditional Curworthy is based on a 17th-century cheese and uses milk from the farm's herd of Friesian cows. The cheese is one of six varieties produced by Rachel Stephens at Stockbeare Farm in Devon.

TASTING NOTES The texture is dense and chewy, with a lovely buttery feel when young, and maturing into a more tangy, peppery flavour.

HOW TO ENJOY Ideal on a cheeseboard, or serve with an Alsace Gewürztraminer, which will complement Curwothy's young, buttery flavour.

ENGLAND Okehampton, Devon
Age 2–6 months
Weight and Shape 450g–2.2kg (1-5lb), drum
Size D. 9–20cm (3½–8in), H. 6–10cm (2½–4in)
Milk Cow
Classification Hard
Producer Curworthy Cheese

Daylesford Cheddar

Created in 2001 using organic milk from the Bamfords Estate in the Cotswolds, it is made in a modern creamery alongside the hugely successful and very elegant Daylesford Organic Farmshop. Now one of a range of award winning organic cheeses.

TASTING NOTES Hard yet chewy, this has a rich full-bodied tang that mellows out to a savoury lingering finish that hints of green grass and red onions

HOW TO ENJOY Versatile in cooking, but it also stands proud on any cheeseboard paired with a not-too-tannic red wine, such as a Pinot Noir or Merlot.

ENGLAND Daylesford, Gloucestershire
Age 9–18 months
Weight and Shape 9kg (20lb), truckle
Size D. 25cm (10in), H. 40cm (16in)
Milk Cow
Classification Hard
Producer Daylesford Organic Creamery

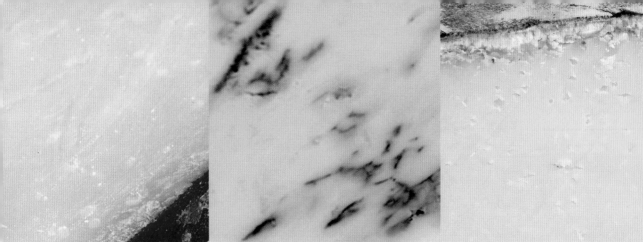

Doddington

Made at Doddington Dairy, situated at the bottom of the Cheviot Hills, this cheese is described by its makers Neill and Jackie Maxwell as lying somewhere between a Leicester and Cheddar. They have been making ice cream and cheeses since 1990 after learning their craft in the Netherlands and France.

TASTING NOTES It has an attractive brick-red rind and a hard, compact, slightly dry texture, with a rich, sweet caramel taste and a long-lasting nuttiness.

HOW TO ENJOY Serve with fruit and nuts, wrapped in warm bread, or grated over salads or pasta, along with a medium-bodied red wine such as a Merlot.

ENGLAND Wooler, Northumberland	
Age 12–14 months	
Weight and Shape 5kg and 10kg, drum	
Size: D. 23cm (9in) and 32cm (12½in), H. 11cm (4⅓in)	
Milk Cow	
Classification Hard	
Producer Doddington Dairy	

Dorset Blue Vinny

Once upon a time, every self-respecting Dorset farmhouse made this cheese – an excellent use for milk left over from making butter. But with changing times, the recipe itself nearly died out, until Mike Davies revived it in the 1980s. He makes it with a combination of skimmed and full milk so it is more moist than the original.

TASTING NOTES As it is unpasteurized and the butterfat content of the milk varies according to the time of year, this cheese is sometimes crumbly and sometimes creamy. It is nutty but not too strong.

HOW TO ENJOY Try with traditional Dorset knob biscuits and a sweet cider.

ENGLAND Stock Gaylard, Dorset	
Age 12–14 weeks	
Weight and Shape 6kg (13lb), round	
Size D. 25cm (10in), H. 30cm (12in)	
Milk Cow	
Classification Blue	
Producer Woodbridge Farm	

Double Gloucester

This iconic cheese can be traced back to the 15th century, when Severn Vale farmers made it from famed Cotswold ewe's milk. Gradually, milk from Gloucester cows replaced it, giving it a superb even texture. Today, it is made throughout England, but not necessarily with Gloucester milk.

TASTING NOTES This hard cheese has a leathery rind and a savoury, mellow flavour. It is made with full-fat milk and coloured deep orange with annatto seeds.

HOW TO ENJOY Eat plain, cook with it, or watch it being rolled down Coopers Hill in Gloucester in May, as per tradition.

ENGLAND All over	
Age Around 4 months	
Weight and Shape Various, wheel	
Size Various	
Milk Cow	
Classification Hard	
Producer Various	

Cheddar

The story of Cheddar can be traced back to the Romans who introduced hard cheeses to England. It was the medieval feudal system, however, that led to the development of the large, buxom traditional British cheeses, because it placed the majority of land in the hands of a few great landowners who could afford to make very large cheeses.

It was not until the 16th century that this hard cheese made in the Mendip Hills near the Cheddar Gorge in Somerset became known as Cheddar. The lush grazing, rolling hills and natural caves offered the ideal conditions for large herds thus the cheesemakers tended to make huge 27–54kg (60–120lb) cheeses requiring 2–3 years to mature.

The lush green *pastures of England's West Country, where Cheddar is situated.*

Since then, it has been emulated throughout the world, especially in Canada, Australia, and New Zealand where the majority is made in blocks rather than elegant clothbound cylinders. But only those made from cows that graze the green and verdant hills of England truly deserve the name Cheddar.

England Dorset, Devon, Somerset	
Age 6–24 months	
Weight and Shape 26kg (56lb), cylinder or block	
Size D. 32cm (12½in), H. 26cm (10½in)	
Milk Cow	
Classification Hard	
Producer Various	

TASTING NOTES To taste an unpasteurized, clothbound Cheddar made from the milk of cows whose diet is fresh grass, clover, buttercups, and daisies, is to taste a piece of England. The bite is firm but yielding like chocolate, the aroma earthy and slightly savoury. The flavour differs from farm to farm, but there is always the rich sweetness of the milk, a classic acidity, sometimes nutty, often with an explosion of flavour in the mouth and a lingering cheese and onion tang.

HOW TO ENJOY For generations, Cheddar has been an integral part of the English diet, in sandwiches, as quick snacks, ploughman's lunches or as huge wedges on cheese platters, embellished with Cox's apples, pickled walnuts, and crusty bread. It is also superb in sauces, melted over baked potatoes, or grated over numerous vegetable dishes and grilled. Best with a Merlot or Pinot Noir.

FARMHOUSE CHEDDAR

Although Cheddar has improved in recent years, it can never achieve the same hardness and depth of flavour as those made by hand in 26kg rounds and aged in cloth like those listed below [R = made with raw milk from a single farm]

Barbers Farmhouse Cheese, Somerset
Belton Cheese, Shropshire
Cheddar Gorge Cheese, Somerset [R]
Cricketer Farm, Somerset
Ford Farm, Dorset
Goulds Chesemakers
Isle of Mull, Scotland [R]
Keen's, Somerset [R]
Lye Cross Farm, Somerset
Montgomery's, Somerset [R]
Quickes Traditional Cheeses, Devon [R]
Westcombe Cheddar, Somerset [R]

Exterior

A fine grey mould grows over the cheesecloth and reduces moisture loss so the cheese can develop its characteristic hard, dense, creamy texture and earthy aroma.

A CLOSER LOOK

Cheddar can be sold as young as six months, when it has a softer texture and mild, almost buttery taste. At 12 months, the texture is firmer, almost chewy, and the taste is more intense. At 18 months, the texture is drier, sometimes with crunchy calcium crystals and the flavour more savoury.

Wedge

CHEDDARING To create the unique texture of Cheddar, the mass of curds is moulded into brick-sized blocks and piled two bricks high. This process is repeated every 15–20 minutes until the bricks flatten out, the acidity rises, and more whey is forced out.

MILLING The flattened bricks are then milled or "minced" to finger-sized pieces and pitched by hand using giant forks to aerate and cool the curd before salting.

The interior is a soft sunshine butter-yellow colour with an orange tinge as it ages.

Interior

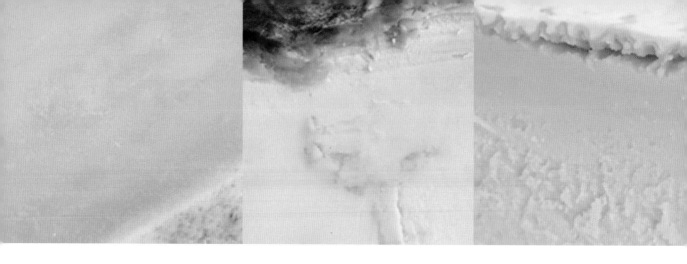

Duddleswell

You would expect a delicious cheese from a farm set in a region officially designated as an Area of Outstanding Natural Beauty. The Hardy family started High Weald Dairy in 1988, in the beautiful surroundings of Ashdown Forest; Duddleswell has echoes of traditional Dales cheeses, with all the nutritional benefits of ewe's milk.

TASTING NOTES Smooth and creamy with a sweet, nutty release, Duddleswell is a hard-pressed cheese with a thin and leathery natural rind.

HOW TO ENJOY Feature as part of a cheeseboard, or instead of pecorino; great with pasta or topping a salad.

ENGLAND Horsted Keynes, West Sussex
Age 3–4 months
Weight and Shape 3.2kg (7lb), truckle
Size D. 24cm (9½in), H. 7–8cm (2¾–3¼in)
Milk Ewe
Classification Hard
Producer High Weald Dairy

Exmoor Blue PGI

Ian Arnett makes a range of traditional handmade hard and soft blue-veined cheeses with vegetarian rennet, using local cow's, sheep's, goat's, and buffalo's milk. Exmoor Blue is the only one with PGI status, which means that it is made according to strict guidelines, including using local unpasteurized Jersey milk.

TASTING NOTES Balance is the key to this semi-soft blue veined cheese, where the zing of the blue still allows other subtle, mildly salty flavours to reach the palate.

HOW TO ENJOY Partake with simple appreciation on the cheeseboard and, if you can find it, Somerset cider brandy.

ENGLAND Taunton, Somerset
Age 4–5 weeks
Weight and Shape 500g (1lb 2oz) and 1.25kg (2¾lb), flat round
Size D. 12cm (4¾in) and 18cm (7in), H. 6cm (2½in)
Milk Cow
Classification Blue
Producer Exmoor Blue Cheese Company

Finn

Charlie Westhead, Haydn Roberts, and the team produce their cheeses in a dairy atop Dorstone Hill, with glorious views over the Wye Valley towards the Black Mountains. As with French double-cream cheeses, 10 per cent additional cream is added to the milk before the cheesemaking begins, giving it a creamy richness.

TASTING NOTES Inside its creamy-white rind lies a soft but firm cheese with a creamy acidity, a salty-sweet mingling, and a hint of mushrooms.

HOW TO ENJOY Bake with it, or savour the extra richness set off to perfection by the plainest of biscuits.

ENGLAND Dorstone, Herefordshire
Age 3 weeks
Weight and Shape 300g (10½oz), round
Size D. 10cm (4in), H. 5cm (2in)
Milk Cow
Classification Soft white
Producer Neal's Yard Creamery

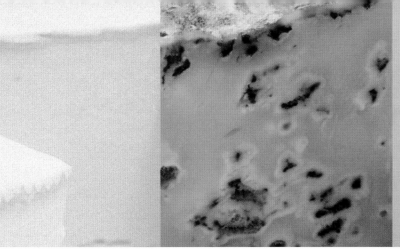

Flower Marie

Kevin and Alison Blunt produce this unique ewe's milk cheese, with its soft rind and moist interior that is often compared to the feel of melting ice cream. They have been making cheese on the farm since 1989; this one lives up to its name – demure-looking, but with a suggestion of naughtiness, captured in a lemony freshness.

TASTING NOTES: The sweetness of the ewe's milk lends a caramel subtlety that is gentle and moist, while the rind has a mushroomy taste and aroma.

HOW TO ENJOY Serve it spread on a chunk of fresh, soft crusty bread, accompanied by a glass of fine port.

ENGLAND Whitesmith, East Sussex	
Age 4–5 weeks	
Weight and Shape 200g (7oz), square	
Size D. 6cm (2½in), H. 5cm (2in)	
Milk Ewe	
Classification Soft white	
Producer Golden Cross Cheese Company	

Fort Grey

Made in the parish of Torteval, on Guernsey, a small ruggedly beautiful island in the English Channel, Fort Grey is named after a local Georgian coastal defence. Fenella Maddison was inspired first by Rick Stein's Food Heroes and then by the legendary Chris Ashby who invented the original recipe.

TASTING NOTES Small, round with splotches of blue-grey on the outside and blue streaks through the rich, buttery Guernsey yellow interior. Mild and spicy with a sea breeze salty edge.

HOW TO ENJOY Tastes best when paired with Brittany cider or a glass of sweet Monbazillac wine.

ENGLAND Channel Islands	
Age 5–8 weeks	
Weight and Shape 150g (5½oz), round	
Size D. 7cm (3in), H. 2cm (¾in)	
Milk Cow Guernsey	
Classification Blue	
Producer Torteval Cheese	

Fowlers Forest Blue

Fowlers can lay claim to the title of oldest cheesemaking family business in England, the keepers of cheesemaking secrets whispered down through the generations. They are also proud of the high-calcium water from the 300m (1,000-ft) borehole, which adds to the cheese's flavour and texture.

TASTING NOTES This is a handcrafted traditional blue cheese, which matures in humidity-controlled cellars. Soft-rinded, firm, and creamy, it is lightly veined, salty, and mildly tangy.

HOW TO ENJOY Melt together with Warwickshire ale and Worcestershire sauce, and spread on toast.

ENGLAND Earlswood, West Midlands	
Age 3 months	
Weight and Shape 5kg (11lb), cylinder	
Size D. 20cm (8in), H. 15cm (6in)	
Milk Cow	
Classification Blue	
Producer Fowlers of Earlswood	

Francis

Working for James Aldridge, affineur and wash rind legend, James McCall always knew he wanted to follow in his footsteps. After a decade or so of making cheese, he has returned to his passion, washing and maturing cheeses including this one made by Lyburn Cheese.

TASTING NOTES Pale pink, sticky rind, dense buttery texture and pungent, farmyardy, savoury notes with a brilliant balance of acidity and richness from the milk. It won Best New Cheese in 2012 proving James definitely has the touch.

HOW TO ENJOY Pair with a dry riesling, local cider or Trappist style beer, or have with local specialities like Dorset Knobs.

ENGLAND Dorset	
Age 6–8 weeks	
Weight and Shape 750g (1lb 10oz), drum	
Size D. 13cm (5in), H. 7cm (3in)	
Milk Cow	
Classification Semi-soft, washed	
Producer James's Cheese	

Golden Cross

Kevin and Alison Blunt's herd of 300 goats graze outside all summer and enjoys a diet of hay all year round, which contributes to continuing success at the British Cheese Awards. From their milk comes a St Maure-style cheese, each log lightly dusted with charcoal and matured to a creamy, full flavour.

TASTING NOTES Sweeter in taste than you might expect, it is soft and delicate, and redolent of those grassy pastures that the goats so enjoy.

HOW TO ENJOY Complemented well by celery on a cheeseboard, it is also an excellent cheese for all sorts of dishes, thanks to its gorgeous texture.

ENGLAND Whitesmith, East Sussex	
Age 3–4 weeks	
Weight and Shape 225g (8oz), log	
Size L. 14cm (5½in), H. 5cm (2in)	
Milk Goat	
Classification Soft white	
Producer Golden Cross Cheese Company	

Hereford Hop

The lightly roasted hops give this cheese its instantly recognizable appearance, but it is the skill of the almost-legendary Charles Martell that ensures the quality under the surface. He has also helped to preserve rare-breed Gloucester cattle and to revive interest in perry, which is like cider but made with fermented pears.

TASTING NOTES Mellow sweetness is thrown into relief by the aroma and taste of the cheese's coat of hops, with a hint of beer permeating through.

HOW TO ENJOY A delightful addition to the cheeseboard, particularly with a dollop of homemade apple chutney.

ENGLAND Dymock, Gloucestershire	
Age 10–12 weeks	
Weight and Shape 2.2kg (5lb), round	
Size D. 22cm (8½in), H. 7cm (2¾in)	
Milk Cow	
Classification Flavour-added	
Producer Charles Martell & Son	

Holy Smoked

Liz Godsell makes a range of handmade cheeses at Church Farm, in the village of Leonard Stanley, including Single Gloucester PDO, using milk from their farm. Her husband Bryan and the extended family help milk, and make, sell, and deliver the cheese.

TASTINGS NOTES It is a young single Gloucester slowly smoked over oak or beech chippings, so the woody smoky aromas are gradually absorbed by the cheese producing a flavour reminiscent of smoked bacon in a creamy onion sauce.

HOW TO ENJOY Smoked cheeses are best grilled on toast, generously grated into baked potato, or served with a cool beer.

ENGLAND Gloucestershire		
Age 4 months		
Weight and Shape 4kg (9lb), round		
Size D. 20cm (8in), H. 6cm (2in)		
Milk Cow		
Classification Flavour-added		
Producer Godsell's Artisan Cheese		

Innes Button

This tiny unpasteurized goat cheese, was the first cheese ever to win Supreme Champion twice at the British Cheese Awards. It is now a favourite of culinary gurus such as Anton Mosimann and Nigel Slater.

TASTING NOTES This is perfection itself – soft and almost mousse-like, it melts in the mouth, releasing its lemony freshness with hints of walnuts and white wine on the finish. Available with ash, pink peppercorns, chopped nuts, and herbs (pictured).

HOW TO ENJOY Savour on its own, spread on soft, warm bread, or grill and serve with a Sauvignon Blanc or Viognier.

ENGLAND Tamworth, Staffordshire		
Age 3–7 days		
Weight and Shape 50g (1¾oz), button		
Size D. 5cm (2in), H. 2.5cm (1in)		
Milk Goat		
Classification Fresh		
Producer Innes Cheese		

Isle of Wight Blue

Guernsey cows that munch on the riches of the Isle of Wight's fertile Arreton Valley help to give this tangy yet mellow cheese its creamy texture. Richard Hodgson gave up a career as a film editor to make cheese, while his mother, Julie, joined him after selling the family's small hotel.

TASTING NOTES It has a thick grey moulded rind, a mellow, nutty paste, which is smooth in texture with a slight spicy bite from the blue.

HOW TO ENJOY Simply enjoy it as it comes, as part of a cheeseboard, or layer it with slices of fresh pear for rather special party canapés.

ENGLAND Sandown, Isle of Wight		
Age 3–5 weeks		
Weight and Shape 230g (8oz), drum		
Size D. 9cm (3½in), H. 4.5cm (1¾in)		
Milk Cow		
Classification Blue		
Producer Isle of Wight Cheese Company		

Kearney Blue

Like many modern day cheeses, this was first made in a kitchen pot near Kearney Village, County Down. It is made from the milk obtained from a few local farms, carefully selected for its quality.

TASTINGS NOTES It has an attractive rustic blue grey rind and the deep yellow interior is buttery with scattered blue blotches. Also has a spicy tang with salty sea spray finish.

HOW TO ENJOY With a rich ruby porter style beer with lashings of hops and plenty of fruit and toffee from Whitewater, Northern Ireland's largest microbrewery.

ENGLAND County Down	
Age 4–6 weeks	
Weight and Shape 550g (1¼lb), round	
Size D. 11cm (4in), H. 5cm (2in)	
Milk Cow	
Classification Blue	
Producer Kearney Cheese Company	

Keltic Gold

Full of pungency and character all at the same time, this cheese from Sue Proudfoot is washed in brine three times a week with local cider until it is ripe. The resulting sticky terra-cotta rind should not be ignored, but instead form part of the pleasure of the eating.

TASTING NOTES Prepare to be deluged by layers of delicious notes, varying from bacon to yeast, with distinct nuttiness in between, and a farmyard finish.

HOW TO ENJOY Make a vegetarian version of a Cornish pasty with apple, onion, and sage wrapped around Keltic Gold, or melt it with a little freshly grated nutmeg for an alpine-style fondue.

ENGLAND Bude, Cornwall	
Age 4–6 weeks	
Weight and Shape 1.5kg (3lb 3oz), drum	
Size D. 20cm (8in), H. 7.5cm (3in)	
Milk Cow	
Classification Semi-soft	
Producer Whalesborough Farm Foods	

Lancashire

One of the great "territorial" cheeses of England, Lancashire comes in three main styles: creamy, tasty, and crumbly, the latter being fast-ripening and high-acidic, a more recent creation. Its history goes back as far as the 13th century, when every farmer's wife made use of surplus milk to make this.

TASTING NOTES Made by combining the curd from three consecutive days, it has a mottled appearance, soft, vaguely lumpy feel in the mouth, and buttery richness balanced by an oniony tang.

HOW TO ENJOY Its meltingly smooth, even consistency makes it ideal for anything from cheese on toast to tasty pies.

ENGLAND Around the Forest of Bowland, Lancashire	
Age 4–12 weeks for "creamy"; 12-plus weeks for "tasty"	
Weight and Shape 20kg (44lb), cylinder	
Size D. 31cm (12¼in), H. 23cm (9in)	
Milk Cow	
Classification Hard	
Producers Various	

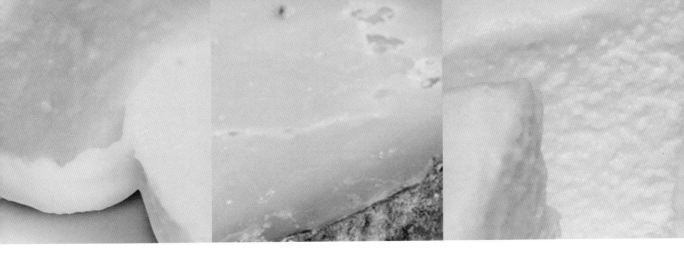

Laverstoke Ciliegine

Laverstoke Park Farm, an organic farm in Hampshire, was founded by former Formula One World Champion Jody Scheckter, who aimed whose aim is to become self-sustaining and self-sufficient. Using milk from over 1,500 water buffaloes, they make yogurt, ice cream, and cheeses from blue to Brie.

TASTINGS NOTES Bright white and glistening, these marble-sized balls of mozzarella have a soft, chicken breast texture. Distinct but delicious earthy notes are characteristics.

HOW TO ENJOY Served as canapés or in a salad with sundried tomatoes, basil, olive oil and balsamic vinegar.

ENGLAND Overton, Hampshire	
Age a few days	
Weight and Shape 10g (¼oz), ball	
Size D. 2cm (¾ in)	
Milk Buffalo	
Classification Fresh	
Producer Laverstoke Park Farm	

Lincolnshire Poacher

Once a traditional folk song, it is now also a cheese invented by Simon Jones and made with his brother, Tim. It was originally a brilliant solution to the abundant supplies of spring milk from their herd of Holsteins, and has become a much-loved modern British cheese. It was Supreme Champion at the British Cheese Awards in 1996.

TASTING NOTES This is similar to an excellent mature, Cheddar-style cheese. Hard and chewy, lively and complex, it offers a full taste experience.

HOW TO ENJOY Eat it plain, grate it, grill it, or bake it with onions, bacon, and potatoes for a fine gratin.

ENGLAND Alford, Lincolnshire	
Age 12–24 months	
Weight and Shape 20kg (44lb), cylinder	
Size D. 23cm (9in), H. 30cm (12in)	
Milk Cow	
Classification Hard	
Producer FW Read & Sons	

Little Ann

Made by Paul Thomas, with a fascination and knowledge of biochemistry, and partner and fellow cheesemaker Hannah Roche, who started Thimble Cheesemakers in 2013. Little Ann was their first, soon to be followed by others using raw milk.

TASTING NOTES Cabecou style, with a lovely creamy Geotricum rind and almost liquid interior that is yeasty with hints of fermenting fruit finishing with delicate, creamy notes.

HOW TO ENJOY This is best served grilled on sourdough bread drizzled with olive oil and paired with a Sancerre or Sancerre Rose.

ENGLAND West Worldham, Hampshire	
Age 10 days	
Weight and Shape 40g (1½oz), cylinder	
Size D. 5cm (2in), H. 1.5cm (½in)	
Milk Cow	
Classification Aged fresh	
Producer Thimble Cheesemakers	

Little Ryding

Previously made by Mary Holbrook of Timsbury, it is now made by the Bartlett brothers, to whom she sold her recipe after deciding to concentrate on goat cheeses. In 2004, using milk from their own flock, James and David's first cheese went on sale, to great applause.

TASTING NOTES Handmade with a Camembert-like rind and creamy middle, this is like a traditional British Sunday lunch on a plate, with flavours of burnt onions and roast lamb, and yet a caramel sweetness, too.

HOW TO ENJOY Serve simply with thin crackers and a side order of homemade caramelised onion chutney.

ENGLAND North Wootton, Somerset
Age 3–8 weeks
Weight and Shape 200g (7oz), round
Size D. 10cm (4in), H. 3cm (1¼in)
Milk Ewe
Classification Soft white
Producer Wootton Organic Dairy

Lord of the Hundreds

Radiating out from the hamlet of Stonegate are the slopes of the Rother Valley, a landscape that leaves clues of its many qualities within the subtleties of this cheese. Cheesemaker Cliff Dyball gave up a career in London as an insurance broker for rewards of a different kind.

TASTING NOTES It has a rustic, reddish-brown rind, that is dusted with grey mould, and has a compact density. Think pecorino; expect a dry, grainy texture, with mild nuttiness alongside a deep burnt caramel sweetness.

HOW TO ENJOY The maker recommends quince jelly as the perfect complement.

ENGLAND Stonegate, East Sussex
Age 6–8 months
Weight and Shape 2.5–4.8kg (5½–10½lb), square
Size D. 18–24cm (7–9½in), H. 7.5–11cm (3–4⅓in)
Milk Ewe
Classification Hard
Producer The Traditional Cheese Dairy

Mayfield

Arthur Alsop and Nicholas Walker started in 2008, using milk from the surrounding farms, making a wide range of cheeses, from Lord London, a soft cheese created to celebrate the 2012 Olympics, to the small Sussex Blue, to the elegant, Swiss-style Mayfield.

TASTINGS NOTES The sunshine yellow interior has large, oval holes and a supple texture. The aroma starts with fermenting fruit and white wine. There is a taste of wild honey, with a touch of nutmeg and an intensely fruity tang.

HOW TO ENJOY Pair with ciders to complement the fruity flavour or serve with a light beer and apple chutney.

ENGLAND Sussex
Age 5–7 months
Weight and Shape 16kg (35lb)–18kg (40lb), boulder
Size D. 40cm (16in), H. 12cm (4in)
Milk Cow
Classification Hard
Producer Alsop & Walker

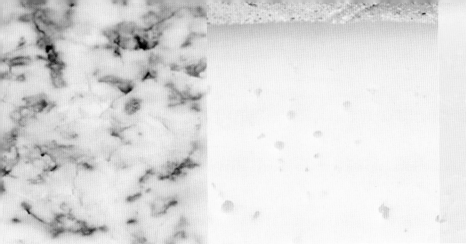

New Forest Blue

Gwyn and Ness Williams use pure Ayrshire milk from a herd grazed on the Hampshire Downs; it is, they say, "the best milk we have ever tasted, and fantastic for cheesemaking". The recipes for their cheeses – including this excellent example – are designed to bring out the milk's charmingly idiosyncratic characteristics.

TASTING NOTES It has a light blue touch, with an attractive sharpness from that extra blue tang.

HOW TO ENJOY Pep up risotto, crumble over salads, or savour the full taste of "Ayrshire" by serving this cheese as simply as possible.

ENGLAND Redlynch, Wiltshire	
Age 6–8 weeks	
Weight and Shape 1.5kg (3lb 3oz), cylinder	
Size D. 17cm (6¾in), H. 11cm (4½in)	
Milk Cow	
Classification Blue	
Producer Loosehanger Cheeses	

Norsworthy

Originally a naval engineer from Durham, Dave Johnson now has his own herd of 180 goats in Devon and makes a series of hard and soft cheeses. Based on a Dutch recipe, Norsworthy is made from unpasteurized milk using the Dutch washed-curd method.

TASTING NOTES Its pleasant and mild taste deepens and lingers. Matured for a month, it develops a fine crusty brown rind and a white paste within that becomes more crumbly as it ripens.

HOW TO ENJOY Delicious served with a chunk of fresh crusty country-style bread, accompanied by an English pale ale or a Merlot.

ENGLAND Norsworthy, Devon	
Age 1 month	
Weight and Shape 2.5kg (5½lb), round	
Size D. 18cm (7in), H. 11cm (4½in)	
Milk Goat	
Classification Semi-soft	
Producer Norsworthy Dairy Goats	

Northumberland

It was a book about sheep and their cheeses that first set Mark Robertson along the artisan cheese road in 1984, and he received so much support and encouragement that he ended up diversifying into goats and cows. During the years, he has taken inspiration from various sources.

TASTING NOTES This Gouda-style cheese, which is, moist, mild, and creamy, with hints of green grass and red onions is also available in flavoured versions.

HOW TO ENJOY It's the perfect choice for making traditional Northumberland pan haggerty, with its layers of potato, onion, and grated cheese.

ENGLAND Blagdon, Northumberland	
Age 12 weeks	
Weight and Shape 2.3kg (5lb), round	
Size D. 20cm (9in), H. 3cm (1¼in)	
Milk Cow	
Classification Hard	
Producer Northumberland Cheese Company	

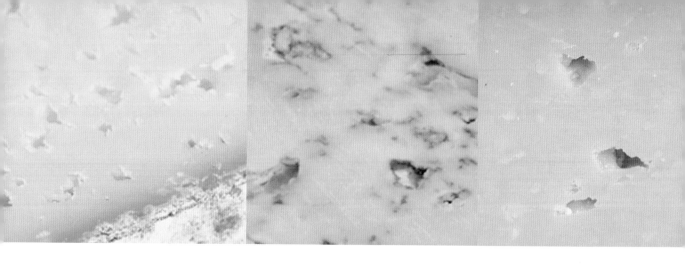

Ogleshield

When Cheddar cheesemaker Jamie Montgomery had two Americans to stay, they all spent some enjoyable hours using his Jersey milk in various "experiments". Thus Jersey Shield was born. Bill Oglethorpe at Neal's Yard Dairy then began another round of experiments, using the washed-rind technique to arrive at this cheese.

TASTING NOTES Beneath the sticky orange rind is a yellow heart with an aroma as robust as its flavour – onion soup and yeasty bread. A cheese to get to know.

HOW TO ENJOY Think of raclette; this is an excellent West Country alternative that melts like a dream.

ENGLAND North Cadbury, Somerset	
Age 4–5 months	
Weight and Shape 5kg (12¼lb), wheel	
Size D. 32cm (12½in), H. 9cm (3½in)	
Milk Cow	
Classification Semi-soft	
Producer JA & E Montgomery	

Old Sarum

With this dairy's cheeses, you know that the Ayrshire cow's milk will produce that characteristic smooth-as-velvet texture. Old Sarum comes in the form of a tall, elegant cylinder with a natural grey-brown rind, a moist interior, and blue-grey veins amid a yellow paste.

TASTING NOTES In the tradition of the Italian soft blue cheese Dolcelatte, this is a sweet-tasting blue that melts in the mouth like rich, spicy butter.

HOW TO ENJOY As an indulgent lunchtime treat, serve in a crusty baguette with crispy, preferably rare-breed bacon.

ENGLAND Redlynch, Wiltshire	
Age 6–8 weeks	
Weight and Shape 1.5kg (3lb 3oz), tall cylinder	
Size D. 17cm (6¾in), H. 11cm (4½in)	
Milk Cow	
Classification Blue	
Producer Loosehanger Cheeses	

Old Winchester

Mike and Judy Smales, who have been making their cheeses for eight years, came up with Old Winchester – still creamy, but with "subtle nuttiness" – to satisfy customers who were looking for a fuller-flavoured cheese. It is also known as Old Smales.

TASTING NOTES Old Winchester's hard, smooth crust protects the hard, almost brittle warm yellow interior, with its distinctive nuttiness and lasting salty-sweet finale.

HOW TO ENJOY Use as either a table cheese or a vegetarian alternative to hard Italian cheeses.

ENGLAND Landford, Wiltshire	
Age 16 months	
Weight and Shape 4kg (9lb), boulder	
Size D. 23cm (9in), H. 7.5cm (3in)	
Milk Cow	
Classification Hard	
Producer Lyburn Farmhouse Cheesemakers	

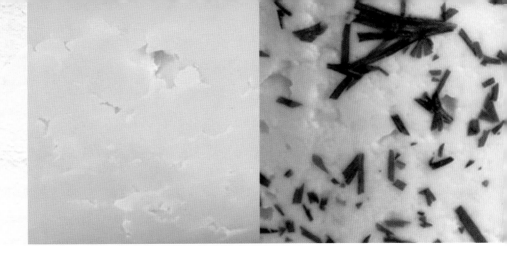

Pablo Cabrito

The Hamptons started making artisanal cheeses in 2008, using milk from their pure Saanen goats. Their passion and commitment to their work, and the quality of their milk results in outstanding cheeses such as this one.

TASTING NOTES The pale grey, soft, wrinkly rind smells mildly goaty like a classic French chèvre, while the interior is smooth, almost velvety as it melts in the mouth. It yields nutty notes and gentle fresh acidity on the finish.

HOW TO ENJOY Perfect on a cheeseboard, accompanied with a rosé or cider from Shropshire's own Wroxeter Vineyard.

ENGLAND Bridgnorth, Shropshire	
Age 2–3 weeks	
Weight and Shape 240g (9oz), log	
Size L. 15cm (6in), H. 5cm (2in)	
Milk Goat	
Classification Aged fresh	
Producer Brock Hall Farm	

Pendragon

Philip Rainbow, one of a handful of producers in Britain to use buffalo's milk, makes this firm Cheddar-style cheese. Pendragon takes its name from strong historical connections Somerset has with the Arthurian myths. It is also available lightly smoked.

TASTING NOTES The hard, waxy yellow paste has a mild sweetness and its understated character appeals to those who like a clean flavour. Being made with buffalo milk means that the cheese is admirably low in cholesterol.

HOW TO ENJOY Assemble a sophisticated cheeseboard, using Pendragon to give variety among cow's and goat's cheeses.

ENGLAND Ditcheat, Somerset	
Age 4–12 months	
Weight and Shape 2kg (4½lb) and 3.5kg (7½lb), round	
Size D. 18cm (7in) and 25cm (10in), H. 7cm (2¾in)	
Milk Buffalo	
Classification Hard	
Producer Somerset Cheese Company	

Perroche

These elegant cylinders, available plain or rolled in fresh herbs, use milk from a farm near Ashleworth in Gloucestershire. Although now produced by Charlie Westhead, Haydn Roberts, and their team, the cheese's name derives from the creamery's previous managers, Perry James and Beatrice Garroche.

TASTING NOTES The gentle process the cheese goes through results in a light, mousse-like texture with a subtle goaty taste and clean, almondy finish.

HOW TO ENJOY Delia Smith describes Perroche as a beautifully mild cheese that grills well.

ENGLAND Dorstone, Herefordshire	
Age 1 week	
Weight and Shape 150g (5½oz), cylinder	
Size D. 6cm (2½in) base, 5cm (2in) top, H. 7cm (2¾in)	
Milk Goat's milk	
Classification Fresh	
Producer Neal's Yard Creamery	

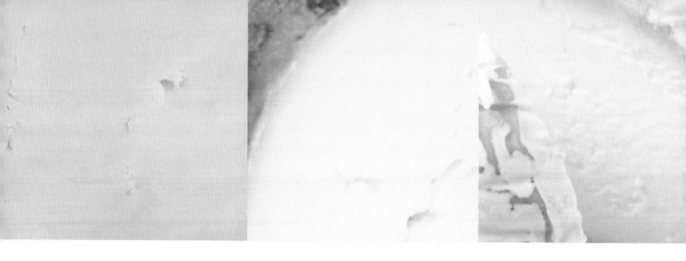

Quickes Hard Goat

The Quicke family has farmed the same land for more than 450 years. Aound 40 years ago, Sir John and his wife, Prue, built the dairy where their daughter Mary continues to produce cheese, including this recently created Cheddar-style goat cheese.

TASTING NOTES Firm, almost chewy, it has a subtle goaty taste and an aromatic, almondy tang with a fresh acidity. This is an excellent alternative for people with an allergy to cow's milk.

HOW TO ENJOY This cooks superbly. Try wilting nettle tops or similar greens in a little water, add with the cheese to a roux of rice flour and milk, then purée.

ENGLAND Newton St Cyres, Devon
Age 6–10 months
Weight and Shape 24kg (53lb), truckle
Size D. 35.5cm (14in), H. 30cm (12in)
Milk Goat
Classification Hard
Producer Quickes Traditional

Rachel

Peter Humphries makes two washed-rind cheeses: Morn Dew, with cow's milk, and this one, made with goat's milk. It looks distinguished, with its fine orange leathery rind, dusted with white, grey, and even yellow moulds – it is the most popular cheese he produces.

TASTING NOTES Rachel is sweet, curvy, and slightly nutty, with a whole raft of taste experiences: rich, tangy, meaty, and savoury. It has a citric sharpness with a sweet nutty finish.

HOW TO ENJOY Savour on its own or in a salad, paired with a glass of Sancerre or a single-varietal cider.

ENGLAND Pylle, Somerset
Age 3 months
Weight and Shape 2kg (4½lb), round
Size D. 18cm (7in), H. 7cm (2¾in)
Milk Goat
Classification Semi-soft
Producer White Lake Cheeses

Ragstone

Another great cheese from Charlie Westhead, Ragstone was originally made in his first creamery based near Sevenoaks in Kent, and it was the nearby Ragstone Ridge that lent its name to this cheese.

TASTING NOTES The wrinkly rind will call to mind a Brie, and it is certainly a lovely-looking product. Creamy yet light on the tongue, it has a hint of mushroomy notes and a lemony tang.

HOW TO ENJOY This is an excellent grilling cheese. Alternatively, bake in the oven, drizzled with a little olive oil, until it is at its melting point. Serve warm and oozy on a bed of mixed leaves.

ENGLAND Dorstone, Herefordshire
Age 3 weeks
Weight and Shape 300g (10½oz), log
Size L. 15cm (6in), H. 5cm (2in)
Milk Goat
Classification Soft white
Producer Neal's Yard Creamery

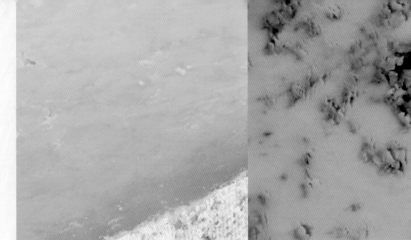

Ravens Oak Wood

Ravens Oak Wood is made at Ravens Oak Dairy, which is now owned by Butlers Farmhouse Cheeses. It is still made by hand at the dairy, however, in small batches to ensure that it retains its smooth, soft texture and farmhouse character.

TASTING NOTES Smooth and soft with a white mould rind, it has a subtle almond flavour when young. This develops into a deeper goaty tang as the cheese ripens.

HOW TO ENJOY Try baking it until it's creamy on the outside but still cool on the inside. If you want the untainted hit of goat, leave to ripen until gooey.

ENGLAND Burland, Cheshire	
Age 6–8 weeks	
Weight and Shape 150g (5½oz), round	
Size D. 7.5cm (3in), H. 4cm (1½in)	
Milk Goat	
Classification Soft white	
Producer Ravens Oak Dairy	

Red Leicester

Named after the city of Leicester, this traditional English cheese is made in a similar way to Cheddar, but coloured with annatto. Prolific by the late 18th century, its quality was partly ascribed to the county's excellent grazing. Farmhouse production in the county had died out by the mid-1900s, until 2005 when the Leicestershire Handmade Cheese Company revived it.

TASTING NOTES The distinctive tangerine-coloured interior is dense, waxy, and smooth, with a sweet, mellow nuttiness that strengthens as it matures.

HOW TO ENJOY Serve on toast or in tarts, or use to add colour to a cheeseboard.

ENGLAND Leicestershire	
Age 4–5 months	
Weight and Shape 10kg (22lb) and 20kg (44lb), wheel	
Size D. 35.5cm (14in) and 46cm (18in), H. 13cm (5in) and 18cm (7in)	
Milk Cow	
Classification Hard	
Producers Various	

Remembered Hills

Made in batches of only 4 cheeses using milk from the Earl of Plymouth's Oakly Park Estate, it beat off 84 British blues to win Best Blue at the 2013 British Cheese Awards. It takes its name from a line in the famous poem "Shropshire Lad" about the blue remembered hills at Shropshire.

TASTINGS NOTES It takes 3 months to mature on beech racks and develop its sticky blue-black rind, thick blue internal streaks, smooth texture, and lively spicy tang with cocoa notes to finish.

HOW TO ENJOY Drizzle it with honey and serve with Mahorall Farm Cider and bread from the well stocked Ludlow Food Centre deli.

ENGLAND Nr Ludlow, Shropshire	
Age 12–15 weeks	
Weight and Shape 10 kg(22lb), cylinder	
Size D. 25cm(10in), H. 23cm (9in)	
Milk Cow	
Classification Blue	
Producer Ludlow Food Centre Cheese	

Stilton PDO

In the early 18th century, the town of Stilton was a major staging post on the London to York road, and the landlord of the Bell Inn in Stilton started serving a soft, blue-veined cheese made in the nearby Leicestershire town of Melton Mowbray.

Such was the popularity of the cheese that Cooper Thornhill, the enterprising landlord, was soon sending Stilton to London, upwards of a thousand a week by the mid-1700s. The cheese was therefore named after the place from which it was made famous, rather than where it was made.

Initially made on small farms, the intricate and time-consuming nature of its production soon influenced Stilton-makers to join forces, and in 1875 the first Stilton was produced by hand in a small factory. In 1910 the Stilton Makers Association was registered as a Trademark, ensuring the cheese could only be made in the counties of Nottinghamshire, Derbyshire, and Leicestershire, and this decision ultimately saved the cheese from mediocrity or even extinction – the fate of other fine British territorial cheeses.

Today, Stilton is one of a handful of British cheeses granted Protected Designation of Origin (PDO) status by the European Commission (see p8). There are just six dairies in the whole country licensed to make Stilton. Colston Basset Dairy and Cropwell Bishop in Nottinghamshire, Long Clawson, Tuxford & Tebbutt, and Websters Dairy in Leicestershire, and Harrington Dairy in Derbyshire, which has granted Stilton accreditation in 2014.

TASTING NOTES Each maker's cheese is slightly different, but all are sharp and aggressive when eaten too young and mellow out to a rich, spicy butter taste with hints of cocoa on the finish and sometimes a touch of walnuts or a slight sharp acidity.

HOW TO ENJOY Ideal for sauces, dressings, and soups, especially broccoli or celery soup, baked in a quiche or tart paired with spinach or crumbled over a grilled steak, or into a salad with a sweet balsamic dressing.

The sweet richness of vintage Port can overpower Stilton. Instead, try a tawny Port or a crisp yet sweet wine like Montbazillac, but not Sauternes, which is too sweet. Alternatively try an aromatic dry Riesling or light beer.

The tradition of pouring Port into Stilton came about to kill the creatures that gathered at the bottom of Stilton bells. Nowadays, with modern refrigeration, there is no need to spoil the Stilton or waste good Port.

The Bell Inn, *which is in the town of Stilton, Peterborough, England.*

ENGLAND Nottinghamshire, Derbyshire, and Leicestershire	
Age 9–14 weeks	
Weight and Shape 7.5 kg (17lb), tall cylinder	
Size D. 20cm (8in), H. 30cm (12in)	
Milk Cow	
Classification Blue	
Producer Various	

A CLOSER LOOK

To create the smooth buttery texture characteristic of Stilton, the freshly drained curds are left to ripen overnight, significantly longer than most other cheeses.

Jagged blue lines radiate erratically from the centre to the outside, like shattered porcelain.

SALTING The curd is milled before being measured into special pans so the salt can be mixed thoroughly by hand.

MOULDING The curds are placed in tall, open-ended, stainless steel, cylindrical moulds and placed on wooden slates where gravity and the weight of the curd gradually force out whey through the holes in the sides of the hoops and through the bottom. Some 77 litres (17 gallons) of milk are required to make one 7.5kg (15lb) Stilton. Once the cheese can stand on its own, it is removed and the curds allowed to drain overnight.

PIERCING At about 6 weeks, each cheese is placed on a special stand and pierced with 18–20 long, narrow stainless steel needles to allow air to enter the body of the cheese.

GRADING Before being released to the retailers, each batch is graded. An "iron" is used to bore into the cheese and extract a plug. By visual inspection and by smell, the grader can determine whether the cheese is up to the mark.

Quarter cylinder

The interior should be straw yellow, not brown or dull.

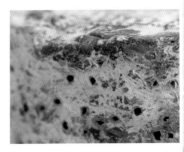

The rind is dry, rough, and crusty, with the pierced holes quite visible.

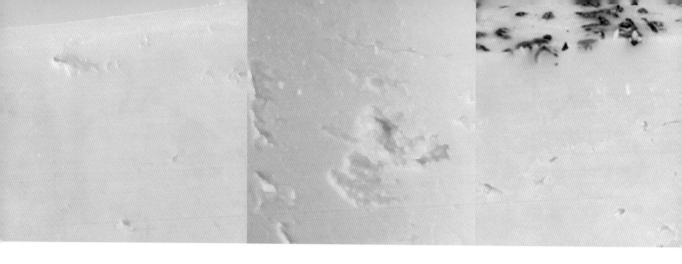

Ribblesdale Original Goat

The late Iain Hill and his wife Christine created this fresh, delicate cheese, and niece Iona now carries on their work. It is made in the Yorkshire Dales' Ribble Valley, where the natural pastures and high rainfall provide excellent grazing for the goats.

TASTING NOTES This cheese has a texture that is similar to a young Gouda and a pale wax cover that conceals a bright white interior.

HOW TO ENJOY Serve on its own, grate it, grill it, or, above all, bake it with figs. Works well with Chardonnay or Merlot.

ENGLAND Horton-in-Ribblesdale, North Yorkshire	
Age 8–12 weeks	
Weight and Shape 2kg (4½lb), boulder	
Size D. 20cm (8in), H. 6cm (2½in)	
Milk Goat	
Classification Hard	
Producer Ribblesdale Cheese Company	

Rosary Plain

Chris and Claire Moody began making cheese in 1986, originally using milk from their own small herd of goats. As they became more successful, however, the pair made the pragmatic decision to buy milk from a herd of pedigree Saanen goats. Their fresh cheese Rosary Plain is a consistent award-winner at the British Cheese Awards.

TASTING NOTES Moist, fresh, meltingly soft, and delightfully aromatic, it also comes flavoured in garlic and herb, pepper-coated, and ash-coated versions.

HOW TO ENJOY Use as a table cheese, for melting or spreading, or add it at the last moment to get a fluffy omelette.

ENGLAND Landford, Wiltshire	
Age 3 days	
Weight and Shape 100g (3½oz), round	
Size D. 5cm (2in), H. 4cm (1½in)	
Milk Goat	
Classification Fresh	
Producer Rosary Goats Cheese	

Sage Derby

Derby is one of England's oldest and most famous cheeses. The custom of adding finely chopped sage, thought to have health-giving properties, to the fresh curd began in the 17th century. Today, most are factory-made, but the West Midlands family producer, Fowlers of Earlswood, still makes Sage Derby traditionally.

TASTING NOTES Softer than Cheddar, this pale yellow cheese has a melted butter taste and a delightful, but subtle, herbal flavour from the sage.

HOW TO ENJOY With its ribbon of herbs, this makes a colourful and distinctive addition to the cheeseboard.

ENGLAND West Midlands	
Age 10–20 weeks	
Weight and Shape 1.5kg (3lb 3oz), round	
Size D. 20cm (8in), H. 10cm (4in)	
Milk Cow	
Classification Flavour-added	
Producers Various	

194

St Eadburgha

The Staceys have farmed at the foot of the Cotswolds for more than 35 years, and named this Camembert-style cheese after the great-granddaughter of Alfred the Great, to whom a local church is dedicated. It is made from the milk of Montbeliarde and Friesian cows that graze in pear orchards and on lush, grassy pastures.

TASTING NOTES This is at its best when it is soft in the middle and the flavour becomes more pungent and meaty.

HOW TO ENJOY It is delicious when warmed until the inside starts to run, or on the cheeseboard with cider, a light ale, or a full-bodied red wine.

ENGLAND Broadway, Worcestershire	
Age 4–12 weeks	
Weight and Shape 175g–3kg (6oz–6½lb), round	
Size D. 9–35cm (3½–13¾in), H. 4cm (1½in)	
Milk Cow	
Classification Soft white	
Producer Gorsehill Abbey Farm	

St Endellion

Started by two farming families in 1996, the creamery – which overlooks the rugged Atlantic coast – has made a name for itself with its innovative approach to cheesemaking. This is a Brie-style cheese made with Cornish double cream.

TASTING NOTES Luxury is the keynote here. As the cheese ripens, the paste softens to a wonderful creamy consistency with a full-bodied flavour, fresh tanginess, and hint of mushroom.

HOW TO ENJOY Leave loosely wrapped for a couple of hours before serving as part of a cheeseboard. It is especially good with a spicy white wine.

ENGLAND Trevarrian, Cornwall	
Age 6 weeks	
Weight and Shape 200g (7oz) and 1kg (2lb 3oz), round	
Size D. 20cm (8in) and 90cm (35½in), H. 3cm (1in) and 3.5cm (1½in)	
Milk Cow	
Classification Soft white	
Producer Cornish Country Larder	

St Oswald

This cheese, another from Mike Stacey who makes St Eadburgha, is named after a former Bishop of Worcester. It is washed in brine and matured for at least one month, and the rind changes from yellow to a sticky orange-brown as it matures. St Oswald is the latest addition to this dairy's repertoire.

TASTING NOTES The smooth, supple paste becomes almost runny and has a full, rich meaty flavour, with onion notes that become stronger as it ages.

HOW TO ENJOY Serve as it comes with a good full-bodied red wine and dried fruit, or put a few dollops in among finely sliced potatoes, then bake.

ENGLAND Broadway, Worcestershire	
Age 1–3 months	
Weight and Shape 350g (12oz) and 2.5kg (5½lb), round	
Size D. 11cm (4½in) and 35cm (13¾in), H. 4.5cm (1¾in)	
Milk Cow	
Classification Semi-soft	
Producer Gorsehill Abbey Farm	

St Swithin's with Lavender

The Nortons have farmed at Frettenham since 1946, using milk from mostly brown Swiss cows to make double cream and a fresh soft cheese called St Swithin's after the local church. It is sold either plain, or topped with lavender or apricot.

TASTINGS NOTES This cheese, tied up with lilac raffia, has a refreshing citrusy tang with mild, creamy back notes, as it melts in the mouth.

HOW TO ENJOY Spread on soft ciabatta and serve with an apple cider, wheat beer, or a luscious Oloroso sherry, which brings out the lavender aroma.

ENGLAND Norfolk	
Age a few days	
Weight and Shape 100 gm (3½oz), round	
Size D. 7cm(2¾in), H 3cm (1in)	
Milk Cow	
Classification Fresh	
Producer Nortons Dairy	

Sharpham Rustic

One of several cheeses produced on an estate that is also famous for its wines, Rustic is made using sweet, rich milk from the Jersey herd. The curd is placed, unpressed, in a colander which gives the cheese its unusual shape and knobbly rind. It is also available flavoured.

TASTING NOTES Deep yellow with a natural mould-coated rind, this moist cheese has a wonderful creamy texture and a buttery sweet flavour balanced by a fresh, gentle acidity.

HOW TO ENJOY Serve on its own, crumbled over warm asparagus or into a roast beetroot and pea shoot salad, with a glass of cider or fruity red wine.

ENGLAND Totnes, Devon	
Age 6–8 weeks	
Weight and Shape 1.7kg (3¾lb), elliptical	
Size D. 18cm (7in), H. 9cm (3½in)	
Milk Cow	
Classification Semi-soft	
Producer Sharpham Partnership	

Shipcord

Suffolk is not traditionally known as a cheesemaking region, so when the Richards family, who were dairy farmers, decided to start cheesemaking in 2006, local cheese lovers greeted them enthusiastically. Each cheese is named after a river meadow on the farm.

TASTING NOTES The curds and whey are scalded, reminiscent of French tommes, giving the cheese a close texture and a "long" creamy amd nutty flavour that develops a tangy acidity as it matures.

HOW TO ENJOY Its creamy texture makes it a perfect snacking cheese, along with crackers, celery, apple, or grapes, but Shipcord also melts and grills well.

ENGLAND Baylham, Suffolk	
Age 6–12 months	
Weight and Shape 4.3–4.8kg (9½–10½lb), wheel	
Size D. 25cm (10in), H. 10cm (4in)	
Milk Cow	
Classification Hard	
Producer Rodwell Farm Dairy	

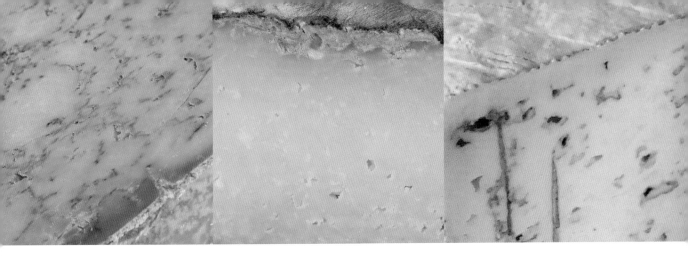

Shropshire Blue

Rather oddly named, as it was actually first created in Inverness, Scotland, in 1970, this cheese is based on the recipe for Stilton with the addition of annatto to give it its attractive mandarin orange colour. It was eventually adopted by the Stilton makers.

TASTING NOTES Milder than Stilton, but equally creamy in texture, its streaks of blue stand out against the orange interior. There is a hint of caramel sweetness behind its spicy, blue tang.

HOW TO ENJOY Spectacular crumbled into salads or melted in soups, this cheese is equally at home on a cheeseboard, with an accompanying port or brown ale.

ENGLAND Leicestershire and Nottinghamshire	
Age 10–13 weeks	
Weight and Shape 7.5kg (17½lb), cylinder	
Size D. 20cm (8in), H. 30cm (12in)	
Milk Cow	
Classification Blue	
Producers Various	

Single Gloucester PDO

One of the few English cheeses with Protected Designation of Origin (PDO), it was rescued from extinction by Charles Martell of Stinking Bishop fame. Traditionally, evening milk was skimmed to make butter, then mixed with full milk the next morning to make the cheese. Producers must have at least one Gloucester cow.

TASTING NOTES Firm but yielding, it has a mild, buttery flavour, with subtle hints of vanilla and nuts, and a gentle acidity.

HOW TO ENJOY Best enjoyed with apples or pears and pickled walnuts, served with perry, a traditional pear cider.

ENGLAND Gloucestershire	
Age 2–3 months	
Weight and Shape 2.25kg (5lb), wheel	
Size D. 22cm (8½in), H. 7cm (2¾in)	
Milk Cow	
Classification Hard	
Producers Various	

Smelly Ha'peth

Sean Wilson took to cheesemaking with the same commitment he showed as Martin Platt in Coronation Street. Passionate about all things local he named his cheeses after old Lancashire sayings - "How's yer Father", "Mouth Almighty" and "Smelly Ha'Peth"–a child covered in muck after a full day's play.

TASTINGS NOTES A sticky, grey-blue crust with chunky blue streaks and smoky notes wafting through the crumbly interior that is both sweet and nutty with a spicy tang on the finish.

HOW TO ENJOY A full bodied red wine would complement this cheese perfectly.

ENGLAND Manchester	
Age 8 weeks	
Weight and Shape 600 gm (1lb5oz), round	
Size D. 11cm (4in), H.5cm (2in),estimate	
Milk Cow	
Classification Blue	
Producer Saddleworth Cheese Co	

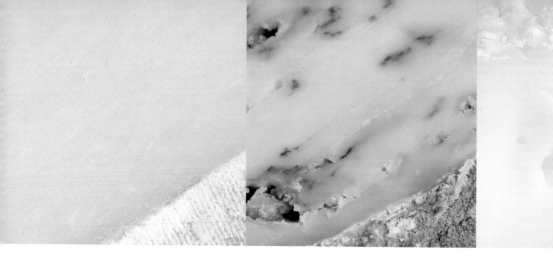

Snodsbury Goat

A joint venture in 2005, between Juliet Harbutt and the Anstey's, this goats cheese is based on Double Gloucester. It is now made by leading cheese wholesalers, Cheese Cellar who bought the recipe and the dairy from Anstey's.

TASTING NOTES Dense with a smooth creaminess, it has a distinct almondy nuttiness rather than the more distinct goaty taste you find in softer goat cheeses, with hints of chicory and wild herbs on the finish.

HOW TO ENJOY Serve on biscuits with some home-made pickle, or grate over salads and soups.

ENGLAND Worcester, Worcestershire	
Age 4–6 months	
Weight and Shape 1.8kg (4lb), drum	
Size D. 20cm (8in), H. 10cm (4in)	
Milk Goat	
Classification Hard	
Producer Cheese Cellar	

Stichelton

Stichelton, the original name for the village of Stilton, provided leading cheesemaker Joe Schneider with his inspiration for this cheese. After his success with Daylesford Cheddar, he set up his own dairy in 2006 to make a blue. It's based on the Stilton recipe, but cannot be called Stilton because it is made with raw milk.

TASTING NOTES Creamy white in colour with bold blue streaks, Stichelton is complex and delicious, and moves from a fruitiness to a spicy sweetness, all carried within a creamy texture.

HOW TO ENJOY Serve on the cheeseboard with biscuits and a glass of port.

ENGLAND Cuckney, Nottinghamshire	
Age 12–14 weeks	
Weight and Shape 7kg (15½lb), cylinder	
Size D. 20cm (8in), H. 30cm (12½in)	
Milk Cow	
Classification Blue	
Producer Stichelton Dairy	

Stinking Bishop

Named after an old variety of pear used to make the perry (pear cider) in which the cheese is washed, Stinking Bishop was created by Charles Martell in 1972. It has become one of the best-known and most-loved English washed rind cheeses, and is even featured in one of Nick Park's Wallace and Gromit films.

TASTING NOTES Rich and meaty, with a hint of sweetness, it is milder than the smell suggests. The supple paste and sticky golden rind are encapsulated in a thin band of wood.

HOW TO ENJOY Ideal on the cheeseboard with pears and a robust red wine.

ENGLAND Dymock, Gloucestershire	
Age 5–8 weeks	
Weight and Shape 500g (1lb 2oz) and 1.5kg (3lb 3oz), round	
Size D. 13cm (5in) and 21cm (8¼in), H. 4.5cm (1¾in) and 5cm (2in)	
Milk Cow	
Classification Semi-soft	
Producer Charles Martell & Son	

Suffolk Gold

Creamy milk from this family-run dairy's small herd of pedigree Guernsey cows (with names such as Madge and Armilla) is used to make this cheese, which is lightly pressed and aged to develop a golden rind. Established in 2004, the dairy also produces, a soft white, blue, and fresh cheeses.

TASTING NOTES The high butterfat content in the Guernsey milk comes through in the mild sweetness and deep yellow colour, while the texture is firm with a few small holes.

HOW TO ENJOY Perfect with oatcakes and an apple or melted under the grill.

ENGLAND Coddenham, Suffolk	
Age 10–12 weeks	
Weight and Shape 3kg (6½lb), wheel	
Size D. 20cm (8in), H. 5cm (2in)	
Milk Cow	
Classification Semi-soft	
Producer Suffolk Farmhouse Cheeses	

Sussex Slipcote

The name derives from an old English word meaning a "little" (slip) piece of "cottage" (cote) cheese, and the organic milk used to make it comes from farms selected by this dairy, which is on the edge of Ashdown Forest. Traditionally made with cow's milk, it is given a sweeter taste here with ewe's milk. It comes in different flavours, including garlic and herb, and peppercorn.

TASTING NOTES This very moist, almost mousse-like cheese has a lemony fresh tang that finishes with sweet notes.

HOW TO ENJOY It's best spread on bread or biscuits, but also a good addition to a baked jacket potato or pasta.

ENGLAND Horsted Keynes, West Sussex	
Age 10 days	
Weight and Shape 100g (3½oz), button	
Size D. 5.5cm (2¼in), H. 4.5cm (1¾in)	
Milk Ewe	
Classification Fresh	
Producer High Weald Dairy	

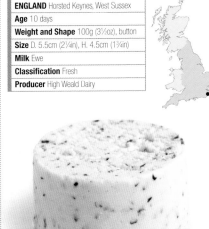

Swaledale Goat

Set up by David and Mandy Read in 1987 and now run by the next generation, who continue to use a recipe that possibly dates back to the back to the 11th century, when it was introduced by Cistercian monks from Normandy.

TASTING NOTES The firm, white paste has a dense, crumbly feel and a sweet taste, with traces of salty brine, with a mild goat flavour. It has a natural brown rind, or is waxed at three days old for a slightly softer texture.

HOW TO ENJOY Choose for subtle flavour in soufflés and tarts, or serve on a plain biscuit with a light ale.

ENGLAND Gallowfields, North Yorkshire	
Age 6–12 weeks	
Weight and Shape 2.5kg (5½lb), round	
Size D. 16cm (6½in), H. 8cm (3¼in)	
Milk Goat	
Classification Hard	
Producer Swaledale Cheese Company	

Yarg Cornish Cheese

One of the most attractive and unusual cheeses created since the revival of British artisan cheeses started in the early 1980s, Yarg Cornish Cheese was first made by Alan and Jenny Gray in Withiel on the edge of Bodmin Moor, Cornwall. Trying to think of a good local name, they eventually decided that Yarg, Gray spelt backwards, sounded Cornish and was uniquely theirs.

In 1984, the Horrell family, who farmed nearby, started making the Yarg and later in partnership with Catherine and Ben Mead who built a new dairy on their farm, Pengreep, in West Cornwall. The Horrells have since retired and all the cheese is now made at Pengreep Dairy.

The Meads returned to the family farm, leaving behind their London careers – Catherine to work on the cheese and Ben to work with the dairy herd. Since then, Ben has invested an enormous amount of time and resources to creating the best possible soil and diversity of pastures resulting in exceptional quality milk from their mixed herd of Ayrshire, Jersey, and Friesian cows. They are an amazing dedicated team and now make 200 tonnes (440,000 pounds) of cheese a year in their highly sustainable bespoke dairy.

TASTING NOTES With age, the nettle casing starts to break down the rind, making it very soft and creamy. As the cheese matures, the fine crumbly texture has a fresh, creamy taste while the edible nettles impart a delicate, slightly mushroomy aroma and a wonderful taste, not so different from spinach or asparagus. Wild Garlic Yarg is similar but softer, with a very subtle taste of garlic.

HOW TO ENJOY Without doubt, Yarg adds style and character to any cheeseboard. It has a low melting point and quickly adds a touch of glamour to crostinis, baguettes, jacket potatoes, pasta, and gratins. Not overpowering, it partners well with fish and is the perfect cheese to use in vegetable pies. The Meads serve it with a local cider, Perry (fermented pear juice), or mild ale. It also goes well with almost any wine – especially fruity whites, or even a dessert wine.

A CLOSER LOOK

Each cheese is a labour of love, made by hand in open vats by a team of dedicated cheesemakers. Every nettle leaf that makes up the unique rind is individually picked – no stems or stalks, no holes or debris, and not a sun scorch mark in sight.

Nettles *are hand-picked locally in May when they don't sting, and are frozen to use later in the year.*

ENGLAND Truro, Cornwall	
Age 6–12 weeks	
Weight and Shape 3.3kg (7lb), wheel	
Size D. 28cm (11in), H. 9cm (3½in)	
Milk Cow	
Classification Flavour-added	
Producer Lynher Dairies	

MATURING The cheeses are matured and carefully monitored to ensure even distribution of the white mould, so each cheese emerges as a unique masterpiece and an example of man's ingenuity working alongside Mother Nature.

NETTLING The freshly formed, pale ivory cheese is taken to the nettling room where the nettles are applied by hand ensuring every leaf overlaps and no cheese is left exposed.

Mild, crumbly, and has a subtle flavour from the nettles.

THE RIND As the cheese ripens, a fine grey mist appears around the jagged edges of the green leaves, making a very attractive, eye-catching surface.

The combination of nettles and moulds speeds up the breakdown of the curd near the rind.

Interior

Ticklemore Goat

Originally conceived by Robin Congdon of Ticklemore Cheeses, this is now made by award-winning cheesemaker Debbie Mumford, a former colleague, on the beautiful 1,000-year-old Sharpham Estate farm, alongside the estate's cow's milk cheeses.

TASTING NOTES The stark-white paste is fine, crumbly, and delicate, and dotted with small holes. The goat flavour comes through as herbaceous with a hint of marzipan.

HOW TO ENJOY This works well in soufflés and tarts, or on the cheeseboard with a fruity red wine, or perhaps a glass of Sharpham rosé.

ENGLAND Totnes, Devon	
Age 2–3 months	
Weight and Shape 1.5kg (3lb 3oz), basket	
Size D. 18cm (7in), H. 8cm (3¼in)	
Milk Goat	
Classification Hard	
Producer Sharpham Partnership	

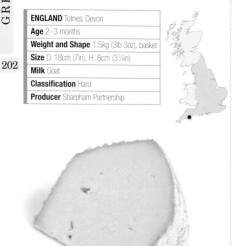

Tunworth

Stacey Hedges uses milk from a local herd of Holstein cows to make this highly acclaimed, Camembert-style cheese – twice awarded Supreme Champion at the British Cheese Awards. Her recent creation, Winslade, is also proving a winner.

TASTING NOTES A wrinkled, white rind with hints of mushrooms, it conceals a sumptuous texture. The flavour is like melted butter, and mushroom soup, with just a dash of sherry.

HOW TO ENJOY For complete melt-in-the-mouth indulgence, warm in the oven until gooey soft, or transport it whole, in its wooden packaging, for a picnic.

ENGLAND Herriard, Hampshire	
Age 6–8 weeks	
Weight and Shape 250g (9oz), round	
Size D. 11cm (4½in), H. 3cm (1¼in)	
Milk Cow	
Classification Soft white	
Producer Hampshire Cheeses	

Tymsboro

Former archaeologist Mary Holbrook developed this cheese, using milk from her own herd, which grazes the Mendip Hills. Following tradition, the goats are milked only from spring through autumn for their period of outdoor grazing. A coating of charcoal and salt gives this cheese an attractive grey-white rind.

TASTING NOTES This is creamy at the edge and drier, dense, and more flavoursome in the middle. It has a subtle flavour of lemon, and almonds, which strengthens and deepens as the cheese matures.

HOW TO ENJOY Eat it with fresh fruit, or melted over poached pears.

ENGLAND Timsbury, Somerset	
Age 3–8 weeks	
Weight and Shape 250g (9oz), truncated pyramid	
Size D. 8cm (3¼in) base; 4cm (1½in) top, H. 7.5cm (3in)	
Milk Goat	
Classification Aged fresh	
Producer Sleight Farm	

Vulscombe

Created in 1982 by Josephine and Graham Townsend, this was one of the first English goat's milk cheeses on the market. Made by lactic fermentation rather than with rennet, Vulscombe has a slightly thicker feel than other, similar cheeses.

TASTING NOTES Unlike most fresh cheeses, it feels thick rather than light in the mouth, but it has a citrussy freshness and a barely discernible herbaceous goaty tang.

HOW TO ENJOY With its decorative bay leaf, it looks good on a cheeseboard. It is easy to spread on biscuits or bread, or try it in a twice-baked soufflé.

ENGLAND Cruwys Morchard, Devon	
Age Up to 5 weeks	
Weight and Shape 170g (6oz), round	
Size D. 7.5cm (3in), H. 4cm (1½in)	
Milk Goat	
Classification Fresh	
Producer Vulscombe Cheese	

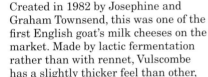

Waterloo

The name is no empty coincidence, as this was originally made on the Duke of Wellington's estate from Guernsey milk. Nowadays, the Wigmores make it with locally sourced milk behind their home, which hides a wonderful dairy that was once a workshop and stables.

TASTING NOTES Bite through the soft, lightly molded rind into the pale, soft paste for a mild, creamy taste when young that matures to a rich, buttery flavour as the cheese ages.

HOW TO ENJOY This is delicious at room temperature with some cold green grapes, or warm it through and serve with a tangy red onion chutney.

ENGLAND Riseley, Berkshire	
Age 4–10 weeks	
Weight and Shape 675g (1½lb), round	
Size D. 16cm (6½in), H. 4.5cm (1¾in)	
Milk Cow	
Classification Soft white	
Producer Village Maid Cheese	

Wedmore

Created by the eminent Chris Duckett, famous for his authentic Caerphilly, Wedmore is a Caerphilly matured with a thin layer of finely chopped chives. Originally made at the Duckett's farm in Wedmore village, it is now made by Tom Calver at Westcombe Dairy, with equal care, and passion for quality.

TASTING NOTES Wedmore is ready to eat after just two weeks, when it is waxy on the surface, but crumbly and moist inside. The mild saltiness is balanced by the tang of chives.

HOW TO ENJOY It is great on its own or paired with a local cider, and can be sweetened with slices of crisp apple.

ENGLAND Westcombe, Somerset	
Age 2 weeks	
Weight and Shape 2kg (4½lb), wheel	
Size D. 17cm (6¾in), H. 7.5cm (3in)	
Milk Cow	
Classification Flavour-added	
Producer Westcombe Dairy Company	

Wensleydale PGI

First crafted by Cistercian monks in 12th century, Wensleydale was gradually perfected by numerous farmers' wives, the legendary Kit Calvert and immortalized by Wallace and Gromit in the 20th century. In 2014, Yorkshire Wensleydale achieved PGI status ensuring it cannot be made outside the designated area.

TASTING NOTES Pale white in colour with a firm yet dense, slightly flaky texture, it has a subtle wild-honey flavour balanced by the cheese's refreshing acidity.

HOW TO ENJOY With crackers. In Yorkshire, they also like to pair that sweetness with a piece of apple pie.

ENGLAND Wensleydale, North Yorkshire	
Age 6–12 weeks	
Weight and Shape 5kg (11lb), cylinder	
Size D. 18cm (7in), H. 18cm (7in)	
Milk Cow, or ewe	
Classification Hard	
Producer Wensleydale Dairy Products	

White Stilton PDO

White Stilton has a Protected Designation of Origin (PDO), meaning it can be made only in Derbyshire, Nottinghamshire, and Leicestershire; other requirements are that it is made from locally produced milk, which must be pasteurized. A popular size for many blended, or flavour-added cheeses.

TASTING NOTES Much underrated, White Stilton has a fresh, creamy mild flavour allied to a fine, crumbly moist texture.

HOW TO ENJOY This cheese, which is often used by makers of blended cheeses, goes very well with a sweet dessert wine, and grapes.

ENGLAND Derbyshire, Nottinghamshire, and Leicestershire	
Age 3–4 weeks	
Weight and Shape 8kg (17½lb), cylinder	
Size D. 20cm (8in), H. 25cm (10in)	
Milk Cow	
Classification Hard	
Producer Various	

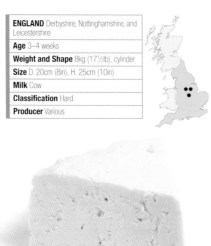

Wiltshire Loaf

Ceri Cryer started in 2005 inspired by the discovery of a recipe for a long forgotten Wiltshire cheese which she put on the map when it won Best Territorial Cheese in 2013 at the British Cheese Awards. She has also named her Royal Wotton Blue in recognition of the army base nearby.

TASTING NOTES Under the light dusting of grey and brown moulds is an open texture like young Caerphilly, buttery yet not rich with refreshing acidity, green grass notes and lingering peppery finish.

HOW TO ENJOY Both Great Bustard or Pigswill, rich in hops and available locally, make great partners.

ENGLAND Wiltshire	
Age 2 months	
Weight and Shape 3 kg (6½lb), wheel	
Size D. 23cm (9in), H. 9cm (3½in)	
Milk Cow	
Classification Hard	
Producer Brinkworth Dairy	

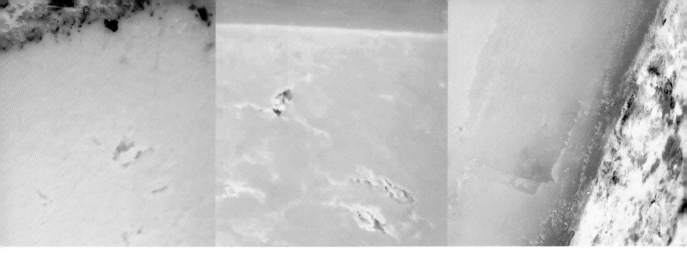

Windrush

Modelled on traditional French methods, Windrush is made by two Australians, Renee and Richard Loveridge, who moved to the Windrush Valley in 2003 and quickly established a dedicated local following. It is also available flavoured with herbs, peppercorns, or garlic.

TASTING NOTES Windrush is only made in small batches. It has a luxurious creamy texture and a lemony fresh tang with hints of fruitiness and white wine.

HOW TO ENJOY Crumble it into tarts or eat simply as it is with a cool Sauvignon Blanc.

ENGLAND Windrush, Oxfordshire	
Age 5 days	
Weight and Shape 115g (4oz), round	
Size D. 6cm (2¼in), H. 3cm (1¼in)	
Milk Goat	
Classification Fresh	
Producer Windrush Valley Goat Dairy	

Winterdale Shaw

The Betts family, farmers since 1495, in Kent make this Cheddar-style cheese,by using only morning milk to retain the freshness and the heat. Matured in their stone cellars deep in the chalky North Downs,it is the first carbon neutral cheese in the UK.

TASTING NOTES Hard and compact yet it melts in the mouth releasing its savoury, cheese and onion tang balanced with the rich creaminess of the milk. Very moorish.

HOW TO ENJOY Kent is famous for its apples and hops so a good strong hoppy beer is the perfect partner along with fresh apples or sweet apple chutney.

ENGLAND Kent	
Age 9–10 months	
Weight and Shape 10 kg (22lb), cylinder	
Size D. 28cm(11in), H. 34cm(13in)	
Milk Cow	
Classification Hard	
Producer Winterdale Cheesemakers	

Woolsery Goat

Woolsery Goat is the result of Annette Lee's dedication to unique artisan cheesemaking, as well as the lush green slopes of Dorset that allow the goats to graze on an abundance of grass and hay.

TASTING NOTES It is moist and open-textured, with a subtle but distinct goaty taste that hints of pine nuts and grass. It has a sea-breeze salty finish.

HOW TO ENJOY Eat on the cheeseboard, together with some apple or pear. It is perfect for a cheese omelette or grated and used in cooking in place of Cheddar.

ENGLAND Up Sydling, Dorset	
Age 8–12 weeks	
Weight and Shape 2.2kg (5lb), cylinder	
Size D. 14cm (5½in), H. 13cm (5¼in)	
Milk Goat	
Classification Hard	
Producer Woolsery Cheese	

Wyfe of Bath

Named after Chaucer's pilgrim from *The Canterbury Tales*, this is made by Graham Padfield, a third-generation farmer, and family pioneer in the cheese world. He has established an excellent reputation in the region for cheesemaking skills.

TASTING NOTES The yellow paste, bounded by a natural brown rind, is smooth and springy with a mild flavour redolent of buttercups and meadows.

HOW TO ENJOY It seems a waste to cook with this excellent award-winning cheese. Instead, serve it on a cheeseboard with crusty bread and a fruity Beaujolais.

ENGLAND Bath, Somerset	
Age 4 months	
Weight and Shape 3kg (6½lb), basket	
Size D. 25cm (10in), H. 38cm (15in)	
Milk Cow	
Classification Semi-soft	
Producer Bath Soft Cheese	

Anster

The Stewart family have farmed at Falside in Fife for over 50 years, but Jane Stewart only started making cheese in 2008 using delicious unpasteurized milk from her herd of home-bred Holstein Friesian cows. They now have a wonderful new cheese dairy where they make their cheeses.

TASTING NOTES Anster has a coarse Cheshire-like texture, and a fresh, fruity tang like sweet apples with a hint of cider. The finish has a lemony tang.

HOW TO ENJOY Try Jane's cheese scone recipe; serve with oat cakes, blackberry jam, a sweet fruit chutney, or finely grate the cheese over roasted parsnips.

SCOTLAND Fife, Scotland	
Age 3–6 months	
Weight and Shape 10 kg (22lb), cylinder	
Size D. 28cm (11in), H. 34cm(13in) estimate	
Milk Cow	
Classification Hard	
Producer St Andrew's Farmhouse Cheese	

Blue Murder

The brainchild of Juliet Harbutt, who wanted to create a cube shaped blue with character, and made by Rory Stone, cheesemaker and owner of Highland Fine Cheese. Using milk collected from the northern dairy herd it definitely stands out from the crowd.

TASTING NOTES It is soft and creamy with hints of gold leaf and the sea breeze on Highland pastures. It has a kick of malt and chocolate, and is mildly spicy.

HOW TO ENJOY Perfect for a cheeseboard, this is also great for a soufflé or blue cheese mousse, and cheese caviar.

SCOTLAND Tain, Highland	
Age 3 months	
Weight and Shape 675g (1½lb), cube	
Size D. 9cm (3½in), H. 9cm (3½in)	
Milk Cow	
Classification Blue	
Producer Highland Fine Cheeses	

Cairnsmore Ewes

Made with milk from the farm's own flock of ewes, Cairnsmore Ewes is aromatic with a rusty-red sandpaper rind. Clothbound and aged for a minimum of six months, it achieves a wonderful full flavour.

TASTING NOTES With hints of old-style caramel toffee, it is moist on the mouth and has hints of boot polish, developing into a salty sweetness. It is very satisfying.

HOW TO ENJOY It is ideal for the cheeseboard, but also good in a Ploughman's lunch with pickled onions and warm crusty bread, or in a quiche with lots of chopped chives.

SCOTLAND Wigtownshire, Dumfries and Gallow	
Age 6–8 months	
Weight and Shape 1.5kg (3lb 3oz), truckles	
Size D. 18cm (7in), H. 23cm (9in)	
Milk Ewe	
Classification Hard	
Producer Galloway Farmhouse Cheeses	

Clava Brie

At Connage Highland Dairy, the Clark family is making some truly wonderful cheeses using their own Jersey Cross, Holstein Friesian, and Norwegian Red cows. They graze on the lush pastures of clover and wild herbs at the banks of the Moray Firth.

TASTING NOTES Under the crusty white rind, the paste is soft and creamy with the subtle taste of sweet meadows and mushrooms. With age, the taste becomes more complex and slightly bitter.

HOW TO ENJOY Serve alongside a hard cheese in a Ploughman's lunch, or melt it onto smoked ham and toasted bread smeared with English mustard.

SCOTLAND Ardersier, Inverness	
Age 3 weeks	
Weight and Shape 250g (9oz) and 1.5kg (2¼lb), round	
Size D. 11cm (4½in) and 25cm (10in), H. 3cm (1in)	
Milk Cow	
Classification Soft White	
Producer Connage Highland Dairy	

Crowdie

Believed to have been introduced by the Vikings, Crowdie was traditionally made by crofters – tenant farmers – with skimmed milk. In Gaelic, it is known as *Gruth*.

TASTING NOTES It has a fresh lemon acidity and the taste of crushed almonds on the top of the mouth. The crumbly and creamy finish hints of freshly baked yeasty bread.

HOW TO ENJOY It is a great alternative to double cream in the Scottish dessert, Cranachan, or spread on oatcakes with fine smoked salmon.

SCOTLAND Tain, Highland	
Age From 2 days	
Weight and Shape 120g (4½oz), log	
Size L. 8cm (3in), H. 4cm (1½in)	
Milk Cow	
Classification Fresh	
Producer Highland Fine Cheeses	

207

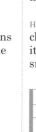

Dunlop

Revived in the mid-1980s by Anne Dorward, Dunlop is now made by a handful of cheesemakers across Scotland. The best are made with traditional Ayrshire milk.

TASTING NOTES Sweet and mild to taste, it has a pale primrose yellow rind and a buttery cheddar paste. At six months, the texture is similar to soft fudge; at 12 months it is firm and fragrant.

HOW TO ENJOY This afternoon tea favourite can be enjoyed with hot scones and Assam tea. Alternatively, add slices to oatcakes with mustard and a dram of whisky. Children love it on toast with warm milk.

SCOTLAND All over	
Age 6–12 months	
Weight and Shape 20kg (44lb), cylinder	
Size D. 30cm (12in), H. 30cm (12in)	
Milk Cow	
Classification Hard	
Producer Various	

Isle of Mull Cheddar

The Reade family farm is on the ruggedly beautiful Isle of Mull, in the Inner Hebrides. Here summers are short, the weather wild, and grain expensive, so the cows' grassy diet is supplemented with the spent grain husks, responsible for the pale colour of the cheese.

TASTING NOTES It has a hard, pale interior with a fermented aroma and taste. It develops a feisty, raw onion and garlic bite that ensures those who taste it return for more.

HOW TO ENJOY A cheese that reflects the quirky nature of its creator, the feed, and the weather, it should be enjoyed with a wee dram of Tobermory whisky.

SCOTLAND Isle of Mull	
Age 6–18 months	
Weight and Shape 24kg (53lb), cylinder	
Size D. 26cm (10in), H 33cm (13in)	
Milk Cow, raw	
Classification Hard	
Producer Isle of Mull Cheese	

Kebbuck

Made by the wonderful people of Camphill Trust near Dumfries, this fine distinctive cheese is washed, then literally hung out to dry in a cloth. After two months, the rind develops a brown, prehistoric appearance.

TASTING NOTES The sponge-like centre with a crispy outer crust has a subtle sweet to peppery taste with a mild finish of beeswax. You can almost taste the cows trampling the grass in the morning dew.

HOW TO ENJOY It is great on a British cheeseboard or simply on its own with Scrumpy cider. It can also be added to the topping of a buttery apple crumble.

SCOTLAND Dumfries, Dumfriesshire	
Age 2 months	
Weight and Shape 800g (1¾lb), various	
Size D. 12cm (5in), H. 6cm (2½in)	
Milk Cow	
Classification Semi-soft	
Producer Loch Arthur Creamery	

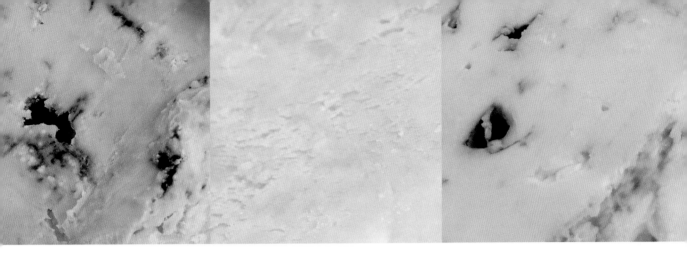

Lanark Blue

Created by Humphrey Errington and now made by daughter Selena, along with two other blues, Dunsyre (cow) and Biggar (goat) and several others. The cheese develops a complex flavour due to the wild heather, and natural pastures on which the ewes graze.

TASTING NOTES It is soft in the centre, has a crumbly outer crust, and is sharp as grapefruit with the meatiness of an aged rib of highland beef. Also has elements of sweetness and steely blues.

HOW TO ENJOY It is great on a cheeseboard with celery hearts and crumbly crackers or grated over a winter salad with hot roasted onions and winter squash.

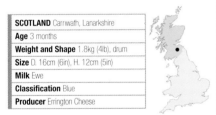

SCOTLAND Carnwath, Lanarkshire	
Age 3 months	
Weight and Shape 1.8kg (4lb), drum	
Size D. 16cm (6in), H. 12cm (5in)	
Milk Ewe	
Classification Blue	
Producer Errington Cheese	

Orkney

Made by Hilda Seator on her farm on the isolated, windswept Orkney Island, it has the consistency, but not the taste, of Wensleydale (see p204). It is a lactic cheese, so no rennet is used.

TASTING NOTES It is pale, with a chewy bite and a lemony zest. There is a hint of butternut squash, and a yeasty breath, like an old brewing room, on the finish.

HOW TO ENJOY It can be enjoyed with a single malt whiskey when crumbled on to oatcakes or alongside traditional fruit cake with a cup of afternoon tea. This good breakfast cheese goes well with boiled gammon and warm, lightly-cooked eggs.

SCOTLAND Kirkwall, Orkney Islands	
Age 4 weeks	
Weight and Shape 3.5kg (7lb 7oz), pressed rounds	
Size D. 12cm (5in), H. 5cm (2in)	
Milk Cow	
Classification Hard	
Producer Grimbister Farm	

Strathdon Blue

Made by Highland Fine Cheese, makers of Caboc (see p210–11), one of Scotland's oldest cheeses, and Blue Murder (see p206), it develops smudges of silver-grey mould and patches of sky blue on the sticky golden rind.

TASTING NOTES It has well-spread blue veining and a slight salt and peppery taste and spicy tang. It can sometimes finish with the essence of mousse-like milky chocolate.

HOW TO ENJOY It is outstanding in twice-baked soufflés with walnuts and dressed salad leaves. It sits well on raisin bread, and is great melted on beef steak.

SCOTLAND Tain, Highland	
Age 3 months	
Weight and Shape 2.8kg (6lb), wheel	
Size D. 30cm (12in), H. 10cm (4in)	
Milk Cow	
Classification Blue	
Producer Highland Fine Cheese	

Caboc

While the Romans played a significant role in improving cheesemaking in England, their influence did not cross the borders into Scotland. Instead, most cheese was made by crofters, and was most likely introduced by the Vikings.

Caboc is similar to Crowdie (see p207), a traditional Scottish cheese made from milk that has curdled naturally without rennet. While Crowdie is made with skimmed milk, Caboc is made with extra cream. It is said to have been created in the 15th century by Mariota de Ile, daughter of the Macdonald, Lord of the Isles, who was forced to flee to Ireland to avoid abduction and marriage by the Campbells. When she returned home to the Isle of Skye, she brought with her the recipe for Caboc, turning the rich milk of the island into a richer and more fitting cheese for the Lord of the Isle and his clan.

Like so many great recipes, it survived by being passed on, generation to generation, but it had all but disappeared until its revival in 1962 by Susannah Stone, a distant descendant of the creator. Using raw milk from their own farm, she set

about recreating the recipe. Today, it is made in exactly the same way at Highland Fine Cheese Company, owned and run by her son Ruaraidh. The milk comes from the most northerly herds on mainland Scotland in Caithness, a barren, treeless area that is fairly flat and exposed to the cold northerly winds. As a result, the cows are of sturdy stock, traditional Friesian with some Ayrshire, and store more fat to protect them from the harsh elements. This gives a protein, and solids-rich milk, ideal for cheesemaking.

TASTING NOTES Made with cream enriched milk, it feels very rich, smooth, and buttery with a nutty taste but slightly sharp finish like sour cream. The toasted pinhead oats give it a nutty yeasty flavour and a pleasant gentle crunchy feel.

HOW TO ENJOY Caboc is at home on any grand dining room cheese table, but is also versatile in the kitchen. Slice onto a blood orange or clementine salad with a handful of bitter salad leaves, or stir into fluffy mashed potatoes served with sliced roast gammon and onion relish. A Stone family favourite is to grill some on haggis from the excellent local butcher, served with a glass of Glenmorangie whisky made just along the road.

Sturdy *Highland cattle*

SCOTLAND Tain, Highland
Age 3 months or more
Weight and Shape 110g (3¾oz), log
Size D. 4cm (1½in), L. 8cm (3¼in)
Milk Cow
Classification Fresh
Producer Highland Fine Cheeses

A CLOSER LOOK

Like many artisan cheeses, Caboc's development was due to the raw materials available – an abundance of milk and Scottish oats.

MILK CHURNS The cream is skimmed from the milk, having been collected from two dairy farms in Caithness, and poured into a small round vat where starter cultures are added, then stirred, and left to slowly ripen in milk churns for upward of three months.

MANUAL PRESSING The cream and milk sours and is then poured into bags and hung to drain.

SHAPING The soft curd is very malleable and is easily shaped into small logs.

THE OATMEAL Rolling the small cheese in toasted pinhead oatmeal was an invention of Susannah's. She felt the flavour was enhanced with the addition of the oatmeal and added a pleasant texture.

The texture is more like double cream than cheese.

Log, sliced

The crunchy oatmeal is the perfect counterbalance to the soft, creamy interior.

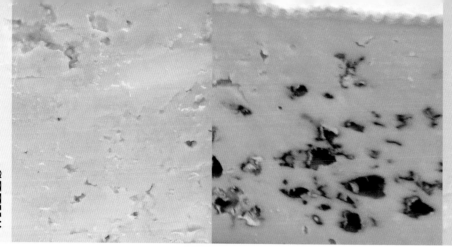

Aberwen

Michael and Caroline McLaren, now own Furnace Farm, which has been in his family since 1874 and in 2010 decided to set up a Welsh Food Centre in the old farm buildings.

TASTINGS NOTES Using milk from a single herd and made to a 300 year old recipe, it is an elegant, clothbound dense, crumbly cheese with a subtle nutty flavour.

HOW TO ENJOY Perfect for Welsh Rarebit or if you are in the area, try Penderyn Welsh whisky or Innkeeper's Tipple traditionally made with wild whinberries, but now with their cultivated cousins, blueberries.

WALES Conwy	
Age 4–5 months	
Weight and Shape 10 kg (22lb), cylinder	
Size D. 25.5cm (10in), H. 22cm (8.5 in)	
Milk Cow	
Classification Hard	
Producer Bodnant Welsh Food	

Boksburg Gold Blue

Steve and Sian Pearce, with over 60 years of experience in the cheese world, founded Carmarthenshire Cheese in 2006. Following the success of their Pont Gar range, they expanded to include two new blues and the hard Llangloffan range.

TASTING NOTES Bright orange curd with streaks of contrasting blue make this cheese stand out. It is smooth, soft, and distinct yet mild with a savoury acidity, which makes this a very appealing blue.

HOW TO ENJOY Like most continental-style blues, it goes well with a sweet wine or a hoppy beer and is great with crunchy fresh celery or in a soufflé.

WALES Carmarthenshire	
Age 11–13 weeks	
Weight and Shape 2.5 kg (5½ lb), wheel	
Size D. 20cm (10in), H. 75mm (3in)	
Milk Cow	
Classification Blue	
Producer Carmarthenshire Cheese	

Cerwyn

Cerwyn is produced on Pant Mawr Farm, situated in the heart of the Preseli Mountains. This was established in 1983 when the Jennings family returned from setting up a dairy enterprise in Libya and North Yemen.

TASTING NOTES It is hard but unpressed, with a smooth, velvety texture, and buttery colour. Its mature flavour has a raw onion tang, and nutty aftertaste.

HOW TO ENJOY It is perfect for the cheeseboard, served with a rich Bordeaux. It is also delicious with fresh fruit and preserves, and excellent in sauces for dishes such as macaroni and cheese, and for grilling on toast.

WALES Clynderwen, Pembrokeshire	
Age 6 months	
Weight and Shape 1.4kg (3lb), wheel	
Size D. 18cm (7in), H. 5cm (2in)	
Milk Cow	
Classification Hard	
Producer Pant Mawr Farmhouse	

Golden Cenarth

Caws Cenarth, in the heart of Wales was started by Gwynfor and Thelma Adams in 1987. Thelma played a leading role in reviving Welsh Caerphilly, and today their son Carwyn continues to make it. They have also created a number of new cheeses, including this modern Welsh classic.

TASTING NOTES A vacherin-style orange, crusty, washed rind cheese, it is supple with hints of meadow flowers, and a strong, savoury almost meaty finish.

HOW TO ENJOY Perfect for a picnic lunch, spread on your favourite crusty bread and serve with charcuterie, a pale ale, or dry riesling.

WALES Pembrokeshire	
Age 4–6 weeks	
Weight and Shape 250gm (9oz), round	
Size D 11cm (4.5in), H. 3.5 (1.5in)	
Milk Cow	
Classification Semi-soft	
Producer Caws Cenarth	

Hafod

Sam Holden, son of the founder of the Soil Association, created Hafod in 2008 on the longest established organic farm in Wales, using a Cheddar recipe and their own Ayrshire cow's milk.

TASTING NOTES The rich, creamy quality of the milk gives the cheese a full yet pure taste, and with age, it becomes hard and chewy with a lively, complex tang and a green, grassy finish.

HOW TO ENJOY It is ideal for the cheeseboard, and delicious with crusty bread and a glass of chilled beer. It has a good melting quality, and is excellent in gratin dishes.

WALES Credigion, West Wales	
Age 12 months	
Weight and Shape 10kg (22lb), cylinder	
Size D. 25cm (10in), H. 25cm (10in)	
Milk Cow	
Classification Hard	
Producer Holden Dairy Farm	

Pant-Ys-Gawn

Made by Abergavenny Fine Foods, the first commercial producers of goat's cheese in Wales, it has proved extremely successful in supermarkets across the country. Named after the family farm where it was first made, it is available with or without fresh herbs.

TASTING NOTES It is a fresh, pure white, clean, and mild-tasting cheese, with a smooth, creamy texture, refreshing, and crisp with a mild goaty finish.

HOW TO ENJOY Spread it thickly on crusty bread; grill it on bruschetta with vine tomatoes; or make a delicious savoury cheesecake mixed with fresh herbs. Serve with Sancerre or rosé.

WALES Abergavenny, Monmouthshire	
Age 3 weeks	
Weight and Shape 100g (3½oz), drum	
Size D. 6cm (2½in), H. 3cm (1in)	
Milk Goat	
Classification Fresh	
Producer Abergavenny Fine Foods	

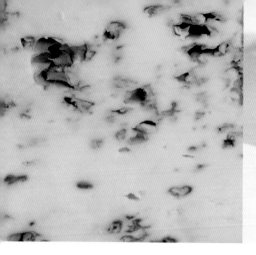

Perl Las

Thelma Adams, a cheesemaker from Wales, started making traditional Caerphilly in 1987 with raw milk from her own herd. Perl Las, which translates from Welsh as "blue pearl", followed in 2001.

TASTING NOTES It has an earthy, mouldy aroma, typical of a true blue, with a smooth, creamy texture. The mellow yet strong taste has a spicy, vaguely herbaceous finish.

HOW TO ENJOY It is a good blue for the cheeseboard, melted on hot fillet steak, or used in a dressing for fresh, crisp salads. Serve Perl Las with a dry Riesling, Tawny Port, or beer.

WALES Boncath, Carmarthenshire	
Age 12–16 weeks	
Weight and Shape 600g (1lb 5oz) and 2.5kg (5½lb), wheel	
Size D. 10cm (4in) and 20cm (8in), H. 8cm (3in) and 10cm (4in)	
Milk Cow	
Classification Blue	
Producer Caws Cenarth	

214

Pont Gar

Carmarthenshire Cheese was founded in 2006 by Steve and Sian Elin Peace. Having worked in the dairy industry for 25 years, they decided to join forces to create their own line of soft cheeses using the excellent local milk.

TASTING NOTES This soft white Brie-style cheese has a mild, velvety texture with a hint of mushrooms, and a sweet buttery taste, with a slight sharpness on the finish. It can also be smoked or made with herbs.

HOW TO ENJOY This cheeseboard classic is delicious with seasonal fruits and nuts. Serve it with a New World Merlot or cider.

WALES Carmarthen, Carmarthenshire	
Age 5 weeks	
Weight and Shape 1.4kg (3lb), wheel	
Size D. 11cm (4½in), H. 4cm (1½in)	
Milk Cow	
Classification Soft white	
Producer Carmarthenshire Cheese Company	

Saval

John Savage at Teifi Farmhouse Cheeses has created a number of hard cheeses, including a traditional Caerphilly, and washed rind cheeses using raw milk. Some have been made in conjunction with Britain's first affineur, James Aldridge.

TASTING NOTES This is a dumpling-shaped cheese with a pink-orange rind. The supple and elastic yellow interior has a distinct, pungent farmyard aroma, and a savoury, meaty finish.

HOW TO ENJOY It is a must for cheese lovers, and is beautifully accompanied by an off-dry Gewürztraminer. It also makes a pungent addition to fondue.

WALES Llandysul, Powys	
Age 6–7 weeks	
Weight and Shape 2kg (4½lb), dumpling	
Size D. 26cm (10in), H. 5cm (2in)	
Milk Cow	
Classification Semi-soft	
Producer Teifi Farmhouse Cheese	

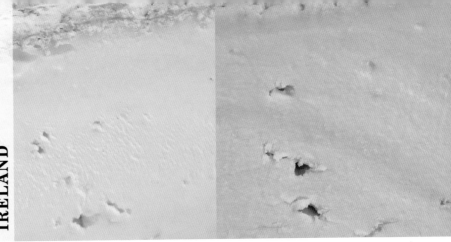

Teifi Farmhouse

After moving from the Netherlands, John Savage set up his dairy in the heart of Wales and modelled his first cheese, Teifi Farmhouse, on Gouda, the cheese of his homeland.

TASTING NOTES The lush, wild pastures in the Teifi Valley give the cheese an exceptional flavour – herbaceous and fruity, with a savoury tang. Smooth and supple when young, it becomes dry, almost brittle with age.

HOW TO ENJOY This classic for any cheeseboard can also be used in cooking where a strong cheese is required. It is perfect with Chardonnay.

WALES Llandysul, Carmarthenshire	
Age 6–12 months	
Weight and Shape 15kg (33lb), boulder	
Size D. 10cm (4in), H. 6cm (2½in)	
Milk Cow	
Classification Hard	
Producer Teifi Farmhouse	

Ardrahan

Founded in Cork by Eugene and Mary Burns in the 1980s to make use of the milk from their own herd, Ardrahan remains one of Ireland's best loved washed-rind cheeses.

TASTING NOTES It is pale golden in the centre with a sticky terracotta rind and has a supple, dense, creamy interior with a sweet-savoury taste and meaty aftertaste that intensifies with age. A smoked version is also produced.

HOW TO ENJOY It melts superbly, so it can be grilled over vegetables or added to an omelette. It is also suitable for a cheeseboard, and can be enjoyed with a glass of beer.

IRELAND Kanturk, Cork	
Age Small: 4–6 weeks, big: 12–14 weeks	
Weight and Shape 1kg (2¼lb), wheel	
Size D. 18cm (7in), H. 10cm (3in)	
Milk Cow	
Classification Semi-soft	
Producer Ardrahan Farmhouse	

Ardsallagh

Jane and Gerard Murphy run the Ardsallagh farm and dairy. Their 400 goats provide the milk that enables them to produce a range of handmade hard and soft cheeses, including an excellent Crottin, as well as yogurt and bottled milk.

TASTING NOTES When young, it has a mild, nutty freshness. With age it becomes hard and can be grated, and it has an almondy mellowness, and aromatic tang on the finish. It is also delicious when smoked.

HOW TO ENJOY On the cheeseboard, Ardsallagh matches reds, like Montepulciano d'Abruzzo, or cider. It's also good for use in quiches and tarts.

IRELAND Carrigtwohill, Cork	
Age 4 months minimum	
Weight and Shape 250g–11kg (9oz–24¼lb), rounds	
Size D. 8–35cm (3–14in), H. 4–12cm (1½–5in)	
Milk Goat	
Classification Hard	
Producer Ardsallagh Goats Products	

215

Caerphilly

The only traditional cheese associated with Wales, Caerphilly was a favourite of the Welsh miners and made on numerous small-scale farms in Glamorgan and Monmouth between the early 1800s and 1914.

Caerphilly Castle *in the historical town of Caerphilly.*

The years after the First World War were tough on the farming community and, with the advent of the railway, farmers were able to sell their milk, rather than having to preserve it as cheese, and subsequently cheese production dwindled. After the Ministry of Food stopped all production of Caerphilly until 1954, traditional Welsh Caerphilly did not reappear until the 1980s. Fortunately, at the turn of the 20th century, some Somerset Cheddar makers, seeing the economic advantages, decided to turn their hands to Caerphilly, as it was ready to sell within a few weeks, compared to 12 months for Cheddar. A few producers, such as Ducketts, Westcombe Farm Dairy – which still make it in the traditional way, continued after the war but made less and less until the artisanal cheese revolution in the 1980s, which coincided with the campaign for traditional cheese by Patrick Rance. Today, only Caws Cenarth, and Caws Caerfai make farmhouse Caerphilly in the Welsh valleys, while Ducketts and Trethowan make theirs in Somerset. Most are matured for a few months rather than a few days and are more likely to be found in top London restaurants than a miner's lunch box.

TASTING NOTES Caerphilly has a delicious fresh taste and sometimes, when the grazing is at its best, its usual herbaceous sweetness is infused, like a rustic béchamel sauce, by the scent of crushed bracken moistened by autumnal rains.

With age, it becomes softer, creamier and more supple as it grows a blueish grey coat, which sometimes sneaks onto the surface of the cheese and indicates it is still alive and well – you just need to scrape it off.

HOW TO ENJOY
Caerphilly's mild, lemony fresh flavour means it can be used in sweet or savoury dishes but especially Welsh Rabbit (also known as Rarebit). The cheese is very good melted on toast or with crusty bread, but it can be mixed with beer, egg, Worcestershire sauce and mustard for an interesting combination. Enjoy with beer, local cider, fruit wine or a white from one of the new Welsh vineyards.

WALES	Dyfed, Ceredigion and Somerset
Age	4 days to 4 months
Weight and Shape	4.5kg (9½lb), wheel
Size	D. 25cm (10in), H. 8cm (3¼ in)
Milk	Cow
Classification	Hard
Producer	Various

A CLOSER LOOK

A simple cheese in appearance and taste, yet what liberates mediocrity into greatness is the quality of the raw materials, the method and, above all, the passion the makers have for their art.

RIND The moulds that grow on the rind of the Caerphilly give it a mottled appearance.

CUTTING THE CURD The curd is cut using special knives, long enough to reach the bottom of the vat. As they are drawn slowly through the milk, they cut the curd in 3 ways, producing 1cm (1/2in) very soft and floppy cubes.

DRAINING THE WHEY
The curd is stirred by hand in the whey until the desired acidity is reached, traditionally determined when an imprint of a hand remains on the pressed curd. The whey is then drained, and the curd cut again and piled into moulds lined with cheesecloth. All this is done by hand. The moulds are stacked three to four cheeses high under the press, separated by metal trays and then pressure is applied. They remain in the press for 20–30 minutes.

MATURING The day after pressing, the cheeses are soaked in a brine bath, dried off, and put in a cold room where they remain for 4–7 days before being sold.

Cheeses that are allowed to mature for 3–4 months develop a magnificent thick grey coat and more complex flavour.

Interior

The interior is a yellow-white colour like a magnolia, with fine, paler, almost white marbling throughout.

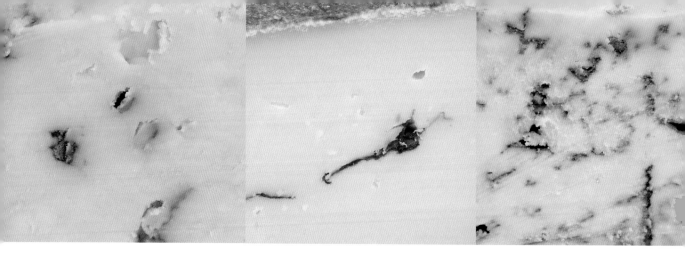

Bellingham Blue

This, one of Ireland's best blue cheeses, is made from raw milk from Glyde Farm's closed herd of Friesians by dedicated cheesemaker Peter Thomas.

TASTING NOTES It is moist with blue-green mould. This natural-rind cheese is mild and gentle when young, then develops a rich, mellow, peppery tang with age.

HOW TO ENJOY Extra mature cheeses work well with a glass of Barolo or Sauternes. It is superb melted over steak, or for stuffing chicken breasts, and is great for soufflés, pasta, and in salads with pears, or pomegranate seeds, and toasted nuts.

IRELAND	Castlebellingham, Louth
Age	6–14 months
Weight and Shape	3kg (6½lb), wheel
Size	D. 20cm (8in), H. 7.5cm (3in)
Milk	Cow
Classification	Blue
Producer	Glyde Farm

Beenoskee

German born Maja Binder produces some of Ireland's most unusual raw milk cheeses at Dingle Peninsula Dairy. The milk is naturally salty, since the cows graze close to the sea, and local seaweed is used for flavouring. Flavoured and seaweed-flecked cheeses are also produced.

TASTING NOTES The crusty rind of seaweed adds a natural, sea-salt flavour to the fudgey, divinely creamy flavour, and there's a warm, spicy paste.

HOW TO ENJOY As a cheeseboard cheese, this needs nothing more than a glass of Alsace Riesling and some quince paste.

IRELAND	Castlegregory, Kerry
Age	6–12 months
Weight and Shape	4–9kg (8lb 13oz–19lb 13oz), wheel
Size	Various
Milk	Cow
Classification	Hard
Producer	Dingle Peninsula Cheese Dairy

Cashel Blue

One of Ireland's best-loved blues, Cashel Blue, is made by the Grubb family at Beechmount Farm with milk from the farm's own pedigree British Friesian herd.

TASTING NOTES This soft, silky, and creamy blue with green-blue marbling has a medium flavour, with a gentle buzz from the mould veining.

HOW TO ENJOY For maximum flavour, serve this cheeseboard cheese at room temperature with a ripe pear and a sweet Semillon or St Emilion wine. It is great melted onto grilled steak, crumbled into salads, or into a smooth celery soup.

IRELAND	Fethard, Tipperary
Age	9–35 weeks
Weight and Shape	1.5 kg (3lb 3oz), drum
Size	D. 13cm (5in), H. 9cm (3½in)
Milk	Cow
Classification	Blue
Producer	J & L Grubb

Coolea

This Gouda-style cheese has received many awards since it first came into production in 1980. It is now made by second-generation cheesemaker Dicky Willems and his wife, Sinead.

TASTING NOTES This smooth, hard, pale-gold cheese has a handful of small holes. It is fruity and mild when young, but intensifies to a rich, nutty caramel spiciness as it ages. Rich milk from hilly grazing adds a herbaceous character to the mix.

HOW TO ENJOY Coolea grates and melts well, and is good in omelettes or salads. Enjoy it with a full-bodied red wine or warming tawny port.

IRELAND Fermoy, Cork
Age 2–24 months
Weight and Shape 4.5kg (10lb) and 9kg (20lb), boulder
Size D. 25cm (10in) and 35cm (14in), H. 10cm (4in)
Milk Cow
Classification Hard
Producer Coolea Farmhouse Cheese

Cooleeney

Cooleeney, Ireland's answer to Camembert, is handmade by a fourth-generation farming family in Tipperary, where lush grazing pastures provide rich, sweet milk.

TASTING NOTES Raw-milk Cooleeney is sensuously rich in texture, with aromas of mushrooms and herbs, a full buttery flavour, and good acidity.

HOW TO ENJOY It should be left out to soften before eating, and is best accompanied with a crusty baguette and grapes. The wine needs to be gentle – a light red Valpolicella would suit.

IRELAND Moyne, Tipperary
Age 8–14 weeks
Weight and Shape 200g (7oz) and 1.7kg (3lb 12oz), round
Size D. 8cm (3in) and 24cm (9½in), H. 2.5cm (1in) and 4.5cm (2in)
Milk Cow
Classification Soft-white
Producer Cooleeney Cheese

Corleggy

Silke Cropp's Corleggy cheese from Cavan was born out of a farmhouse cheese revolution that helped put Ireland on the culinary map. Goats and cows dine out on the nearby drumlin pastures that are rich with herbs.

TASTING NOTES Corleggy has notes of lush sweet grass and wild herbs. Its natural rind is brine-washed and flavourful.

HOW TO ENJOY This cheese is perfect with plums or figs. It also grates well and can be used in sauces or soufflés.

IRELAND Belturbet, Cavan
Age 2–4 months
Weight and Shape 400g (14oz) and 1kg (2¼lb), cylinder
Size D. 10cm (4in) and 16cm (6in), H. 12cm (5in)
Milk Goat
Classification Hard
Producer Corleggy Cheeses

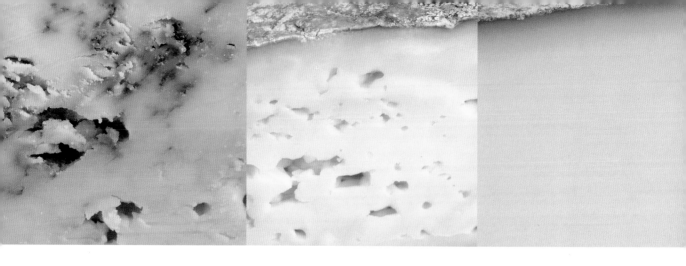

Crozier Blue

Ireland's first ewe's milk blue cheese, Crozier Blue, was developed in 1993. It is a sister to Cashel Blue and is similar in taste to Roquefort (see pp82–83).

TASTING NOTES The Crozier flock of British Friesland ewes graze on limestone to give the soft, creamy, and subtly crumbly cheese a steely dry piquancy and peppery punch.

HOW TO ENJOY Crozier Blue can be served as a first course with ripe pears, walnuts, and delicate salad leaves or after dinner with a glass of late-bottled vintage Port or Tokaji. Use it on blue-cheese pizza, in a quiche, or added to risotto.

IRELAND Fethard, Tipperary	
Age 10–35 weeks	
Weight and Shape 1.5 kg (3lb 3oz), drum	
Size D. 13cm, (5in), H.10cm (4in)	
Milk Ewe	
Classification Blue	
Producer J & L Grubb	

Durrus

It is one of the original "big four" west Cork cheeses. Thirty years later, Jeffa Gill still makes her washed-rind cheese in Dunmanus Bay, using time-honoured methods and raw milk.

TASTING NOTES This orange-hued washed rind cheese is speckled with tiny holes. It is smooth, creamy, and sensuously textured, with sublime grassy flavours and warm fruity notes that become nuttier and richer with age.

HOW TO ENJOY Durrus is superb after dinner with Sancerre or Merlot. Durrus Melt, a type of fondue, is a classic modern Irish recipe.

IRELAND Durrus, Cork	
Age 3–8 weeks	
Weight and Shape 250g–1.4kg (9oz–3lb), round	
Size D. 10–17cm (4–6½in), H. 5–6cm (2–2½in)	
Milk Cow	
Classification Semi-soft	
Producer Durrus Cheese	

Glebe Brethan

David and Mairead Tiernan first made this wonderful hard, creamy cheese in 2004. Its strengths have been attributed to the excellent milk from their herd of Montbéliarde cows.

TASTING NOTES When young, this smooth and golden yellow cheese with intermittent holes is fruity and creamy. Ageing adds spice, nuttiness, and a gentle aromatic buzz, finished with a zesty tang.

HOW TO ENJOY This versatile cheese can be enjoyed as it comes with just an Alsace Pinot Gris. It is also nice in tartlets with caramelized onions or in a smooth fondue or sauce.

IRELAND Dunleer, Louth	
Age 6–24 months	
Weight and Shape 40–45kg (88lb 3oz–99lb 3oz), wheels	
Size D. 60–66cm (23½–26in), H. 10cm (4in)	
Milk Cow	
Classification Hard	
Producer Glebe Brethan Farmhouse	

Grace

Grace is one of a line of organic fresh cheeses packed in jars, covered with sunflower oil, and flavoured with various herbs and spices.

TASTING NOTES It has a very fresh, soft, creamy taste with herbaceous grassy notes from the sunflower oil. The other cheeses in the line are flavoured with olives, nettles, chives, or pepper.

HOW TO ENJOY Eat on crusty bread, crackers, or sandwiches with peppery salad leaves and tomatoes. It's good for jacket potatoes, as an instant dip, or as a base for smoked salmon pâté, and it makes an excellent luxurious cheesecake.

IRELAND Ladestown, Westmeath	
Age A few days	
Weight and Shape 150g (5½oz), glass jar	
Size No size	
Milk Cow	
Classification Fresh	
Producer Moonshine Dairy Farm	

Gubbeen

Gubbeen is a farmhouse cheese made with milk from the farm's herd of Friesian and Kerry Cows. The orange sticky bacteria on the rind, which has been named *Gubbeenensis*, is now world famous.

TASTING NOTES It is washed in brine. Gubbeen is smooth and creamy, with tiny holes. It has gentle herb and floral notes with a meaty finish.

HOW TO ENJOY Match Extra Mature Smoked Gubbeen with Christmas cake. After dinner, it is superb with Chianti or Bordeaux. Gubbeen melts well for pizzas, mashed potatoes, and omelettes.

IRELAND Schull, Cork	
Age 12–16 weeks	
Weight and Shape 500g–4.5kg (1lb 2oz–9lb 15oz), round	
Size D. 12cm–30cm (5–12in), H. 5–10cm (2–4in)	
Milk Cow	
Classification Semi-soft	
Producer Gubbeen Cheese	

Killeen Goat

Marion Roeleveld makes Killeen, with cows' and goats' milk from a recipe she learnt while working in Holland. The goats' milk comes from partner Haske's wonderful herd that started in 1990 with ten kid goats, which now has 200 to cope with the demand for the milk.

TASTING NOTES Winner of Best Goat 2014 and Best Irish Cheese 2012, it has a compact pale ivory interior with savoury notes reminiscent of marmite and a nutty almond finish.

HOW TO ENJOY Supple like young Gouda, it grills superbly, but is best served with a handful of Irish cheeses and a glass of Guinness.

IRELAND Co Galway	
Age 8–12 weeks	
Weight and Shape 5 kg (11lb), round	
Size D. 24cm (9in), H 10cm (4in) estimate	
Milk Goat	
Classification Hard	
Producer Killeen Farmhouse Cheese	

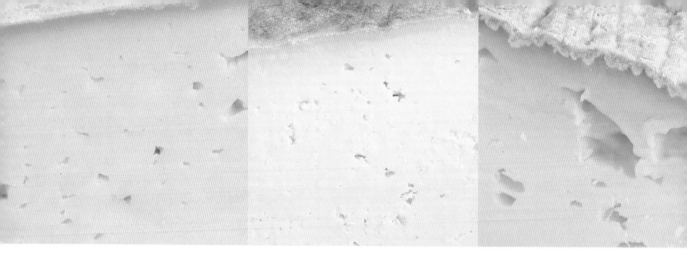

Knockdrinna Gold

Helen Finnegan only started making cheese in 2004, but she has already won awards for her goat's and ewe's milk cheeses, and more recently, for her cow's milk cheese, Lavistown (see p222).

TASTING NOTES Knockdrinna Gold is creamy and nutty. Its rind is washed with organic white wine, lending a rich golden colour and citrussy notes. A soft creamy goat's cheese and semi-soft ewe's milk cheese are also produced.

HOW TO ENJOY On the cheeseboard or a mixed cheese platter, it is best served with a grassy Sauvignon Blanc. It is ideal baked in a goat's cheese tart.

IRELAND Stoneyford, Kilkenny	
Age 2 months	
Weight and Shape 3 kg (6½lb), round	
Size D. 23cm (9in), H. 8cm (3in)	
Milk Goat	
Classification Semi-soft	
Producer Knockdrinna Farmhouse Cheese	

Lavistown

More than a quarter of a century ago, Lavistown was first made at Lavistown House by Olivia Goodwillie. It is now made by Helen Finnegan at Knockdrinna.

TASTING NOTES This low-fat Caerphilly style cheese has a thin, leathery, pale-cream rind dusted with white, grey, and pink moulds. It is tangy and fresh when young, but becomes more crumbly with a hint of spice with age.

HOW TO ENJOY Pair it with wedges of dessert apples and a glass of ale. It adds something special to apple pie or can be placed underneath the mincemeat before baking your Christmas mince pies.

IRELAND Stoneyford, Kilkenny	
Age 3 weeks–70 days	
Weight and Shape 3.5kg (7lb 11oz), wheel	
Size D. 23cm (9in), H. 9cm (3½in)	
Milk Cow	
Classification Hard	
Producer Knockdrinna Farmhouse Cheese	

Milleens

Ireland's first farmhouse artisan cheese, Milleens, was created in 1976 by Veronica Steele. Veronica nicknamed the smallest Milleens a "*dote*" – an Irish term for something cherished.

TASTING NOTES It is a washed-rind cheese with an orange-pink hue and inviting soft texture that becomes unctuously runny. The flavour is mushroomy and herbaceous, with full woodland aromas.

HOW TO ENJOY Serve with good bread, preferably Irish soda, and a glass of Barolo or Claret. Milleens can be added at the last minute to risotto or melted into vegetable soups, such as broccoli or cauliflower.

IRELAND Eyeries, Cork	
Age 2–3 months	
Weight and Shape 250g (9oz) and 1.25kg (2¾lb), round	
Size 10cm (4in) and 23cm (9in), H. 3cm (1in) and 4cm (1½in)	
Milk Cow	
Classification Semi-soft	
Producer Milleens Cheese	

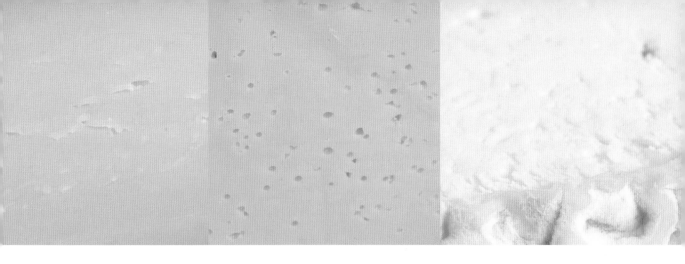

Mossfield Organic

This award-winning, organic farmhouse cheese is from Offaly, where the farm's Friesian and Rotbunt herd is kept on a variety of grazing, which adds subtle nuances to the milk.

TASTING NOTES This Gouda-style cheese has a moist, supple consistency and elegant mellow notes, becoming full-bodied and crumbly as it ages. It is also available with tomato and herbs as well as garlic and basil.

HOW TO ENJOY Mossfield is great for the cheeseboard, with a glass of claret, or in tarts and quiches. The flavoured alternatives add zest to baked potatoes.

IRELAND Clareen, Offaly
Age 3–9 months
Weight and Shape 5kg (11lb), wheels
Size D. 29cm (11½in), H. 10cm (4in)
Milk Cow
Classification Semi-soft
Producer Mossfield Organic Cheese

St Gall

In Fermoy, Cork, Frank, and Gudrun Shinnick have developed a superb range of farmhouse cheeses, including this hard cheese made with raw cow's milk.

TASTING NOTES It has a naturally hard rind, a rich gold colour, and small holes punctuating the creamy consistency. Sweet milky flavours are rounded with toasty, almost biscuity, notes and a fresh, spicy acidity to finish.

HOW TO ENJOY This needs no adornment, just a glass of decent red wine. In cooking, it melts well for Welsh Rarebit, mixed with chopped spring onions or tomatoes.

IRELAND Fermoy, Cork
Age 3–6 months
Weight and Shape 5kg (11lb), round
Size D. 30cm (12in), H. 10cm (4in)
Milk Cow
Classification Hard
Producer Fermoy Natural Cheeses

St Tola Log

St Tola is made from fresh, sweet, organic, goat's milk from the Burren region of Clare. They make a wide range of goats' milk cheese including an award winning Crottin and a hard cheese.

TASTING NOTES This classic chevre-style log has a pale, wrinkly rind tinged with pink and a silky texture with a subtle nutty, goaty flavour and crisp finish.

HOW TO ENJOY Serve it grilled or fresh with sourdough bread and grapes, or with slices of pear and a white Bordeaux. Crumble it into salads or serve on warm toasted brioche drizzled with honey, and enjoy with a Sauternes.

IRELAND Burren, Clare
Age 3–5 weeks
Weight and Shape 1kg (2¼lb), log
Size L. 21cm (8½in), H. 8cm (3in)
Milk Goat
Classification Aged Fresh
Producer Inagh Farmhouse Cheese

LOW COUNTRIES

BELGIUM Belgium has a long tradition of dairy farming and small-farm cheese production, but in the Middle Ages, trading in silks and spices overshadowed cheesemaking. Subsequently, milk and cream were more often used for making butter and chocolate. However, the 1960s saw a return of the artisan cheesemakers, and many traditional recipes were revived. The new era is characterized by flavour and diversification, with an increasing number of goat's milk cheeses.

THE NETHERLANDS Cheese has been made in The Netherlands since prehistoric times, but it was the Romans who introduced hard cheeses, which would become Gouda and Edam. They also engineered the dykes and canals that created the huge meadows underpinning the Dutch dairy industry.

From the Middle Ages, Dutch cheese was traded in domestic and foreign markets. Cheesemakers were quick to incorporate newly discovered exotic spices (such as cumin, caraway, and cloves) into their cheeses.

GRONINGEN

WADDENZEE

FRIESLAND

DRENTHE

NOORD-HOLLAND

OVERIJSSEL

FLEVOLAND

GELDERLAND

UTRECHT

THE NETHERLANDS

ZUID- HOLLAND

PRODUCED THROUGHOUT THE COUNTRY
Edam,
Geitenkaas Met Kruiden,
Gouda,
Kernhem,
Leidse Kaas,
Maasdam,
Nagelkaas

NOORD-BRABANT

ZEELAND

ANTWERPEN
Postel

LIMBURG

NORTH SEA

Bio or Pas de Bleu,
Pas de Rouge

WEST VLAANDEREN
Rubens
OOST-VLAANDEREN

VLAAMS BRABANT

LIMBURG

Keiems Bloempje

Passendale

BRUSSEL

BELGIUM

BRABANT WALLON

Hervé ★

LIÈGE

N

HAINAUT

NAMUR

Chimay à la Bière,
Vieux Chimay

LUXEMBOURG

DIEKIRCH

LUXEMBOURG

GREVEN-MACHER

LUXEMBOURG

Key
★ AOC, DOC, DOP, PGI, or PDO cheeses
🧀 Produced only here
🧀 Produced throughout the region

50 miles

50 km

Bio or Pas de Bleu

Made with organic, raw milk by the Hinkelspel dairy cooperative (*hinkelspel* means "hopscotch" in English). Its slightly sticky rind is red-brown and covered in grey, blue, and some white moulds.

TASTING NOTES The pale yellow, creamy interior has a mass of well-spread blue streaks. It has an intense steely blue tang, long-lasting and very peppery, with an acidic bite and spicy overtones.

HOW TO ENJOY Delicious with autumn fruit such as sweet grapes and Doyenné pears, or in a salad with chicory and nuts. Pair with sweet white wines.

BELGIUM Oost-Vlaanderen	
Age 8–10 weeks	
Weight and Shape 800g–1kg (1¾lb–2¼lb), drum	
Size D. 10cm (4in), H. 10cm (4in)	
Milk Cow	
Classification Blue	
Producer Coöperatieve Het Hinkelspel	

Chimay à la Bière

In 1850, a group of Cistercian monks set about building Scourmont Abbey and establishing a herd of Friesian cows to make butter and, later, Trappist cheeses such as this one, which is washed in Chimay Trappist beer. Today, the milk used comes from 250 producers in the region.

TASTING NOTES The firm leathery rind has a heady aroma of hops and the farmyard, while the creamy, supple interior is fruity, with a distinct taste of toasted hops continuing on the finish.

HOW TO ENJOY This is a superb melting cheese, or serve it simply, accompanied by a Belgian beer, ideally from Chimay.

BELGIUM Chimay, Hainaut	
Age 4 weeks	
Weight and Shape 2kg (4⅓lb), wheel	
Size D. 19cm (7½in), H. 6cm (2½in),	
Milk Cow	
Classification Semi-soft	
Producer Chimay Fromage	

Herve PDO

Probably the most famous of Belgium's cheeses, this is named after the town where it is made and is similar to Limburger. Washed repeatedly in brine over 3 months, the rind becomes sticky and covered in orange-brown mould. Herve Remoudou is richer and stronger.

TASTING NOTES Its pale yellow interior is springy and creamy. The flavour ranges from surprisingly sweet and mellow, to strong and spicy.

HOW TO ENJOY Its pungency demands a strong companion, so enjoy with dark breads, and wash down with Belgian-style Trappist beers and ales.

BELGIUM Hervé, Liège	
Age 3 months minimum	
Weight and Shape 200g (7oz), brick	
Size L. 6cm (2½in), W. 6cm (2½in), H. 5cm (2in)	
Milk Cow	
Classification Semi-soft	
Producer Hervé Société	

225

Keiems Bloempje

"Keiems" refers to a part of the city of Diksmuide, a region of lush meadows formed by the intricate system of dykes and canals, or *polders*, while "Bloempje" is the Walloon for "flower" and refers to the *Penicillium candidum* bloom that coats the cheese. Some types are flavoured with herbs and garlic.

TASTING NOTES Made from raw organic milk, it has a thick, creamy texture, a mushroomy aroma, and a milky taste with a mushroom and green grass finish.

HOW TO ENJOY Try it grilled on bread or spread on crispbreads with a sweet homemade chutney; complement with Chardonnay or a light beer.

BELGIUM Diksmuide, West Vlaanderen	
Age 4–8 weeks	
Weight and Shape 350g (12oz) or 7kg (15½lb), round	
Size D. 11cm (4¼in), H. 4cm (1½in)	
Milk Cow	
Classification Soft white	
Producer Het Dischhof	

226

Pas de Rouge

The name Pas de Rouge refers to a hop in Belgium's version of the playground game of hopscotch. This washed rind Trappist-style cheese is made with organic raw cow's milk and has a red-orange leathery rind that develops a white mist of *Penicillium* mould as it matures.

TASTING NOTES Pas de Rouge is supple and buttery, with small, scattered holes. It has a lightly farmyardy aroma and overtones of hazelnut, with a meaty taste as it comes of age.

HOW TO ENJOY Eat it like the locals: with brown bread, butter, and coffee or a typical Belgian Trappist beer.

BELGIUM Ghent, Oost Vlaanderen	
Age 6–8 weeks	
Weight and Shape 2.5kg (5½lb), round	
Size D. 22cm (8¾in), H. 7cm (2¾in)	
Milk Cow	
Classification Semi-soft	
Producer Coöperatieve Het Hinkelspel	

Passendale

This popular Flemish cheese, based on an old monastic recipe, resembles a loaf of bread. Its distinctive caramel brown rind is lightly dusted with white mould. It is named after the village made infamous by the Battle of Passendale in World War I.

TASTING NOTES It is firm yet pliable, with very small and irregular holes and a pale yellow creamy interior that has a buttery taste becoming more mellow with age.

HOW TO ENJOY A stalwart of the continental breakfast buffet with cold hams and smoked meats and sausages. Serve with light beers or white wines.

BELGIUM Passchendaele, West Vlaanderen	
Age 3–6 months	
Weight and Shape 3kg (6½lb), round	
Size D. 15cm (6in), H. 7cm (2¾in)	
Milk Cow	
Classification Semi-soft	
Producer Bongrain	

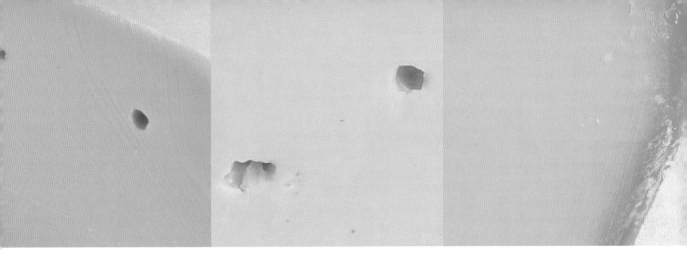

Postel

This orange-rinded cheese is handmade by the monks at the Abbey of Postel using milk from their own herd of some 160 cows and others from nearby farms. Needless to say, this cheese is not made in high volumes, but is much loved by those in the know.

TASTING NOTES It is hard and quite dry with a dark, earthy yellow colour. Postel is a nutty-flavoured cheese, with hints of spices, such as cloves and nutmeg, intensifying with age.

HOW TO ENJOY Pair with a bottle of Postel beer, obviously. This is a good cheese for grating, as a snack, or as a topping for baked jacket potatoes.

BELGIUM Mol, Antwerpen	
Age 12–24 months	
Weight and Shape 4kg (8¾lb), loaf	
Size L. 27cm (10¾in), W. 13cm (5¼in), H. 11cm (4¼in)	
Milk Cow	
Classification Hard	
Producer Abbey of Postel	

Rubens

This distinctive washed-rind cheese is named in honour of the 17th-century Flemish Baroque painter Peter Paul Rubens. The recipe was revived in the 1960s and is now one of the most popular of all the Belgian cheeses.

TASTING NOTES Beneath the reddish-brown protective rind lies a firm yet supple paste with small holes. It has a rich, smooth flavour, with a subtle sweet-savoury taste.

HOW TO ENJOY Like all semi-soft cheeses, Rubens grills and bakes well, and it is easy to slice for snacks or breakfast. Try it with slices of fresh apple, and serve with cider or a light red wine.

BELGIUM West Vlaanderen	
Age 8–12 weeks	
Weight and Shape 3kg (6½lb), oval	
Size D. 30cm (12in), H. 9cm (4½in)	
Milk Cow	
Classification Semi-soft	
Producers Bongrain	

Vieux Chimay

Like Chimay à la Bière, this is made at Scourmount Abbey. Annatto is added to the milk to give the finished cheese a warm tangerine colour. With its flattened ball shape and thin golden brown crust, it makes for an attractive addition to a cheeseboard.

TASTING NOTES Although this cheese is described as hard, Vieux Chimay has a soft, chewy melt-in-the-mouth texture. The flavour is buttery with a hint of hazelnuts and a distinct but pleasant bitterness to the finish.

HOW TO ENJOY The makers recommend it melted into a lobster risotto and paired with a glass of Chimay Tripel beer.

BELGIUM Chimay, Hainaut	
Age 6 months	
Weight and Shape 3kg (6½lb), flattened ball	
Size D.17cm (6¾in), H.11cm (4¼in)	
Milk Cow	
Classification Hard	
Producer Chimay Fromage	

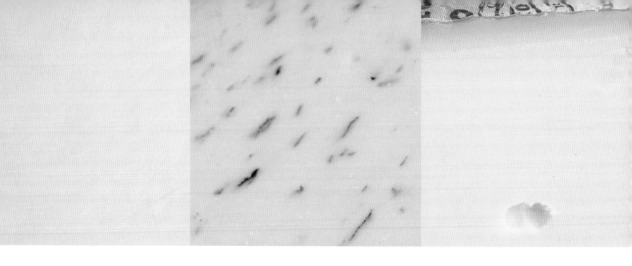

Edam

Edam, which was first shipped from the Port of Edam north of Amsterdam in 1439, is made with skimmed milk. Its distinctive red waxed coat is a familiar sight on deli counters the world over. The majority is exported since the Dutch prefer Gouda.

TASTING NOTES Beneath the thin rind it has a supple, smooth texture and sweet, milky, buttery flavour, becoming more flavoursome and firmer with age.

HOW TO ENJOY This simple cheese is equally at home as a snack, in sandwiches, grilled, grated, or served at breakfast with chocolate and eggs, as they do in the Netherlands.

THE NETHERLANDS All over	
Age 1–12 months	
Weight and Shape 1kg (2¼lb), ball	
Size D. 10cm (4in), H. 10cm (4in)	
Milk Cow	
Classification Semi-soft	
Producer Friesland Campina	

228

Geitenkaas Met Kruiden

Cheese lovers visiting Amsterdam should make time to visit one of the amazing cheese shops. Less well-known hard goat's cheeses such as this one are definitely worth trying. The name means "goat's cheese with nettles".

TASTING NOTES It is supple like young Gouda, with a stark white interior that is scattered with flecks of chopped nettles. It has a subtle almond flavour from the goat's milk and a slight grassy, earthy finish.

HOW TO ENJOY Great as a snack or on a cheeseboard, paired with a cool beer.

THE NETHERLANDS All over	
Age 3–6 months	
Weight and Shape 8kg (17lb 10oz), boulder	
Size D. 20cm (8in), H. 10cm (4in)	
Milk Goat	
Classification Flavour-added	
Producer Various	

Kernhem

This modern Dutch cheese is named after the Kernhem Estate, a mystical place where, according to legend, a white lady or ghost is regularly seen. Unlike most other Dutch cheeses, Kernhem is made with added cream and has a sticky orange-coloured rind from frequent washings in brine.

TASTING NOTES Kernhem's paste is soft and gooey, with a pronounced farmyard aroma; a nutty, creamy flavour; and a penetrating savoury finish.

HOW TO ENJOY This is a cheese that cries out for tangy pickles, cold meats, and a glass of white wine.

THE NETHERLANDS Gelderland	
Age 5–6 weeks	
Weight and Shape 2.5kg (5½lb), round	
Size D. 20cm (8in), H. 5cm (2in)	
Milk Cow	
Classification Semi-soft	
Producer Friesland Campina	

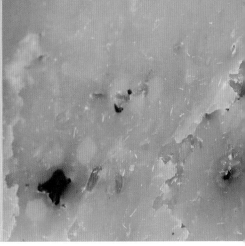

Leidse Kaas AOC

Named after Leiden, its town of origin, the rind is imprinted with crossed keys, the city's emblem. It is similar to Gouda, but made with semi-skimmed milk and is scattered with cumin seeds. Spices such as cumin, cloves, and peppercorns were introduced in the 1600s by early Dutch explorers.

TASTING NOTES The dense, compact sunshine-yellow interior feels dry yet creamy and mellow. It is perfectly balanced by the aromatic cumin.

HOW TO ENJOY It is excellent with all drinks, such as beer and aromatic wines. It also adds a pleasant spice-filled note to salads, soups, and vegetable dishes.

THE NETHERLANDS All over	
Age 2–12 months	
Weight and Shape 10kg (22lb), boulder	
Size D. 30cm (12in), H. 10cm (4in)	
Milk Cow	
Classification Flavour-added	
Producer Various	

Maasdam

This Swiss-style cheese was originally created in the Netherlands as a less expensive alternative to Emmental, but its sweet, fruity taste, large holes, and bulging upper side proved very popular. Production continues to grow, with leading brand Leerdammer now sold across the world.

TASTING NOTES It is very supple and elastic with large holes, and its sweet, fermenting fruit flavour is a result of the special bacteria added to the milk.

HOW TO ENJOY It is a definite favourite for all the family as a snacking cheese or in sandwiches, salads, and fondue. Pair with light fruity whites and rosé.

THE NETHERLANDS All over	
Age 4–12 weeks	
Weight and Shape 10kg (22lb), boulder	
Size D. 30–40cm (12–15½in), H. 15–20cm (6–8in)	
Milk Cow	
Classification Semi-soft	
Producer Various	

Nagelkaas

Originally made in Friesland it is a Gouda in which fresh cloves and cumin have been added to the fresh curd and aged together. The cloves resemble nails so they are called *kruidnagels*, or "spicy nails", and the cheese is known as "nail cheese". Its equivalent without cloves is known as Kanterkaas.

TASTING NOTES Despite being made from skimmed milk with only a 23 per cent fat content, the cheese possesses a pronounced hot, spicy, aromatic taste and a firm, creamy texture. It becomes a deep yellow with age.

HOW TO ENJOY Use sparingly in salads and hot dishes, and complement with beer.

THE NETHERLANDS All over	
Age 4–12 months	
Weight and Shape 8kg (17lb 10oz), boulder	
Size D. 30cm (12in), H. 10cm (4in)	
Milk Cow	
Classification Flavour-added	
Producer Various	

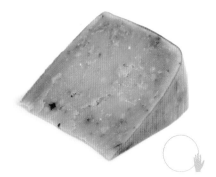

Gouda

The long-keeping properties of the Dutch cheeses, especially Gouda, and the geographical position of The Netherlands on the west coast of Europe meant, historically, the cheeses could be shipped to France and further afield. By the 12th century their popularity had spread across Europe and later became an essential item on the explorers' shopping list when they took to the seas.

Evidence of their importance can be seen in the existence of weigh-houses and formal markets in virtually every town, such as the beautifully restored example in Gouda. Built in 1668, it was where the farmers brought their cheeses to be weighed and quality checked to estimate their tax. Today, you can find out your weight in cheese at the weekly markets in summer in Gouda, Alkmaar, and Edam.

What differentiates Gouda and Edam (see p228) from other cheeses is that some of the whey is replaced with hot water in the vat once the curd has been cut – a process known as washing the curd. This removes lactose from the curd, producing a sweeter, more mellow and slightly more elastic curd.

The fresco on the outside of the Gouda weigh-house.

THE NETHERLANDS All over	
Age 4 weeks–3 years	
Weight and Shape 200g–20kg (7oz–44lb), wheel	
Size Various	
Milk Cow	
Classification Hard	
Producer Various	

The best are the Boerenkaas, Farmhouse Gouda, made with raw milk by small farmers when the weather permits the cattle to stay outside and graze the fresh grasses of the polders, a remarkable landscape of dykes and windmills.

Over the centuries, other European countries have adopted this style of cheesemaking, most notably Sweden. In the last century, Dutch immigrants in America, Australia, and New Zealand have started making farmhouse versions that meticulously retain the old methods – though regulations prevent most from using raw milk.

TASTING NOTES At only a few months old, Gouda is supple with a sweet fruity taste, becoming firmer and fruitier, and by 18 months, the interior, with its small holes, has become deep yellow, hard, almost brittle and granular. Each bite reveals more of its complex character, from fruity to a hint of cocoa and groundnut, while the feel in the mouth is rich and smooth. Boerenkaas Gouda has a more outspoken taste that differs from farm to farm.

HOW TO ENJOY Young Gouda is ideal for sandwiches, snacks, and salads. The stronger taste of aged Gouda lends itself to the cheeseboard or cooked in hot dishes from gratins to tarts and pasta alongside a good Dutch beer or a robust red like Pinot Noir or Barolo.

A CLOSER LOOK

The Netherlands produce 730 million kilos of cheese, out of which 500 million is exported. About 60 per cent of Dutch cheese produce is Gouda.

Young Gouda has a distinctive polished yellow rind.

Young Cheese

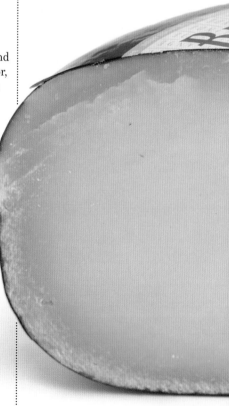

WASHING THE CURD In order to wash the curd, some of the whey is drained and replaced by warm water. This is stirred in, and some more of the whey, now diluted, is drained off and replaced by more water. The water removes the lactose (milk sugars) from the curd. When the water is hot, it scalds the curd and so expels additional moisture. The result of this activity is to keep the acidity of the curd at a lower level than would normally be the case since the activity of the lactic bacteria is reduced.

ADDING FLAVOUR The founding of the Dutch East Indies Company in the 17th century opened up the spice trade. The Dutch were quick to utilize these new and aromatic flavours in their cheeses – particularly cumin, caraway, peppercorns, and cloves.

VERTICAL PRESS The cheeses are removed from their moulds, stacked in vertical presses, and lightly pressed for a few hours or even days.

Aged Gouda, aged for a minimum of 18 months, has a black waxed rind.

With age, the interior becomes hard, dry, and a deep sunshine yellow.

Mature Cheese

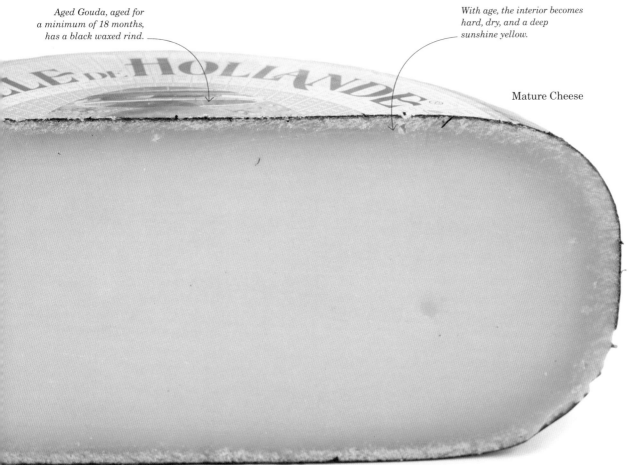

GERMANY, AUSTRIA, AND SWITZERLAND

N

GERMANY In the Alpine regions of Bayern (Bavaria), cheesemaking was influenced by the Swiss, and before them, the Romans. Allgäu, the heart of German cheesemaking, draws its inspiration from the Swiss with its famous Allgäuer Emmentaler, which was introduced to the area in 1821. An abundant supply of high-quality milk allows Bayern to produce 75 per cent of Germany's cheeses, making it one of Germany's most important milk and cheese regions.

In the northern regions of Germany, traditional cheeses are often fresh or lactic-acidified milk products, as seen in The Netherlands and Denmark or with Trappiste cheeses. Although many cheeses are produced in Bayern, some of Germany's more famous cheeses, such as Altenburger Ziegenkäse, are produced in the northern parts of Germany.

AUSTRIA Since the climate and pastures in Western Austria (Vorarlberg and Tirol) are similar to those in Switzerland, it is no wonder that the border-sharing cheesemakers have been swapping recipes for centuries. In the east, the influence came from the Balkans, which is why fresh-style cheeses are more prevalent.

SWITZERLAND The great cheeses of Switzerland, famous throughout the world, can trace their history back to before the coming of the Romans. The first reference to cheesemaking was made in 33BCE, when the Rhaetians made "cheese" for the long, hard winter. Records show that by the Middle Ages, Swiss cheeses were being traded across much of Europe.

In modern times, despite much of the production moving to large factories, most Swiss cheeses are still made in small dairies or cooperatives. This is due to the primary objective of the Swiss agricultural policy – maintaining the landscape that characterizes Switzerland.

SCHLESWIG-HOLSTEIN
Schichtkäse

MECKLENBURG-VORPOMMERN

GERMANY
PRODUCED THROUGHOUT THE COUNTRY
Tilsiterkäse

NIEDERSACHSEN
Harzer Käse

BRANDENBURG

SACHSEN-ANHALT
Harzer Käse

NORDRHEIN-WESTFALEN

SACHSEN
Altenburger Ziegenkäse ★

THÜRINGEN
Harzer Käse,
Altenburger Ziegenkäse ★

HESSEN

RHEINLAND-PFALZ

SAARLAND

BAYERN
Allgäuer Bergkäse ★,
Allgäuer Emmentaler ★,
Limburger,
Weisslacker

BADEN-WÜRTTEMBERG

Tête de Moine ★,
Vacherin Mont d'Or ★

Tomme Vaudoise,
Vacherin Fribourgeois ★

Sbrinz ★   Appenzeller   Bavaria Blu

Appenzeller   Bachensteiner   Bio Paulus

Gruyère ★   Vorarlberger Bergkäse ★

Tomme Vaudoise   Hobelkäse   Sbrinz ★   **AUSTRIA**

Sbrinz ★   Chorherrenkäse,   Tiroler Graukäse ★,
                 Tiroler Graukäse ★   Weinkäse

SWITZERLAND   Schabziger
PRODUCED THROUGHOUT THE COUNTRY   Chorherrenkäse,
Emmentaler,   Tiroler Graukäse ★
Mutschli,
Raclette   **LIECHTENSTEIN**

Valle Maggia

Hobelkäse

100 miles

100 km

Key
★ AOC, DOC, DOP, PGI, or PDO cheeses
   Produced only here
   Produced throughout the region

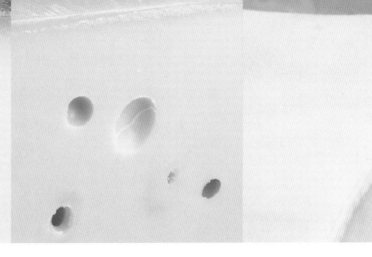

Allgäuer Bergkäse PDO

Allgäu is known for its Swiss-style cheeses, introduced in 1841 by two Swiss cheesemakers. Bergkäse, or mountain cheese, is like a little Emmentaler (see pp240–41) with smaller holes and made in alpine huts during late spring and summer.

TASTING NOTES Dense with small holes, it has a sweet, buttery taste becoming more intense and slightly salty.

HOW TO ENJOY This is perfect for a Bavarian *Brotzeit*, an afternoon meal accompanied with sausage slices, bacon, and dark bread. Enjoy with a fine Bavarian beer.

GERMANY Bayern	
Age 3-6 months	
Weight and Shape 25kg (55lb 2oz), wheel	
Size D. 50cm (20in), H. 10cm (4in)	
Milk Cow	
Classification Hard	
Producer Various	

Allgäuer Emmentaler PDO

Allgäu cheeses use milk from the brown Allgäu cattle that graze the spring meadows that are rich in alpine flowers. This is based on the Swiss Emmentaler (see pp240–41), but is smaller and ripens more quickly.

TASTING NOTES Most cheeses are sold at around three months old, when they are supple, golden yellow, and mild with a hint of hazelnut.

HOW TO ENJOY Perfect for breakfast, snacks, cheese plates and cooking, it is typically served with tea, coffee, or beer. In Germany, thin slices of cheese are laid on or between white bread slices.

GERMANY Bayern	
Age 3–6 months	
Weight and Shape 80kg (176lb 6oz), wheel	
Size D. 90cm (35½in), H. 110cm (43½in)	
Milk Cow	
Classification Hard	
Producer Various	

Altenburger Ziegenkäse PDO

Sachsen and Thüringia in eastern Germany were home to this cheese. Very little of it was produced until German reunification, but it is now available all over the country.

TASTING NOTES Soft and creamy, and pure white in colour, typical of goat's cheese. It has a very pleasant, mild flavour and a goaty finish that is not too pronounced. The interior is punctuated with caraway seeds.

HOW TO ENJOY Perfect for cheeseboards, salads, or drizzled with sweet mustard to bring out the flavour. Enjoy it with a liqueur or a light white wine.

GERMANY Sachsen and Thüringia	
Age 4 weeks	
Weight and Shape 300-500g (10 oz–1lb 2oz), round	
Size D. 20cm (8in), H. 10cm (4in)	
Milk Goat with some cow	
Classification Soft-white	
Producer Altenburger Land	

233

Bavaria Blu

This cheese is a fusion of Camembert and Gorgonzola: it has a thick, white coat and the blue mould is injected into the young cheese, a technique developed in Germany in the 1970s. Made with extra cream, Bavaria Blu is often referred to as the blue cheese for people who don't like blue cheese.

TASTING NOTES Considerably milder than Gorgonzola or Camembert, it has a very rich, creamy taste, and subtle spicy blue finish. The blue splodges through the interior make it very appealing.

HOW TO ENJOY Served on most German cheeseboards with a white Rhine wine such as Riesling and a nutty bread.

GERMANY Allgäu, Bayern	
Age 4–6 weeks	
Weight and Shape 1.5kg (3lb 3oz), round	
Size D. 30cm (12in), H. 7cm (3in)	
Milk Cow	
Classification Blue	
Producer Käserei Champignon	

Harzer Käse

Although this cheese has been made for centuries from soured skimmed milk on small farms throughout Germany, butter was always more important than cheese. The best known types are Harzer, along with Olmützer Quargel (pictured), Handkäse, and Mainzer.

TASTING NOTES Several of these "coins" are assembled into a roll, and are then separated for eating. When fresh, the paste is lemony sharp, but at about three weeks, it becomes more mellow.

HOW TO ENJOY Mixed with vinegar, salt, and onion, it is called "hand cheese with music". With dark German bread and cider, it is a satisfying afternoon meal.

GERMANY The Harz mountain range (Niedersachsen, Sachsen-Anhalt, and Thüringen)	
Age 2–4 weeks	
Weight and Shape 100g (3½oz), coin	
Size L. 10cm (4in), D. 5cm (2in)	
Milk Cow	
Classification Fresh	
Producer Various	

Limburger

This washed-rind cheese was originally made in Belgium's Limbourg region. It became so popular that, since 1830, the majority of it has been made in Germany, mostly using the excellent local milk from the Allgäu region.

TASTING NOTES Its sticky orange-brown rind and intense farmyardy smell comes from being washed in special bacteria. The taste is significantly milder, but still farmyardy and meaty.

HOW TO ENJOY Served as "Brotzeit", which is afternoon tea with boiled jacket potatoes and butter, or with vinaigrette and slices of onion, dark bread, and beer or cider.

GERMANY Bayern	
Age 6–12 weeks	
Weight and Shape 150g (5oz), brick	
Size L. 12cm (5in), W. 4cm (1½in), H. 3.5cm (1in)	
Milk Cow	
Classification Semi-soft	
Producer Various	

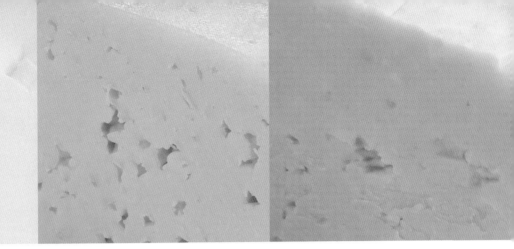

Schichtkäse or Handkäse

This lactic cheese (which curdles without rennet) is made in northern Germany from a very old recipe using skimmed milk. Similar to quark, but dryer, it is made of layers of curd – the top and bottom layers from skimmed milk; the middle layer from whole milk.

TASTING NOTES It is an acquired taste that is vaguely aromatic and tart, with a texture similar to cottage cheese. The middle layer of the cheese looks more yellow because it is higher in fat.

HOW TO ENJOY It is suitable for breakfast in place of quark or yogurt. Spread on a slice of dark bread as a snack. It also goes perfectly with tea or coffee.

GERMANY Schleswig-Holstein
Age A few days
Weight and Shape 100–500g (3½oz–1lb 2oz), packets or pots
Size Various
Milk Cow
Classification Fresh
Producer Various

Tilsiterkäse

Named after the town of Tilsit (now Sowjetsk in Russia), this cheese was apparently created by mid-19th century Dutch immigrants who were trying to re-create their famous Gouda. Brick-shaped, it can be waxed or made with added cream, herbs, pepper, or caraway seeds. Swiss Tilsit is round and firmer, with pea-sized holes.

TASTING NOTES Butter-yellow, springy, and sliceable, with many uneven slits, it ranges in flavour from mild and sweet-savoury to strong and meaty.

HOW TO ENJOY It is ideal for breakfast, sandwiches, and snacks along with a beer, Riesling, Sylvaner, or fruity red.

GERMANY All over
Age 12–18 weeks
Weight and Shape 4kg (8½lb), brick
Size Various L. 30cm (12in), W. 15cm (6in), H. 15cm (6in) (pictured)
Milk Cow
Classification Semi-soft
Producer Various

Weisslacker

This cheese was invented in 1874, and its name means "white lacquer cheese", which denotes its shiny, glass-like white rind. It is soaked in brine, and is not unlike feta. This cheese is also known as Bayerische Bierkäse (Bavarian beer cheese), as it goes extremely well with this brew.

TASTING NOTES After two days in brine, it is crumbly and has a surprisingly strong smell and tang with a salty bite.

HOW TO ENJOY Cut it into chunks and serve with Bretzels (chewy pretzels), vinaigrette, and a lot of onions. This is a hearty meal best washed down with a lot of beer. Also used in "Maultaschen".

GERMANY Bayern
Age 3–6 weeks
Weight and Shape 500g–1kg (1lb 2oz–2¼lb), brick
Size L. 10–12cm (4–5in), W. 10–12cm (4–5in), H. 6–10cm (2½–4in)
Milk Cow
Classification Fresh
Producer Various

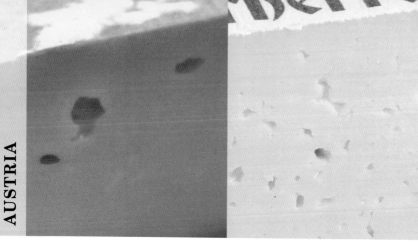

Bachensteiner

The small mountain village cooperative of Sibratsgfäll, founded in 1907, sits on the edge of the Bregenz Forest at an altitude of 930m (3,051ft), nestled between majestic mountains. Cows here graze a variety of grasses and herbs in the meadows producing rich, sweet milk.

TASTING NOTES Hand-washed in brine, it has a sticky pink-orange rind and a rich, creamy interior with tiny holes. The taste and aroma is farmyardy, meaty with a sweet spicy finish.

HOW TO ENJOY Great with hoppy Austrian beer or an aromatic white wine. Serve with crusty, dark bread and mountain ham or with sliced pickled onion.

AUSTRIA Vorarlberg	
Age 2–4 weeks	
Weight and Shape 210g (7oz), brick	
Size L. 14cm (5.5in), H. 4.5cm (2in)	
Milk Cow	
Classification Semi-soft	
Producer Sibratsgfälle Cooperative	

Chorherrenkäse

Bearing the imprint of a wide cross, this cheese is dipped in white wax giving it a distinctive appearance and is sometimes known as Amadeus in other countries. It was originally made in Tirol, and based on the old monastery or Trappist style cheeses, where the fresh milk was combined with sweet buttermilk.

TASTING NOTES Supple with small holes, it has a smooth texture and a pleasant milky or lactic aroma. Its taste has a hint of herbs and meadow flowers.

HOW TO ENJOY A pleasant, undemanding cheese for the cheeseboard, breakfast table or buffet. Pair with Trappist style beer or local Grüner Veltliner wine.

AUSTRIA Tirol	
Age 4–6 weeks	
Weight and Shape 800g (1¾lb), loaf	
Size D. 25cm (10in), H. 18cm (7in)	
Milk Cow	
Classification Semi-soft	
Producer Bergland Voitsberg	

Bio Paulus

In 1924, Friar Leonhard brought the recipe for this Trappiste style cheese to the monastery of Schlierbach in Upper Austria, where it is still made by the monks. They now make a range of cow, goat, and ewes milk cheeses, all organic since 1999.

TASTING NOTES Brine washed, it has a pale red-orange rind and smooth, deep yellow interior with a spicy full bodied taste and a farmyardy aroma typical of Trappiste cheese.

HOW TO ENJOY It is great on a cheeseboard with crisp bread for an afternoon snack. Pair it with a red Zinfandel, Merlot, or Pinot Noir, or a full-bodied white wine.

AUSTRIA Upper Austria Salzburg	
Age 3–6 weeks	
Weight and Shape 150g (5½oz), round	
Size D. 12cm (4⅓in), H. 3.5cm (1⅓in)	
Milk Cow, organic	
Classification Semi-soft	
Producer Schlierbach Monastery	

Tiroler Graukäse PDO

Made with skimmed milk and soured naturally using a lactic starter rather than rennet, this cheese from Tirol is pressed, then milled and pressed again. There is also a version of Graukäse made in Steiermark.

TASTING NOTES In the first few days, it is curd-like and crumbly, but left at room temperature for a few days, it ripens and becomes smooth, softer, and almost runny. The taste is lemony fresh.

HOW TO ENJOY In Tirol, it is served with vinegar, pumpkin seed oil, and onion rings. The version from Steiermark is grated over flat cake on buttered bread. Try with salads and sautéed potatoes.

AUSTRIA Tirol and Steiermark	
Age 4 weeks	
Weight and Shape 2kg (4½lb), block	
Size L. 15cm (6in), W. 15cm (6in), H. 15cm (6in)	
Milk Cow	
Classification Hard	
Producers Various	

Vorarlberger Bergkäse PDO

The Vorarlberg Mountains overshadow Lake Constance. Their high pastures, carpeted with wild flowers and grasses, provide superb grazing for the cattle during the summer months. They produce rich, flavoursome milk to make this bergkäse (mountain cheese).

TASTING NOTES The rind is thick and the paste supple. The grazing gives this cheese its buttery yellow colour and subtle taste of wild honey with a savoury, salty undercurrent that comes with age.

HOW TO ENJOY Vorarlberger is equally at home as a snack, in a fondue, or grilled, complemented by a fruity Chardonnay.

AUSTRIA Vorarlberg	
Age 6–8 months	
Weight and Shape 50kg (110lb), wheel	
Size D. 50cm (20in), H. 12cm (5in)	
Milk Cow	
Classification Hard	
Producer Various	

Weinkäse

This cheese was born in Leibnitz, in a dairy near the Slovenian border, where, by chance, a new cheese that was temporarily stored in a nearby wine cellar absorbed the wonderful aromas. Today it is made in nearby Enns Valley and washed with red wine to create an almost black rind dusted with white mould.

TASTING NOTES It tastes of fermenting fruit with a slightly lemony tang and a hint of the Zweigelt wine, balanced by a smooth, tender texture.

HOW TO ENJOY Serve as an eye-catching cheeseboard addition with crusty bread. Pair it with a red Zweigelt wine.

AUSTRIA Steiermark	
Age 6–8 weeks	
Weight and Shape 1kg (2¼lb), round	
Size D. 20cm (8in), H. 5cm (2in)	
Milk Cow	
Classification Semi-soft	
Producer Schärdinger Group	

Appenzeller

Made in the hilly pre-alps of Switzerland for more than 700 years, this cheese has a brown-orange aromatic rind from washing with a closely-guarded secret blend of cider, white wine, herbs, and spices. It is still made in small village dairies but marketed under a joint brand name.

TASTING NOTES The "classic" at six months has nutty notes and a spicy finish. Later the cheese becomes more aromatic, and sold as "Surchoix or even better "Extra".

HOW TO ENJOY Popular for breakfast when young or the cheeseboard when aged. Served with crusty bread, cider, beer, or a racy red wine such as Dole or Fitou.

SWITZERLAND Appenzell Ausserrhoden, Appenzell Innerrhoden, St Gallen, and Thurgau	
Age 6–8 months	
Weight and Shape 8kg (17lb 10oz), wheel	
Size D. 35cm (14in), H. 12cm (5in)	
Milk Cow	
Classification Semi-soft	
Producer Various	

238

Gruyère AOC

Switzerland's most popular cheese is named after the picturesque village of Gruyère, near Fribourg, and can trace its history back to 1072. The best, Gruyere d'Alpage, are made in the mountains in summer, when the cows graze the alpine pastures.

TASTING NOTES At four months, it is firm and dense, with a nutty flavour. At eight months, it has a wonderful complexity that is rich, strong, nutty, and earthy.

HOW TO ENJOY This essential ingredient for fondue can also be grated over pasta, salads, or vegetables, or into sauces. Serve with walnuts, fruity bread, and a Dole or Burgundy red wine.

SWITZERLAND Fribourg	
Age From 12 months	
Weight and Shape 40kg (88lb), wheel	
Size D. 70cm (27½in), H. 15cm (6in)	
Milk Cow	
Classification Hard	
Producer Various	

Hobelkäse

During the summer in Bern and Valais, cows graze in the mountains pastures and the farmers, each with a few cows, pool their milk to make this cheese. In autumn, they return home and share the cheeses at the annual "Chästeilet", a major event for the farmers and tourists.

TASTING NOTES Cut into paper-thin slices with a cheese-rake, Hobelkäse reveals the exquisite aroma of the flowery meadows captured in the milk.

HOW TO ENJOY It is traditionally served thinly sliced and rolled with a prickling white wine from the Lake Gteneva vineyards as an apéritif.

SWITZERLAND Bern and Valais	
Age 18 months	
Weight 10kg (22lb), wheel	
Size D. 50cm (20in), H. 15cm (6in)	
Milk Cow	
Classification Hard	
Producer Various	

Mutschli

Using a surplus of cow's, goat's, and occasionally ewe's milks, village dairies around the country produce this cheese. Significantly smaller than most Swiss cheeses, it comes in various shapes and sizes.

TASTING NOTES Beneath the washed yellow to brown rind, is a soft, mild paste, with few or no holes, and a light yellow colour. Mutschli is a pleasant cheese and a children's favourite.

HOW TO ENJOY In central Switzerland, Mutschli is typically fried in a pan and served with boiled potatoes, similar to Raclette. Otherwise, it is eaten mostly as part of breakfast or as a snack.

SWITZERLAND All over
Age 5 weeks
Weight and Shape 900g (2lb), round
Size D. 15cm (6in), H. 5cm (2in)
Milk Cow, goat, or ewe
Classification Semi-soft
Producer Various

Raclette

The name originates from the French word *racler*, meaning "to scrape", and relates to the process of grilling the cheese and scraping it onto bowls of piping-hot potato. It is now made throughout Switzerland. Raw-milk cheeses from the valleys are stamped with their origin, for instance Bagnes, Orsières, Goms, and others.

TASTING NOTES A brown, leathery washed rind encases a smooth, supple paste with a rich, fruity savoury flavour that tastes like liquid gold when grilled.

HOW TO ENJOY Serve on top of steaming potatoes, with pickled cucumbers and onions, and a local white or red wine.

SWITZERLAND All over
Age 6 months
Weight and Shape 6kg (13¼lb), wheel
Size D. 45cm (18in), H. 10cm (4in)
Milk Cow
Classification Semi-soft
Producer Various

Sbrinz AOC

Sbrinz today is not very different from the one described by the Roman writer Pliny in 70BCE as "Caseus Helveticus", or "Swiss cheese". Although it is very hard, it is less crumbly than Parmigiano-Reggiano (see pp128–29) because it is made with full-fat milk.

TASTING NOTES This very hard and grainy cheese has a distinct aroma from the flowery meadows, with spicy, slightly salty undercurrents.

HOW TO ENJOY It is superb grated into pasta and soups, or serve accompanied by a fruity Swiss or Burgundy red or white wine, or even Champagne, as an apéritif.

SWITZERLAND Luzern, Obwalden, and Nidwalden
Age 18–48 months
Weight 30–40kg (66–88lb), wheel
Size Various D. 40cm (15½in), H. 30cm (12in) (pictured)
Milk Cow
Classification Hard
Producer Various

Emmentaler

One of the great classics of the cheese world, Emmentaler can trace its history back to 1293, but was first recorded by name in 1542 when the recipe was given to the people of Langehthal in the Emme valley.

At the beginning of each summer, farmers would take their small herds of cows to the summer pastures, known as *alpage*. Far from the nearest markets, they needed to make a cheese that required months to mature, so they pooled their milk, creating huge slow-ripening cheeses, which could ripen in the chalets until the cows returned to the valleys at the beginning of autumn.

Little has changed since then, except that Emmentaler is now made all over Switzerland where there are high pastures, and takes place in mountain chalets or small owner-operated cooperatives. Hence, as you travel through the magnificent Alps, you can still see the timber-built chalets with their colourful flower boxes, wooden balconies, and tiny windows and the peaceful cows with their hand-painted bells grazing meadows abundant with wild flowers, grasses, and herbs. It is this that makes Swiss Emmentaler unique and impossible to emulate despite many copies the world over. Over winter, the cattle are housed in barns and fed a diet of hay, which makes the milk more concentrated and intense – but the colour is a paler yellow and the cheeses often smaller.

TASTING NOTES When first cut, a perfume like a million meadow flowers is released. If you squeeze a small piece, you can feel its supple texture. As it warms you can taste the hushed tones of the Alpine meadows, the sweetness of ripe, fermenting fruit and herbaceous white wine that tingles on the palate. If you find one that has a tiny "tear" of moisture trapped in the holes, it will be as near to perfect as you could find.

HOW TO ENJOY Great for snacking, sandwiches, for breakfast, and on a cheeseboard, but comes into its own in a fondue where it is rich, creamy, and wonderfully stretchy while its sweet, nutty nature is underlined. Its stringy texture when cooked means, unlike most hard cheeses, it does not break down in sauces but lends itself to being grated or grilled – especially in a Croque Monsieur.

With its immense flavour and firm texture, Emmentaler can be served with big red or white wines or even a crisp, fruity white Swiss wine.

Cattle grazing *in the summer Alpage.*

SWITZERLAND All over		
Age 4–18 months		
Weight and Shape 75–100kg (165–220lb), wheel		
Size D. 80–100cm (31½–39in), H. 16–27cm (6–10½in)		
Milk Cow		
Classification Hard		
Producer Various		

A CLOSER LOOK

About 1,000 litres (1,760 pints) of milk is needed for one cheese. Consequently, like all the big mountain cheeses of Europe, they are made by cooperatives rather than individuals.

RIND The distinctive, repeating pattern on the rind guarantees authenticity to the consumer.

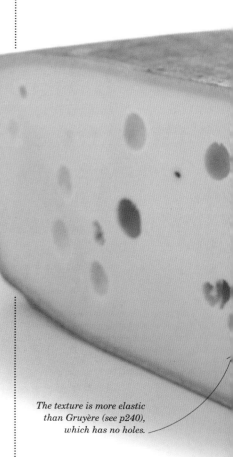

The texture is more elastic than Gruyère (see p240), which has no holes.

CUTTING THE CURD The milk is warmed in a large vat, traditionally a huge copper kettle, and three different starter cultures are stirred into the milk. The curd is cut with wires strung in a giant frame. In the traditional hemispherical vats a "figure of eight" motion is required to cut the curd evenly into rice-sized pieces.

KNEADING AND PRESSING The curd is kneaded so it fills a large hoop and is put into a press. It is then turned and the diameter of the hoop is reduced. The process is repeated six or more times.

GRADING After 6–12 months, a grader using a special hammer, like a tuning fork, will tap each cheese and, from the resonance or echo, can ascertain the size, distribution, and even shape of the holes – and therefore its quality. The best are stamped in red with the Alpine horn blower (common to all Swiss cheeses) and the words "Switzerland" and "Emmentaler". The sides are branded with a unique identification number for traceability.

Quarter wheel

The propionic bacteria present during maturation gives off bubbles of carbon dioxide, and, unable to escape, these create the small holes characteristic of the cheese.

Schabziger or Sapsago

This unique and very distinctive lime green zero-fat cheese has been made since the 11th century, when the local monks introduced fenugreek. Skimmed-milk curds are aged for a few weeks, then finely ground and mixed with the ground fenugreek seeds. It is also known as Sapsago in the USA.

TASTING NOTES Pressed into a small, truncated cone, it has a powerful, racy, almost eye-watering spicy tang.

HOW TO ENJOY Mix with butter in equal parts, spread over crusty white bread with onions or fresh chives. It spices up baked potatoes, fondues, and soups. Cider or Pinot Noir work well with it.

SWITZERLAND Glarus	
Age 8 weeks	
Weight and Shape 100g (3½oz), truncated cone	
Size D. 5cm (2in), H. 10cm (4in)	
Milk Cow	
Classification Fresh	
Producer Geska	

Tête de Moine AOC

First made in the 12th century by monks at Bellelay monastery, its production shifted to farms owned by the monastery when the cheese was given to the Church as a tithe. Originally named Bellelay after the monastery, it was renamed "head of the monks" in recognition of enthusiastic consumption.

TASTING NOTES Dense, smooth, and yellow as the result of meadow flowers, it has a buttery, slightly savoury taste that is revealed when pared into rosettes with the *girolle* machine.

HOW TO ENJOY Using a *girolle*, guests create rosettes, and enjoy them with a Lake Geneva white and fresh walnuts.

SWITZERLAND Jura	
Age 8 months	
Weight and Shape 600–800g (1lb 5oz–1¾lb), cylinder	
Size D. 12cm (5in), H. 18cm (7in) (pictured)	
Milk Cow	
Classification Hard	
Producer Various	

Tomme Vaudoise

Made in French-speaking Switzerland, this cheese has a thin, wrinkled rind dusted with white mould. The raw cow's milk version, Tomme Fleurette, develops reddish-brown patches that break down the curd until it is almost liquid. Goat's milk versions are sold as Tomme de Chèvre.

TASTING NOTES Vaudoise is mild and creamy with a hint of mushrooms from the rind, while Fleurette has a more intense, rustic flavour as it softens.

HOW TO ENJOY Great with crispy bread, especially caraway or walnut, and a Vully or Chablis, or dip in breadcrumbs and lightly fry, and serve with salad.

SWITERLAND Vaud and Fribourg	
Age 4–6 weeks	
Weight and Shape 100–150g (3½–5oz), disc	
Size: D. 16cm (6in), 3cm (1in) (pictured)	
Milk Cow or goat	
Classification Soft white	
Producer Various	

Vacherin Fribourgeois AOC

Vacherin Fribourgeois, not to be confused with Vacherin Mont d'Or, is a dense, deep yellow cheese. Produced in the canton of Fribourg, it first came to fame in 1448, when it was served to the daughter of the Scottish king and wife of the Duke Sigismund of Austria.

TASTING NOTES Supple and nutty, it has a long, tender aftertaste of alpine flowers and freshly cut hay. Its flavours intensify when the cheese is melted.

HOW TO ENJOY At its best in *fondue au vacherin*, made with three vacherins of different ages – like the best-ever cheese soup. Pair with Pinot Noir.

SWITZERLAND Fribourg	
Age 9 weeks–6 months	
Weight and Shape 6–8kg (13¼lb–17lb 10oz), wheel	
Size D. 45cm (18in), H. 11cm (4½in) (pictured)	
Milk Cow	
Classification Semi-soft	
Producer Various	

Vacherin Mont d'Or AOC

This is produced from September until March, when the cows come down from the mountains to spend winter in the warm barns of individual farmers. In the summer, their milk is combined to make huge wheels of Gruyère.

TASTING NOTES Encircled by aromatic spruce bark, the almost liquid interior hints of farmyards, meadow flowers, and white wine, with a woody tang.

HOW TO ENJOY Spoon direct from the box, or make a little hole in the rind, pour in some white wine, and put the whole box in the oven at 220°C (425°F/Gas 7) for 30 minutes. Serve with a dry white.

SWITZERLAND Vaud	
Age 6–10 weeks	
Weight and Shape 400g (14oz) and 1kg (2¼lb), round	
Size D. 18cm (7in), H. 8cm (3in) (pictured)	
Milk Cow	
Classification Semi-soft	
Producer Various	

Valle Maggia

Produced in villages in the valley of Maggia on the southern side of the Swiss Alps, all the cheeses are round and covered with a thick grey mould. They are named after the particular valley in which they are produced, such as Verzasca, Piora, and Bedretto.

TASTING NOTES The ivory paste has tiny little holes and a smooth, buttery taste. There is also sometimes a subtle fragrance of the smoke that drifts into the storeroom from the farmer's fire.

HOW TO ENJOY It is perfect sustenance for walking and hiking, enjoyed with dried pork or venison sausage, particularly with the local Merlot wine.

SWITZERLAND Ticino	
Age 6 months	
Weight and Shape 6–8kg (13¼lb–17lb 10oz), round	
Size D. 40cm (15½in), H. 12cm (5in) (pictured)	
Milk Cow, sometimes mixed with goat or ewe	
Classification Semi-soft	
Producer Various	

SCANDINAVIA

Scandinavia is known for its long, dark winter days and all-day summer sunlight. Being isolated for much of the year and having short grazing times, farmers found it essential to preserve their most precious source of protein, often in the form of whey cheese. In Lapland, the far-north region of Scandinavia, the milk of the reindeer is still used to make cheese, and the exceptionally rich milk produces cheese with an earthy, gamey flavour.

N

DENMARK Denmark, the most southern of the Scandinavian countries, has a milder maritime climate and flat meadows that are home to comfort-loving cows. Denmark has a thriving dairy industry, with cheeses exported around the world.

NORWAY With the exception of a long, narrow strip of grazing land bordering the sea, Norway is made up of forests, rugged mountains and the Tundra in the north, which is why goats, rather than cows, prevailed.

SWEDEN Sweden's well-established dairy industry dates back to the 9th century when Benedictine monks, who were sent to convert the war-mongering Vikings to a more peaceful way of life, introduced cheesemaking.

FINLAND Finland, which has one-third of its landmass in the Arctic Circle, has a thriving dairy industry that features many European-style cheeses, as well as its own unique reindeer cheese (Juustoleipä) that is toasted in front of the fire.

LATVIA Since ancient times, Latvia has been at the crossroads between the East and the West, North and South, from the Vikings to the Greeks. The result is a unique economic, cultural, and culinary environment, where cheese plays an important role. Janu Siers takes a centre stage on the most popular holiday Ligo or St John's Day celebrating the summer solstice.

LITHUANIA With a past that is unescapably complex, today Lithuania is independent and a full member of the European Union, sharing its border with multiple nations. A land of rivers, lakes, and meadows, with the average dairy herd of only 10, many rural households still make their own cheese but most is made in large factories like Dziuga, which was established in 1904.

FINLAND
PRODUCED THROUGHOUT THE COUNTRY
**Juustoleipä,
Oltermanni,
Turunmaa**

100 miles

100 km

SWEDEN
PRODUCED THROUGHOUT THE COUNTRY
**Ädelost,
Grevéost,
Herrgårdsost,
Hushållsost,
Mesost,
Prästost,
Västerbottenost**

Ridder

Gammelost

NORWAY
PRODUCED THROUGHOUT THE COUNTRY
**Jarlsberg,
Nökkelost**

Gjetost

LATVIA
PRODUCED THROUGHOUT THE COUNTRY
**Janu Siers or John's Cheese,
Snowballs or "Sniega bumbas",
Klasiskais,
Trikantlers Reserve,
Krievijas or Russian Cheese**

Dziuga

LITHUANIA

Samsø

DENMARK
PRODUCED THROUGHOUT THE COUNTRY
**Bla Castello,
Danablu
Danbo
Havarti**

Esrom ★

Key
★ AOC, DOC, DOP, PGI, or PDO cheeses
⬒ Produced only here
⬭ Produced throughout the region

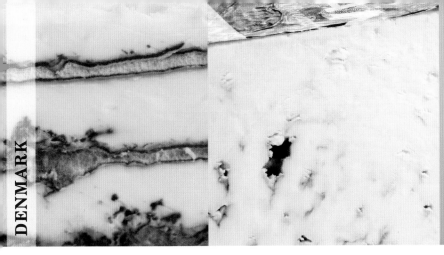
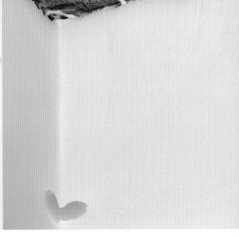

Bla Castello

Developed in the 1960s to meet demand for mild creamy blue cheese, Bla Castello, also known as Blue Castello, has a unique rind that can develop a combination of red and blue-green moulds.

TASTING NOTES This rich and buttery cheese has a Brie-like texture, mild spicy accents of blue veins, an aroma that hints of mushrooms, and a flavour that develops steadily but never becomes too strong.

HOW TO ENJOY Ideal for younger palates, and eats well on bread and, of course, Danish crisp-bread. Matches well with Danish beer.

DENMARK All over	
Age 8–10 weeks	
Weight and Shape 150g (5½oz), half moon, and 1.6kg (2¼lb), round	
Size D. 11.5cm (4½in) and 20cm (8in), H. 5.5cm (2in) and 6cm (2½in)	
Milk Cow	
Classification Blue	
Producer Tholstrup	

Danablu

Invented in the early 20th century as an alternative to the imported French blues, and is now available worldwide. Danablu, also known as Danish Blue, is one of the most popular cheeses in Denmark.

TASTING NOTES This mature blue has deep purple-blue streaks, a smooth yet crumbly, moist texture, and a full flavour that is fresh with a sharp, salty, almost metallic blue bite and creamy finish.

HOW TO ENJOY A cheeseboard stalwart, pairs well with grapes, apples or tomatoes, or try it with olives and pickles. It needs a slightly sweet wine or hoppy ale to offset its salty tang.

DENMARK All over	
Age 2–3 months	
Weight and Shape 3kg (6½lb), drum or block	
Size D. 20cm (8in), H. 10cm (4in)	
Milk Cow	
Classification Blue	
Producer Rosenborg	

Danbo

This milder version of Samsø (see p246) is one of Denmark's most popular cheeses, and is made with semi-skimmed milk. The smooth, barely formed yellow rind is often covered in red or orange wax. It is also known as King Christian or Christian IX in the United States.

TASTING NOTES It is pale, with a pleasant aroma. The pliable interior is smattered with small holes, and the taste is slightly sweet and nutty.

HOW TO ENJOY This breakfast cheese is also great for sandwiches and for general snacking. It partners well with dark breads such as Pumpernickel, and beers, apple juice, and ciders.

DENMARK All over	
Age 6–12 months	
Weight and Shape Various	
Size Various	
Milk Cow	
Classification Semi-soft	
Producer Various	

Esrom PGI

First made by Cistercian monks in the 12th century, this was reintroduced by the Danish Cheese Institute in 1951. Formerly named Danish Port Salut, it was renamed Esrom after the ancient abbey in which it was first made. Esrom was granted PGI status in 1996.

TASTING NOTES Esrom is pale lemon in colour, with small holes, and tastes sweet and buttery; it becomes more pungent with age, while still retaining its sweetness. Some styles are made with garlic or pepper.

HOW TO ENJOY It is ideal in a traditional Danish open sandwich, or eaten with cold cuts of hams and *charcuterie*.

DENMARK Hovedstaden	
Age 21–28 days	
Weight and Shape 200g–2kg (7oz–4½lb), brick	
Size Various. L. 22cm (8½in), W. 12cm (5in), H. 6cm (2½in) (pictured)	
Milk Cow	
Classification Semi-soft	
Producer Various	

246

Havarti

Probably Denmark's most famous cheese, Havarti was invented in the mid-1800s by Hanne Neilsen, who was the wife of a farmer from New Zealand. She travelled through Europe to learn cheesemaking and invented this masterpiece, with its added cream. It was originally named "Havarthi", after her farm.

TASTING NOTES It is sweet, mellow, and very creamy, with a buttery aroma that becomes sharper and saltier, with hints of hazelnut. Some contain caraway seeds.

HOW TO ENJOY This great snacking cheese is ideal for Danish open sandwiches, slicing and grilling, or adding to salads.

DENMARK All over	
Age 4–12 weeks	
Weight and Shape 4.5kg (10lb), blocks or drums	
Size Various. L. 11cm (4½in), W. 6cm (2½in), H. 5cm (2in) (pictured)	
Milk Cow	
Classification Semi-soft	
Producer Various	

Samsø

This semi-soft cheese was created in the early 19th century when the king of Denmark invited Swiss cheesemakers to share their skills with Danish farmers. A pale elastic-textured cheese with irregular-shaped holes based on Emmental was the result. It is named after the Danish island of Samsø, a traditional Viking meeting place.

TASTING NOTES It is mild and buttery when young. As it ages, Samsø develops a sweet-sour pungency and distinct hazelnut flavours.

HOW TO ENJOY Samsø is perfect for a fondue, melted on top of boiled potatoes, or sliced on a chunk of rye bread.

DENMARK Samsø, Mitjylland	
Age 8–12 weeks	
Weight and Shape Various, wheel or rectangle	
Size Various	
Milk Cow	
Classification Semi-soft	
Producer Various	

Gammelost

Gammelost, which means "old cheese", is so named because it grows a green-brown mould traditionally achieved by wrapping the cheese in straw soaked in gin and juniper berries. It is made with very low-fat skimmed milk, mainly in Sogn og Fjordane and Hardanger.

TASTING NOTES It is sharp and aromatic with a brittle, granular texture and a sharp pungent tang reminiscent of aged Camembert or Danish Blue. Its brownish yellow interior is flecked with erratic, uneven streaks of blue.

HOW TO ENJOY This after-dinner favourite is robust enough to enjoy with strong digestives such as schnapps or grappa.

NORWAY Vestlandet	
Age 4–5 weeks	
Weight and Shape 3kg (6½lb), drum	
Size D. 10cm (4in), H. 20cm (8in)	
Milk Goat	
Classification Hard	
Producer Various	

Gjetost

Made in the Gudbrandsdalen Valley using milk, cream, and whey, Gjetost has the colour of French mustard and the texture of fudge. It was once made using only goat's milk – *gjet* means "goat" in Norwegian. To differentiate the styles today, those made with pure cow's milk are called mysost, but ekta gjetost is made with pure goat's milk.

TASTING NOTES This is not to everyone's taste, but Norwegians love its sweet caramel and peanut butter flavours, and its unique aromatic, goaty taste.

HOW TO ENJOY Gjetost is traditionally eaten thinly shaved on hard flatbread, or with spiced fruit cake at Christmas.

NORWAY Østlandet	
Age From a few days	
Weight and Shape 250–500g (9oz–1lb 2oz), cylinder	
Size Various. L. 15cm (6in), W. 6cm (2½in), H. 4cm (1½in) (pictured)	
Milk Goat or cow	
Classification Fresh	
Producer Various	

Jarlsberg

First produced in the 1860s in Jarlsberg and Vestfold county, it was revived in the mid-1900s. It is made from the rich milk produced from cow grazing in high summer pastures, and it has large round holes and a lemony-yellow colour.

TASTING NOTES It was inspired by Swiss Emmental, but Jarlsberg is softer, more supple, sweeter, and less nutty, with a fermenting fruit tang to the finish.

HOW TO ENJOY Try sliced in salads or as a party snack. This versatile cheese is also great in sandwiches with smoked ham, grilled on toast, or melted like raclette and served with crudités.

NORWAY All over	
Age 1–15 months	
Weight and Shape 10kg (22lb), wheel or block	
Size: Various	
Milk Cow	
Classification Semi-soft	
Producer Tine	

247

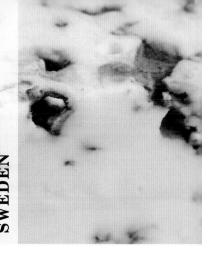

Nökkelost

This cheese, which is based on the Dutch Leidse Kaas (see p229), is made with partially skimmed milk and scattered with finely chopped cumin seeds and cloves. Although it has been made in Norway since the 17th century, it is named after the crossed keys (*nökkel*) that are the emblem of the Dutch city of Leiden.

TASTING NOTES It is springy yet firm, and has a creamy feel and a warm spicy flavour that hints of Christmas.

HOW TO ENJOY It adds a warm spiciness to tarts and baked vegetables, or serve simply with fresh apples and pears, pumpernickel, and beer.

NORWAY All over	
Age 12 weeks	
Weight and Shape 10kg (22lb), wheel or block	
Size Various	
Milk Cow	
Classification Flavour-added	
Producer Tine	

Ridder

It is a semi-soft cheese that is washed in brine that is mixed with annatto, which gives it a sticky, orange rind. Swedish cheesemaker Sven Fenelius invented this cheese, which is named after the Norwegian word for "knight", in 1969. It is now available worldwide.

TASTING NOTES This sweet, buttery yet sharp, and slightly nutty cheese has a dense, pliable, pale yellow interior. As it ages, it becomes more pungent.

HOW TO ENJOY It makes an excellent dessert cheese when young, especially when served with fresh summer berries. It tastes more mellow when it is grilled or baked.

NORWAY Vestlandet	
Age 12–15 weeks	
Weight and Shape 3.25kg (7lb), wheel	
Size D. 15cm (6in), H. 5–7cm (2–3in)	
Milk Cow	
Classification Semi-soft	
Producer Tine	

Ädelost

Ädelost, or "noble cheese", is Sweden's only original blue and was created as an alternative to the imported French blues. It is characterized by blue-grey pockets and short broken veins that are scattered through its pale, creamy interior. The thin, pale rind is dusted with grey, white, and blue moulds.

TASTING NOTES Adelost's high-moisture texture emphasizes the sharp, spicy, blue bite and salty tang of the cheese.

HOW TO ENJOY Crumble over salads or mix with extra virgin olive oil and balsamic vinegar to make a piquant salad dressing. Serve with a hoppy beer or local schnapps.

SWEDEN All over	
Age 8–12 weeks	
Weight and Shape 2.5kg (5½lb), drum	
Size D. 18cm (7in), H. 10cm (4in)	
Milk Cow	
Classification Blue	
Producer Various	

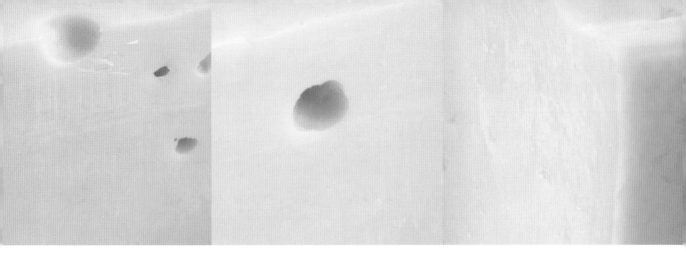

Grevéost

This commercially produced cheese, with its pale yellow, dense interior and various sizes and shapes of holes, is based on Emmental (see pp240–41). It plays a daily role in Swedish cooking because its mild, sweet flavour appeals to both young and old.

TASTING NOTES This sweet and nutty cheese is firm to the bite, with a dense and pliable texture, but it lacks Emmental's depth.

HOW TO ENJOY Spread brioche with butter and fill with thin slices of the cheese and smoked ham. It works well as a snack, grilled, or grated into béchamel-type sauces.

SWEDEN All over	
Age 40 weeks	
Weight and Shape 15kg (33lb), wheel	
Size D. 35cm (14in), H. 10–14cm (4–5½in)	
Milk Cow	
Classification Semi-soft	
Producer Various	

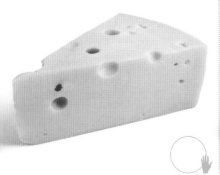

Herrgårdsost

Created in the early 20th century as a local alternative to Gruyère (see p238), Herrgårdsost derives its name from the Swedish for "manor house". Although based on Gruyère, it is softer and more supple, with smaller round holes.

TASTING NOTES The pale yellow interior has a thin rind that is most often waxed. It is nutty and has a similar taste to mild Cheddar (see pp178-79), its zingy tang intensifies with age.

HOW TO ENJOY Like Gruyère, this is an excellent eating and cooking cheese. Try it with pickled gherkins to accentuate its tangy character, and match it with a fruity white wine.

SWEDEN All over	
Age 4–24 months	
Weight and Shape 12–18kg (33lb–39lb 11oz), round	
Size Various. D. 40cm (15½in), H. 12cm (5in) (pictured)	
Milk Cow	
Classification Semi-soft	
Producer Various	

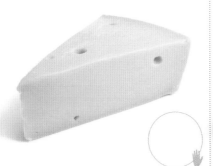

Hushållsost

Hushållsost means "household cheese" in Swedish, and with more than 700 years of history behind it, it is one of the country's best-known and most-used cheeses. Unlike many Swedish cheeses, it is made unashamedly with full-fat milk.

TASTING NOTES This mild and creamy cheese has a straw-coloured interior, a lemon-fresh finish, an open texture with small irregular holes, and a barely formed rind.

HOW TO ENJOY It is popular as part of the traditional breakfast buffet, and is also great for sandwiches, pizzas, tarts, and even melted on top of casseroles.

SWEDEN All over	
Age 4–12 weeks	
Weight and Shape 3kg (6½lb), drum	
Size D. 20–25cm (8–10in), H. 5–8cm (2–3in)	
Milk Cow	
Classification Semi-soft	
Producer Various	

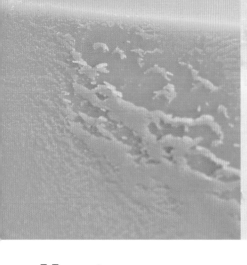

Mesost

This whey cheese came about from the need of the Scandinavian producers to use every element of their milk. The whey is cooked so that the proteins and fats separate. The remaining liquid evaporates, leaving behind a sticky brown caramelised mass of sugars. Sometimes cream or milk is added to increase the yield.

TASTING NOTES It is an acquired taste to those not bought up on it. The cheese is sweet with a creamy, caramel fudge flavour and bitter aftertaste.

HOW TO ENJOY It is usually served at breakfast with toast or bread, or as a snack.

SWEDEN All over	
Age From a few days	
Weight and Shape 1kg–8kg (2lb 4oz–17lb 6oz), blocks	
Size Various	
Milk Cow, goat, or ewe	
Classification Fresh	
Producer Various	

Prästost

Prästost or "priest cheese" dates from the 16th century when farmers paid a tithe to the local church in the form of goods, including milk. Once paid the farmer's wife converted the balance of the milk into cheese and sold it at the local market to recoup some costs. Today it is factory made.

TASTING NOTES It is supple with rice-sized holes and a squishy texture, and its robust, sweet-sour flavour leaves a sharp, fruity tingle on the palate.

HOW TO ENJOY Try it sprinkled on hearty soups, on chilli con carne, or as an extra dimension to a cheeseboard with a fruity red.

SWEDEN All over	
Age Up to 12 months	
Weight and Shape 12kg–15kg (26lb 5oz–33lb), wheels	
Size Various. D. 10cm (4in), H. 5–7cm (1–3in) (pictured)	
Milk Cow	
Classification Semi-soft	
Producer Various	

Västerbottenost

Swedish cuisine is all about converting the bounty of the brief summer harvest into food that will last through the long, harsh winter. As a result, hard cheeses were made in homes and small dairies across Sweden. Västerbottenost, a mass-produced cheese invented in the mid-19th century, is modelled on these traditional cheeses.

TASTING NOTES It is hard and granular like aged Cheddar, with small irregular holes and a fruity tangy that becomes more savoury with age.

HOW TO ENJOY This great after dinner cheese is best served with beer, schnapps, or red wine.

SWEDEN All over	
Age Up to 12 months	
Weight and Shape 20kg (44lb), wheel	
Size D. 50cm (20in), H. 20cm (8in)	
Milk Cow	
Classification: Hard	
Producer Various	

Juustoleipä

Juustoleipä ("cheese bread") is a unique cheese that was once made in homes using cow or reindeer milk. The curd was pressed into flat wooden platters then toasted in front of an open fire, hence the name. Today it is commercially made with cow's milk.

TASTING NOTES Beneath the lightly toasted rind, the whitish-yellow interior is floppy and squeaky on the palate, with hints of coconut, pineapple, sweet milk, and eggs.

HOW TO ENJOY It is rarely found outside Finland, where it is grilled, and served with fruit jam for breakfast, or dropped into a cup of coffee, but not consumed.

FINLAND Finland and Lapland	
Age From a few days	
Weight and Shape 800g (28oz), round and flat	
Size D. 14cm (5½in), H. 1.5cm (½in)	
Milk Cow or reindeer	
Classification Fresh	
Producer Various	

Oltermanni

This Havarti-style cheese is made by Valio, a large dairy owned by Finnish dairy farmers. They produce the cleanest milk in the EU due to their crystal clear water and freedom from industrial pollution. Outside Finland, it is sometimes sold as Baby Muenster, or Finlandia Cheese.

TASTING NOTES Similar to Turunmaa, it has a barely formed rind and small, irregular holes.

HOW TO ENJOY Like many Scandinavian cheeses, it is served at breakfast, sliced on rye bread, or grilled.

FINLAND All over	
Age 1–3 months	
Weight and Shape 1.1kg (2lb 4oz), cylinder	
Size D. 11cm (4½in), H. 10cm (4in)	
Milk Cow	
Classification Semi-soft	
Producer Valio	

Turunmaa

This cheese was originally made as a breakfast cheese in the grand manor houses of Turku, Finland's ancient 16th century capital. This Havarti-style cheese has a firm yet open texture and a richness that comes from the excellent grazing in the area.

TASTING NOTES It is chewy and creamy, with tiny eyes and a rich, deep buttery taste with a savoury tang like grilled Cheddar on the finish. It is like a delicious but slightly rubbery omelette.

HOW TO ENJOY Typically served at breakfast in Scandinavia, it is good with slices of smoked ham, and cold meats.

FINLAND All over	
Age 8–12 weeks	
Weight and Shape 6–10kg (13–22lb), drum	
Size D. 10–15cm (4–6in); H. 5–7cm (2–3in)	
Milk Cow	
Classification Semi-soft	
Producer Valio	

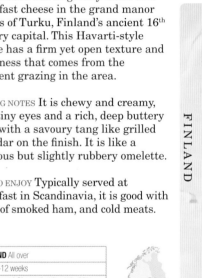

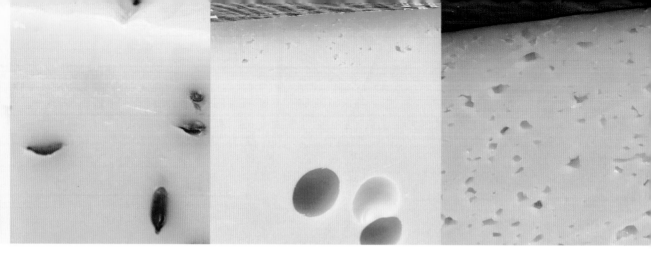

Janu Siers

This once-a-year treat, is made by heating cottage cheese and milk together until it curdles, this is then combined with melted butter, and beaten alongwith eggs, salt and caraway seeds. This is then stirred and shaped into a round.

TASTING NOTES It is a moist, chewy cheese with a texture that lies somewhere between Halloumi and Edam. It has a mildly citrus zing, with a taste reminiscent of scrambled eggs, offset by the exotic flavour of the caraway.

HOW TO ENJOY Made in homes across Latvia, it is best served with rye bread.

LATVIA All over	
Age 1–4 weeks	
Weight and Shape 425gm (15oz), round	
Size D. 11cm (4in), H. 4cm (1½in)	
Milk Cow	
Classification Unique	
Producer Various	

Klasiskais

Milk and milk products play an essential part of Latvian cuisine as described in a traditional poem, 'milk I was eating, milk I was drinking, in the milk I washed my mouth'. This classic Emmental-style cheese is also available flavoured with fenugreek seeds.

TASTING NOTES It has a yellow coloured dense, supple interior with irregularly shaped, hazelnut-sized holes and an intensely sweet, and fruity aroma. It tastes like fermented pears, similar to a young Emmentaler or Maasdam.

HOW TO ENJOY It grills and slices well, is ideal for breakfast, and cheese platters. Also good in sandwiches and salads.

LATVIA All over	
Age 2–6 months	
Weight and Shape 5kg (11lb), round	
Size D. 26cm (10in), H. 10cm (4in)	
Milk Cow	
Classification Semi-soft	
Producer Trikata Cooperative Dairy	

Krievijas or Russian Cheese

One of the most popular cheeses in Latvia, it is based on the recipe for Tilsit, a cheese that originated in a town in Kaliningrad Oblast. Much loved by the locals, it is used in the kitchen much as the English use Cheddar or the Dutch use Gouda.

TASTING NOTES Butter-yellow with an elastic texture, it is buttery and sweet-savoury, when young.It becomes stronger and aromatic with age, hinting of white wine and fruit.

HOW TO ENJOY Perfect for making snacks like spicy cheese biscuits, serve with local, dark rye breads, and dark beer.

LATVIA All over	
Age 90 days	
Weight and Shape 5kg (11lb),wheel or block	
Size D. 26cm (10in), H. 7.5cm (3in)	
Milk Cow	
Classification Hard	
Producer Trikata Cooperative Dairy	

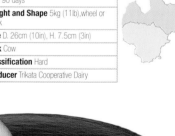

Sniega bumbas

"Trikātas siers" or Three Cats Cheese is one of the oldest dairies in Latvia and is now a cooperative owned by 600 Latvian farmers, producing an increasing range of diverse cheeses including these cheeses flavoured with garlic or rolled in tomato, basil, and herbs.

TASTING NOTES These are small fluffy white balls of cows' milk, loosely packed in oil and infused with garlic. The tomato and herb combinations are equally successful.

HOW TO ENJOY An excellent appetizer, combine with vegetables, add to salads or spread bread or biscuits.

LATVIA All over	
Age From a few days	
Weight and Shape 40g (1½oz), balls	
Size D. 2cm (1in)	
Milk Cow	
Classification Fresh	
Producer Trikata Cooperative Dairy	

Trikantlers Reserve

A recent survey showed Latvians could only name 2 cheeses, Edam and Tilsit. So Trikata set up an online Academy to educate and inspire the conservative Latvians to try new cheeses.

TASTING NOTES Aged for a minimum of 8 months, it has a deep yellow-orange coloured, smooth interior, scattered with tiny holes, and a full bodied nutty taste alongwith fruity notes on the finish.

HOW TO ENJOY The full flavour needs a full bodied red, and makes it a great ingredient for sauces, salads, roasted vegetables and gratins.

LATVIA All over	
Age 8–10 months	
Weight and Shape 5kg (11lb), round	
Size D. 26cm (10in), H. 7.5cm (3in)	
Milk Cow	
Classification Hard	
Producer Trikata Cooperative Dairy	

Dziugas

Named after Dziugas, a local giant, it is similar in style to Parmesan and is made only between spring and autumn, when the small herds graze the natural pastures, in and around the Zemaitijos National Park. Believed to give strength and joy to those who consume it.

TASTING NOTES A hard, pale yellow cheese with a thin, edible crust. At 24 months it is savoury, with crunchy crystals. At 36 months, the flavour is intense and fruity with a mouth watering tingle

HOW TO ENJOY Popular in the Baltics for cooking, it is served in rough chunks with pears, grapes and hazelnuts but is equally at home on a cheeseboard.

LITHUANIA Telsiai	
Age 12–36 month	
Weight and Shape 4.2–4.5kg (9¼–10lb), wheel	
Size D. 22–24cm (8½–9½in), H. 9–10cm (3½–4in)	
Milk Cow	
Classification Hard	
Producer Dziugas Cooperative	

EASTERN EUROPE
AND THE NEAR EAST

POLAND

**PRODUCED THROUGHOUT
THE COUNTRY**
**Bryndza ★,
Oscypek ★,
Redykołka**

**CZECH
REPUBLIC**

**PRODUCED
THROUGHOUT
THE COUNTRY**
**Abertam,
Brynza**

SLOVAKIA

**PRODUCED THROUGHOUT
THE COUNTRY**
**Bovski ★,
Bryndza ★,
Mohant,
Nanoski,
Ostiepok,
Sir,
Tolminc ★**

HUNGARY
**PRODUCED
THROUGHOUT
THE COUNTRY**
**Balaton,
Kashkaval,
Lake Balaton,
Liptauer**

ROMANIA

**PRODUCED
THROUGHOUT
THE COUNTRY**
**Ardalena,
Brânză,
Cascaval ★,
Teleme**

🧀 **Turoš**

CROATIA
**PRODUCED THROUGHOUT
THE COUNTRY**
**Kolan,
Sir**

SLOVENIA

SERBIA

**PRODUCED
THROUGHOUT
THE COUNTRY**
**Brenca,
Kačkavalj,
Manur,
Urda**

BULGARIA

**PRODUCED
THROUGHOUT
THE COUNTRY**
**Kashkaval:,
Sirene**

**BOSNIA&
HERZEGOVINA**

🧀 **Škripavac**

Paski Sir

MONTENEGRO

MACEDONIA
**PRODUCED
THROUGHOUT
THE COUNTRY**
Kashkaval

ADRIATIC SEA

Kaseri ★

Tulum

GREECE

🧀 **Galotiri ★**

AEGEAN SEA

ALBANIA
**PRODUCED
THROUGHOUT
THE COUNTRY**
Kaçkavalli

🧀 **Kaseri ★**

Kaseri ★

**PRODUCED THROUGHOUT
THE COUNTRY**
**Anthotyros ★,
Feta ★,
Kefalotyri ★,
Manouri,
Myzithra**

🧀 **Galotiri ★**

**BOSNIA&
HERZEGOVINA**

Graviera ★

IONIAN SEA

Graviera ★

🧀 **KRITI**

N

200 miles

200 km

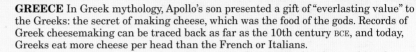

GREECE In Greek mythology, Apollo's son presented a gift of "everlasting value" to the Greeks: the secret of making cheese, which was the food of the gods. Records of Greek cheesemaking can be traced back as far as the 10th century BCE, and today, Greeks eat more cheese per head than the French or Italians.

The variety of mountain and maritime natural pastures plus the sun-kissed climate provide ideal conditions for the tenacious native goats and hardy sheep that provide the milk for some of the world's oldest and greatest cheeses.

EASTERN EUROPE Since 552CE, Eastern Europe's borders changed frequently and numerous forces occupied the region, which led to a melting pot of culinary influences, from Roman to Russian and Turkish to Central Asian. As a result, borders are blurred and cheeses with similar names and recipes are found throughout the region.

When post-war communism led to mass production, small producers all but died out, but since the Iron Curtain dropped, artisan cheesemakers have re-emerged. The Eastern European dairy industry is now thriving, with many small traditional creameries producing a variety of European and local cheeses.

ISRAEL AND THE NEAR EAST Although archaeological sites dating from 7000BCE show signs that the domestication of the then-evolving sheep and goat population could have led to the development of the first cheeses for this region, the harsh climate prevented the creation of the sophisticated cheeses that were seen in Europe.

In the 1980s, interest in cheese beyond just fresh and salted or dried styles started a new wave of artisan and industrial cheeses. European-trained cheesemakers were able to upgrade the quality and awareness of traditional cheeses and produce European-style cheeses.

BLACK SEA

Tulum

TURKEY
PRODUCED
THROUGHOUT
THE COUNTRY
Beyaz Peynir

SYRIA

LEBANON
PRODUCED
THROUGHOUT
THE COUNTRY
Akkawi

CYPRUS
PRODUCED
THROUGHOUT
THE COUNTRY
**Anari,
Halloumi**

Turkeez

Inbar

Ketem

ISRAEL

PRODUCED
THROUGHOUT
THE COUNTRY
**Labane,
Zfatit**

MEDITERRANEAN SEA

Key	
★	AOC, DOC, DOP, PGI, or PDO cheeses
	Produced only here
	Produced throughout the region

Anthotyros DOC

This cheese has been made for centuries using the whey of ewe's and goat's milk, or a mix of both, with the addition of small quantities of cream. It is widely available throughout Greece as a soft or a hard cheese.

TASTING NOTES When fresh, it is creamy and lemony with a unique floral taste; when aged, it develops grey moulds and is dry with a stronger, salty tang and a hint of smoke on the finish.

HOW TO ENJOY It is traditionally used in savoury or sweet pasties, and when aged, it is grated over hot savoury dishes. It is especially tasty when paired with fresh figs.

GREECE All over	
Age A couple of days up to 12 months	
Weight and Shape 350g (12oz), ball or truncated cone	
Size Various	
Milk Ewe and goat	
Classification Fresh and Aged fresh	
Producer Various	

Graviera DOC

This is one of the most popular Greek cheeses. It is based on Gruyère (see p238) but can be made with cow's, goat's or ewe's milk, depending on the season. Graviera from Krìti (Crete) is made using ewe's milk and some goat, while Graviera Naxos is made with cow's milk with a little ewe or goat.

TASTING NOTES The Cretan Graviera is sweet and fruity like Emmental, with a delicate fragrance and burnt caramel finish. The Naxos version is richer, creamier and more nutty.

HOW TO ENJOY This classic all-round table cheese can also be baked in cheese pastries.

GREECE Naxos and Kriti	
Age 3–5 months	
Weight and Shape 2–8kg (4½–17½lb), drum	
Size Various	
Milk Ewe, goat, or cow	
Classification Hard	
Producer Various	

Kaseri DOC

One of the oldest cheeses in the world, Kaseri is produced using a mix of goat's and ewe's milk (minimum 80 per cent ewe's). It is an aged "pasta filata" or stretched curd cheese, similar to Italian Provolone (see p130), which gives it a stringy texture when cooked.

TASTING NOTES This firm but supple cheese has no rind and tastes salty, yet sweet and pungent, with a dry feel in the mouth.

HOW TO ENJOY This table cheese is great for melting and grilling. Try on top of pitta bread and smothered in fresh vine-tomato pulp and olives for your own Greek-style pizza.

GREECE Thessalia, Mitilini island, and Xanthi	
Age 12 weeks	
Weight and Shape 1–9kg (2–20lb), wheel	
Size Various	
Milk Ewe and goat	
Classification Semi-soft	
Producer Various	

256

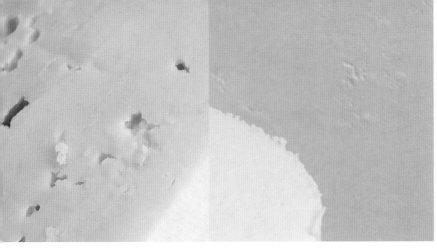

Galotiri DOC

Galotiri is one of the oldest Greek cheeses. It is predominantly made with ewe's milk, typically for household consumption rather than on a commercial scale. The fresh curds from successive days are placed in barrels and sealed with fat or hung from the rafters in sacks to drain until needed. If mould grows, it is scraped off to allow the whey to escape and the cheese to breathe.

TASTING NOTES It is soft and spreadable with a refreshing, slightly sour and brackish taste, which is much appreciated by the Greeks.

HOW TO ENJOY Use it in various traditional dishes, especially in spreads with herbs or spices.

GREECE Epirus and Thessalia		
Age Few days to a few months		
Weight and Shape Various, small pots		
Size Various		
Milk Ewe, or ewe and goat		
Classification Fresh		
Producer Various		

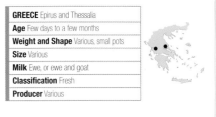

Myzithra

Myzithra is the ancestor of all Greek whey cheeses because it has been made for thousands of years from the whey of Feta (see pp258–59) and Kefalotyri (see p257). It comes in two types: fresh Myzithra is unsalted or slightly salty and similar to cottage cheese, while the aged one is dry, salty, and firm.

257

TASTING NOTES It is mild and refreshing when fresh, but has a nuttier and more salty taste and a dusty, grey mouldy rind when aged.

HOW TO ENJOY Fresh Myzithra makes deliciously light sweet or savoury dishes, while the dried version is ideal for grating over savoury dishes, such as pasta and pastries.

GREECE All over		
Age From a couple of days		
Weight and Shape 1–2kg (2.5–4.5lb) (fresh), 500g–1.5kg (1–3lb) (dried), pear		
Size Various		
Milk Ewe and goat		
Classification Fresh and aged fresh		
Producer Various		

Kefalotyri DOC

This cheese has been made throughout Greece since the Byzantine era and is referred to as a "male or first cheese", a term used to describe cheeses made with full milk. "Female or second" cheeses are made with whey.

TASTING NOTES This firm but dry cheese has numerous irregular holes, a fresh taste and a distinct tang of ewe's milk. It also has a herbaceous tang on the finish, which is reminiscent of olive oil.

HOW TO ENJOY It is traditionally used in the classic Greek dish "saganaki", where thick slices are fried, sometimes covered in egg and breadcrumbs, and served with a squeeze of lemon.

GREECE All over		
Age 3–4 months		
Weight and Shape 6–8kg (13–17½lb), drum		
Size Various		
Milk Ewe, and ewe and goat		
Classification Hard		
Producer Various		

Manouri

This very old and popular Greek white, or fresh, cheese is made from the drained whey from Feta (see pp258–59) production, with the addition of larger quantities of milk than used in Anthotyros.

TASTING NOTES It is similar to Feta but smoother, creamier, and less salty. Manouri is drained in cloth sacks and generally sold in logs.

HOW TO ENJOY Its low salt content means it is used in savoury and sweet dishes, particularly pastries such as "spanakopita", a baked spinach and cheese filo pastry pie, or sweet pastries. Also, simply serve drizzled with honey.

GREECE All over		
Age From a few days		
Weight and Shape 500g (1lb), log		
Size L. 25cm (9½in), H. 7cm (3in)		
Milk Ewe or goat		
Classification Fresh		
Producer Various		

Feta PDO

According to Greek mythology, the gods sent Apollo's son to teach the Greeks the art of cheesemaking. However, the first, but no less magical, record of cheesemaking was Homer's Odyssey. Written in the 8th Century, Homer describes seeing Cyclops the giant making ewe's milk cheese in his cave, a simple recipe that would later become Feta.

Feta, granted protection in 2002 under the EU protected name scheme PDO (see p8), can now only be made in the mountainous regions of Macedonia, Thrace, Epirus, Thessaly, Sterea Ellada, Peloponnesus, and Mytilini from ewe's or goat's milk because it is in these areas that the herds still graze freely. As you watch the agile goats and the patient sheep grazing the steep rugged hills and scrubby, rock-strewn pastures, it is easy to see why the comfort-loving cow never made Greece its home! There are no pesticides, insect repellents, or other pollutants used and you can still catch the sound and a glimpse of the herds passing through small villages on the way to new pastures.

The hardy goats graze the rugged landscape of Greece's mountainous regions.

GREECE All over	
Age	2 months minimum
Weight and Shape	Various
Size	Various
Milk	Goat or ewe
Classification	Fresh
Producer	Various

To those used to seeing sheep grazing ankle-deep in grass and clover it is hard to imagine they can eke out sufficient food to survive, let alone produce milk for cheese from their diet of wild herbs, flowers, and tenacious grasses. But it is precisely why they produce some of the thickest, most aromatic milk in the world. The scent of the thyme, marjoram, and pine is captured and concentrated in the tiny fat globules in the milk.

TASTING NOTES Firm and compact yet easily crumbled, Feta has no rind and a myriad of small holes. Very white if made with pure goat's milk, it has a very fresh taste that hints of wild herbs, white wine, and a slightly goaty tang. Ewe's milk Feta feels slightly richer and creamier and is more ivory white. The taste is reminiscent of roast lamb, lamb fat, and lanolin, like unwashed wool. Both have a salty tang on the finish and a depth of flavour from the grazing.

HOW TO ENJOY Feta is consumed at every meal in Greece – for example in pastries and pies such as Spanokopitta, the delicious cheese and spinach pies found all over Greece; in salads, usually with olives, tomatoes, raw onion, and olive oil; or mixed with almost any combination of fresh or cooked vegetables. It does not dissolve completely when baked or grilled, giving its lightness to endless Greek dishes.

If you find Feta too salty, simply soak a chunk in cold water or milk for 10–15 minutes. This removes the excess salt but does not mask its favour.

A CLOSER LOOK

Feta is produced in homes, small family-run dairies, and large industrial units, but all must respect the traditional recipe protected by the PDO status. It is an important component of the Greek diet, connected with the history and traditions of the country.

Feta is usually cut into small blocks and vacuum packed along with a little brine. Originally, shepherds who lived far from the sea where salt was bought would store their cheeses in olive oil.

CUTTING THE CURD Once the starter culture and rennet have done their job, the soft floppy curd is cut into 1–2cm (½in)cubes using what looks like a giant wooden comb or square harp.

DRAINING The curds and whey are poured onto large draining tables with low sides. Traditionally it would have been put in a basket woven from reeds and left to drain; now the curd is turned 2–3 times over the next few hours and salted to speed up the expulsion of the whey.

The colour changes depending on the ratio of the different milks used. Goat's milk is more white, whereas ewe's milk is more ivory.

Block of Feta

It crumbles easily, making it perfect for salads.

Cascaval PDO

Made across Eastern Europe with similar names in Hungary, Bulgaria, Macedonia, Serbia and particularly Romania, where they make around 23 varieties. It is similar in style to the Italian cheese Cacicavallo. Its colour varies from pale yellow to yellow-brown, and it has a natural thin rind.

TASTING NOTES It is flexible and crumbly, with a salty, sharp, almost bitter taste. There is also a hint of caramelized onions in the aftertaste.

HOW TO ENJOY Traditionally a table cheese, it can be fried, baked in pastry dishes, or grated over vegetables.

ROMANIA All over		
Age 8 weeks		
Weight and Shape 7–9kg (15lb 7oz–19lb 13oz), irregular round		
Size D. 5–11.5cm (2–4½in), H. 3–3.5cm (1in)		
Milk Ewe, or ewe and cow		
Classification Hard		
Producer Various		

Bryndza PGI

Bryndza, which was originally from the Carpathain Mountain region, was probably introduced by the Greeks. Similar cheeses are made throughout Eastern Europe.

TASTING NOTES Similar to Feta (see pp258–259), but softer, spreadable, and not as salty. It has a lemony acidity and varies from soft to firm to crumbly depending on its age and the type of milk used.

HOW TO ENJOY Spread on warm granary bread or crumble over baby salad leaves and tomatoes. Served as part of the traditional dish *bryndzové halušky* (potato dumplings with Bryndza).

SLOVAKIA All over		
Age 4 weeks or more		
Weight and Shape 100–300g (3½–10oz), block		
Size L. 7.5–12cm (3–5in), W. 5–10cm (2–4in), H. 3.5cm (1in)		
Milk Ewe, goat, or cow		
Classification Fresh		
Producer Various		

Oštiepok PGI

A table cheese, made from ewe's milk, this is very similar to the Polish Oszczypek or Oscypek cheese. The curds are pressed into beautiful, hand-crafted wooden moulds giving each a unique identity, then stored in the eaves of the house where it absorbs smoke from the fire below.

TASTING NOTES This cheese is smoky, slightly salty with a caramel taste from the milk. The rind ranges from a pale straw coloured to deep orange-brown, depending on the age and smoking.

HOW TO ENJOY It combines well with cured meats as well as sausages, and is used extensively in local dishes.

SLOVAKIA All over		
Age 1–4 weeks		
Weight and Shape 150g–2kg (5½oz–4½lb), various shapes		
Size Various		
Milk Ewe		
Classification Hard		
Producer Various		

Beyaz Peynir

Known as "white cheese", this Feta-like cheese is made and consumed in large quantities all over Turkey. The recipe varies slightly from place to place, and it can be made from ewe's, goat's or cow's milk.

TASTING NOTES The taste varies from season to season depending on the mix of milks used. It can vary from salty to very salty and hard to soft, but the creamier version produced in Marmara is much sought after.

HOW TO ENJOY It plays a major role in Turkish cuisine for breakfast, salads, snacks, or as a filling in vegetable and pastry dishes.

TURKEY	All over	
Age	Minimum of 3 months	
Weight and Shape	250g–1kg (9oz–2¼lb), various	
Size	Various	
Milk	Ewe, goat, or cow	
Classification	Fresh	
Producer	Various	

Tulum

One of the world's oldest cheeses, Tulum, is made by packing specially cured goat's skins with fresh curd over a period of weeks. The skins are stitched up and left to age for three months, before being slit open for the cheese to be served from the skins.

TASTING NOTES It is surprisingly mild with aromatic or sweet flavours that depend on the milk and the seasons. Erzincan, the most common variety, can be strong and somewhat bitter.

HOW TO ENJOY This relatively expensive artisan cheese is best served simply drizzled with olive oil alongside fruit, figs, olives, or fresh vegetables.

TURKEY	Eastern Anatolia and Aegean regions	
Age	From 3 months	
Weight and Shape	500–600g (1lb 2oz–1lb 5oz), pots or blocks	
Size	L. 10cm (4in), W. 10cm (4in), H. 10cm (4in)	
Milk	Ewe, goat, or a mixture	
Classification	Fresh	
Producer	Various	

Anari

Anari is made using whey from Halloumi, plus some goat or ewe's milk to improve the texture and taste. Traditionally, if it is not consumed fresh, it is salted and dried in the warm, dry air, which today happens by gentle heating.

TASTING NOTES This chalky-white cheese is soft, moist, and creamy with a very delicate, milky taste. Dried Anari is very hard and salty.

HOW TO ENJOY Fresh Anari is served with fruit or carob-based syrups, or used to make sweet and savoury pastries called *bourekia*. Dried Anari is grated over salads, pasta, or sauces.

CYPRUS	All over	
Age	From a few days to a few months	
Weight and Shape	Various, pots or blocks	
Size	L. 10cm (4in), W. 10cm (4in), H. 10cm (4in)	
Milk	Goat and ewe	
Classification	Fresh	
Producer	Various	

261

Halloumi

Born out of a need to preserve milk and provide protein during the winter months when the sheep and goats stopped producing milk, Halloumi was, and still is, a vital part of the Cypriot diet.

What gives Halloumi its unique place in culinary history is not only its ability to keep its shape and not melt when cooked, but also the source of its milk – the amazing Mouflon breed of sheep, which were introduced in the Neolithic period and over thousands of years adapted to its environment and became an integral part of the community. Sadly, Mouflon sheep are now considered an endangered species although in other parts of the world they are bred for hunting and sport.

Handsome-looking, they have a red-brown rough coat and striking thick spiral horns that arch back over the head.

Some Halloumi is still made traditionally in rural areas, but following huge international demand most is now produced in factories. Although they adhere to the traditional recipe using goat's and ewe's milk, most mix it with some cow's milk, as it is not seasonal and is less expensive, however, this impacts on the taste.

Cyprus has applied for PDO status for Halloumi.

TASTING NOTES Salty and tangy with a bouncy texture but, when cooked, the milk sugars in the cheese caramelize on the outside giving it a sweet onion taste, while the texture is supple, springy and squeaky.

The flavour of the cheese varies according to the seasons and type of milk used. The best are made with raw goat's and ewe's milk during the spring and summer months when the free-ranging animals graze on a myriad of wild flowers, herbs, grasses, and scrubby bushes that cover the rocky island.

HOW TO ENJOY The main ingredient in a Cypriot breakfast, starter, or lunch, Halloumi is usually served alongside fresh fruit, such as melon and figs, or with vegetables. It is the only cheese that does not melt when heated, thanks to its unique texture, and is excellent cut into thick slices and barbecued or fried as a canapé.

It is essential not to use oil when frying Halloumi, as this seals the cheese and stops the milk sugars from escaping, resulting in the cheese losing its sweet caramel flavour.

The Mouflon sheep, *introduced during the Neolithic period.*

CYPRUS	All over
Weight and Shape	250g (12oz), blocks
Size	L. 12cm (5in), H. 6cm (2½in)
Milk	Goat, ewe, or cow
Classification	Fresh
Producer	Various

A CLOSER LOOK

Halloumi is similar to the Italian *pasta filata cheeses*, which are stretched. Halloumi is kneaded, however, which gives it a unique, dense texture.

HEATING Traditionally, raw goat's or ewe's milk, or a combination of both, was heated in a cauldron. Today, some cow's milk is usually mixed in and pasteurized in stainless steel vats.

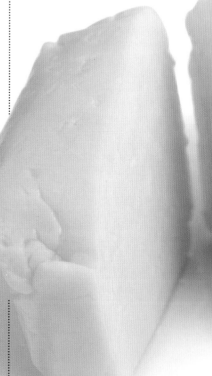

The early formed rind is shiny from the brine in which it is stored.

CUTTING THE CURDS
The curds are cut with knives or wires on a frame and stirred in the hot whey to harden them and expel more whey.

The firm, dense texture is easy to slice for frying or grilling.

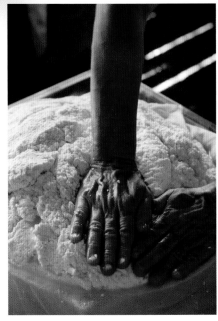

KNEADING The still slightly rubbery curds are cut into plastic moulds and kneaded and pressed by hand to remove the excess whey and create the texture.

Block of cheese, sliced

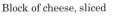

264

Akkawi

Like Feta (see pp258–59), Akkawi is sometimes soaked in water to remove the salt so that it can be used in sweet dishes. The name originates from the port town Acre. It is still made in many homes, but is increasingly made commercially in Europe for the Arab market.

TASTING NOTES It is very white and firm with some small holes and a fresh, salty taste. It feels slightly fatty when made with cow's milk.

HOW TO ENJOY It is very versatile and is a staple ingredient of many Lebanese and Middle Eastern dishes, from salads to pastries, or simply as a snack.

LEBANON All over		
Age 1–3 months		
Weight and Shape Various, blocks		
Size Various. L. 11–15cm (4½–6in), W. 10–15cm (4–6in), H. 4cm (1½in) (pictured)		
Milk Ewe or cow		
Classification Fresh		
Producer Various		

Inbar

After a visit to a Swiss dairy, Michal Melamed became fascinated with making cheese. She and her husband then moved to the Galilee, where they built their dairy in Kibbutz Reshafim to make ewe and goat cheeses. Inbar is a tribute to Alpine-style cheeses.

TASTING NOTES It is firm yet supple with a hard, dry rind, and a delicate, yet aromatic, slightly nutty taste. It is also flavoured with black pepper, thyme, red wine, mustard seeds, and even chillies.

HOW TO ENJOY It is good on a cheeseboard or sliced thinly for sandwiches. Grate and grill in vegetable dishes.

ISRAEL Kibbutz Reshafim, Emek Hama'ayanot		
Age From 2 months		
Weight and Shape 2kg (4½lb), round		
Size D. 25cm (10in), H. 7–8cm (3–4in)		
Milk Ewe		
Classification Flavour-added		
Producer Shirat Roim Dairy		

Ketem

Daniel and Anat Kornmehl, as part of a new generation of Israeli cheesemakers, have created a variety of European-style goat's cheeses in the Negev desert. Ketem ("spot" in English) is based on the much-loved French cheese, Pelardon (see p72).

TASTING NOTES Beneath its wrinkled white rind, it is firm yet creamy. It melts in your mouth. When young, it is distinctly goaty but mild. Once mature it is strong, aromatic, sharp, and very stormy in character.

HOW TO ENJOY Although it is best served as part of a cheeseboard, it is also good grilled or baked.

ISRAEL Tlalim, Ramat HaNegev		
Age 2–3 weeks		
Weight and Shape 160g (5½oz), round		
Size L. 10cm (4in), W. 10cm (4in), H. 3cm (1in)		
Milk Goat		
Classification Aged fresh		
Producer Kornmehl Family Dairy		

Labane

Throughout the Middle East, Labane is made in many households by draining thick, full-fat yoghurt overnight in cloth. It is one of the basic ingredients of Eastern Mediterranean cuisine. Without a doubt, the best are made with ewe's milk, but some are now made with cow's milk.

TASTING NOTES This deliciously rich and velvety smooth cheese has a mildly lemony fresh tang. Those made with ewe's milk have a lovely sweetness.

HOW TO ENJOY It is traditionally eaten at breakfast, or served with olive oil, fresh local herbs, pine nuts and pitta bread.

ISRAEL All over		
Age A few hours		
Weight and Shape 250g (9oz) and 500g (1lb 2oz), pots		
Size No size		
Milk Cow, ewe, goat, or a mixture		
Classification Fresh		
Producer Various		

Turkeez

The Barkanit family dairy, established in 1978, was one of the first in Israel. The family learnt their skills in Europe. This attractive cheese, which is made from the milk of their own ewes and goats that graze the pastures of Harod Valley, is one of their best.

TASTING NOTES It is velvety, with a fresh acidity and a hint of salt, while the walnuts provide a crunchy, nutty balance. With age it has a taste reminiscent of Roquefort (see pp82–83).

HOW TO ENJOY Use on cheeseboards, or break it into chunks and use in fruit salads, with smoked meats or grilled over pears. Pair it with sweet wines.

ISRAEL Kfar Yehezke'el, Gilboa		
Age From a few days		
Weight and Shape 150g and 500g (5½oz and 1lb 2oz), truncated cone		
Size D. 10cm and 20cm (4in and 8in), H. 7cm and 15cm (3in and 6in)		
Milk Ewe and goat		
Classification Fresh		
Producer Barkanit Dairy		

Zfatit

This popular Israeli cheese was first made in Safed (*Zfat* in Hebrew) in the 19th century by the Hame'iry family. It is now made in small baskets by various producers in Israel and around the world.

TASTING NOTES It bears the imprint of the baskets, and is a little spongy but high in moisture with a silky texture. The combination of milky sweetness and salt makes it irresistible. It is often flavoured with herbs and spices.

HOW TO ENJOY It is best on a sunny morning with a dash of olive oil, fresh tomatoes, basil, grated pepper and warm sourdough bread.

ISRAEL All over		
Age From a few days		
Weight and Shape 250g (9oz), round		
Size D. 20cm (8in), H. 5cm (2in)		
Milk Cow		
Classification Fresh		
Producer Various		

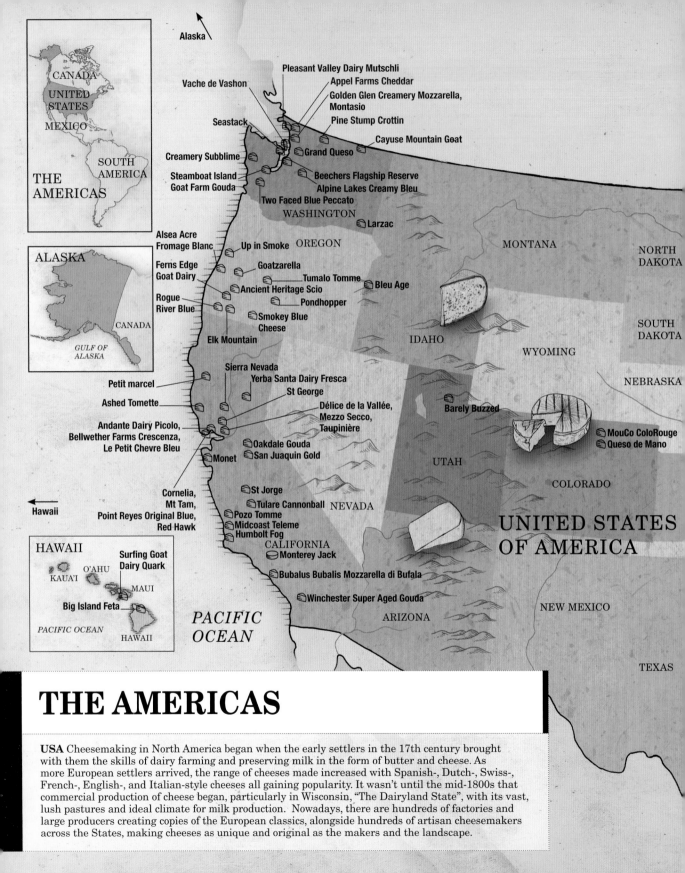

THE AMERICAS

Alaska

CANADA
UNITED STATES
MEXICO

SOUTH AMERICA

THE AMERICAS

ALASKA

CANADA

GULF OF ALASKA

Pleasant Valley Dairy Mutschli
Vache de Vashon
Appel Farms Cheddar
Golden Glen Creamery Mozzarella, Montasio
Pine Stump Crottin
Seastack
Cayuse Mountain Goat
Grand Queso
Creamery Subblime
Beechers Flagship Reserve
Steamboat Island Goat Farm Gouda
Alpine Lakes Creamy Bleu
Two Faced Blue Peccato

WASHINGTON

Larzac

Alsea Acre Fromage Blanc
Up in Smoke
OREGON
Ferns Edge Goat Dairy
Goatzarella
Tumalo Tomme
Bleu Age
Rogue River Blue
Ancient Heritage Scio
Pondhopper
Smokey Blue Cheese
Elk Mountain

MONTANA
NORTH DAKOTA
SOUTH DAKOTA

IDAHO
WYOMING
NEBRASKA

Petit marcel
Sierra Nevada
Yerba Santa Dairy Fresca
St George
Ashed Tomette
Délice de la Vallée, Mezzo Secco, Taupinière
Andante Dairy Picolo, Bellwether Farms Crescenza, Le Petit Chevre Bleu
Oakdale Gouda
San Juaquin Gold
Monet

Barely Buzzed
UTAH
MouCo ColoRouge
Queso de Mano
COLORADO

St Jorge
Cornelia, Mt Tam, Point Reyes Original Blue, Red Hawk
Tulare Cannonball
NEVADA
Pozo Tomme
Midcoast Teleme
Humbolt Fog
CALIFORNIA
Monterey Jack

UNITED STATES OF AMERICA

Bubalus Bubalis Mozzarella di Bufala

Winchester Super Aged Gouda
ARIZONA
NEW MEXICO

HAWAII
O'AHU
KAUA'I
Surfing Goat Dairy Quark
MAUI
Big Island Feta
PACIFIC OCEAN
HAWAII

PACIFIC OCEAN

← Hawaii

TEXAS

THE AMERICAS

USA Cheesemaking in North America began when the early settlers in the 17th century brought with them the skills of dairy farming and preserving milk in the form of butter and cheese. As more European settlers arrived, the range of cheeses made increased with Spanish-, Dutch-, Swiss-, French-, English-, and Italian-style cheeses all gaining popularity. It wasn't until the mid-1800s that commercial production of cheese began, particularly in Wisconsin, "The Dairyland State", with its vast, lush pastures and ideal climate for milk production. Nowadays, there are hundreds of factories and large producers creating copies of the European classics, alongside hundreds of artisan cheesemakers across the States, making cheeses as unique and original as the makers and the landscape.

VERMONT

MAINE

Shelburne Cheddar

Vaquero Blue

Bayley Hazen Blue,
Constant Bliss,
Winnimere

VERMONT

Grafton Cheddar

Cabot Clothbound

NEW
HAMPSHIRE

Coupole

Blythedale Farm Camembert

Bourrée

Tarentaise

Soft Wheel,
Twig Farm Square Cheese

Tarentaise

Vermont Ayr

Ascutney Mountain Cheese

NEW YORK

West West Blue

Dorset

Vermont Shepherd

MASSACHUSETTS

MINNESOTA

Trader Lake Cedar

WISCONSIN

MAINE

City of Ships

VERMONT

Rosemary's Waltz,
R&R Cheddar

Hubbardston Blue

NEW HAMPSHIRE

Kunik

MASSACHUSETTS

Ocooch Mountain
Mona

American Grana

Battenkill Brebis

Ewe's Blue

Great Hill Blue

Big Woods Blue

Bad Axe

Alpine

NEW YORK

RHODE ISLAND

Cave Aged Marisa

MICHIGAN

Green Peppercorn Chevre,
Triple Cream Wheel

Brigid's Abbey,
Hooligan

Chèvre in Blue

Pleasant Ridge Reserve

Bleu Mont Cheddar

Eden

CONNECTICUT

Gruyère Surchoix

Grand Queso

Tumbleweed

IOWA

Bridgewater Round

PENNSLYVANIA

5 Spoke Creamery Browning Gold

Telford Reserve

NEW JERSEY

Maytag Blue

OHIO

DELAWARE

Frisian Farms Mature Gouda

INDIANA

Mountain Top Bleu

ILLINOIS

WEST
VIRGINIA

MARYLAND

Huckleberry Blue

Old Kentucky Tome,
Wabash Cannonball

Everona Piedmont

KANSAS

Dirt Lover

VIRGINIA

MISSOURI

Appalachian,
Grayson

KENTUCKY

Awe Brie

NORTH CAROLINA

TENNESSEE

OKLAHOMA

Clemson Blue

ARKANSAS

Belle Chèvre

SOUTH
CAROLINA

ALABAMA

GEORGIA

ATLANTIC OCEAN

Blanca Bianca,
Hoja Santa

LOUISIANA

Thomasville Tomme

Hopelessly Bleu

MISSISSIPPI

GULF OF MEXICO

N

FLORIDA

200 miles

200 km

Key

★ AOC, DOC, DOP, PGI, or PDO cheeses

Produced only here

Produced throughout the region

CANADA Canada's cheese history dates back to 1635, when French colonists first produced cheese. Throughout the centuries, immigrants from Europe, the Middle East, and even India brought with them their favourite recipes, adding diversity and complexity to the variety of cheeses.

Until the 1990s, most cheeses were made on small farms for local consumption or in huge factories that produced blocks of strong Cheddar. The renaissance of artisan cheesemakers, who used cow's, goat's, and ewe's milk, led Canadians to discover and voice their pride in their country's exceptional cheeses. Nearly 200 cheese companies exist today, which reflects increasing consumption.

Key
- ★ AOC, DOC, DOP, PGI, or PDO cheeses
- Produced only here
- Produced throughout the region

ARCTIC OCEAN

BEAUFORT SEA

BAFFIN BAY

YUKON TERRITORY

NORTHWEST TERRITORIES

NUNAVUT

LABRADOR SEA

NEWFOUNDLAND

QUEEN CHARLOTTE ISLANDS

HUDSON BAY

CANADA
PRODUCED THROUGHOUT THE COUNTRY
Cheddar Curds

ALBERTA

QUÉBEC

NEWFOUNDLAND AND LABRADOR

Avonlea Clothbound Cheddar

Sieur de Duplessis

Le Paillasson de l'isle d'Orléans

Bouquetin de Portneuf, La Sauvagine

BRITISH COLUMBIA

Baby Blue

Old Grizzly

Harvest Moon

MANITOBA

SASKAT-CHEWAN

ONTARIO

Le Délice des Appalaches

Le Cendré des Prés — Allegretto

Le Sabot de Blanchette

VANCOUVER ISLAND

La Barre du Jour, Le Cru des Erables

PRINCE EDWARD ISLAND

Dragon's Breath Blue

NOVA SCOTIA

NEW BRUNSWICK

Seven-Year-Old Orange Cheddar

Bleu Bénédictin

Le Cabanon

Prestige

Oka Classique

Raclette de Compton au Poivre

Comfort Cream

Piacere

PACIFIC OCEAN

500 miles

500 km

N

ATLANTIC OCEAN

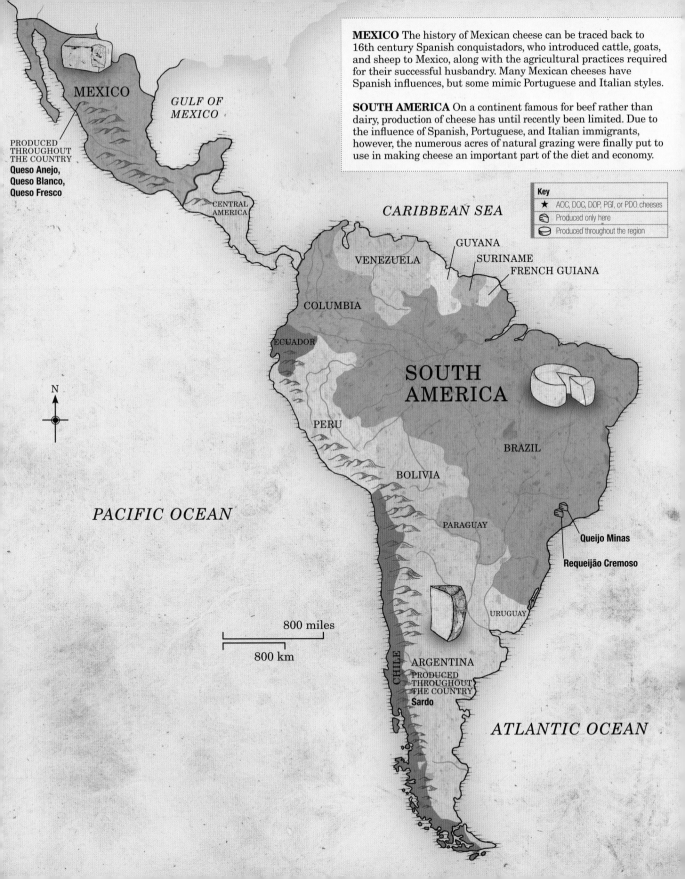

MEXICO The history of Mexican cheese can be traced back to 16th century Spanish conquistadors, who introduced cattle, goats, and sheep to Mexico, along with the agricultural practices required for their successful husbandry. Many Mexican cheeses have Spanish influences, but some mimic Portuguese and Italian styles.

SOUTH AMERICA On a continent famous for beef rather than dairy, production of cheese has until recently been limited. Due to the influence of Spanish, Portuguese, and Italian immigrants, however, the numerous acres of natural grazing were finally put to use in making cheese an important part of the diet and economy.

MEXICO

GULF OF
MEXICO

PRODUCED
THROUGHOUT
THE COUNTRY
**Queso Anejo,
Queso Blanco,
Queso Fresco**

CENTRAL
AMERICA

CARIBBEAN SEA

VENEZUELA

GUYANA
SURINAME
FRENCH GUIANA

COLUMBIA

ECUADOR

SOUTH
AMERICA

PERU

BRAZIL

BOLIVIA

Key

★	AOC, DOC, DOP, PGI, or PDO cheeses
	Produced only here
	Produced throughout the region

PARAGUAY

Queijo Minas

Requeijão Cremoso

PACIFIC OCEAN

N

800 miles

800 km

URUGUAY

CHILE

ARGENTINA
PRODUCED
THROUGHOUT
THE COUNTRY
Sardo

ATLANTIC OCEAN

Alpine

In 1972, a group of educators, farmers, and artisans decided to buy a farm and offer urban-based children a hands-on experience of what it means to be 'stewards of the land'. Based on Rudolf Steiner's concept of biodynamic farming, it has hosted more than 13,000 children.

TASTING NOTES A rinded, mountain-style organic cheese made from rich, sweet golden milk. As the cheese ages, its supple texture and buttery, mellow taste becomes nutty, more complex and firm.

HOW TO ENJOY It melts superbly and makes for a perfect snack. Pair with a mild, younger red wine or a dry, not too sharp white.

USA Ghent, New York	
Age Regular 6–8 months; Aged 12 months plus	
Weight and Shape 3.6–10kg (8–22lb), wheel	
Size D. 23–30cm (9–12in), H. 10cm (4in)	
Milk Cow, organic	
Classification Hard	
Producer Hawthorne Valley Farm	

270

Alsea Acre Fromage Blanc

The mild Oregon climate provides the Alsea Acre family farm with the ideal environment to create European-style cheeses all year.

TASTING NOTES The pure goat's milk flavours arrive with a zesty fresh taste, alongside hints of citrus and pine nuts. The finish is a complex and creamy taste on the palate.

HOW TO ENJOY Sprinkle over fresh salad greens with green grapes, roasted almonds, and toasted crostini. Enjoy with a chilled glass of Roussanne.

USA Alsea, Oregon	
Age From a few days	
Weight and Shape 225g (8oz), tubs	
Size No size	
Milk Goat	
Classification Fresh	
Producer Alsea Acre	

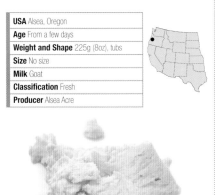

American Grana

In 1979, Errico Auricchio left the family cheese company and set up Bel Gioioso to create quality Italian cheeses. Today they have over 27 cheeses, and are consistent winners at the American Cheese Society Awards. American Grana is a Parmesan-style cheese made using raw milk, gathered from local farms.

TASTING NOTES Made in huge rounds that are matured on wooden shelves in special caves. Hard and grainy with a sweet, nutty flavour that intensifies with age.

HOW TO ENJOY Eat on its own or use for grating. Pair with a strong beer or your favourite red.

USA Green Bay, Wisconsin	
Age 18–24 months	
Weight and Shape 31.75kg (70lb), drum	
Size D. 37cm (14½in), H. 20cm (8in)	
Milk Cow	
Classification Hard	
Producer Bel Gioioso	

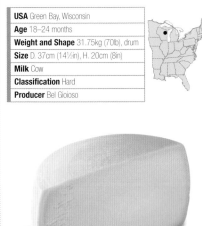

Andante Dairy Picolo

The cheesemakers at California's Andante Dairy are inspired by the various musical tempos of the cheesemaking process. This luxurious triple-cream cheese combines Jersey milk and crème fraîche.

TASTING NOTES Made with fresh cow's milk, Picolo has a pleasantly tart and sweet taste inspired by spring. When properly aged, it melts in the mouth.

HOW TO ENJOY Drizzle wedges of Picolo with citrus honey and accompany with a sweet baguette and a glass of sparkling Prosecco.

USA Petaluma, California	
Age 2–4 weeks	
Weight and Shape 125g (4½oz), round	
Size D. 5cm (2in), H. 4cm (1½in)	
Milk Cow	
Classification Soft white	
Producer Andande Dairy	

Appalachian

Meadow Creek Dairy, located in the mountainous parts of south western Virginia, draws inspiration from various traditional European cheeses. Appalachian loosely resembles a French Tomme (see pp89–91).

TASTING NOTES The flavour is very delicate and raw with strong vegetal notes and a spicy finish. The texture is dense and chewy with a musty strong aroma.

HOW TO ENJOY Appalachian melts well, making it the perfect cooking cheese. However, the flavour is robust enough to serve the cheese on its own.

USA Galax, Virginia	
Age 60 days	
Weight and Shape 4.5kg (10lb) wheel	
Size D. 23cm (9in), H. 5cm (2in)	
Milk Cow	
Classification Semi-soft	
Producer Meadow Creek Dairy	

Appel Farms Cheddar

Handmade at Appel family's farm in Washington state using the cheddaring technique of authentic English Cheddar (see pp178–79). The milk comes from a large herd of cows fed on grass and corn. They also make Feta, Gouda, and yogurt, which they sell at their farm shop.

TASTING NOTES Aged for three months minimum, the flavours go from mild to sharp to extra sharp, a bit like raw onion. Also available with garlic and dill, black pepper, and bacon.

HOW TO ENJOY Excellent in a homemade mac and cheese, paired with a fine Pilsner.

USA Ferndale, Washington	
Age 3–6 months	
Weight and Shape 2.25kg (5lb), wheel	
Size D. 25cm (10in), H. 6cm (2½in)	
Milk Cow	
Classification Hard	
Producer Appel Farms	

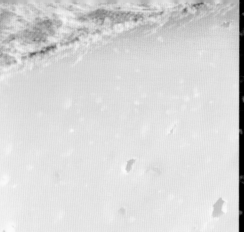
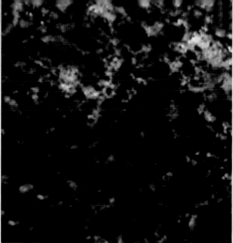

Ascutney Mountain Cheese

The Cobb Hill cheesemakers are part of a community of 23 households making agricultural products. They produce two raw milk cheeses from a small herd of Jersey cows. The farm uses no chemical fertilizers, additives or feeds.

TASTING NOTES Although it is loosely based on alpine cheeses, Ascutney Mountain is not quite as dense but still has a firm texture. The mild initial flavour develops towards a pineapple-like sweet and sour finish.

HOW TO ENJOY The sweet taste favours a good hoppy beer, like an IPA, and some savoury chutney.

USA Hartland, Vermont	
Age 6–10 months	
Weight and Shape 4.5kg (10lb), wheel	
Size D. 38cm (15in), H. 12cm (5in)	
Milk Cow	
Classification Hard	
Producer Cobb Hill Cheese	

Ashed Tomette

Since 1976, Ana and Gilbert Cox have been making award-winning cheese from their herd of Alpine, La Mancha, and Nubian dairy goats on their farm just north of the town of Willits in Mendocino County.

TASTING NOTES The striking ash-covered disc has a firm yet flaky texture, with a cream-white centre that has a subtle goaty taste and nutty overtones.

HOW TO ENJOY Match with a hearty Cabernet, then serve with a seasonal fresh fruit platter and warm crunchy sweet baguettes.

USA Willits, California	
Age 2–4 weeks	
Weight and Shape 60g (2oz), disc	
Size Various	
Milk Goat	
Classification Fresh	
Producer Shamrock Artisan Goat Cheese	

Awe Brie

Although Awe Brie is influenced by Western European cheesemakers, it is produced on a farm in the rolling hills of Kentucky. It is the first Brie made within the United States to be produced using raw milk. In fact, all of Kenny's Farmhouse cheeses are made using raw milk, piped fresh from the milking barn for processing.

TASTING NOTES The cheese is ripened to 60 days. Its snow-white exterior conceals a golden interior that has a silky texture and robust flavour.

HOW TO ENJOY Bourbon and slices of fresh pear are perfect to serve alongside a cheeseboard of Awe Brie.

USA Austin, Kentucky	
Age 60 days	
Weight and Shape 900g (2lb), wheel	
Size Various	
Milk Cow	
Classification Soft white	
Producer Kenny's Farmhouse Cheese	

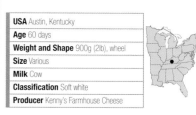

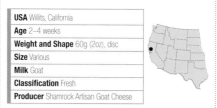

Barely Buzzed

It is hand-rubbed with a blend of South American and Indonesian finely ground coffee beans and French lavender buds, mixed with oil to suspend the dry ingredients in the rub. Barely Buzzed is aged in caves on Utah blue spruce. Its unusual name comes courtesy of a contest held by Beehive Cheese Company in 2007.

TASTING NOTES It is a smooth Cheddar-style cheese with a nutty flavour. The rub and sweet Jersey milk imparts hints of butterscotch, caramel, and coffee.

HOW TO ENJOY This is ideal paired with stout and crusty whole grain bread.

USA Uintah, Utah	
Age 3–4 months	
Weight and Shape 4.1–5kg (9–11lb), wheel	
Size D. 25cm (10in), H. 7.5cm (3in)	
Milk Cow	
Classification Flavour-added	
Producer Beehive Cheese Company	

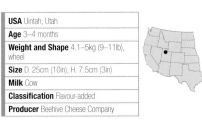

Battenkill Brebis

Karen Weinberg and husband Paul Borghard began in 1990, with just 2 sheep. Today their herd of 500 grazes on pastures of clovers, fescue, wild oregano, timothy, and cattails, from April to September; the result - award-winning cheeses.

TASTING NOTES This Basque-style raw milk cheese is cloth wrapped, with a rind flecked with natural bacteria. Supple and dense with herbaceous notes when young; aged, it is sweet and tastes of brazil nuts.

HOW TO ENJOY Serve with fresh bread or grilled or grated on salads, soups or pasta. Pair with a light beer.

USA Shushan, New York	
Age 4–18 months	
Weight and Shape 2.7kg (6lb), round	
Size D. 20cm (8in), H. 12–15cm (5–6in)	
Milk Ewe	
Classification Hard	
Producer 3 Corner Field Farm	

Bayley Hazen Blue

The Kehlers have only been producing cheese from a pure Ayrshire herd since 2002, but the complexity and sophistication of their products speaks to the incredible amount of research and training they have undergone as they strive for perfection.

TASTING NOTES This medium-strong and relatively dry blue cheese delivers a complex flavour. The blue is upfront and slightly peppery, while the cheese's finish is long and creamy.

HOW TO ENJOY It is complemented well by Port or sweet wines, and is best served as part of a cheeseboard.

USA Greensboro, Vermont	
Age 4–6 months	
Weight and Shape 1.8kg (4lb), drum	
Size D. 15cm (6in), H. 23cm (9in)	
Milk Cow	
Classification Blue	
Producer Jasper Hill Farm	

Beechers Flagship Reserve

In 2003, Kurt Beecher followed his passion for artisan cheeses and opened Beecher's shop in the heart of Seattle's Pike Place Market. Eight years later he opened a new cheesemaking "kitchen", café and restaurant in the heart of New York, using the produce of local herds from southern Albany.

TASTING NOTES A a traditionally made Cheddar (see pp178–79), it is aged for at least 16 months. Dense, chewy with bold, savoury notes, and sharp lingering tang.

HOW TO ENJOY Serve with a soughdough loaf, along with your favourite beer or a robust red.

USA Seattle, Washington	
Age 15 plus months	
Weight and Shape 7.2kg (16lb), cylinder	
Size D. 20cm (8in), H. 23cm (9in)	
Milk Cow	
Classification Hard	
Producer Beechers Handmade Cheese	

Belle Chèvre

Located in Elkmont, Alabama, Fromagerie Belle Chèvre is among the relatively few cheesemakers in the southern United States. Nonetheless, the creamery has gathered more than 50 awards throughout the years for its fresh goat's milk cheeses.

TASTING NOTES This traditional French-style chèvre is very rich and smooth, with a tangy flavour and distinct herbaceous finish.

HOW TO ENJOY It marries well with almost any preserve and is perfect for any recipe that calls for fresh chèvre. Alternatively, serve plain with almonds, walnuts, and a crisp white wine.

USA Elkmont, Alabama	
Age Fresh	
Weight and Shape 225g (8oz), log	
Size D. 2.5cm (1in), L. 5cm (2in)	
Milk Goat	
Classification Fresh	
Producer Fromagerie Belle Chèvre	

Bellwether Farms Crescenza

This cheese is modelled on the famous Italian cheese Crescenza (see p114), right down to its traditional square shape, but it has a twist of California coastal sea breeze flavour.

TASTING NOTES This handmade cheese goes to market at one week of age. It is milky white and high in moisture. The rich Jersey milk gives it a creamy flavour balanced by a pleasant tartness and yeasty finish.

HOW TO ENJOY Dollop with a spoonful of homemade apricot compote, serve with a crunchy fresh baguette, accompanied with a crisp Pinot Blanc.

USA Petaluma, California	
Age 1 week	
Weight and Shape 1.5kg (3lb 3oz), square	
Size D. 30cm (12in), H. 1cm (½in)	
Milk Cow	
Classification Fresh	
Producer Bellwether Farms	

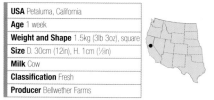

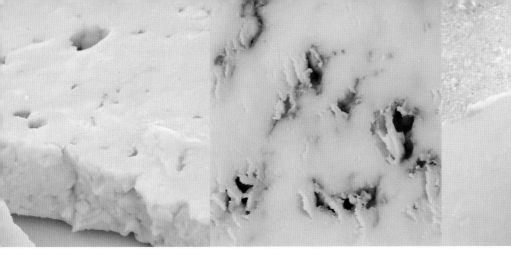

Big Island Feta

Dick Threlfall, a retired farrier who shod horses for more than 35 years, focuses on the feta, the herd, and the machinery; while Heather, having worked in the veterinary field, milks the goats and makes the soft cheeses.

TASTING NOTES The pleasant slight tang has a hint of unusual flavours because the goats browse on pastures as well as tropical vegetation including bamboo shoots and macadamia tree leaves.

HOW TO ENJOY Create a Hawaiian salad with toasted whole macadamia nuts, fresh-picked spinach and sweet island pineapple, and pair with a chilled Kona Brewing Big Wave golden ale.

USA Honokaa, Hawaii	
Age 3–12 weeks	
Weight and Shape 450g (1lb), block	
Size Various	
Milk Goat	
Classification Fresh	
Producer Hawaiian Island Goat Dairy	

Big Woods Blue

Despite losing much of their herd in a devastating fire on the farm in 2005, the Reads have been slowly rebuilding with the help of the local community and Slow Food groups. They continue to produce this magnificent raw milk cheese for blue lovers.

TASTING NOTES This creamy and mild cheese is both very approachable for blue-shy tasters and complex and surprising for veterans. The robust and only slightly salty cheese melts in the mouth like milk chocolate.

HOW TO ENJOY The complexity of this cheese deserves to be matched with a great vintage port.

USA Nerstrand, Minnesota	
Age 4–6 months	
Weight and Shape 3.2kg (7lb), round	
Size D. 15cm (6in), H. 12cm (5in)	
Milk Ewe	
Classification Blue	
Producer Shepherd's Way Farms	

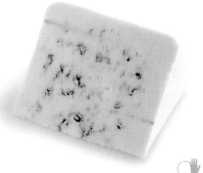

Blanca Bianca

Paula Lambert has spent more than 20 years working with cheese, drawing particular inspiration from her travels in Italy. The Mozzarella Company was founded to produce fresh mozzarella, but production now includes many of Paula's own creations, including this cheese washed with white wine.

TASTING NOTES Rich and full-flavoured, the chewy paste fills the mouth and nose with sweet floral tastes. While not a particularly powerful washed-rind cheese when young, it develops a strong but pleasing punch as it matures.

HOW TO ENJOY Try with dark walnut raisin bread and a light beer.

USA Dallas, Texas	
Age 2 months	
Weight and Shape 675g (1½lb), flat wheel	
Size D. 18cm (7in), H. 5cm (2in)	
Milk Cow	
Classification Semi-soft	
Producer Mozzarella Company	

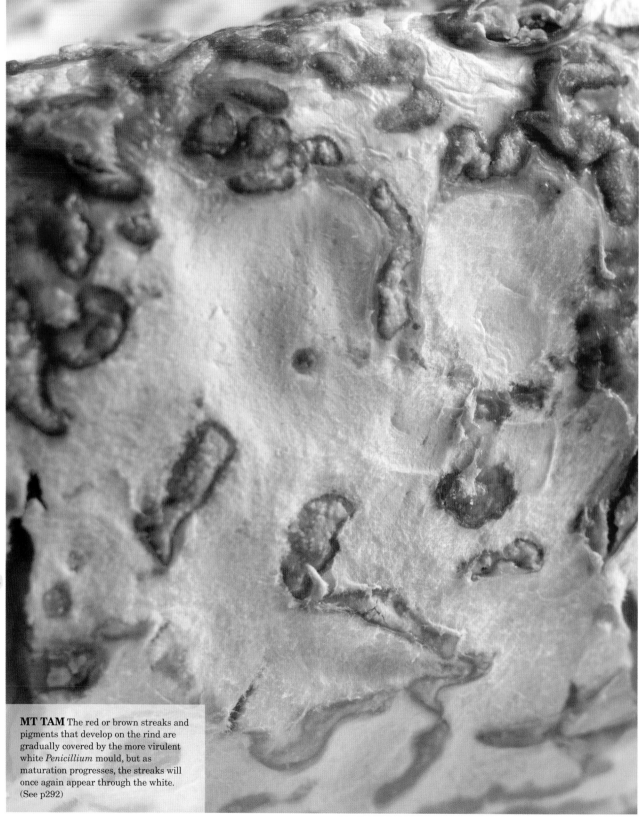

MT TAM The red or brown streaks and
pigments that develop on the rind are
gradually covered by the more virulent
white *Penicillium* mould, but as
maturation progresses, the streaks will
once again appear through the white.
(See p292)

Bleu Mont Cheddar

Willie Lehner is a second generation cheesemaker who trained in England and Switzerland. He buys milk from local certified organic producers and makes cheese off-site at other producers' cheesemaking facilities. All his cheeses are then transferred to a custom-built cave on his property to ripen.

TASTING NOTES With a very pleasant and tasty element of freshly turned earth, this handmade clothbound Cheddar has a medium-strong flavour with good grassy notes and a nice lingering finish.

HOW TO ENJOY Savour on its own with some chutney and dried figs or dates.

USA Blue Mounds, Wisconsin	
Age 12–18 months	
Weight and Shape 3.6kg (8lb), drum	
Size D. 15cm (6in), H. 10cm (4in)	
Milk Cow	
Classification Hard	
Producer Bleu Mont Dairy	

Blythedale Farm Camembert

Becky and Tom Loftus at Blythedale Farm in Corinth, Vermont, have been producing Camembert and Brie-style cheeses since 1994. They have stuck with their tried-and-true recipe, using milk from their herd of Jersey cows to produce this well-regarded cheese.

TASTING NOTES While possessing the typical rich creamy flavour you would expect in a Camembert-style cheese, it has a softer and wetter rind, as well as a tarter initial flavour.

HOW TO ENJOY Use to make a great ham and Camembert sandwich on a baguette, or serve with crackers and champagne.

USA Corinth, Vermont	
Age 4 weeks	
Weight and Shape 225g (8oz), round	
Size D. 12cm (5in), H. 2.5cm (1in)	
Milk Cow	
Classification Soft white	
Producer Blythedale Farm	

Bourrée

Dancing Cow Farm began producing cheese in 2006. Unlike many artisanal cheesemakers, after the cheese is made, Steve and Karen Getz hand the job of ripening over to the experts in the cellars at Jasper Hill so that they can focus on maintaining high milk quality standards.

TASTING NOTES Although it is a washed-rind cheese, its aroma is relatively mild and floral. The texture is smooth, rich, and somewhat sticky on the palate, with a peanut-like flavour that grows more intense as it finishes.

HOW TO ENJOY Bourrée is best served with a strong ale and some chutney.

USA Bridport, Vermont	
Age 3 months	
Weight and Shape 450g (1lb), round	
Size D. 10cm (4in), H. 5cm (2in)	
Milk Cow	
Classification Semi-soft	
Producer Dancing Cow Farmstead Cheese	

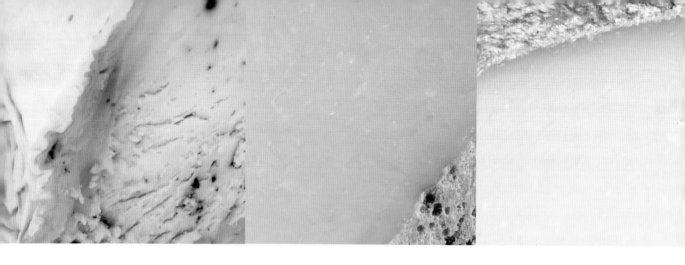

Bridgewater Round

Zingerman's has built its ever-growing reputation on selling flavoursome, traditionally made foods, including a huge variety of cheeses. In doing so, they have managed to both educate and inspire their staff and customers. It was almost inevitable that they would turn their hand to cheesemaking.

TASTING NOTES It is made with added cream and spiked with freshly ground black pepper. Bridgewater Round has a rich, silky feel and taste, with a hint of mushrooms on the finish.

HOW TO ENJOY This star of the cheeseboard is complemented by nuts, dried fruit, and a crisp, fruity Chinon.

USA Ann Arbor, Michigan
Age 4–8 weeks
Weight and Shape 225g (8oz), round
Size Various
Milk Cow
Classification Soft white
Producer Zingerman's

Cabot Clothbound

Cabot Creamery can trace its origins back to 1919, when a cooperative of 94 local farmers was formed in Vermont. This raw-milk cheese is a handmade traditional bandaged Cheddar (see pp178–79) that is cave-aged in the cellars at Jasper Hill Farm.

TASTING NOTES It is initially sweet and buttery on the palate, but its finish is much more savoury and heavy; rather than a classic Cheddar acidity, it has a fuller, rounder sour bite.

HOW TO ENJOY Serve simply with some hearty bread, homemade chutney, and a beer. Big red wines work well, too.

USA Montpelier, Vermont
Age 12 months or more
Weight and Shape 5.4kg (12lb), cylinder
Size D. 46cm (18in), H. 10cm (4in)
Milk Cow
Classification Hard
Producer Cabot Creamery Cooperative

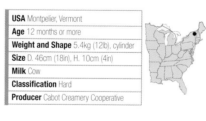

Cave Aged Marisa

Sid Cooke is the master cheesemaker at the helm of this large Wisconsin creamery, which produces dozens of varieties of cheese yet crafts each one with great care and attention. The majority are made using cow's milk, but this one uses ewe's milk.

TASTING NOTES This dense medium-firm natural rind cheese has an intense floral aroma and a very sweet initial flavour. As the flavour develops, it becomes more savoury. There is a hint of lanoline on the finish.

HOW TO ENJOY It is great served with black fruit preserves or quince paste and good hearty dark bread.

USA La Valle, Wisconsin
Age 6 months
Weight and Shape 2.7kg (6lb), round
Size D. 30cm (12in), H. 10cm (4in)
Milk Ewe
Classification Hard
Producer Carr Valley Cheese Company

278

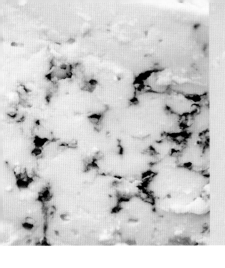

Chèvre in Blue

Established in 1988, MontChevre offers outstanding cheeses at great value while promoting sustainable farming. It is the largest goat's cheese producer in North America, with the milk suppliers in Wisconsin and Iowa. Their cheeses are natural, with no additives.

TASTING NOTES The deep purple streaks stand out against the stark white, crumbly interior. Its herbaceous, aromatic character, derived from the goat's milk, is offset by the strong spicy finish of the blue.

HOW TO ENJOY Perfect spread on your favourite bread or cracker, or crumbled in salads. Enjoy with a sweet wine.

USA Belmont, Wisconsin	
Age 2–3 months	
Weight and Shape 1.8kg (4lb), drum	
Size D. 18cm (7in), H. 10cm (4in)	
Milk Goat	
Classification Blue	
Producer MontChevre	

City of Ships

This small producer keeps her business local, buying milk from nearby farms and supplying cheese to local outlets, but the high-quality milk and expert ripening make this worth seeking out.

TASTING NOTES Highly complex flavours cover all of the senses. Initially sweet, it yields to herbal and sea-salty flavours, building to a strong lingering butterscotch finish that coats the tongue. The texture is tight and chewy, with a faint crunch.

HOW TO ENJOY To savour the best of its myriad flavours, serve it on its own or with other medium-strength cheeses, and mild biscuits with gentle textures.

USA Phippsburg, Maine	
Age 8 months	
Weight and Shape 2.7kg (6lb), rounded wheel	
Size D. 28cm (11in), H. 10cm (4in)	
Milk Cow	
Classification Hard	
Producer Hahn's End	

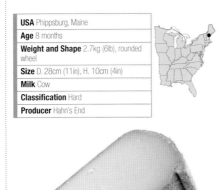

Clemson Blue

Now produced at Clemson University, Clemson Blue dates back to 1941, when the cheese was aged in an abandoned railroad tunnel under Stumphouse Mountain. Since the late 1950s, the entire making and ripening process has taken place on campus.

TASTING NOTES The texture is medium-grained and slightly clumpy, but on the palate it quickly opens up into an exceptionally smooth creaminess. Its medium blue flavour is well balanced against the buttermilk sweetness.

HOW TO ENJOY Its moderate intensity allows it to be paired with both sweet wines and fruitier reds such as Merlot.

USA Clemson, South Carolina	
Age 6 months	
Weight and Shape 900g (2lb), flat disc	
Size D. 25cm (10in), H. 2.5cm (1in)	
Milk Cow	
Classification Blue	
Producer Clemson University	

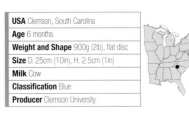

Constant Bliss

The name comes from American Revolutionary history and seems improbably fitting because the cheese is aged just to the US legal minimum of 60 days and offers a rare glimpse into the world of soft raw-milk cheeses that are typically unavailable in the United States.

TASTING NOTES The thin dry rind has a stony aroma and slight bitterness enveloped by the paste's salty, buttery almost popcorn-like flavour. With age, it becomes soft and rich, but not runny.

HOW TO ENJOY Feature on a cheeseboard with other premium cheeses. Even better, serve with Champagne and caviar.

USA	Greensboro, Vermont
Age	60 days
Weight and Shape	225g (8oz), cylinder
Size	D. 5cm (2in), H. 7.5cm (3in)
Milk	Cow
Classification	Soft white
Producer	Jasper Hill Farm

Cornelia

Made at Point Reyes Farmstead, and delivered to the Murray's Cheese Shop NY, it is matured in their washed rind caves. Here for the next few months, the cave master will work his magic bringing out its hidden character, like the great affineurs have done for centuries in Europe.

TASTING NOTES The leathery rind, dusted with fine white mould, hides a supple, almost liquid, buttery interior with tiny holes. It has hints of cheese sauce, and a roasted peanut finish.

HOW TO ENJOY Perfect on a cheeseboard or with cooked meats, accompanied by a medium-bodied red or Trappiste beer.

USA	Pt Reyes Station, California
Age	6 months
Weight and Shape	450g (1lb), round
Size	D. 10cm (4in), H. 4cm (1½in)
Milk	Cow
Classification	Semi-soft
Producer	Point Reyes Farmstead

Coupole

Allison Hooper's cheesemaking journey began in the 1970s in France. By 1985, she had formed Vermont Butter and Cheese Company, where they make a variety of award-winning dairy products, with Bob Reese. Coupole, sprinkled with ash, exhibits all the best qualities of a French-style goat's cheese.

TASTING NOTES It is soft and smooth, but not runny. It has just enough punch to remind you of the goat's milk from which it is made, but is mild enough to charm first-time goat's cheese tasters.

HOW TO ENJOY It is perfect on a cheeseboard. Try it in a salad with nuts, pears, and a spicy salad green.

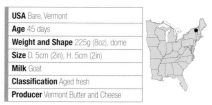

USA	Bare, Vermont
Age	45 days
Weight and Shape	225g (8oz), dome
Size	D. 5cm (2in), H. 5cm (2in)
Milk	Goat
Classification	Aged fresh
Producer	Vermont Butter and Cheese

Dirt Lover

Green Dirt farm above the Missouri River Valley is owned by Sarah Hoffmann and Jacqueline Smith and provides a complexity of grazing to cope with extremes of weather from steep slopes to low areas of dense shape and water meadows. Ideal for creating award-winning farmstead cheeses and grass-fed lamb.

TASTING NOTES The name refers to the layer of charcoal ash under the white crust. Dense, creamy with a hint of lanolin when young, becoming richer and earthy with a lemony finish, as it matures.

HOW TO ENJOY Try it with a lightly oaked Chardonnay, rosé, or a local beer.

USA Weston, Missouri	
Age 2–8 weeks	
Weight and Shape 140g (5oz), cylinder,	
Size D. 7.5cm (3in), H. 5cm (2in)	
Milk Ewe	
Classification Soft white	
Producer Green Dirt Farm	

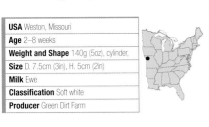

Dorset

Located in Champlain Valley, the dairy was Vermont's first cheese cooperative founded by Consider Stebbins Bardwell. Now it makes numerous cheeses using milk from their own goats and 2 local Jersey herds.

TASTING NOTES Lightly brine washed, this Taleggio-style cheese with orange-pink rind dusted with white mould has a farmyardy aroma. Its supple, yellow interior is sweet and buttery and gently pungent with a meaty, beef stock finish.

HOW TO ENJOY It opens up at room temperature and pairs well with cider, beer or an aromatic white and a bowl of fresh walnuts.

USA West Pawlet, Vermont	
Age 60 days	
Weight and Shape 900g (2lb), round	
Size D. 20cm (8in), H. 2.5cm (1in)	
Milk Cow	
Classification Semi-soft	
Producer Consider Bardwell Farm	

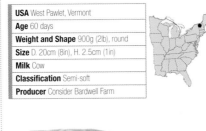

Eden

Located just an hour north of New York City, Sprout Creek Farm makes a wide variety of cheeses from its mixed herd using traditional methods and sustainable farming practices. The milk is produced seasonally. In harmony with its cheesemaking ventures, the farm also offers educational workshops to increase understanding of good farming practices.

TASTING NOTES Lightly washed in brine, it has an apple tartness to its flavour, with a long and full savoury finish. The texture is supple and chewy.

HOW TO ENJOY This cheese is perfect to serve with cider.

USA Poughkeepsie, New York	
Age 3 months	
Weight and Shape 3.6kg (8lb), flat wheel	
Size D. 35cm (14in), H. 5cm (2in)	
Milk Cow	
Classification Semi-soft	
Producer Sprout Creek Farm	

Elk Mountain

The production of this semi-soft cheese is based on the method used to make European mountain-style cheeses such as Tomme des Pyrénées (see p90). This American version is named after Elk Mountain, near the Rogue River in Oregon, where it is made.

TASTING NOTES It is best eaten when it has aged six months. This cheese is washed in a local Wild Mountain Oregon beer, and the paste has a very buttery flavour and firm texture.

HOW TO ENJOY A true pairing of this Oregon cheese would be with a savour of fig preserves. Enjoy the pair with an Elk Mountain Ale.

USA Rogue River, Oregon	
Age 6 months	
Weight and Shape 3.6kg (8lb), wheel	
Size D. 23cm (9in), H. 11cm (4½in)	
Milk Goat	
Classification Semi-soft	
Producer Phoila Farm	

Everona Piedmont

The Piedmont region of Virginia is in the foothills of the ancient Blue Ridge Mountains, and Dr Pat Elliot has operated a full-time ewe farm here since 1992, alongside her farm-based family medical practice. Everona also produces the ewe's milk cheese Stony Man, as well as a variety of "infused" versions of Piedmont, and a wine-washed cheese, Pride of Bacchus.

TASTING NOTES Beneath the brown-grey rind it is warm yellow with a nutty sweetness along with even floral tones, and a smooth buttery finish.

HOW TO ENJOY Pair with a hoppy beer or Merlot, along with slices of fresh pear.

USA Rapidan, Virginia	
Age: 3–6 months	
Weight and Shape 675g (1½lb) and 2.7kg (6lb), wheel	
Size Various D. 20cm (8in), H. 7.5cm (3in) (pictured)	
Milk Ewe	
Classification Hard	
Producer Everona Dairy	

Ewe's Blue

Located in New York State's Hudson Valley, Old Chatham has grown since 1993 to become one of the largest ewe dairies in the United States. Its line of sophisticated and well-executed cheese and yogurt products are widely available throughout the United States.

TASTING NOTES Similar in style to Roquefort (see pp82–83), it is moist and creamy with pockets of blue-green mould and fruity, buttery notes; it has a more mineral-like character and less saltiness than its French counterpart.

HOW TO ENJOY Try it crumbled on top of salad greens, or enjoy it simply, with French bread and a glass of Sauterne.

USA Old Chatham, New York	
Age 6–8 months	
Weight and Shape 1.8kg (4lb), wheel	
Size D. 23cm (9in), H. 5cm (2in)	
Milk Ewe	
Classification Blue	
Producer Old Chatham Sheepherding Company	

Frisian Farms Mature Gouda

Making farmstead Gouda in the Dutch tradition is part of Frisian Farms' commitment to its Dutch ancestry. It is located just outside Pella, Iowa, a predominantly Dutch community that has preserved its Dutch culture, including traditional windmills, a historical village, and an annual tulip festival. The Gouda is available in young, mature, and smoked versions.

TASTING NOTES Each golden wheel is filled with nutty flavours and fruity essences, with a sweet cream finish.

HOW TO ENJOY Savour with a Riesling, fresh grapes, and wheat crackers.

USA Oskaloosa, Iowa	
Age 6–8 weeks minimum	
Weight and Shape 9.1kg (20lb), wheel	
Size D. 35cm (14in), H. 15cm (6in)	
Milk Cow	
Classification Hard	
Producer Frisian Farms	

Goatzarella

Fifty Alpine and Nubian goats provide the organic milk for this supple, elastic mozzarella-style cheese. The goats are also the family pets and all know their names. Goatzarella is one of several goat's milk cheeses made by Fraga Farm, including a chèvre and a feta.

TASTING NOTES Made with vegetarian rennet, it is rich in cream with a grassy meadow flavour and finishes with a silky texture on the palate.

HOW TO ENJOY Use for cooking rather than for the cheeseboard. It grates and melts superbly. Try it on fresh herbed foccacia with tomatoes and olive oil, paired with an Oregon Pinot Noir.

USA Sweet Home, Oregon	
Age 2–6 weeks	
Weight and Shape 225g (8oz), square	
Size L. 23cm (9in), W. 23cm (9in), H. 7.5cm (3in)	
Milk Goat	
Classification Fresh	
Producer Fraga Farm Goat Cheese	

Grafton Cheddar

The Grafton Coop, founded in 1892 by a group of dairy farmers, is now part of the Grafton-based Windham Foundation, which promotes Vermont's rural communities. Their "Queen of Quality" clothbound Grafton Cheddar uses Jersey milk from a single, grass-fed herd from Farms for City Kids Foundation. It is aged in Grafton's own caves for a minimum of six months.

TASTING NOTES Dense, compact and sunshine yellow from the milk, it has grassy yet sweet overtones which become more intense and savoury.

HOW TO ENJOY Superb for cooking, a robust red is its perfect accompaniment.

USA Grafton, Vermont	
Age 6–18 months	
Weight and Shape 9kg (20lb), wheel	
Size D. 27cm (10½in), H. 12cm (5in)	
Milk Cow	
Classification Hard	
Producer Grafton Village Cheese	

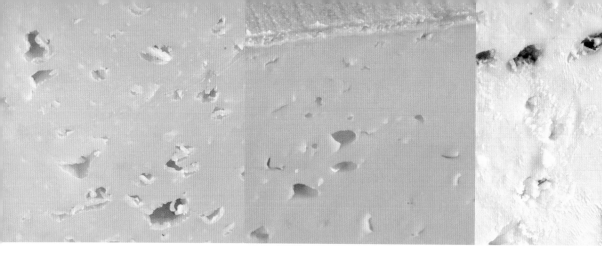

Grand Queso

The Roths' mission when they began producing cheese in the United States was not to import cheese, but rather to utilize the traditions and technology. Although Grand Queso is reminiscent of Spanish Manchego (see pp162–163), it has its own unique flavour profile.

TASTING NOTES It has a full, rounded taste and aroma that is sweet and very buttery, while the texture is gummy and slightly oily, but not heavy.

HOW TO ENJOY Grand Queso is a terrific option in Spanish and Mexican recipes calling for a hard full-flavoured cheese. Serve it grated over bruschetta topped with sun-dried tomatoes.

USA Monroe, Wisconsin	
Age 6 months	
Weight and Shape 2.25kg (5lb), wheel	
Size D. 15cm (6in), H. 12cm (5in)	
Milk Cow	
Classification Hard	
Producer Roth Käse USA	

Grayson

Meadow Creek Dairy is located in the Blue Ridge Mountains of southwest Virginia, at an altitude of 850m (2800ft). According to the cheesemakers, it is the great air and water quality, along with ecologically responsible farming, that result in exceptionally high milk quality.

TASTING NOTES This intensely strong-smelling washed cheese possesses an appropriately strong vegetal flavour. Its firm texture holds up well on the palate, and it finishes surprisingly cleanly.

HOW TO ENJOY Grayson's intensity demands strong flavours to match, such as crackers with black pepper or rye bread with onion confit.

USA Galax, Virginia	
Age 4 months	
Weight and Shape 3.6kg (8lb), square	
Size D. 18cm (7in), H. 5cm (2in)	
Milk Cow	
Classification Semi-soft	
Producers Meadow Creek Dairy	

Great Hill Blue

This old dairy farm located south of Boston has been in the family for more than a generation. The dairy purchases Jersey and Holstein milk from several surrounding farms, but it is neither pasteurized nor homogenized. The resulting cheese has won numerous awards since its launch in 1996.

TASTING NOTES It has a surprisingly tight texture that opens on the palate like cool butter. Tangy, with a good blue punch, it is just salty enough to complement the natural sweetness.

HOW TO ENJOY It is delightful on its own or in a salad with apples and bacon; pair with aromatic Riesling or Viognier.

USA Marion, Massachusetts	
Age 6 months	
Weight and Shape 3.6kg (8lb), drum	
Size D. 23cm (9in), H. 10cm (4in)	
Milk Cow	
Classification Blue	
Producer Great Hill Dairy	

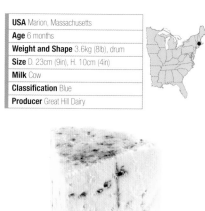

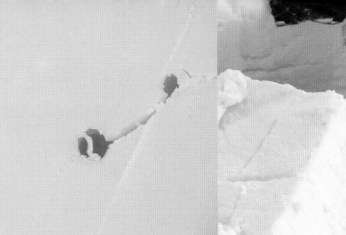

Green Peppercorn Chèvre

Coach Farm has acquired a reputation for outstanding quality in the past few years and has won numerous international awards. They make regular appearances at many of New York City's great farmers markets.

TASTING NOTES Firm and crumbly, it has a lemony sourness that is perfectly accented, but not overpowered, by the mild green peppercorn flavour. The finish is delicate and clean.

HOW TO ENJOY Delicate yet complex, it is ideal with a summer salad of fresh greens and ripe tomatoes.

USA Pine Plains, New York	
Age 30 days	
Weight and Shape 1.35kg (3lb), brick	
Size L. 30cm (12in), H. 10cm (4in)	
Milk Goat	
Classification Soft white	
Producer Coach Farm	

Gruyère Surchoix

The Roth family came to the United States from Switzerland in 1990 to capitalize on the great milk produced in Wisconsin. The family had been in the cheese business for generations, and the result is an American Gruyère that is of similar quality to the Swiss original, but with distinctive character.

TASTING NOTES The pale white cheese has an aroma of dried apples with a hint of mustiness. The flavour continues in that direction, but the lengthy finish turns to a meaty saltiness.

HOW TO ENJOY It is the perfect choice for fondue. Alternatively, serve with a selection of dry salamis and Riesling.

USA Monroe, Wisconsin	
Age 9–19 months	
Weight and Shape 7.3kg (16lb), wheel	
Size D. 35cm (14in), H. 12cm (5in)	
Milk Cow	
Classification Hard	
Producer Roth Käse USA	

Hoja Santa

Paula Lambert has been making mozzarella at her creamery near Dallas for more than 20 years and has developed a line of Italian-inspired cheeses. This fresh cheese is similar to a French Banon (see p34), but wrapped in the Mexican hoja santa leaf.

TASTING NOTES It has a very fine curd that feels light and clean in the mouth. The natural woody sassafras flavour that comes off the leaf differentiates it from other fresh chèvre cheeses.

HOW TO ENJOY It is delicious on toast, but, to really bring out the flavour of the hoja santa leaves, try this with some Chardonnay.

USA Dallas, Texas	
Age 4 weeks	
Weight and Shape 225g (8oz), drum	
Size D. 5cm (2in), H. 4cm (1½in)	
Milk Goat	
Classification Fresh	
Producer Mozzarella Company	

USA

Monterey Jack

Also known as Monterey Sonoma Jack or, colloquially, "Jack", Monterey Jack was given its official title by the Food and Drug Administration in 1955 to encompass all the varieties then on the market. A debate has raged as to who created Monterey Jack and the characters behind the story are as smooth, colourful, and sharp as the cheese itself.

In the mid-1800s, Dona Juana Cota de Boronda made and sold a cheese called Queso del Pais door-to-door to help feed her family of 15 children. Meanwhile, Domingo Pedrazzi of Carmel Valley is known to have created a similar cheese that required the application of pressure from a device called a "housejack". He named it Pedrazzi's Jack Cheese.

It was the shrewd and less-than-popular local businessman David Jacks, however, who laid claim to Monterey Jack cheese and, it is said, stole the idea of Queso del Pais and started major production using milk from his 14 dairy ranches in the 1890s. Jacks marketed the cheese as Jacks' Cheese.

What is not in doubt is that David Jacks was the first person to manufacture the cheese on a large scale. However, according to research by Wendy Moss in 1966, it was the Franciscan monks in the 1700s who brought the recipe from Spain, via Mexico –a soft, creamy cheese known as Queso Blanco Pais.

Today, Monterey Jack is one of the best-loved American cheeses. It accounts for about 10 per cent of all cheese production in California.

TASTING NOTES Young Jack is very mild with a lactic taste. It is sometimes flavoured with spices, pimientos, or Jalapeño peppers. The Farmstead version is almost runny, has an earthy, mushroomy aroma, and a sweet creamy taste that hints of hazelnuts, with a citrus tang.

Mezzo Secco is a firmer fresh Jack. Dry Jack is the firmest of the Jacks. It first appeared in the 1930s as an alternative to Parmesan. Aged for 7–12 months or longer, it has a deep yellow-gold interior with a grainy, brittle texture and a deep full-bodied tang that is sweet and nutty. The best example is the Dry Jack made by Ig Vella of Vella Cheeses in Sonoma – a legend in his own lifetime.

HOW TO ENJOY The supple texture of Young Jack is perfect for grilling, snacking and numerous Mexican-style dishes. Young Jack is perfect with a cool beer or cider. Dry Jack is great for sauces, omelettes, soufflés, or grated on pasta, tacos and enchiladas. Dry Jack needs the depth of one of California's great red wines.

A CLOSER LOOK

There are numerous Jacks on the market, and flavoured ones are gaining in popularity. Young, Mezzo Secco, or Dry – the process remains largely the same – the difference is in the maturing.

MEASURING THE CURDS Once the whey has been drained, the curds are carefully measured and placed in square pieces of cheesecloth, then knotted, ready for shaping.

Drums of Dry Jack *mature on wooden racks of a cellar. Dry Jack is usually aged for 7–12 months.*

USA California	
Age 1–12 months	
Weight and Shape 2.5kg (5½lb) drum	
Size Various	
Milk Cow	
Classification Semi soft (Monterey Jack); Hard (Dry Jack)	
Producer Various	

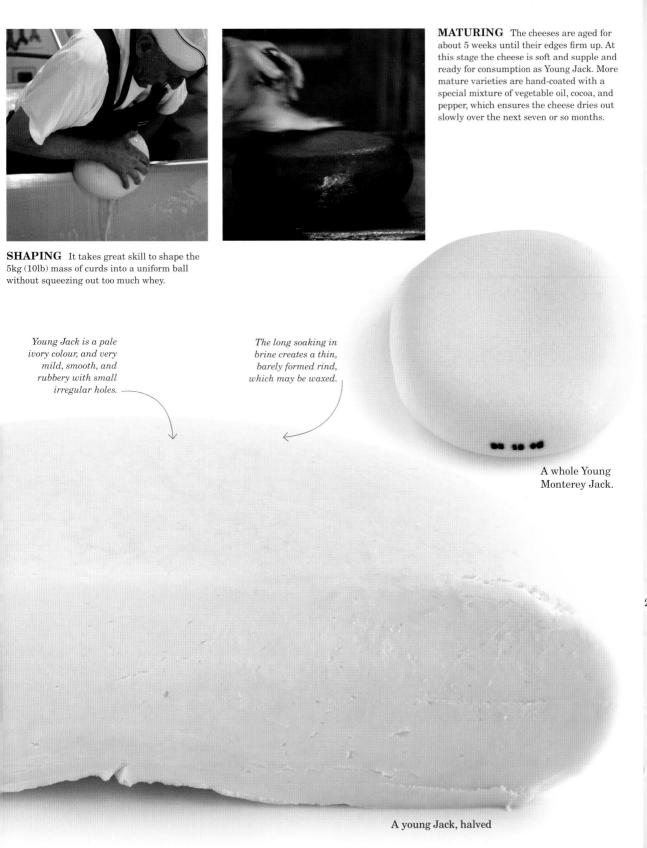

MATURING The cheeses are aged for about 5 weeks until their edges firm up. At this stage the cheese is soft and supple and ready for consumption as Young Jack. More mature varieties are hand-coated with a special mixture of vegetable oil, cocoa, and pepper, which ensures the cheese dries out slowly over the next seven or so months.

SHAPING It takes great skill to shape the 5kg (10lb) mass of curds into a uniform ball without squeezing out too much whey.

Young Jack is a pale ivory colour, and very mild, smooth, and rubbery with small irregular holes.

The long soaking in brine creates a thin, barely formed rind, which may be waxed.

A whole Young Monterey Jack.

A young Jack, halved

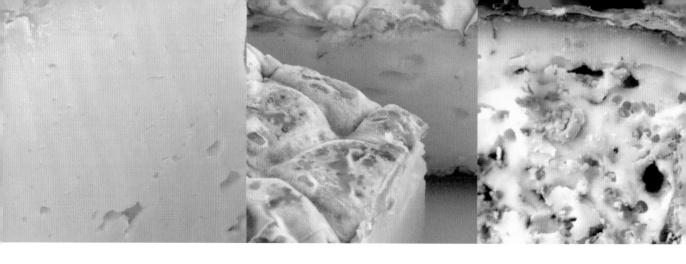

Hooligan

Hooligan, a washed-rind basket-moulded cheese, is made by Mark Gillman, school teacher turned cheesemaker, who is a regular at New York's Union Square farmers' market. Cato Corner keeps its own herd of about 40 hormone- and antibiotic-free Jersey cows.

TASTING NOTES Cato Corner's best-known and most pungent cheese, its aroma is intense and slightly yeasty, the texture firm but moist, with a slight grittiness from the rind, and it melts on the palate, with a creamy sweet finish.

HOW TO ENJOY It is excellent melted on toast with a little tomato or on its own with a good-quality Belgian ale.

USA Colchester, Connecticut	
Age 60 days	
Weight and Shape 450g (1lb), wheel	
Size D. 15cm (6in), H. 7.5cm (3in)	
Milk Cow	
Classification Semi-soft	
Producer Cato Corner Farm	

Hubbardston Blue

Now operated by the Kilmoyers, Westfield Farm has been producing high-quality goat's milk cheeses in all shapes, sizes, and types since 1971. Hubbardston is a surface-ripened blue cheese; the bright blue mould grows on the outside rather than internally, but as it ages the blue is overlaid with a distinctive gunmetal grey rind.

TASTING NOTES It is very soft and creamy, sometimes runny, and is not particularly pungent, with mushroom-like flavours and a mild blue finish.

HOW TO ENJOY This very approachable blue works well with wholemeal crackers, fresh figs, and a sweet white.

USA Hubbardston, Massachusetts	
Age 30–40 days	
Weight and Shape 225g (8oz), round	
Size D. 7.5cm (3in), H. 2.5cm (1in)	
Milk Goat	
Classification Blue	
Producer Westfield Farm	

Huckleberry Blue

Wes Jarrell and Leslie Cooperband founded Prairie Fruit Farm in 2003, with a focus on organic and sustainable farming. They have a herd of about 70 goats. Huckleberry is wrapped in sycamore leaves, which are soaked in pear brandy. It is sold with or without them.

TASTING NOTES Raw-milk, aged blue-veined cheese with a natural rind. Named after one of the more strong-willed goats, it is bold, and beautiful in appearance, flavour, and finish.

HOW TO ENJOY Have it with a glass of pear brandy, or cider.

USA Champaign, Illinois	
Age 2–3 months	
Weight and Shape 2.25kg (5lb), drum	
Size D. 14cm (5½in), H. 12cm (5in)	
Milk Goat	
Classification Blue	
Producer Prairie Fruit Farm	

Humboldt Fog

Mary Keehn's search in the 1970s for a healthy source of milk for her family led her to become one of America's best known artisan cheesemakers. "Humboldt Fog" and "Bermuda Triangle" are two of her iconic creations.

TASTING NOTES Named after the local ocean fog, its pure white crusty mould hides a fine layer of black ash covering, which is present inside the cheese as well. It has a creamy, smooth texture and a taste which is reminiscent of almonds and white wine.

HOW TO ENJOY Serve with fresh salad greens, or as a dessert, with baked pears. Pair with Pinot Gris or a wheat beer.

USA Arcata, California
Age 6–8 weeks
Weight and Shape 5kg (11lb) and 2.25kg (5lb), round
Size D. 20cm (8in), 11cm(4¼in), H. 5cm (2in), 9.5cm (3¾in)
Milk Goat
Classification Soft white
Producer Cypress Grove Chèvre

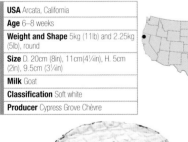

Kunik

Nettle Meadow is currently home to more than 100 goats, in addition to a multitude of other farm animals that have been rescued or retired over the years. This cheese is an unusual triple-cream blend of goat's milk and cream from the farm's Jersey cows.

TASTING NOTES This remarkably sweet, honey-like cheese has a mouthfeel ranging from custard when fresh to butter if the cheese has dried a bit.

HOW TO ENJOY Kunik is perfectly suited to very dark breads such as rye, where the sweetness of the cheese will really shine and cries out for an accompanying glass of Champagne.

USA Warrensburg, New York
Age 2–4 weeks
Weight and Shape 300g (10oz), round
Size D. 10cm (4in), H. 5cm (2in)
Milk Goat with cow's milk cream
Classification Soft white
Producer Nettle Meadow Goat Farm

Larzac

Along the Touchet River in southwest Washington State's Walla Walla Valley lies the home of the first farmstead ewe's milk dairy using recipes based on cheeses from southern France. Larzac has an attractive thin layer of fine wood ash through the centre.

TASTING NOTES Each batch is handmade to achieve a delicate soft texture, then cellared for a month to complete the aging that highlights the fresh sweet goat milk flavours in each cheese.

HOW TO ENJOY Larzac is perfect sliced over fresh butterleaf greens, roasted golden beetroot, and olive oil, and paired with a crisp Pilsner beer.

USA Dayton, Washington
Age 4–6 weeks
Weight and Shape 225g (8oz), truncated cone
Size D. 10cm (4in), base, 5cm (2in), top, H. 7.5cm (3in)
Milk Goat
Classification Aged fresh
Producer Monteillet Fromagerie

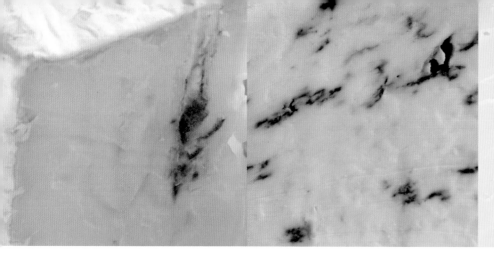

Le Petit Chèvre Bleu

One of the oldest continuously producing cheese companies in the Unites States, Marin French, is located within California's Sonoma County. It shows a strong French influence in each of its cheeses.

TASTING NOTES Aged for 30 days, this triple-cream Brie-style cheese strikes a good balance between rich flavours and delicate fine blue veining. It has a creamy texture, with a subtle mild, white pepper spicy taste.

HOW TO ENJOY Spread on buttered toast in the morning, and savour with apricot preserves and fresh pear juice, or pair with a full-bodied Cabernet Sauvignon.

USA Petaluma, California
Age 30 days or more
Weight and Shape 115g (4oz), round
Size: D. 5.5cm (2 ¼in), H. 4cm (1 ¾in)
Milk Goat
Classification Blue
Producer Marin French Cheese Company

Maytag Blue

It is certainly one of the most famous and oldest original American cheeses but despite high demand, it is still produced by hand as it was when it was first made in 1941. Although the cheese is cave-aged, it always remains bleach white in appearance.

TASTING NOTES This Roquefort-like blue is made with cow's milk. Maytag has an enigmatic flavour. Initially creamy and steely blue, it yields to a lemon-tart-like sweet-sourness on the finish.

HOW TO ENJOY Apart from being a cheeseboard star, this sturdy cheese is perfect for salads, melted on fillet steak, or even baked into fruit-based desserts.

USA Newton, Iowa
Age 4 months
Weight and Shape 1.8kg (4lb), drum
Size: D. 18cm (7in), H. 10cm (4in)
Milk Cow
Classification Blue
Producer Maytag Dairy Farms

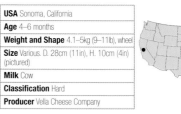

Mezzo Secco

Mezzo Secco is not as hard as dry Monterey Jack, but is firmer than a young, soft Jack. It was first created in the 1920s, in the days before the advent of refrigeration, when perishable foods were stored in "ice boxes" and cheese had to fend for itself.

TASTING NOTES Mezzo Secco's supple, dense golden interior has a rich and nutty full flavour, enhanced by a black pepper and vegetable oil coating.

HOW TO ENJOY This is still a great choice for picnics, or slice and serve it over chargrilled lamb burgers with a glass of Californian Pinot Noir.

USA Sonoma, California
Age 4–6 months
Weight and Shape 4.1–5kg (9–11lb), wheel
Size: Various. D. 28cm (11in), H. 10cm (4in) (pictured)
Milk Cow
Classification Hard
Producer Vella Cheese Company

Mona

The cooperative began operating in 1997 to "to enhance the quality of life for co-op member families by sustainably producing, and marketing premium sheep dairy products." Now it has around 12 dairies and produces a few products under its own label.

TASTING NOTES Covered with an edible coating, it is aged for around 6 months. Its firm yet moist texture is crumbly and has a warm buttery taste with hints of caramel from the ewe's milk, along with a nutty finish.

HOW TO ENJOY Grate over pasta or grill, and serve with an American Pinot Noir or a sweet wine.

USA River Falls, Wisconsin		
Age 6 months		
Weight and Shape 5.4kg (12lb), wheel		
Size D. 35.5cm (14in), 12cm (5in)		
Milk Ewe and cow		
Classification Hard		
Producer Wisconsin Sheep Dairy Cooperative		

Monet

Decorated with fresh marigold, borage, and viola flowers, the French chèvre-style Monet produced by Dee Harley is a true artist's palatte that reflects the beautiful gardens that surround this coastal California dairy.

TASTING NOTES This fresh and clean chèvre's soft, smooth texture is the result of the gentle handling of the fresh goat's milk, and has hints of spring grass flavour year-round.

HOW TO ENJOY With its floral decoration, it makes a stunning centrepiece for a cheeseboard. Serve with a garden-fresh salad and a crisp Pinot Grigio.

USA Pescadero, California		
Age 1–3 weeks		
Weight and Shape 225g (8oz), ball		
Size D. 7.5cm (3in), H. 2.5cm (1in)		
Milk Goat		
Classification Fresh		
Producer Harley Farms Goat Dairy		

MouCo ColoRouge

This particular cheesemaker enjoys the changing of the seasons. The flavours within the cheese change as it ages and evolves. ColoRouge is rubbed with a brine solution to create the red-orange rind with its distinctive haze of white mould.

TASTING NOTES It is hand-ladled to create a soft and creamy texture beneath the smear rind, and has mild buttery overtones that develop into complex and spicy notes.

HOW TO ENJOY Spread ColoRouge over crispy toast, and serve with a rich tawny port and halved fresh red and green grapes.

USA Fort Collins, Colorado		
Age 3–8 weeks		
Weight and Shape 225g (8oz), round		
Size D. 7.5cm (3in), H. 2.5cm (1in)		
Milk Cow		
Classification Semi-soft		
Producer MouCo Cheese Company		

Mountain Top Bleu

Firefly Farms originally kept its own herd of goats, but ultimately decided to buy milk from a local Amish cooperative in Pennsylvania so they could focus exclusively on cheese production. They make several varieties, but this small blue is particularly unusual.

TASTING NOTES The relatively uncommon pyramid shape hints at Mountain Top Bleu's unique flavour. While subtle, the bluing is well balanced against grassy, bright, and enjoyably goaty flavours. Its texture is soft and velvety.

HOW TO ENJOY The cheesemaker suggests serving this with poached figs. A white Port would do well on the side.

USA Bittinger, Maryland	
Age 5 weeks	
Weight and Shape 225g (8oz), pyramid	
Size D. 10cm (4in), H. 7.5cm (3in)	
Milk Goat	
Classification Blue	
Producer FireFly Farms	

Mt Tam

Named after Mt Tamalpais, a small mountain located on the Marin County coast of northern California just to the north of San Francisco Bay, Cowgirl Creamery's signature triple-cream cheese is made with organic cow's milk from the Straus Family Dairy.

TASTING NOTES Under the thick, white bloomy rind, Mt Tam is creamy and dense in texture, with a rich flavour and a pleasant fruity finish.

HOW TO ENJOY Mt Tam goes extremely well with a golden Pilsner or a Fumé Blanc, dried apricots, and fresh-baked crunchy Pugliese bread.

USA Point Reyes, California	
Age 3–4 weeks	
Weight and Shape: 60g (2oz), round	
Size D. 7.5cm (3in), H. 5cm (2in)	
Milk Cow	
Classification Soft white	
Producer Cowgirl Creamery	

Oakdale Gouda

Dutch-born Walter and Lenneke Bulk re-create the cheeses of their homeland, Gouda (see pp230–231) and Edam (see p228), in central California. It is available plain or flavoured with peppercorns, garlic, mustard, or jalapeño peppers.

TASTING NOTES Aged to perfection for about ten weeks, the cheese has flavours that share elements of butterscotch and toasted almonds.

HOW TO ENJOY Create a golden grilled sandwich on French bread with a slice of country ham; serve with Sangiovese and fresh or dried fruit.

USA Oakdale, California	
Age 2–4 months	
Weight and Shape 4.1–5kg (9–11lb), boulder	
Size D. 23cm (9in), H. 7.5cm (3in)	
Milk Cow	
Classification Hard	
Producer Oakdale Cheese Company	

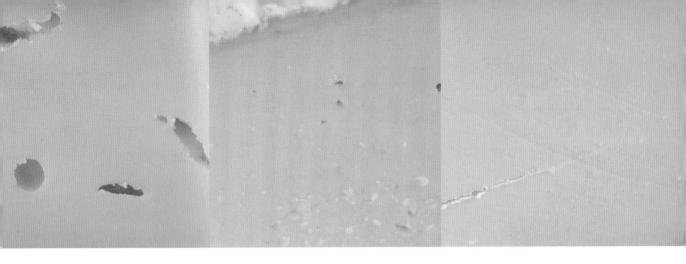

Ocooch Mountain

Hidden Springs, located in a part of Wisconsin known as the Driftless Area, operates in close cooperation with its surrounding Amish neighbours, utilizing traditional sustainable methods. The high-quality milk is sourced from a herd of East Friesian and Lacaune ewes that thrive in this terrain.

TASTING NOTES This very firm-textured cheese is crumbly and slightly grainy on the palate, with a fat, sweet, and very nutty flavour. It has a delightful aroma of sheep on open pastureland.

HOW TO ENJOY Ocooch is delicious with honey and almonds, or on its own with a good red Burgundy.

USA	Westby, Wisconsin
Age	4 months
Weight and Shape	900g (2lb), wheel
Size	D. 12cm (5in), H. 6cm (2⅓in)
Milk	Ewe
Classification	Hard
Producer	Hidden Springs Creamery

Old Kentucky Tome

This cheese from Capriole, which was founded by Judy and Larry Schadd, is based on the mountain Tommes of Europe, but has a thinner rind dusted with a fine powdery white mould. The quality of the cheeses exhibit the great care with which the Schadds keep their herd of more than 400 goats.

TASTING NOTES Its pure white, smooth texture feels light on the palate, and it has slightly goaty notes, with a hint of toasted walnut on the finish.

HOW TO ENJOY Robust enough to stand up to many flavours, but Judy suggests a yellow tomato and ginger preserve. Pair with Pinot Noir or other soft reds.

USA	Greenville, Indiana
Age	4–8 months
Weight and Shape	1.8kg (4lb), drum
Size	D. 25cm (10in), H. 10cm (4in)
Milk	Goat
Classification	Soft white
Producer	Capriole Farmstead Goat Cheeses

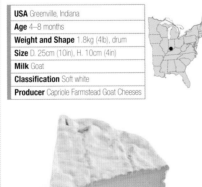

Pleasant Ridge Reserve

Produced in the style of European mountain cheeses from May through October. It is named after a land formation on the farm, and is the only cheese to have won Best of Show at the American Cheese Society three times.

TASTING NOTES Brine washings and the unique micro-flora of the raw milk help develop its complex flavours and dense, supple texture. Young, it has the fruity sweetness of an aromatic wine, after months in the ripening caves it becomes savoury, and more intense.

HOW TO ENJOY Perfect on a cheeseboard or used like Gruyère. Goes well with crisp fruity, whites.

USA	Dodgeville, Wisconsin
Age	8–12 months
Weight and Shape	5.4kg (12lb), wheel
Size	D. 30cm (12in), H. 7.5cm (3in)
Milk	Cow
Classification	Hard
Producer	Uplands Cheese Company

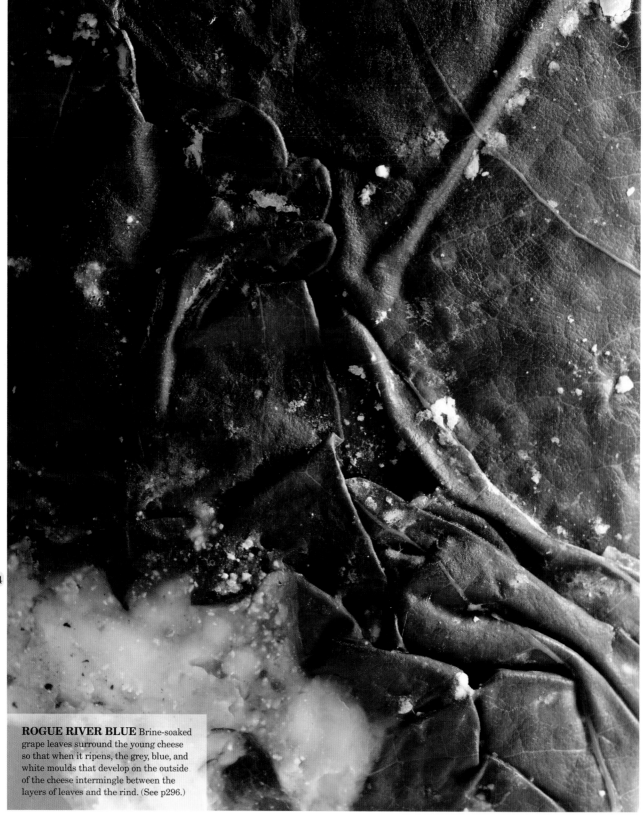

ROGUE RIVER BLUE Brine-soaked grape leaves surround the young cheese so that when it ripens, the grey, blue, and white moulds that develop on the outside of the cheese intermingle between the layers of leaves and the rind. (See p296.)

Point Reyes Original Blue

Since its debut in 2000, this Original Blue cheese, made in Point Reyes, California, has become a mainstay on cheeseboards and the recipient of numerous cheesemaking awards.

TASTING NOTES This blue cheese has a pleasant tang, with salty ocean flavours developing as the blue-grey veins mature throughout the creamy, smooth white wheel. The taste becomes more robust with age.

HOW TO ENJOY Crumble over a warm dish of green beans sprinkled with pancetta and savour the taste while enjoying a glass of California Cabernet.

USA Point Reyes, California	
Age 6–8 months	
Weight and Shape 2.7kg (6lb), wheel	
Size Various	
Milk Cow	
Classification Blue	
Producer Point Reyes Cheese	

Pondhopper

After a visit to Brazil, Flavio DeCastilhos became fascinated with the local Italian style artisan cheeses. It resulted in the successful Tumalo Farms in the Cascade Mountains where they make 12 artisan cheeses, mostly from goat's milk. Adding a unique touch, Pondhopper is washed in beer from a local microbrewery.

TASTING NOTES Pale yellow-white with a few tiny eyes it is smooth and supple with a hoppy taste balanced by a nutty taste and fresh, herbaceous tang typical of goat's milk cheeses.

HOW TO ENJOY A natural partner for a nutty, hoppy ale, and yeasty bread.

USA Bend, Oregon	
Age 2–12 weeks	
Weight and Shape 4.1kg (9lb), wheel	
Size D. 25cm (10in), H. 7.5cm (3in)	
Milk Goat	
Classification Hard	
Producer Tumalo Farms	

Queso de Mano

Cheesemaker Jim Schott start in 1989 with just 5 goats. By 2007, he had formed a partnership with Colorado Correction Industries to cope with demand. This has proved hugely successful for all. Queso de Mano was its first raw-milk cheese.

TASTING NOTES An aged Spanish style hard cheese it is slightly grainy with a supple texture, and aromatic tang from the goats milk and a distinct taste of toasted almonds on the finish.

HOW TO ENJOY Serve thin slices with *membrillo*, toasted almonds or figs along with a Fino or a dry sherry or a hoppy beer.

USA Longmont, Colorado	
Age 4–6 months	
Weight and Shape 2.7kg (6lb), drum	
Size D. 15cm (6in), H. 10cm (4in)	
Milk Goat	
Classification Hard	
Producer Haystack Mountain Goat Dairy	

USA

295

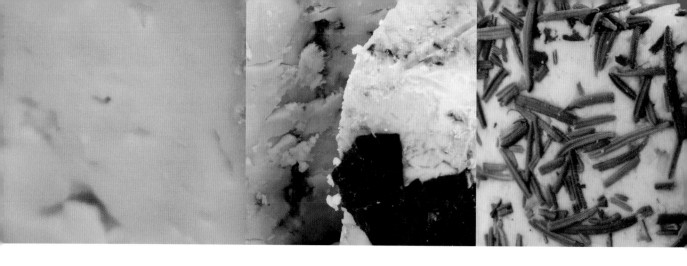

Red Hawk

In the early 1990s, friends Peggy Smith and Sue Conley launched Tomales Bay Foods in Pt. Reyes Station to help farms get their products to the Bay Area's finest chefs. Today they offer over 200 cheeses from America, and Europe, including their own successful brand, Cowgirl Creamery.

TASTING NOTES This triple cream cheese is washed in brine, giving the rind its distinctive sunset orange-red colour, which gives Red Hawk its bold appearance and pungent flavour and aroma.

HOW TO ENJOY Goes well with an IPA beer, Dry Riesling or cider.

USA Pt Reyes Station, CA California
Age 4–5 weeks
Weight and Shape 300g (10oz), round
Size D. 10cm (4in), H. 5cm (2in)
Milk Cow
Classification Semi-soft, Washed
Producer Cowgirl Creamery

Rogue River Blue

Rogue Creamery, founded in the 1930s by one of America's great cheesemakers Thomas Vella, continues to enjoy great success. Under the management of David Gremmels, in 2008 Rogue River became the first American raw-milk cheese to be certified for export.

TASTING NOTES Wrapped in grape leaves and soaked in pear brandy, it has great intensity and depth of flavour. Firm, yet moist and smooth in the mouth, it is less salty than many blues, and is creamy and sweet with a spicy finish.

HOW TO ENJOY Pair with dessert wines and pears or use in desserts such as poached pears or calvados soufflé.

USA Central Point, Oregon
Age 6–8 months
Weight and Shape 2.25kg (5lb), drum
Size D. 15cm (6in), H. 10cm (4in)
Milk Cow
Classification Blue
Producer Rogue Creamery

Rosemary's Waltz

Silvery Moon Creamery was founded in 2003 by Jennifer Betencourt who, after studying cheesemaking at Cornell, formed a partnership with Smiling Hill Farm. Although located in a relatively commercial area of Maine, the farm still works the same pristine pastures that have remained in the hands of the same family since the 1700s.

TASTING NOTES It is very fresh and clean, with a crumbly texture. It picks up the flavours of the rosemary and juniper on the rind without being overpowered.

HOW TO ENJOY Its mildness makes it a good base for numerous recipes. Try it shaved over baked sweet potato slices.

USA Westbrook, Maine
Age 1 month
Weight and Shape 1.35kg (3lb), wheel
Size D. 18cm (7in), H. 7.5cm (3in)
Milk Cow
Classification Fresh
Producer Silvery Moon Creamery

R&R Cheddar

Founded in the 1700s, Smiling Hill Farm is ancient by American standards. Their Holstein cows graze on pastures free of chemical fertilizer and pesticides. Silvery Moon Creamery partnered with Smiling Hill in 2003, adding artisan cheeses to its existing dairy business.

TASTING NOTES This mild cheese is full of interesting subtlety, with a chewy texture and tight grain. The flavour is sweet and full. Rather than salty or savoury on the finish, it has an earthy minerality.

HOW TO ENJOY The texture and age make it ideal for melting in sandwiches. Enjoy on its own with a strong lager.

USA Westbrook, Maine
Age 6 months minimum
Weight and Shape 7.7kg (17lb), drum
Size D. 35cm (14in), H. 10cm (4in)
Milk Cow
Classification Hard
Producer Silvery Moon Creamery

St George

This is made to honour the island of São Jorge in the Azores, where Mary and George Matos are originally from. The Matos family now makes its Portuguese-style raw milk, farmstead cheeses in Santa Rosa, California.

TASTING NOTES A perfect balance of creamy dense and rich flavours, with a firm Cheddar-like texture that offers hints of earthy meadow, enhanced over time with crunchy crystals that round out the full flavour of the Jersey cream.

HOW TO ENJOY It is a marvellous choice for macaroni cheese with sun-dried tomatoes and olive oil, complemented by a glass of Barbera.

USA Santa Rosa, California
Age 6–10 months
Weight and Shape 4.1–7.3kg (9–16lb), wheel
Size Various
Milk Cow
Classification Hard
Producer Matos Cheese Factory

St Jorge

The Fagundes family makes cheeses based on those from the Azores, a group of small islands west of Portugal, where Isabel Fagundes made cheese in the late 1800s. St Jorge, the family's first, was released in 2000 and, like all their cheese, is made only with morning milk from their farm.

TASTING NOTES With a texture between Cheddar and Gouda, this raw milk cheese is long in flavour and slow to mature. After the initial sharp bite, it mellows to a creamy, sweet-fruity tang.

HOW TO ENJOY This excellent grating cheese also makes a tasty snack with a glass of Cabernet Sauvignon.

USA Hanford, California
Age Up to 3 years
Weight and Shape 2.7–3.6kg (6–8lb), wheel
Size D. 25cm (10in), H. 10cm (4in)
Milk Cow
Classification Hard
Producer Fagundes Old World Cheese

San Joaquin Gold

Named after the San Joaquin Valley in California, this American original is inspired by Swiss-mountain cheeses. It is produced with the milk of Holstein Farmstead cows, keeping with the cheesemaker's concept of creating cheese in the European tradition.

TASTING NOTES It is aged for 16 to 24 months to create a full-flavoured cheese with a buttery golden colour and a crumbly texture. As it ages, the complex flavours of nuts and grass arise to the palate.

HOW TO ENJOY Grate it into a creamy pasta dish and serve with a full-bodied San Juaquin Syrah.

USA	Modesto, California
Age	16–24 months
Weight and Shape	13.6kg (30lb), wheel
Size	Various
Milk	Cow
Classification	Hard
Producer	Fiscali Farmstead Cheese

Seastack

The rock formations covering the coastal lines of the Pacific Northwest are the inspiration for the cheeses produced at the Mt Townsend Creamery in Washington.

TASTING NOTES The coating of vegetable ash and sea salt prior to ripening is the key to the balance of flavours in this soft white cheese. It is a one-of-a-kind cheese, with a silky texture and earthy flavours that become piquant as it ages.

HOW TO ENJOY This perfect picnic and hiking cheese is served with a fresh, crusty baguette, Viognier and dried fruit. Equally, it makes a delicious finale to a fine meal with friends.

USA	Port Townsend, Washington
Age	4–6 weeks
Weight and Shape	225g (8oz), round
Size	Various
Milk	Cow
Classification	Soft white
Producer	Mt Townsend Creamery

Shelburne Cheddar

Shelburne Farms is a non-profit organization. They have been making cheddar since 1980, on their 1,400-acre working farm, forest, and National Historic Landmark, in Shelburne. This cheddar is made with brown Swiss cows' raw milk, and then aged at Jasper Hill.

TASTING NOTES Hand wrapped and carefully aged for more than a year in cheesecloth, it has a dense, crumbly texture and buttery feel with a sharp raw onion savoury bite, and deep, warm yellow colour.

HOW TO ENJOY Taste it on site where you can view the cheesemaking at the Farm Barn, from mid-May to mid-October.

USA	Shelburne, Vermont
Age	12–14 months
Weight and Shape	10kg (22lb), drum
Size	D. 33cm (13in), H. 12cm (5in)
Milk	Cow
Classification	Hard
Producer	Shelburne Farms

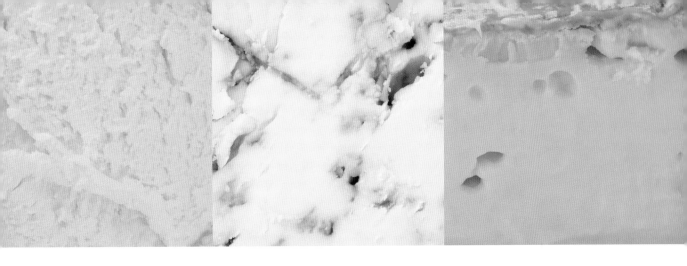

Sierra Nevada Cream Cheese

Named after the Sierra Nevada Mountains, California, the cheesemakers of the same name also produce a variety of natural and organic cheeses, including a Cheddar and various flavoured Jack cheeses. However, their best cheese is this authentic, old-style cream cheese.

TASTING NOTES Sierra Nevada has a full-cream flavour and texture, with hints of sweet grass, butter, and a sea-salty tang on the finish.

HOW TO ENJOY Spread on a bagel or fold into an omelette with smoked salmon and chive blossoms, alongside a glass of California Sauvignon Blanc.

USA Willows, California	
Age 1–3 weeks	
Weight and Shape 200g (7oz), container	
Size No size	
Milk Cow	
Classification Fresh	
Producer Sierra Nevada	

Smokey Blue Cheese

Rogue Creamery age their cheeses in Roquefort-style caves, and after their success with Oregon Blue, the first blue made on the West Coast, its producers decided to be the first to smoke a blue. Smokey Blue was born.

TASTING NOTES This cheese is smoked over a bed of local hazelnut shells, giving the robust, spicy blue a hint of hazelnuts with a touch of creamy caramel and smoke on the finish.

HOW TO ENJOY The marriage of this smoked blue with a bottle of chocolate stout and slices of a stoneground-wheat baguette is a great way to enjoy a sunny afternoon.

USA Central Point, Oregon	
Age 3 months	
Weight and Shape 2¼kg (5lb), wheel	
Size Various	
Milk Cow	
Classification Blue	
Producer Rogue Creamery	

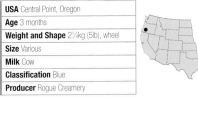

Soft Wheel

Michael Lee started out as a cheese retailer, but since 2005, he has been producing his own cheese from a small herd of 25 goats. Respectful of seasonality, this cheesemaker often supplements his supply of milk with cow's milk from neighbouring farms.

TASTING NOTES Soft Wheel is a pungent, washed-rind cheese. The rind is thick but soft and sticky, while the inside is rich and goaty with hints of chestnuts.

HOW TO ENJOY Spread on warm crusty bread and serve with dried fruit and nuts alongside an Alsace-style aromatic white wine or wheat beer.

USA West Cornwall, Vermont	
Age 80 days	
Weight and Shape 675g (1½lb), wheel	
Size D. 12cm (5in), H. 5cm (2in)	
Milk Goat and cow	
Classification Semi-soft	
Producer Twig Farm	

Surfing Goat Dairy Quark

The farm is located on the sunny Hawaiian slopes of Maui's Haleakala Crater, providing the herd of goats with native vegetation, as well as pasture, to forage on, and adding distinctive regional flavours to the milk.

TASTING NOTES It is smooth on the palate, with a sweet creamy taste and pleasant tangy goat milk finish.

HOW TO ENJOY Serve the Quark with fresh mango slices and macadamia nuts over salad greens. For a true tropical experience, complement with a Kona Brewing Co. Fire Rock Pale Ale.

USA Kula, Maui, Hawaii	
Age A few days	
Weight and Shape 225g (8oz), jar	
Size No size	
Milk Goat	
Classification Fresh	
Producer Surfing Goat Dairy	

Tarentaise

John and Janine Putnam, who trained in Haute-Savoie, France, offer an excellent American interpretation of Alpine cheeses. They have shared the recipe and strict milk quality controls with neighbouring Spring Brook Farms to expand production.

TASTING NOTES The golden colour translates into the flavour, with toasty caramel notes and a touch of acidity on the finish. It has a cherry-like aroma when freshly cut. The texture is initially medium dry, but relaxes in the mouth.

HOW TO ENJOY Pair with Vin de Savoie and some fresh apples. It also grills like Raclette and makes a great fondue.

USA North Pomfret, Vermont	
Age 8 months	
Weight and Shape 8.2kg (18lb), wheel	
Size D. 50cm (20in), H. 10cm (4in)	
Milk Cow	
Classification Hard	
Producer Thistle Hill Farm	

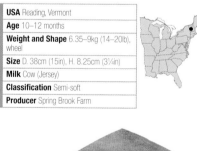

Tarentaise

Following a trip to England, Karli and Jim Hagedorn were inspired to create the Farms for City Kids Foundation at Spring Brook Farm. A place where city kids spend time learning while helping out. Neighbours, Thistle Hill, gave them the recipe to expand production.

TASTING NOTES Tarentaise has a brown-orange rind, and pale, dense, elastic interior with tiny holes. It has distinct farmyard notes, with hints of nuts and a peppery, spicy finish. A winner at the 2014 American Cheese Society awards.

HOW TO ENJOY Pair with crunchy pickles and a rich brown ale or melt over boiled potatoes and serve with cured meats.

USA Reading, Vermont	
Age 10–12 months	
Weight and Shape 6.35–9kg (14–20lb), wheel	
Size D. 38cm (15in), H. 8.25cm (3¼in)	
Milk Cow (Jersey)	
Classification Semi-soft	
Producer Spring Brook Farm	

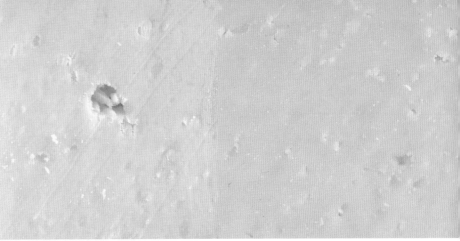

Taupinière

Laura Chenel, recognized as the "pioneer" of American goat cheese, started making goat cheese in the late 1970s. In 2006, she sold the company to a French family, committed to carrying on her legacy. Made in the historic town of Sonoma, it is based on the traditional French cheese, Poitou-Charentes, and means "molehill", referring to its shape.

TASTING NOTES Pleasantly chalky, with a mild goat taste, it has a thin dusting of charcoal ash beneath the stark white crusty rind. As the cheese ages, a creamy layer develops under the rind.

HOW TO ENJOY Great on a cheeseboard, pair with Sancerre or Pouilly Fume.

USA Sonoma, California	
Age 2–6 weeks	
Weight and Shape 250g (9oz), molehill	
Size D. 7.5cm (3in), H. 5.5cm (2.5in)	
Milk Goat	
Classification Soft white	
Producer Laura Chenel's Chèvre	

Telford Reserve

Located just outside Philadelphia, Necessity Farm, believe in traditional sustainable farming, with their small, grass-fed herd producing beautiful raw milk from which they make about ten cheeses, alongside other farm products. Their range includes sausages to free-range chickens, that are sold almost exclusively into the local community.

TASTING NOTES Deliciously complex, with a tart bite and a long butterscotch finish typical of premium aged Gouda. It has a firm texture.

HOW TO ENJOY Beer, preferably good lager, is the best match. Serve with sourdough bread, country ham, and hot mustard.

USA Philadelphia, Pennsylvania	
Age 10 months	
Weight and Shape 3.6kg (8lb), wheel	
Size D. 40cm (16in), H. 12cm (5in)	
Milk Cow	
Classification Hard	
Producer Necessity Farm and Dairy	

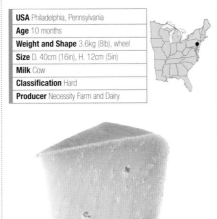

Thomasville Tomme

Sweet Grass Dairy is located on the beautiful wooded terrain in southern Georgia. The Littles keep a small herd of goats and Jersey cows, from which they produce several different styles of cheese. This one is modelled after traditional tommes of the Pyrenees.

TASTING NOTES Although relatively mild in flavour, this cheese has an appealing simplicity that is best compared to farm-fresh milk: clean, rich, slightly sweet, and perfectly balanced. The texture is chewy and semi-soft.

HOW TO ENJOY Its mellow flavour lends richness to recipes like macaroni and cheese, without being overpowering.

USA Thomasville, Georgia	
Age 3–6 months	
Weight and Shape 4.1kg (9lb), wheel	
Size D. 30cm (12in), H. 12cm (5in)	
Milk Cow	
Classification Semi-soft	
Producer Sweet Grass Dairy	

SMOKEY BLUE CHEESE The holes where the stainless steel rods have penetrated are clearly visible. These create fine tunnels that allow air to reach the interior, encouraging the blue mould added to the milk to turn blue. (See p299)

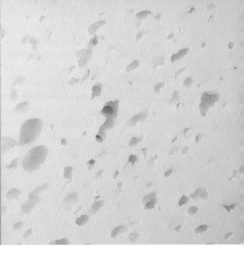

Trader Lake Cedar

Dave and Mary Falk, farming organically since 1986, aim to exist in harmony with the environment through proper stewardship of the land and livestock. 100 acres of their land is devoted to grazing their specially bred sheep and a small herd of French Alpine goats and another 100 is a wildlife habitat.

TASTING NOTES Aged in fresh air caves on cedar boards, the cheese is imbued with its woody aroma. It is supple, silky with small holes, and a nutty flavour that ends with a peppery, woody undertone.

HOW TO ENJOY Rosé, crisp whites, or bubbles make good partners.

USA Grantsburg, Wisconsin	
Age 2½ months or more	
Weight and Shape 1.8kg (4lb), flying saucer	
Size D. 20cm (8in), H. 7.5–10cm (3–4in)	
Milk Sheep and Goat (blend)	
Classification Semi-soft	
Producer Love Tree Farmstead	

Triple Cream Wheel

Coach Farm produces exceptional milk from its large herd of Alpine goats and makes a wide range of products. Given the relatively small yield, every drop of cream goes into producing this 75 per cent fat triple-cream goat's cheese.

TASTING NOTES It is dense, rich, sweet, and buttery, with a subtle tart finish and barely a hint of the goat's milk. It does not exhibit a tendency to become runny or soupy, as is sometimes the case with triple-cream cheeses.

HOW TO ENJOY This cheese is too delicate to cook, so try it with Champagne. To indulge, smear on toast points and top with caviar.

USA Pine Plains, New York	
Age 20–30 days	
Weight and Shape 2kg (4½lb), wheel	
Size D. 18cm (7in), H. 7.5cm (3in)	
Milk Goat	
Classification Soft white	
Producer Coach Farm	

Tumalo Tomme

Tumalo Tomme is named after Tumalo in Oregon's Cascade Mountains; the "tomme" comes from the style of artisan cheeses produced mainly in the French Alps that bear this name. It is made with raw milk from a mixed herd of Alpine, La Mancha, and Saanen goats.

TASTING NOTES The pine essence from the aging planks is reflected in the pastoral flavours that complement the earthy components of this washed-rind cheese. The finish has floral overtones.

HOW TO ENJOY Pear cider enhances the flavours of Tumalo Tomme, especially when served with pear compote and crusty walnut bread.

USA Redmond, Oregon	
Age 6 months	
Weight and Shape 1.8–2kg (4–4½lb), wheel	
Size D. 17cm (6½in), H. 7.5cm (3in)	
Milk Goat	
Classification Semi-soft	
Producer Juniper Grove Farm	

Tumbleweed

5 Spoke Creamery's first "spoke" of inspiration came from the belief that like riding a bicycle, balance is the key to a healthy lifestyle for people and animals too. Their cows graze on a unique terroir of grasses, herbs, producing sweet, herbaceous raw milk.

TASTING NOTES A cross between French Cantal and Cheddar, it comes into its own after 12 months in the cave. Hard, compact, and pale yellow, it has a fruity acidity which is balanced by the rich sweetness of the milk.

HOW TO ENJOY Goes well with fresh figs, or honey with a touch of balsamic vinegar, paired with a bold Tempranillo.

USA Port Chester, New York	
Age 12–14 months	
Weight and Shape 4.5kg (10lb), square	
Size L. 20cm (8in), W. 20cm (8in), H. 20cm (8in)	
Milk Cow	
Classification Hard	
Producer 5 Spoke Creamery	

Twig Farm Square Cheese

Not able to rely fully on the availability of goat's milk, Twig Farm sometimes follows the traditional practice of supplementing its supply with cow's milk. But for certain cheeses, including this one, it uses milk from its own herd only. Tying it in cheesecloth forms its irregular square shape.

TASTING NOTES Hazelnuts are the leading flavour, which rolls into a surprisingly mellow, sweet finish. The rind carries a certain pungency, but this does not penetrate the firm, dense paste.

HOW TO ENJOY Perfect with a honey derived from nut or herbal blossoms.

USA West Cornwall, Vermont	
Age 2–3 months	
Weight and Shape 900g (2lb), flat square	
Size L. 10cm (4in), W. 10cm (4in), H. 5cm (2in)	
Milk Goat	
Classification Hard	
Producer Twig Farm	

Vaquero Blue

This organic farm produces a wide range of handmade ewe's milk or mixed ewe's and cow's milk cheeses. Many, including this one, are cave-aged on the property. Their strictly seasonal production means that many of Willow Hill's cheeses come and go quickly, but patience is rewarded with exceptional quality and dynamic flavors.

TASTING NOTES Its appearance speaks volumes about the cave ripening, but this medium-strong, slightly musty blue is buttery and smooth on the palate.

HOW TO ENJOY Ideal for crumbling into salads or grilling on your favorite steak. Paired with a Merlot or Dry Riesling.

USA Milton, Vermont	
Age 6 months	
Weight and Shape 1.8kg (4lb), cylinder	
Size D. 12cm (5in), H. 15cm (6in)	
Milk Ewe and Cow	
Classification Blue	
Producer Willow Hill Farm	

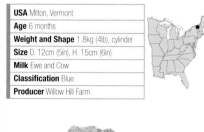

Vermont Shepherd

Aside from producing this excellent cave-aged ewe's milk cheese, Major Farms has served as a training ground for many aspiring cheesemakers. To highlight the importance of terroir, each wheel of cheese is delivered with a certificate detailing the herd's activity on the day of production.

TASTING NOTES Deliciously sweet and concentrated, its texture is very dense and relaxes nicely in the mouth. True to Pyrenean style, it has a long sweet-savoury finish, with a hint of woolliness.

HOW TO ENJOY The classic pairing is with a black cherry conserve, but it works equally well with quince paste.

USA Putney, Vermont	
Age 6 months	
Weight and Shape 1.35kg (3lb), convex drum	
Size D. 15cm (6in), H. 9cm (3½in)	
Milk Ewe	
Classification Hard	
Producer Major Farms	

Wabash Cannonball

Capriole, founded by Judy Schadd, has an ever-evolving line of French-style goat's cheeses distinctively its own. The Wabash Cannonball has been a success for years and was an American Cheese Society award winner in 1995.

TASTING NOTES It is firm and slightly dry, with a thin white rind dusted with ash. This surface-ripened cheese has a goaty and slightly acidic flavour, and the rind lends a pleasant muskiness. The finish is rich and buttermilky.

HOW TO ENJOY It is ideal with dried fruits and sparkling wine. Bread and crackers distract from the flavour, so it is best to enjoy this one on its own.

USA Greenville, Indiana	
Age 3–10 weeks	
Weight and Shape 115g (4oz), flattened ball	
Size D. 4cm (1½in)	
Milk Goat	
Classification Aged fresh	
Producer Capriole Farmstead Goat Cheese	

West West Blue

After 30 years of "cheese whispering" for others, Peter Dixon, with wife Rachel, is now making his own raw milk cheeses which are aged in an old root cellar. Inspired by traditional Gorgonzola (see p108–09), West West Blue is a blend of fresh curd from two consecutive days.

TASTING NOTES The layered curd ripens at different rates, creating a mottled, earthy texture. The blue streaks impart a spicy, salt and pepper tang. Some are aged by Crown Finish Caves for the New York market.

HOW TO ENJOY In a bar in New York or a field in Vermont, with a Merlot, light hoppy ale or Dry Riesling.

USA Westminster West, Vermont	
Age 5–10 months	
Weight and Shape 8kg (18lb), wheel	
Size D. 30cm (12in) H. 15cm (6in)	
Milk Cow	
Classifiaction Blue	
Producer Parish Hill Creamery	

Winnimere

Available only from mid-winter through spring, this cheese is always worth waiting for, and its slight variability from year to year always stirs excitement for the cheese to become available. Like Jasper Hill's other cheeses, the beer-washed Winnimere reflects European training.

TASTING NOTES It has a sweet pungency, with hints of wet stone. The sweet flavour has an almost bacon-like smokiness to it, while the texture is so velvety with a soft rind.

HOW TO ENJOY It is best with sweet beer or cider. Make sure it is ripe and at room temperature when you serve it so it is almost liquid.

USA	Greensboro, Vermont
Age	2 months
Weight and Shape	550g (1¼lb), round
Size	D. 15cm (6in), H. 5cm (2in)
Milk	Cow
Classification	Semi-soft
Producer	Jasper Hill Farm

306

More Cheeses of the USA

The following cheeses are rare, largely because they are only available seasonally or because they are produced in very remote areas. Although it has proved impossible to photograph them, they are important and interesting examples of cheeses of the USA, so we are including them. So, read, savour, and seek out.

Alpine Lakes Creamy Bleu

The milk for this blue cheese comes from a herd of mixed East Friesland and Locaune ewes. It is then infused with the traditional *Penicillium roqueforti* mould to create a pristine, true blue flavour and a rustic appearance.

TASTING NOTES Alpine Lakes Creamy Bleu is ripened and brought to market when 60 days old. By then it is rich, smooth, and creamy to taste with an ivory centre streaked with blue. It intensifies in flavour with age.

HOW TO ENJOY Serve on a cheeseboard with fresh plums, cherries, and a crusty Walnut Levaine loaf alongside an aromatic, crisp white Port.

USA	Leavenworth, Washington
Age	2–3 months
Weight and Shape	225g (8oz), round
Size	D. 6cm (2½in), H. 5cm (2in)
Milk	Ewe
Classification	Blue
Producer	Alpine Lakes Sheep Cheese

5 Spoke Creamery Browning Gold

The name 5 Spoke Creamery was inspired by the ambling bicycle journeys around the world of two friends, which they likened to the journey of discovery when making cheese. All the cheeses are handmade in the farmstead tradition, and produced on site from the raw milk of a closed herd of grass-fed cows.

TASTING NOTES This hard cheese is aged for 24 months until it is full of rich buttery flavours and has a firm Cheddar-like texture.

HOW TO ENJOY Ideal when paired with toasted almonds, a fresh-baked sweet baguette and a golden ale.

USA	Port Chester, New York
Age	24 months
Weight and Shape	4–4.9kg (9–11lbs), cylinder
Size	D. 16cm (6in), H. 19cm (7½in)
Milk	Cow
Classification	Hard
Producer	5 Spoke Creamery

Ancient Heritage Scio

The cheesemakers at Ancient Heritage Dairy were impressed by the flavour and texture of traditional, European ewe's milk cheese, so they decided to recreate one at home in Oregon. Ancient Heritage Scio was produced in honour of old-world cheesemakers.

TASTING NOTES The distinct flavours of this two-month aged, raw ewe's milk cheese stand out as a sweet, moist, and dense taste on the palate with a hint of roasted nuts in the finish.

HOW TO ENJOY Ancient Heritage Scio is pleasantly delicious when paired with almonds, fresh-baked wheat breads and a nutty brown ale.

USA	Scio, Oregon
Age	60 days
Weight and Shape	2.25kg (5lb), wheel
Size	D. 23cm (9in), H. 7.5cm (3in)
Milk	Ewe
Classification	Semi-soft
Producer	Ancient Heritage Dairy

Bad Axe

Hidden Springs Farm is a sustainable ewe dairy in the rolling hills of western Wisconsin, combining an old-fashioned, all-natural farmstead with just enough modern equipment and science to keep quality at its peak. Bad Axe is named after the river that flows through the Westby Valley.

TASTING NOTES It is a delectably creamy and sweet semi-soft cheese. The flavour of the ewe's-milk cream stays pleasantly on the palate.

HOW TO ENJOY It pairs perfectly with a fresh baguette stuffed with rocket and tomatoes and served up for an afternoon picnic.

USA Westby, Wisconsin	
Age 8–12 weeks	
Weight and Shape 2.7kg (6lb), wheel	
Size D. 15cm (6in), H. 7.5cm (3in)	
Milk Ewe	
Classification Semi-soft	
Producer Hidden Springs Creamery	

Bleu Age

Rollingstone Chèvre was the first farmstead goat cheese producer in Idaho. From the first goat, purchased to provide milk for the family, their herd has expanded to more than 300, from which they now make a variety of wonderful cheeses, including this unusual external blue mould one.

TASTING NOTES Beneath the thick, midnight-blue *Penicillium roqueforti* coat is a thin, almost liquid, sweet layer, then a firmer nutty interior. It has a distinct, but not strong, goaty taste and a spicy blue tang.

HOW TO ENJOY Serve with walnuts, slices of fresh pears and a dry Riesling.

USA Parma, Idaho	
Age 30 days	
Weight and Shape 175g (6oz), round	
Size D. 7.5cm (3in), H. 5cm (2in)	
Milk Goat	
Classification Blue	
Producer Rollingstone Chèvre	

Cayuse Mountain Goat

Clare Paris makes raw goat's and ewe's milk cheeses including Shepherd's Gem, a hard ewe's milk cheese; Rosa Rugosa, a semi-soft ewe's and goat's milk cheese; and Cayuse, which is named after a mountain summit in Okanogan County.

TASTING NOTES It has a dense, creamy texture and a complex, yet subtle, character that has all the nutty and herbaceous attributes of a hard goat cheese without the feral goaty taste associated with French-style chèvre.

HOW TO ENJOY It is best on a cheese plate with charcuterie, herbed olives, and a flavourful Zinfandel.

USA Tonasket, Washington	
Age 5–7 months	
Weight and Shape 1.8–2.25kg (4–5lb), wheel	
Size D. 20cm (8in), H. 7.5cm (3in)	
Milk Ewe and goat	
Classification Semi-soft	
Producer Larkhaven Farmstead Cheeses	

Creamery Subblime

This cheese owes its name not just to its flavour, but to "Subby", a La Mancha doe in the farm's herd that once broke her neck and resembled a submarine while healing. All Estrella Family Creamery cheeses are made with raw milk and the animals graze on organically maintained pastures.

TASTING NOTES When aged for two months to semi-soft perfection, it has a delicate hint of goat and a tang of coastal salt air on the finish.

HOW TO ENJOY It is best with a baguette, apple slices, a drizzle of wild honey and a Washington State Chardonnay to highlight the elegant flavours.

USA Montesano, Washington	
Age 60 days	
Weight and Shape 225g (8oz), round	
Size Various	
Milk Goat	
Classification Semi-soft	
Producer Estrella Family Creamery	

Ferns' Edge Goat Dairy

Ferns' Edge Dairy is nestled in the foothills of Mount Zion in the Cascade Hills of Oregon. The fresh, artisan cheese of the same name is handcrafted using the milk of the organic farm goats and seasoned with some of their home-grown herbs.

TASTING NOTES This fresh-flavoured chèvre is made by hand to create a delicate and soft texture, which is followed by a sweet cream finish.

HOW TO ENJOY Serve with fresh pears, some blanched almonds and a sweet baguette, and wash it down with a crisp glass of Viognier.

USA Lowell, Oregon	
Age 1–3 weeks	
Weight and Shape 115g (4oz), log	
Size Various	
Milk Goat	
Classification Fresh	
Producer Ferns' Edge Goat Dairy	

Golden Glen Creamery Mozzarella

Golden Glen Creamery is the only farmstead producer on the Washington coast that hand-makes and stretches fresh mozzarella.

TASTING NOTES It is moist and creamy to start, with a rich flavour and a delicate texture that reflects the gentle process by which the cheese was made.

HOW TO ENJOY Toss in a salad with rocket leaves, serve as a snack with a dribble of fresh pesto, or add to a fresh tomato and garlic pasta dish. Add a bottle of rich Washington Syrah to create a fine meal.

USA Bow, Washington	
Age 2–10 days	
Weight and Shape 225g (8oz), ball	
Size Various	
Milk Cow	
Classification Fresh	
Producer Golden Glen Creamery	

Hopelessly Blue

One of the few artisan cheesemakers in Texas, Sara Bolton established Pure Luck Farm & Dairy in 1979. Carried on by her daughters, they now have around 100 Nubian and Alpine goats. Produced between March and October, Hopelessly Blue is named after one of the sisters who refused to eat it.

TASTING NOTES Don't be put off by the thick, grey blue crust as it hides a cream-like interior with streaks of pale blue. Surprisingly mild, it tastes like sweet spicy butter and becomes bolder with age.

HOW TO ENJOY Best with a big red, rustic bread, fresh apples or pears.

USA	Dripping Springs, Texas
Age	8–12 weeks
Weight and shape	800g (1½lb), drum
Size	D. 12cm (5in), H. 4–5cm (1½–2in)
Milk	Goat
Classification	Blue
Producer	Pure Luck Farm & Dairy

Midcoast Teleme

The Original Teleme was created by Giovanni Peluso, but the tradition continues to this day thanks to the work of third-generation cheesemaker Frankin Peluso. It is still made using rice flour that has been coated within the state of California.

TASTING NOTES This fresh, butcher's-block shaped cheese is aged for one week in order to yield a velvety smooth, moist texture and a fresh clean flavour.

HOW TO ENJOY Italian salami, Teleme, and a sourdough baguette make a classic San Francisco North Beach sandwich. Enjoy it with a glass of old vine Zinfandel.

USA	San Louis Obispo, California
Age	1 week
Weight and Shape	3kg (6½lb), block
Size	L. 20cm (8in), W. 20cm (8in), H. 7.5cm (3in)
Milk	Cow
Classification	Fresh
Producer	Franklin's Cheeses

Montasio

Although this American cheese is based on the norteastern Italian cheese of the same name, it has a flavour and style of its own that is influenced by the grazing and coastal breeze of Samish Bay. The milk used comes from their own organic herd of Jersey, Dutch Belted, and Shorthorn cows.

TASTING NOTES It is firm to the touch, with a rich creamy taste that becomes more flavourful, and complex with age.

HOW TO ENJOY Grate it over warm ravioli or fresh cooked spinach pasta, and serve with a glass of Sangiovese.

USA	Bow, Washington
Age	6–9 months
Weight and shape	4kg (8lb 13oz), wheel
Size	D. 25cm (10in), H. 9cm (3½in)
Milk	Cow
Classification	Hard
Producer	Samish Bay Cheese

Pine Stump Crottin

This Crottin is made in the traditional French way, where the curd is gently ladled into moulds and allowed to drain off without pressing. Over time it creates a snow-white, round drum with a thin white rind.

TASTING NOTES When young, this goat's cheese is delicate and soft. As it ages, it becomes dense and strengthens in flavour, maintaining its original earthy tones.

HOW TO ENJOY Warm it and sprinkle with cracked black pepper, combine with olive oil over frisée greens, and serve with a fruity Marsanne.

308

USA	Omak, Washington
Age	Over 60 days
Weight and shape	115–225g (4–8oz), drum
Size	D. 9–10cm (3½–4in), H. 7.5cm (3in)
Milk	Goat
Classification	Aged fresh
Producer	Pine Stump Farms

Pleasant Valley Dairy Mutschli

This original Washington creation is an artisan cheese that is produced from the milk of this family farmstead's cows. Mutschli was first made to be an American version of Swiss cheese, with the same smooth texture but no holes.

TASTING NOTES The raw milk offers a mild but sweet milk flavour that finishes with a hint of toasted walnuts.

HOW TO ENJOY Use it to create a rich warm dish of potatoes au gratin with fresh parsley, red onions and toasted walnuts. Complement and accentuate its flavours with a nutty brown ale.

USA	Ferndale, Washington
Age	8 – 12 weeks
Weight and Shape	900g–2.7kg (2–6lb), rounds
Size	Various
Milk	Cow
Classification	Hard
Producers	Pleasant Valley Dairy

Pozo Tomme

Jim and Christine Macquire started making cheese in earnest when they moved to their small ranch near San Luis Obisbo in 1999. There they established their mixed herd of ewes and goats, and soon after, they created Pozo Tomme, their flagship cheese.

TASTING NOTES This semi-soft cheese develops a thin natural rind and old world flavours that vary from earthy undertones to a distinct nuttiness. With age it becomes firm and is rich in butterscotch flavours.

HOW TO ENJOY Serve on its own, or when aged, grate over grilled vegetables or risotto, accompanied by a Pinot Grigio.

USA	Santa Margarita, California
Age	2–4 months
Weight and Shape	2.25–2.7kg (5–6lb), wheel
Size	Various
Milk	Ewe
Classification	Semi-soft
Producer	Rinconada Dairy

Steamboat Island Gouda

Jason Drew, a supporter of the Slow Food movement, established Steamboat Island Goat Farm in 2006. His intention was to create handmade goat's cheeses that could be produced with integrity and would support his community and family farm.

TASTING NOTES Farm Gouda is a Cheddar-style cheese with a full flavour of goat's milk, along with balanced meadow and floral undertones and a nutty background.

HOW TO ENJOY Serve with sourdough rolls or as a great alternative to cow's milk Cheddar. It is excellent with a Pilsner.

USA Steamboat Island, Washington	
Age 2–6 months	
Weight and Shape 900g–4.5kg (2–10lb), round	
Size Various	
Milk Goat	
Classification Hard	
Producer Steamboat Island Goat Farm	

Two Faced Blue Peccato

The name refers to the fact that it is made using a combination of two milks: raw ewe's and cow's. It is one of several blues made in the century-old barn on the banks of the Chehalis River.

TASTING NOTES A vein of musical blues runs through each wheel, inspired by the notes of the cheesemaking. The taste is a blend of earthy and floral flavours, encompassed in a soft, natural, and blue-grey rind.

HOW TO ENJOY Eat with fresh figs, honey, and toasted walnut bread for a late afternoon cheeseboard, alongside a Washington state Pinot Noir.

USA Doty, Washington	
Age 3 months	
Weight and Shape 4.5kg (10lb) wheel	
Size Various	
Milk Ewe and cow	
Classification Blue	
Producer Willapa Hills Farmstead Cheese	

Up in Smoke

The underlining character of the various cheeses produced by River's Edge Chevre is attributed to the abundance of grazing in the meadows alongside the Siletz River and the surrounding woodlands. Up in Smoke is, as the name suggests, smoked, then wrapped in smoked maple leaves that have been sprinkled with bourbon.

TASTING NOTES The combination of smoke, maple leaves, and hints of bourbon provide an unusual but elegant contrast to the lemony fresh tang and creamy texture of the cheese.

HOW TO ENJOY Serve with crusty bread or maple-toasted walnuts and smoked ale.

USA Logsden, Oregon	
Age 1–3 weeks	
Weight and Shape 140g (5oz), ball	
Size D. 7cm (3in), H. 5cm (2in)	
Milk Goat	
Classification Fresh	
Producer River's Edge Chevre	

Vache de Vashon

Influenced by the Alpine regions of France, Italy and Switzerland, Sea Breeze has created their own unique cellar-aged regional and original raw-milk cheeses.

TASTING NOTES The essence of apples and pears tease the palette, with a sweet and delicate, rich, buttery texture on the finish.

HOW TO ENJOY You can appreciate Vache de Vashon with a dry cider or Sauvignon Blanc, along with sweet, butter pound cake for dessert.

USA Vashon Island, Washington	
Age 2–4 months	
Weight and Shape 900g–1.35kg (2–3lb), wheel	
Size Various	
Milk Cow	
Classification Semi-soft	
Producer Sea Breeze Farm	

Widmers Cellar Brick Cheese

Joe Widmer, a third-generation cheesemaker in the town of Theresa, Wisconsin, makes a large variety of cheeses, including this aged brick, a Wisconsin original first made in 1877 that is washed or smeared to create the orange-coloured sticky rind.

TASTING NOTES The flavour changes from mild and sweet with a subtle nuttiness to pungent and tangy when aged. It is also available as a spread.

HOW TO ENJOY Slice for Pumpernickle sandwiches with mustard and shaved onions, or shred over roasted root vegetables, served with a pale ale.

USA Theresa, Wisconsin	
Age 8–12 weeks	
Weight and Shape 2.25kg (5lb), brick	
Size Various	
Milk Cow	
Classification Semi-soft	
Producer Widmers Cellars	

Yerba Santa Dairy Fresca

The family originally came from Peru where they made cheese. They moved to the United States, and in 1986, bought a farm where they strive to create a model of sustainable agriculture and excellent goat's cheeses.

TASTING NOTES This crumbly Feta-style cheese is freshly made and delivered to market daily. It has a creamy taste and brine flavours.

HOW TO ENJOY Eat a chef's sandwich of Fresca, olives, and roasted red peppers and enjoy with a California Zinfandel.

USA Lakeport, California	
Age 1–2 weeks	
Weight and Shape 115g (4oz) and 225g (8oz), containers	
Size Various	
Milk Goat	
Classification Fresh	
Producer Yerba Santa Dairy	

Allegretto

This washed-rind cheese is produced in Québec's far north Abitibi region, an unusual location for dairy sheep production. Its producers believe that the pasture's shorter growing season and the Nordic microclimate give the milk a richer, sweeter taste.

TASTING NOTES The large wheel has an off-white paste with a few pinholes. Its nutty aroma and sweet, full flavour make it very morish.

HOW TO ENJOY Melt on a special raclette grill, or under an ordinary grill, and scrape onto a crusty baguette, or try it with steamed asparagus. Serve with an amber ale, a dry Riesling, or Zinfandel.

CANADA La Sarre, Québec	
Age 60–75 days	
Weight and Shape 3.5kg (7½lb), wheel	
Size D. 30cm (12in), H. 10cm (4in)	
Milk Ewe	
Classification Semi-soft	
Producer Fromagerie La Vache à Maillotte	

Avonlea Clothbound Cheddar

This Prince Edward Island Dairy, well known for its delicious ice cream and funky cow-inspired T-shirts, has moved into cheesemaking using traditional clothbound Cheddar techniques.

TASTING NOTES The grey-green rind bears the impressions of the cloth. The aroma is of fruit and nuts and has the taste of lingering herbs. The cheese's off-white interior is dense yet crumbly because of its long ageing.

HOW TO ENJOY Melt on open-faced roast beef sandwiches, grate into cider and maple syrup soup, or mix into mashed potatoes. Enjoy with ale or Merlot.

CANADA Charlottetown, Prince Edward Island	
Age 12–18 months	
Weight and Shape 8kg (17½lb), tall cylinder	
Size D. 24cm (9½in), H. 20cm (8in)	
Milk Cow	
Classification Hard	
Producer COWS Inc.	

Baby Blue

Using raw and pasteurized milk, the Grace sisters produce a range of blue, hard, soft white, and fresh cheeses from their farm on Salt Spring Island, including this Brie-style blue.

TASTING NOTES The delicate subtle blue flavour has a sweet milky aroma, a buttery texture, and a slight cultured cream finish. Its richness and yellow interior are derived from the unique qualities of the Jersey milk.

HOW TO ENJOY Savour with a glass of Pilsner, Sauvignon Blanc, or Icewine. Melt over poached pears with toasted walnuts for a succulent dessert.

CANADA Salt Spring Island, British Columbia	
Age 30–45 days	
Weight and Shape 160g (5½oz), round	
Size D. 5cm (2in), H. 5cm (2in)	
Milk Cow	
Classification Blue	
Producer Moonstruck Organic Cheese	

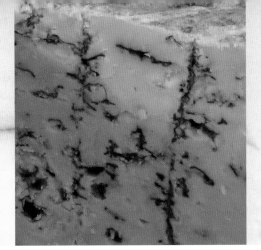

La Barre du Jour

Québec cheesemakers are creating new versions of European classics. This is a goat's milk version of the Swiss Raclette (see p239) and has a thin layer of red Espelette chilli through the centre like a spicy Morbier (see p67).

TASTING NOTES The flavours are delicate and mild – until your taste buds detect the heat and spiciness of the chilli.

HOW TO ENJOY This delicious melting cheese can be used in a spicy version of raclette with steamed vegetables, grilled sausage, or prawns. A dark beer or a Merlot would be a good match.

CANADA Mont-Laurier, Québec	
Age 45–60 days	
Weight and Shape 1.7kg (4lb), wheel	
Size D. 20cm (8in), H. 4cm (1½in)	
Milk Goat	
Classification Flavour-added	
Producer Fromagerie Le P'tit Train du Nord	

Bleu Bénédictin

Produced at Abbaye Saint-Benoît-du-Lac, a Benedictine monastery set among woodlands on the edge of a lake, this blue won Grand Champion at the 2000 Canadian Cheese Grand Prix.

TASTING NOTES Blue Bénédictin has pronounced streaks and patches of blue-green veins throughout the off-white paste, an aroma of mould and salt, and a lingering spicy, salty tang.

HOW TO ENJOY Serve melted over a juicy steak with a red wine jus. Many Canadian sommeliers match this champion with another Canadian icon: Icewine. The wine's sweetness perfectly balances the saltiness of the cheese.

CANADA Saint-Benoît-du-Lac, Québec	
Age 3–5 months	
Weight and Shape 1.8kg (4lb), wheel	
Size D. 20cm (8in), H. 10cm (4in)	
Milk Cow	
Classification Blue	
Producer Abbaye Saint-Benoît-du-Lac	

Bouquetin de Portneuf

This artisanal farmstead cheese, which is based on the famed Crottin de Chavignol (see p53), is eaten from 10 days old up to 2 months old. The change in its flavour profile is quite amazing.

TASTING NOTES Creamy when young with a rich, lingering flavour and a slight herbal, barnyard aroma; the older cheese is more dense in consistency, with light brown and grey moulds on the rind and a piquant aftertaste.

HOW TO ENJOY Melt the young cheese into scrambled eggs with chives, or try with chanterelles, leeks, and puréed garlic. Chardonnay or Pilsner matches well.

CANADA Saint-Raymond de Portneuf, Québec	
Age 10–60 days	
Weight and Shape 95g (3½oz), cylinder	
Size D. 5cm (2in), H. 5cm (2in)	
Milk Goat	
Classification Aged fresh	
Producer Ferme Tourilli	

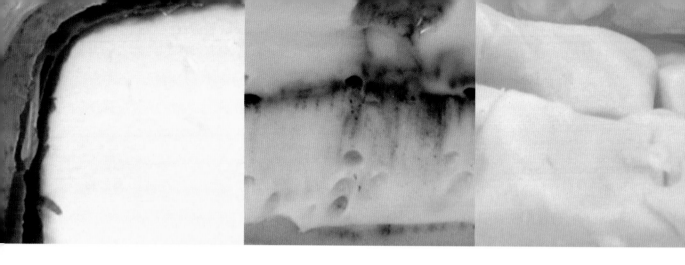

Le Cabanon

This artisanal farmstead cheese is made by Fromagerie La Moutonnière, one of the pioneers in ewe's milk cheese in Québec. It is wrapped in both maple and grape leaves that have been soaked in alcohol, such as eau de vie.

TASTING NOTES Upon unwrapping the small cheese from its leafy cover, you discover an ivory-white rindless cheese. A slight herbal aroma introduces you to a lingering grassy flavour, and the soft paste melts delicately on the palate.

HOW TO ENJOY Serve with a crisp Viognier white wine, whole roasted garlic cloves, and a sliced baguette, or crumble into salads with a light vinaigrette.

CANADA Sainte-Hélène-de-Chester, Québec	
Age 30 days	
Weight and Shape 130g (4½oz), round	
Size D. 10cm (4in), H. 4cm (1½in)	
Milk Ewe	
Classification Aged fresh	
Producer Fromagerie La Moutonnière	

Le Cendré des Prés

This Camembert-style cheese was first made by Fromagerie Domaine Féodal in 2001. It is produced using local Ayrshire cow's milk and has a decorative layer of maple ash running through its centre.

TASTING NOTES The soft, creamy off-white paste has a sweet aroma and mushroom flavour; the ash adds a great visual component when the cheese is cut. The rind is soft and slightly spongy.

HOW TO ENJOY The cheesemaker suggests stuffing the cheese into a filo-wrapped seared pork tenderloin. Bake until the dough is golden. Riesling, Beaujolais, or Pilsner is best savoured with this dish.

CANADA Berthierville, Québec	
Age 45–55 days	
Weight and Shape 1.5kg (3lb 3oz), wheel	
Size D. 20cm (8in), H. 4cm (1½in)	
Milk Cow	
Classification Soft white	
Producer Fromagerie Domaine Féodale	

Cheddar Curds

Eastern Canadian Cheddar makers discovered that the fresh unpressed curds were a delicious "squeaky" and salty snack popular with their regular patrons. Goat's and ewe's milk versions are now appearing in shops.

TASTING NOTES The white or orange-coloured curds must be "squeaky" to be good. Some are flavoured with garlic powder, barbecue or souvlaki spices, herbs, or maple seasoning.

HOW TO ENJOY As a snack, still warm from the vat, or in the Québec dish *poutine* – French fries with white Cheddar curds, topped with a brown velouté sauce. Enjoy with an ale.

CANADA All over	
Age Best within 48 hours of being made	
Weight and Shape 250g (9oz) bags, finger-shaped	
Size No size	
Milk Cow, goat, or ewe	
Classification Fresh	
Producer Various	

Comfort Cream

Niagara Peninsula's Upper Canada Cheese Company, the first in the recent wave of new artisanal cheesemakers in Ontario, produces this Camembert-style cheese. It is made using milk from a single herd of local Guernsey cows.

TASTING NOTES The warm yellow paste has a subtle mushroom aroma, and the rich Guernsey milk gives the supple interior a delicate, buttery flavour.

HOW TO ENJOY Bake in buttery filo dough with local wine jelly. Remove the rind, and melt the paste with other cheese to produce a variation of a Normandy seafood fondue. Serve with a Niagara Peninsula Chardonnay.

CANADA Jordan Station, Ontario	
Age 30–45 days	
Weight and Shape 300g (10oz), wheel	
Size D. 12cm (5in), H. 4cm (1½in)	
Milk Cow	
Classification Soft white	
Producer Upper Canada Cheese Company	

Le Cru des Erables

Influenced by the aromas of its surroundings, this washed-rind cheese is made in an old maple syrup shanty – where the sap is boiled and reduced to a thick, sweet syrup – then washed in a local maple sap liqueur.

TASTING NOTES Beneath the pale pink-orange rind, the light yellow paste has a smooth, satiny texture, while the full, persistent flavour has beefy undertones and a slight barn aroma.

HOW TO ENJOY Melt over mushrooms sautéed with garlic, or serve on a grilled slice of baguette as a great winter snack. Matches well with amber ale or Baco Noir red wine.

CANADA Mont-Laurier, Québec	
Age 45–60 days	
Weight and Shape 1kg (2¼lb), wheel	
Size D. 20cm (8in), H. 3cm (1in)	
Milk Cow	
Classification Semi-soft	
Producer Les Fromages de l'Érablière	

Le Délice des Appalaches

Named after the nearby Appalaches mountain range, the cheese is washed with ice cider, a unique frozen apple-based Québec drink. Apples are left to freeze outdoors, before being pressed to produce this regional speciality.

TASTING NOTES It has a pale-orange rind, supple and velvety texture, the scent of apples and nuts, and a mild flavour with a slight lactic aftertaste.

HOW TO ENJOY Serve with an apple-based beverage such as hard cider, Calvados, or ice cider. It melts very well, making it ideal for fondue or in béchamel sauces to accompany pork dishes.

CANADA Plessisville, Québec	
Age 45–60 days	
Weight and Shape 200g (7oz), square	
Size L. 12cm (5in), W. 20cm (8in), H. 5cm (2in)	
Milk Cow	
Classification Semi-soft	
Producer Fromagerie Éco-Délices	

CANADA

Dragon's Breath Blue

This small black bell of blue cheese is covered in a thick black wax coating. It is made by Maja and Willem van den Hoek, who recommend that you slice off the top and inhale, and, if there is any mould under the wax, mix it in.

TASTING NOTES Under the black wax, the white paste has a few holes. It has a spicy blue aroma, with a subtle creamy saltiness and lingering flavours, but no bitterness or harshness – despite what its name might imply.

HOW TO ENJOY Stuff it into ravioli with leeks or stir it into freshly cooked pasta, or use as a topping for dried apricots. Match to Icewine, beer, or dry Riesling.

CANADA Upper Economy, Nova Scotia	
Age 30–45 days	
Weight and Shape 200g (7oz), cylinder	
Size D. 6cm (2½in), H. 7.5cm (3in)	
Milk Cow	
Classification Blue	
Producer That Dutchman's Farm	

Harvest Moon

Gitta Sutherland makes this washed-rind cheese only at the full moon. Poplar Grove is in British Columbia's Okanagan Valley, renowned for its bountiful harvest of apples, nuts, and grapes.

TASTING NOTES The pale yellow paste has a buttery aroma, supple, silky texture; and a delicate cream flavour. The pale orange rind, characteristic of washed cheeses, gives it a slight salty aroma.

HOW TO ENJOY Serve on a cheese platter with frozen grapes and candied or spicy walnuts. It goes well with a wheat beer or Okanagan Chardonnay.

CANADA Penticton, British Columbia	
Age 30–40 days	
Weight and Shape 190g (7oz), wheel	
Size D. 10cm (4in), H. 2.5cm (1in)	
Milk Cow	
Classification Semi-soft	
Producer Poplar Grove Cheese Company	

OKA Classique

One of Canada's best-known cheeses was originally produced at the Trappist monastery in Oka, Québec, using methods taught to the monks by a visiting brother from the Abbaye Port-du-Salut in France. Agropur, the province's largest dairy cooperative, now produces it commercially.

TASTING NOTES Washed in brine, this has a tangerine coloured sticky rind with a light yellow pinholed paste, and a nutty, salty aroma. With age, it becomes more meaty, piquant, and farmyardy.

HOW TO ENJOY Great on a cheeseboard, in tarts, or melted on potatoes. A Belgian-style beer is a good accompaniment.

CANADA Oka, Québec	
Age 45–75 days	
Weight and Shape 2.5kg (5lb), wheel	
Size D. 25cm (10in), H. 5cm (2in)	
Milk Cow	
Classification Semi-soft	
Producer Agropur Cooperative	

Old Grizzly

This aged traditional Gouda-style cheese is made by an award-winning Dutch artisanal cheesemaker within sight of Alberta's Rocky Mountains. All of Sylvan Star's cheeses are made with milk from its own herd.

TASTING NOTES During the two-year maturing period, the milk proteins caramelize to a light brown colour. When you break a piece off the large boulder-shaped wheel, a sweet cultured-cream aroma is evident and the cheese has a sweet-savoury tang.

HOW TO ENJOY Grate over potatoes, soups, pasta, and casseroles, or use in sauces. Match with a big red or a strong beer.

CANADA Red Deer, Alberta	
Age 2 years	
Weight and Shape 10kg (22lb), wheel	
Size D. 36cm (14in), H. 10cm (4in)	
Milk Cow	
Classification Hard	
Producer Sylvan Star Cheese	

Le Paillasson de l'isle d'Orléans

This simple fresh cheese was introduced in 1635 by the first French colonists on the Ile d'Orléans near Québec City. It had all but died out until being revived in 2003 by Jocelyn Labbe.

TASTING NOTES Lemon fresh with the sweetness of fresh milk and a hint of saltiness, this cheese has a firm but moist texture that is perfect for grilling.

HOW TO ENJOY Serve fresh with fruit, or pan-fried with maple-caramelized apples, smoked salmon, and mesclun. Try with sautéed onions and shiitake mushrooms. A light white wine works well with this salty cheese.

CANADA Ile d'Orléans, Québec	
Age 3–10 days	
Weight and Shape 115g (4oz), disc	
Size D. 7cm (3in), H. 1cm (½in)	
Milk Cow	
Classification Fresh	
Producer Les Fromages de l'isle d'Orléans	

Piacere

Similar to a Corsican Fleur du Maquis (see p58), this cheese is coated with rosemary, summer savory, juniper berries, chilli, and a touch of grey-green mould, and is made with ewe's milk produced by local Mennonite farmers.

TASTING NOTES Piacere's white interior has a delicate, slightly sweet flavour that balances well with the lingering flavours provided by the herb- and spice-coated rind. With age, the paste becomes very soft and creamy.

HOW TO ENJOY Superb on a cheeseboard, but Piacere also melts well when baked or grilled. A fruity white or a Merlot would be a good complement.

CANADA Millbank, Ontario	
Age 30–45 days	
Weight and Shape 750g (1lb 10oz), wheel	
Size D. 20cm (8in), H. 2.5cm (1in)	
Milk Ewe	
Classification Aged fresh	
Producer Monforte Dairy	

Prestige

Fromages Chaput make an interesting range of raw cow's and goat's milk cheeses based on French artisan recipes. Prestige is a large aged fresh cheese that is made to appeal to those who like a distinctly "goaty" cheese.

TASTING NOTES The smooth, dense white interior is covered in black olivewood ash overlaid by white and grey moulds, adding complexity to the cheese's fresh, aromatic, and slightly peppery taste.

HOW TO ENJOY Perfect for a cheeseboard grilled on crusty bread and served with thinly sliced cucumber or leafy green salad. Both Sauvignon Blanc and dry Riesling make good partners.

CANADA Châteauguay, Québec		
Age 45–60 days		
Weight and Shape 1.8kg (4lb), wheel		
Size D. 17.5cm (7in), H. 12.5cm (5in)		
Milk Goat		
Classification Aged fresh		
Producer Fromages Chaput		

Raclette de Compton au Poivre

Farmed and improved by four generations of Bolducs, La Station has a herd of 70 Holstein cows that is carefully managed, and fed a complex organic diet. Their raw milk is used in making their award-winning French mountain-style cheeses.

TASTINGS NOTES The copper-coloured washed rind, hides a supple, elastic interior with tiny holes. Its flavours range from buttery sweet to savoury, with umami notes.

HOW TO ENJOY Best when melted over boiled potatoes, or onto a crusty bread, and paired with charcuterie and pickles.

CANADA Compton, Quebec		
Age 3–4 months		
Weight and Shape 3.5kg (8lb), wheel		
Size D. 26cm (10in), H. 6cm (2½in)		
Milk Cow, organic		
Classification Semi-soft		
Producer Fromagerie Le Station		

Le Sabot de Blanchette

The Guitels have been making raw and pasteurized cheese from their own herd of cows and goats since 1995, using recipes from their homelands, France and Switzerland. Included among these is Le Sabot, based on the cheeses of the Loire.

TASTING NOTES The soft, satiny texture with a delicate sweetness counteracts the lactic goaty aromas. As it ages, blue moulds appear on the thin wrinkly rind.

HOW TO ENJOY This attractive cheeseboard choice also grills and bakes superbly, especially in quiches and tarts. Serve with crisp whites, rosé, or light beer.

CANADA Saint-Roch-de-l'Achigan, Québec		
Age 30–45 days		
Weight and Shape 150g (5½oz), pyramid		
Size D. 4cm (1½in), H. 7cm (3in)		
Milk Goat		
Classification Aged fresh		
Producer Fromagerie La Suisse Normande		

La Sauvagine

Made by La Fromagerie Alexis de Portneuf, a large-scale producer of numerous cheeses, La Sauvagine is a double cream cheese washed in brine. It won Grand Champion at the 2006 Canadian Cheese Grand Prix.

TASTING NOTES The added cream makes it almost runny, rich, and buttery, with a hint of mushrooms. The washed orange rind with its dusting of white has a rustic, farmyardy taste.

HOW TO ENJOY This is superb on its own, but its supple texture means it also melts well, especially when grilled. The creamy richness goes well with ale or a juicy red from Cahors.

CANADA Saint-Raymond-de-Portneuf, Québec		
Age 30–45 days		
Weight and Shape 1kg (2¼lb), wheel		
Size D. 20cm (8in), H. 3cm (1in)		
Milk Cow		
Classification Semi-soft		
Producer La Fromagerie Alexis de Portneuf		

Seven-Year-Old Orange Cheddar

Pine River, a farmer-owned cooperative was established in 1885 on the banks of the river of the same name near Lake Huron. Today, Cheddar is its main business. It is coloured with annatto, to give it a bright mandarin-orange colour, then aged for seven years.

TASTING NOTES The long, slow ageing process causes calcium crystals to form, providing a flavour burst and sharp tang. The texture is hard, dry and crumbly.

HOW TO ENJOY This extremely versatile hard cheese is regularly found served with apple pie, an Ontario favourite. Enjoy with strong ale, stout, or porter.

CANADA Pine River, Ontario		
Age 7 years		
Weight and Shape 2.5 kg, (5½lb), block		
Size L. 30cm (12in), W. 25cm (10in), H. 45cm (18in)		
Milk Cow		
Classification Hard		
Producer Pine River Cheese and Butter Co-op		

Sieur de Duplessis

Pressed and washed in brine, then aged for a period of up to nine months, Sieur de Duplessis is Atlantic Canada's only unpasteurized ewe's milk cheese.

TASTING NOTES The mottled golden brown rind surrounds a firm, dense pale yellow interior that has the sweet, nutty taste of ewe's milk, with floral notes from the pastures. As the cheese ages, the flavour becomes more intense, with a rich meaty finish.

HOW TO ENJOY Although this is almost too good to cook, it has all the versatility of a hard cheese and lends its sweetness to any dish. Match with a full-bodied white, fruity red, or Indian Pale Ale.

CANADA Sainte-Marie-de-Kent, New Brunswick		
Age 3–9 months		
Weight and Shape 2kg (4½lb), wheel		
Size D. 20cm (8in), H. 10cm (4in)		
Milk Ewe		
Classification Hard		
Producer La Bergerie aux 4 Vents		

Queso Anejo

Meaning "aged cheese", Queso Anejo is simply an aged version of Queso Fresco, or "fresh cheese" and was originally made purely with goat's milk, though nowadays it is more likely to be made with goat's and cow's milk, due to demand.

TASTING NOTES It becomes firm, chewy, yet crumbly with age and has mild herbacious notes that are heightened when cooked, A salty bite, and definitely hot when rolled in paprika.

HOW TO ENJOY Grated or shredded onto various dishes including Chilli con carne, enchiladas, and tacos. It is also great crumbled over salads.

MEXICO All over	
Age 2–8 months	
Weight and Shape 5–10kg (6½lb–11lb) rounds or blocks	
Size Various	
Milk Goat or Cow and Goat	
Classification Hard	
Producer Various	

Queso Blanco

Simply meaning "white cheese", this skimmed cow's milk cheese is prevalent throughout Mexico and Latin America. Resembling a cross between salty cottage cheese and Mozzarella, it is made by coagulating the milk with lemon juice and scalding the curds before pressing and kneading them.

TASTING NOTES Lemon fresh and with a buttery mild flavour, it's firm and elastic to the bite.

HOW TO ENJOY Used as a topping for spicy dishes such as enchiladas and empanadas, or crumbled over soups or salads. In Peru, it is melted with spices to make a cold sauce for boiled potatoes.

MEXICO All over	
Age From a few days	
Weight and Shape Various	
Size Various	
Milk Cow	
Classification Fresh	
Producer Various	

Queso Fresco

Introduced by the Spanish, it means simply "fresh cheese" and is consumed within a few days as it has high moisture content. Made by curdling cow's and goat's milk then lightly pressing the cheese, it is made in homes and large factories.

TASTING NOTES It is very white, creamy, spongy, slightly grainy, and mild with a fresh lemony acidity and slight saltiness, somewhere between ricotta and feta.

HOW TO ENJOY Crumbled over enchiladas or used as a filling in many Mexican dishes, it softens and becomes creamy when heated, but it will not melt.

MEXICO All over	
Age From 1 to 5 days	
Weight and Shape Various	
Size L. 9cm (3½in) W. 9cm (3½in), H. 2.5cm (¾in)	
Milk Cow or Goat	
Classification Fresh	
Producer Various	

318

Queijo Minas

A household staple in the hilly Minas Gerais region of Brazil that produces more coffee and milk than any other state in Brazil. Made by thousands of small producers, the cheese arrived in the region with the Portuguese explorers of the 1500s.

TASTING NOTES Soft and moist with a very mild salty tang and hint of lemon on the palate, it becomes yellow with a white centre with age, and develops a deeper tang and slight bitterness.

HOW TO ENJOY Usually eaten at breakfast with French bread, it can also be used as a filling in the traditional *Pão de queijo*, bread buns stuffed with cheese.

BRAZIL Minas Gerais	
Age From 4 to 10 days (to a few months when aged)	
Weight and Shape Various	
Size D. 9cm (3½in), H. 5cm (2in)	
Milk Cow	
Classification Fresh and aged fresh	
Producer Various	

Requeijão Cremoso

This very popular and now mass-produced cheese can be traced back to an Italian immigrant named Mario Silvestrini who developed the cheese back in 1911. The cheese is made to a secret recipe and is now synonymous with the large manufacturer Catupiry.

TASTING NOTES Soft white, tangy, and creamy, this cheese is easily spreadable, with the consistency of cream cheese but without the sweet taste.

HOW TO ENJOY A great snacking cheese, it can be eaten on bread or biscuits, as a stuffing in savoury pastries or even on pizzas. It can also be used as a dessert.

BRAZIL Minas Gerais	
Age From 4 to 10 days (to a few months when aged)	
Weight and Shape Various	
Size D. 12cm (5in), H. 4cm (1½in)	
Milk Cow	
Classification Fresh	
Producer Laticinios Catupiry® Ltda	

Sardo

It takes its name and basic recipe from the famous Italian sheep's milk cheese Pecorino Sardo (see p126), which it emulates, and although its hard, grainy texture is similar, it is made with cow's milk and the thin rind is waxed with red or black wax.

TASTING NOTES Hard but less grainy than Italian Pecorino, it has a richness in the mouth and sharp, salty taste with a lingering raw onion bite on the finish.

HOW TO ENJOY Excellent grating cheese, it is sprinkled onto various local dishes as well as pasta and salads, or thinly sliced as a snack.

ARGENTINA All over	
Age 9–18 months	
Weight and Shape 3–5kg (6½lb–11lb) drum	
Size D. 16cm (6in), H. 11cm 4½in)	
Milk Cow	
Classification Hard	
Producer Various	

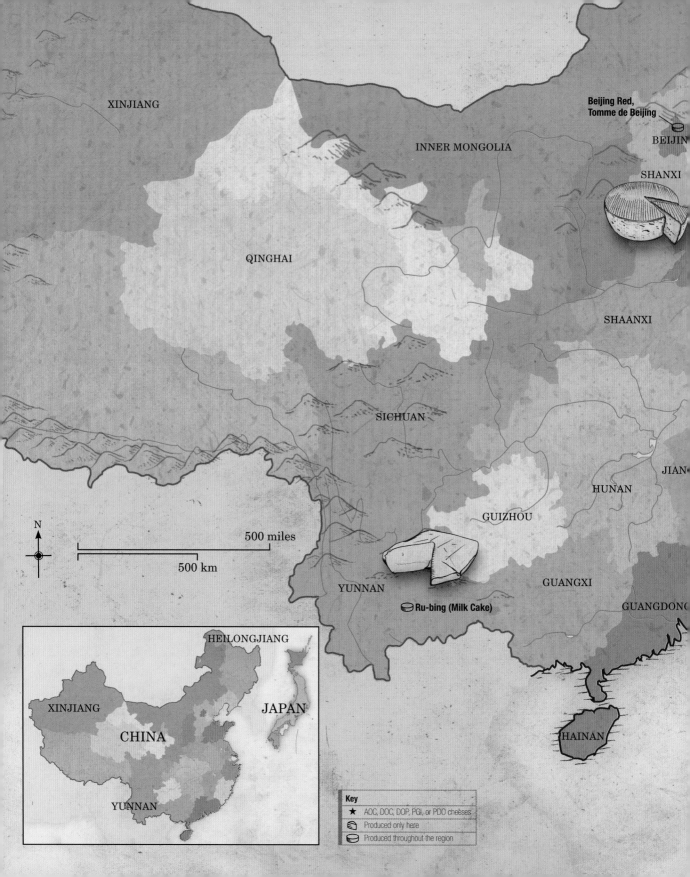

XINJIANG

INNER MONGOLIA

**Beijing Red,
Tomme de Beijing**

BEIJIN

SHANXI

QINGHAI

SHAANXI

SICHUAN

JIAN

HUNAN

GUIZHOU

YUNNAN

GUANGXI

⬤ Ru-bing (Milk Cake)

GUANGDONG

N

500 miles

500 km

HEILONGJIANG

JAPAN

XINJIANG

CHINA

HAINAN

YUNNAN

Key

★ AOC, DOC, DOP, PGI, or PDO cheeses
▱ Produced only here
⬤ Produced throughout the region

CHINA AND JAPAN

CHINA It is widely believed that ancient Chinese avoided dairy products to draw a line between themselves and the barbarians who roamed their borders or maybe it was because of their prolific use of soya milk. Whatever their reasons, dairy products were virtually unknown until the 20th century and cheese is still viewed with suspicion except in Yunnan Province. However, as the Western diet intrudes on tradition, the need for milk has risen dramatically, yet, with over 1.7 million dairy farms, production cannot keep pace with demand.

JAPAN Initially, most cheeses were processed, but since the year 2000, subsidies and technical support from the government has led to an increase of cheesemakers. As a result, Japan's northernmost island, Hokkaido, now boasts more than 100 cheesemakers, and overall there are nearly 200 small farms and factories producing cheese across Japan. Most cheeses are based on classic European cheeses like Camembert, Emmental, and Edam but increasingly, the cheese makers are experimenting and washing cheese in sake or green tea or decorating them with cherry blossom and selling them in their own small shops and cafés.

LIAONING

SHANDONG

JIANGSU

ZHEJIANG

PUJIAN

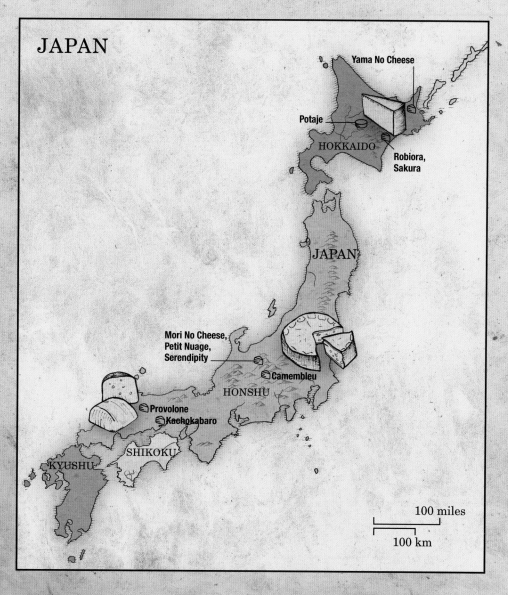

JAPAN

Yama No Cheese

Potaje

HOKKAIDO

Robiora, Sakura

JAPAN

Mori No Cheese, Petit Nuage, Serendipity

Camembleu

HONSHU

Provolone

Kachokabaro

SHIKOKU

KYUSHU

100 miles

100 km

Beijing Red

Finding Beijing's only cheesemaker in a city of 24 million people and six ring roads was no easy feat but worth it. Liu Yang went to France to get a degree, but came back a cheesemaker determined to introduce cheese to the Chinese. This was one of my favourites.

TASTINGS NOTES Its sticky terracotta rind, washed in white wine, quickly dries out and flakes in Beijing's heat but the interior is supple, smooth and savoury with a hint of wine.

HOW TO ENJOY In the beautiful formal gardens of the Summer Palace with a glass of white wine or beer listening to traditional Chinese music.

CHINA Beijing	
Age 3–5 weeks	
Weight and Shape 125g (4½oz), round	
Size D. 8.5cm (3in), H. 2.5cm (1in)	
Milk Cow or Goat	
Classification Semi-soft, washed	
Producer Le Fromager de Pekin	

Ru-bing or Milk Cake

This fresh, lightly salted cheese is made by hundreds of small producers for their own use or to sell at local markets and to restaurants. Ru-shan or "milk fans" are made by stretching and wrapping the curd around sticks to dry.

TASTINGS NOTES Curdled with vinegar, the curds are soft and slightly elastic with a delicate milky flavour that hints of goat milk, and a texture somewhere between tofu and Halloumi.

HOW TO ENJOY Typically pan-fried and dipped in rose-petal jam, or salt and Sichuan pepper. Also found stir-fried with Yunnan ham or other ingredients. Makes great street food.

CHINA Yunnan Province (SW China)	
Age From a few days	
Weight and Shape Various, square or brick shaped	
Size Various	
Milk Goat or Ewe	
Classification Fresh	
Producers Various small and large producers	

Tomme de Beijing

During his time in Corsica, Liu Yang spent time with various artisan cheesemakers learning unique cheese skills and the secret of bringing out the best in milk. He has put these into practice in his own country where cows graze on dry feed and supplements.

TASTINGS NOTES More like the mountain cheeses of northern Italy, it has a firm paste with small scattered holes. The flavour is fresh, with mouth-watering acidity and notes of vanilla and liquorice with a nutty or buttery finish.

HOW TO ENJOY With eight very different cow and goat milk cheeses, these make a superb Chinese cheeseboard.

CHINA Beijing	
Age 3–4 months	
Weight and Shape 850g–1kg (1¾lb–2¼lb), round	
Size D. 18cm (7in), H. 6cm (2½in)	
Milk Cow	
Classification Hard	
Producer Le Fromager de Pekin	

Camembleu

Established over 30 years ago Atelier make a range of excellent, raw milk cheeses including one washed in miso, another in sake lees. This is basically a Camembert with broken streaks of purple-blue mould through the centre.

TASTINGS NOTES The combination of the mild, creamy, slightly mushroomy taste of the Camembert type cheese goes well with the spicy, slightly mouldy taste and aroma of the blue. The rind is fluffy rather than crusty.

HOW TO ENJOY The Japanese seem to love it with jam or honey and almost any cheese goes well with a light Japanese beer or a glass of sake.

JAPAN Mihari, Nagano	
Age 3–4 weeks	
Weight and Shape 250g (9oz), round	
Size D. 11cm(4in), H. 3.5cm(1in)	
Milk Cow – Jersey – Holstein	
Classification Blue	
Producers Atelier de Fromage	

Kachokabaro

Say the name aloud and you realize it is Caciocavallo, the Italian cheese made in the shape of a small gourd. Made by one of Japan's most renowned cheesemakers, Yoshida Farm, who also make a Camembert, ricotta, fresh mozzarella, and rakoret (raclette).

TASTING NOTES It has a hard edible rind, firm, straw-coloured fibrous texture, and is slightly sour with a rich lingering milky flavour when young. With age the taste becomes dense with *umami*.

HOW TO ENJOY Cut into chunks and put on a brochette, then grill or grate and use in various recipes.

JAPAN Kaga-gun Kibi Chuo, Okayama	
Age 2–3 months	
Weight and Shape 500g–850g (1lb 2oz–1lb 14oz), teardrop or pear	
Size D. 11cm (4⅓in), L. 15cm (5⅞in)	
Milk Cow	
Classification Semi-soft, pasta filata	
Producer Yoshida Farm	

Mori No Cheese

A Japanese original, this washed-rind cheese has a sticky, mandarin-orange rind dusted with blue-grey moulds. Made from the milk of a single herd of brown Swiss cows that graze the high mountain pastures giving the cheese a darker colour and richer taste. *Mori* is the Japanese word for "forest" so the name literally means, "cheese of the forest".

TASTING NOTES Supple with lots of small eyes, both aroma and taste are reminiscent of fallen leaves in the forest with a wonderful strong robust flavour.

HOW TO ENJOY Excellent with medium- to full-bodied red wine or rice wine.

JAPAN Matsumoto, Nagano	
Age 3–8 weeks	
Weight and Shape 250–300g (9–10½oz), round	
Size Various, D. 10.5cm (4⅓in), H. 3.5cm (1½in)	
Milk Cow	
Classification Semi-soft	
Producer Shimuzu Farm	

Provolone

The expense of importing cheese from Europe has led to the development of many great Japanese alternatives such as this one, which is based on the famous Italian stretched curd cheese of the same name (see p130).

TASTING NOTES It has a sweet, melted butter taste, a fine, slightly smoked wax-covered rind, and a subtle smoky aroma.

HOW TO ENJOY The taste is more intense when cooked. Try baking it on rice cakes, especially those made with local rice, *Nitamai*, or on local beef, *Oku-Izumo*, and serve with soy sauce. It also works well when baked with honey.

JAPAN Unnan, Shimane		
Age 1–3 months		
Weight and Shape 380g (13oz), drum		
Size D. 8cm (3in), H 4.5cm (2in)		
Milk Cow		
Classification Semi-soft		
Producer Kisuki Nyugyo		

Robiora

Based on the popular Italian cheese of the same name (see p134), Robiora means "to become red" in Italian, and refers to the reddish hue that develops on the rind as a result of washing with "Grappa" or grape-based spirit. It is produced in Shiranuka Farm which is situated near the coast on the East Side of Hokkaido.

TASTING NOTES It is a strong pungent, meaty cheese with the classic supple texture of washed rind cheeses.

HOW TO ENJOY It is delicious grilled on oysters, with potatoes, and full-bodied red wine or with locally made grape jam.

JAPAN Shiranuka Gun, Hokkaido		
Age 4–8 weeks		
Weight and Shape 1–1.5kg (2¼lb–3lb 3oz), round		
Size D. 22cm (8½in), H. 3.5cm (1in)		
Milk Cow		
Classification Semi-soft		
Producer Shiranuka Farm		

Sakura

The cherry blossom, known as *Sakura* in Japan, that for just a week every year paints the country a candy floss pink, inspired the cheesemaker to create Japan's first original cheese. Produced on the co-operative, Kyodo Gakusha Shintoku Farm.

TASTING NOTES Mild, lemony with a melt-in-the-mouth feel. When ripe it becomes creamy beneath the soft rind and the aroma deepens.

HOW TO ENJOY This elegant addition to a cheeseboard can be served with green tea or red wine, such as Pinot Noir. It is also great with grilled Kobe beef.

JAPAN Shiranuka Gun, Hokkaido		
Age 2–4 weeks		
Weight and Shape 90g (3oz), round		
Size D. 6.5cm (2¾ in), H. 3cm (1in)		
Milk Cow		
Classification Soft White		
Producer Kyodo Gakusha Shintoku Farm		

Petit Nuage

Based on the Corsican cheese Brocciu, Petit Nuage is made from the whey of Brown Swiss cows. Its name, "small cloud" in French, refers to its small size, and white appearance. After draining, the fresh cheese is turned out of its moulds bearing the imprint of the basket weave.

TASTING NOTES Made by heating the fresh whey, this cheese is very white and very mild with the sweetness of milk. The light, delicate almost mousse-like fine curd feels like eating a cloud.

HOW TO ENJOY It is delicious as a dessert with jam or honey or in savoury dishes, such as pasta or quiche.

JAPAN Matsumoto, Nagano	
Age 2–10 days	
Weight and Shape 200g (7oz), flat round	
Size D. 9cm (3½in), H. 3.5cm (1in)	
Milk Cow	
Classification Fresh	
Producer Shimuzu Farm	

Serendipity

Produced from spring to autumn, from goats that graze on the Japanese Alps in the village of Hakuba. Once formed they are removed from their small round moulds, and preserved in pots in rice oil and locally grown herbs. It is owned by Australian Robert Alexander who fell in love with Japan.

TASTING NOTES Its mild taste combines well with the herbs and subtle rice oil gives a delicate flavour to the cheese.

HOW TO ENJOY Best enjoyed with some of the oil on fresh bread, or spread on rice crackers with a glass of rosé. It is also good when had in salads.

JAPAN Matsumoto, Nagano	
Age From 10 days to a few months	
Weight and Shape 160g (5½oz), jars	
Size D. 5.2cm (2in), H 3.5cm (1in)	
Milk Goat	
Classification Fresh	
Producer Kaze No Tani Farm	

Yama No Cheese

Yama literally means "cheese of the mountain" and is loosely based on the cheeses made in the French Alps. It is made on the most eastern part of Hokkaido. Look out for the 16 months plus, with a green label.

TASTING NOTES Long affinage gives it a firm, compact texture and a complex, nutty, rich lingering flavour and aroma. Its deep yellow colour is the result of the lush, green summer pastures.

HOW TO ENJOY Delicious on a cheese plate served with coffee, roasted green tea, salad, or with Hakushaku potatoes.

JAPAN Shibetsu Gun, Hokkaido	
Age 6–18 months	
Weight and Shape 10–11kg (22½–24¼lb), wheel	
Size D. 36cm (14in), H 10cm (4in)	
Milk Cow	
Classification Hard	
Producer Mitomo Farm	

Potaje

The name Potaje or "potage" means "kitchen garden", as the rosemary and thyme that cover the cheese are from the garden. The goats at Ranran Farm graze against the beautiful backdrop of the Tokachi Millennium Forest, giving the milk a sweet, mild taste.

TASTING NOTES Light and crumbly texture with a subtle, aromatic taste from the lovely goat's milk infused with the scent of the fresh herbs. A lemony finish.

HOW TO ENJOY This cheese is best suited for a cheeseboard, but can be crumbled and grilled over fresh vegetables, especially courgettes or aubergines.

JAPAN Tokachi Millennium Forest	
Age From 7–10 days	
Weight and Shape 90g (3oz), round	
Size D. 6cm (2½in), H. 3.5 (1in)	
Milk Goat	
Classification Fresh	
Producers Ranran Farm, Yagi Cheese	

NORTHERN TERRITORY

QUEENSLAND

AUSTRALIA

SOUTH AUSTRALIA

NEW SOUTH WALES

GREAT AUSTRALIAN BIGHT

N

200 miles

200 km

Washington Washrind
Woodside Edith

Holy Goat La Luna,
Holy Goat Pandora

Richard Thomas Fromage Blanc,
Yarra Valley Dairy Persian Fetta

VICTORIA

Shaw River
Buffalo Mozzarella

Meredith Blue

Ironstone Extra

Gunnamatta Gold

Gippsland Blue,
Jenson's Red Washed
Rind,
Strzelecki Blue

Roaring Forties,
Stormy

BASS STRAIT

Healey's Pyengana

Heidi Farm Gruyère,
Heidi Farm Raclette

TASMANIA

Bruny Island C2,
Bruny Island Lewis

INDIAN OCEAN

NORTHERN
TERRITORY

CORAL SEA

AUSTRALIA

WESTERN
AUSTRALIA

SOUTH
AUSTRALIA

QUEENSLAND

PACIFIC OCEAN

NEW SOUTH
WALES

VICTORIA

TASMAN SEA

TASMANIA

NEW ZEALAND

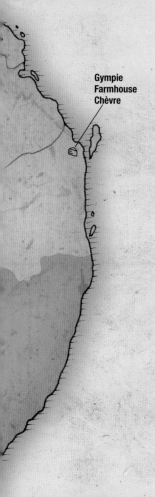

CORAL SEA

Gympie
Farmhouse
Chèvre

AUSTRALIA AND NEW ZEALAND

AUSTRALIA Australian dairy farming began when the first fleet landed in Sydney Cove in 1788, but it was not until the end of the gold rush, almost a century later, that cooperatives made Cheddar and butter for export.

Milk production mostly takes place in the southeastern coastal regions. Although low-cost industrial production, quarantine and protective trade policies once created barriers to the production of artisanal cheeses, demand has resulted in adaptations of European recipes to Australian conditions during the past two decades. The making and importing of raw milk cheese has only become legal in the last few years.

NEW ZEALAND European migrants to New Zealand in the early 1800s had to bring cattle and cheesemaking skills with them. Small-scale family production of Cheddar and Cheshire gave way to farmer-owned cooperatives, and the first dairy factory opened in Edendale, South Island, in 1882. With refrigerated shipping, Cheddar became a major export by the 1840s; by the 1920s, cheese and butter were being exported to England.

When Dutch cheesemakers migrated to New Zealand in the 1980s with their traditional recipes, the revival of small-scale artisan cheesemaking began. With a growing awareness of the wider cheese world, cheesemakers began producing alternatives to the great cheeses of Europe and creating unique artisanal cheeses.

TASMAN SEA

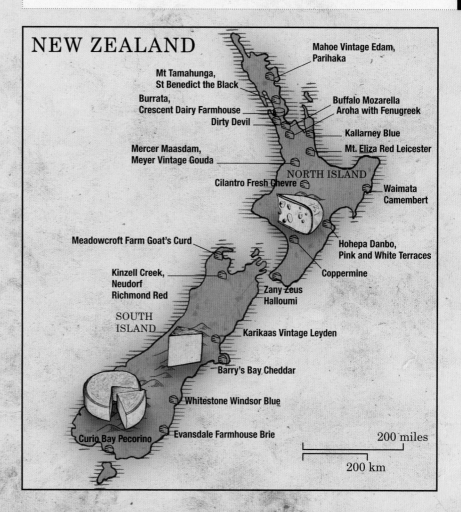

NEW ZEALAND

Mahoe Vintage Edam,
Parihaka

Mt Tamahunga,
St Benedict the Black

Burrata,
Crescent Dairy Farmhouse

Dirty Devil

Buffalo Mozarella
Aroha with Fenugreek

Kallarney Blue

Mt. Eliza Red Leicester

Mercer Maasdam,
Meyer Vintage Gouda

NORTH ISLAND

Cilantro Fresh Chevre

Waimata
Camembert

Meadowcroft Farm Goat's Curd

Hohepa Danbo,
Pink and White Terraces

Kinzell Creek,
Neudorf
Richmond Red

Coppermine

Zany Zeus
Halloumi

SOUTH
ISLAND

Karikaas Vintage Leyden

Barry's Bay Cheddar

Whitestone Windsor Blue

Evansdale Farmhouse Brie

Curio Bay Pecorino

200 miles

200 km

Key
★ AOC, DOC, DOP, PGI, or PDO cheeses
🛢 Produced only here
🛢 Produced throughout the region

328

Bruny Island C2

Nick Haddow, who is passionate about cheese, studied extensively in Europe before settling on Bruny Island, south of Hobart, with his partner Leonie in 2005. C2 was his first cheese, named after the vat in which it was created.

TASTING NOTES At its best, when it is at least nine months old, it develops a deliciously rich complex nutty flavour with a hint of caramel and a mouth-tingling tang.

HOW TO ENJOY It is an ideal cheese for sauces or grilling, or as it is on a cheeseboard. Match with a dry Tasmanian Riesling.

AUSTRALIA Bruny Island, Tasmania	
Age 9–12 months	
Weight and Shape 7kg (13lb), drum	
Size D. 20cm (8in), H. 18cm (7in)	
Milk Cow	
Classification Hard	
Producer Bruny Island Cheese Company	

Bruny Island Lewis

This quirky cheese by Nick Haddow is based on a mountain recipe he studied in Savoie, France. As no milk is produced on the island, the cheese is made from the milk from a single herd of Saanen goats near Cygnet on the mainland. It is named after a beloved family goat that once guarded the vegetable patch next to the dairy.

TASTING NOTES Ripened under an elegant thick natural slate-coloured rind, the pure white dense interior is subtly nutty with fresh herbal overtones.

HOW TO ENJOY Enjoy simply with crusty sourdough bread and a glass of chilled Tasmanian sparkling wine.

AUSTRALIA Bruny Island, Tasmania	
Age 4–6 months	
Weight and Shape 1.5kg (3lb 3oz), drum	
Size D. 12cm (5in), H. 7cm (3in)	
Milk Goat	
Classification Hard	
Producer Bruny Island Cheese Company	

Gippsland Blue

Created in 1981 at Hillcrest Farm in Gippsland, this natural grey rind cheese was the first artisan Australian blue. Based on Gorgonzola (see pp108–09), its milk comes from the farm's Holstein Friesian cows. It is matured on wooden shelves in special underground cellars built deep beneath the farm dairy.

TASTING NOTES This rich and creamy blue is at its best when it develops a soft and sticky texture that is punctuated with steely blue veins.

HOW TO ENJOY This very seasonal cheese – recommended from late autumn to early summer – is best enjoyed with an Australian late-harvest sweet wine.

AUSTRALIA Neerim South, Victoria	
Age 2–3 months	
Weight and Shape 5.5kg (12lb), wheel	
Size D. 15cm (6in), H. 24cm (9½in)	
Milk Cow	
Classification Blue	
Producer Tarago River Cheese	

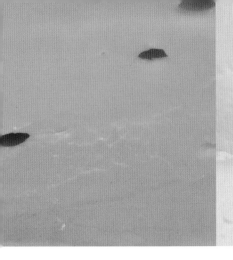

Gunnamatta Gold

Created by Trevor and Jan Brandon at the tiny Red Hill Cheesery on Victoria's Mornington Peninsula, this cheese is handmade using organic milk. Open to the public, the cheesery is only an hour away from Melbourne and takes its name from one of the peninsula's best surf breaks.

TASTING NOTES Beneath the slightly sticky terra-cotta rind lies a soft and creamy cheese with a delicious rich finish and a hint of smoke.

HOW TO ENJOY Like all intense washed-rind cheeses, it needs a spicy, aromatic wine, such as a Mornington Peninsula Pinot Noir, and crusty bread.

AUSTRALIA Mornington Peninsula, Victoria	
Age 4–5 weeks	
Weight and Shape 250g (9oz), round	
Size D. 10cm (4in), H. 3cm (1in)	
Milk Cow	
Classification Semi-soft	
Producer Red Hill Cheese	

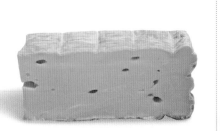

Gympie Farmhouse Chèvre

Camille Mortaud learned his craft in the Poitou-Charentes region of France, renowned for its aged fresh cheeses, and follows the traditions at Conondale, in the hinterland behind the Sunshine Coast in southeast Queensland, using milk sourced from nearby Kingaroy.

TASTING NOTES The rind turns a grey dusty blue the longer the cheese is aged and can be quite strong; the interior has a delightful savoury flavour with a delicious lingering goaty finish.

HOW TO ENJOY Perfect with crusty bread and a crisp dry white wine, or serve grilled along with a wild rocket salad.

AUSTRALIA Gympie, Queensland	
Age 3–4 weeks	
Weight and Shape 110g (4oz), log	
Size D. 5cm (2in), L. 6cm (2½in)	
Milk Goat	
Classification Aged fresh	
Producer Gympie Farm Cheese	

Healey's Pyengana

Dating back to 1901, this venerable cheese from the lush George River Valley is the oldest surviving traditional clothbound Australian cheese. Originally made by a cooperative, the "washed curd" Colby recipe was adopted by the Healey family and is now handmade from the milk of its herd of Holstein Friesian cows.

TASTING NOTES The large wheels are matured for at least a year until the moist, open texture develops herbal hints of pasture and honey.

HOW TO ENJOY Ideal with crusty bread and a Tasmanian cider or Pinot Noir.

AUSTRALIA Pyengana, Tasmania	
Age 9–18 months	
Weight and Shape 18.5kg (40½lb), wheel	
Size D. 30cm (12in), H. 20cm (8in)	
Milk Cow	
Classification Hard	
Producer Pyengana Cheese Factory	

Heidi Farm Gruyère

Weighing in at 30kg (66lb), this is Australia's largest handmade artisan cheese, and has won many accolades since it was launched by Swiss migrant and cheesemaker, Frank Marchand. Heidi Farm is now owned by National Foods, but the cheese is still handmade.

TASTING NOTES Sold at various ages, but is at its best when aged for at least a year, when its smooth concentrated texture develops an intensely rich, slightly nutty flavour with a hint of honey.

HOW TO ENJOY This wonderful melting or grilling cheese is particularly good as a base for macaroni cheese. Great with a full-bodied red wine.

AUSTRALIA Exton, Tasmania		
Age 9–12 months		
Weight and Shape 30kg (66lb), wheel		
Size D. 46cm (18in), H. 10cm (4in)		
Milk Cow		
Classification Hard		
Producer Heidi Farm		

Heidi Farm Raclette

Very successfully adapted in the 1980s by farmer and master cheesemaker, Frank Marchand from the traditional Swiss raclette, this uses Friesian milk from several local farms and has since won many national awards.

TASTING NOTES Beneath the cheese's sticky, slightly smelly terra-cotta rind lies a creamy pliable interior with a melange of grassy farm flavours and a hint of sweetness.

HOW TO ENJOY A delicious table cheese, or enjoy cut in half and grilled in the traditional manner in front of a hot grill. Serve it with Pink Eye potatoes and a dry Riesling.

AUSTRALIA Exton, Tasmania		
Age 2–4 months		
Weight and Shape 4kg (8lb 13oz), wheel		
Size D. 30cm (12in), H. 7cm (3in)		
Milk Cow		
Classification Semi-soft		
Producer Heidi Farm		

Holy Goat La Luna

Holy Goat was established at Sutton Grange Organic Farm in 2001, when Carla Meurs and Anne-Marie Monda returned from studying artisanal goat's cheese in Europe. All cheeses are handmade in their small dairy, using organic milk from a herd of 60 very pampered goats.

TASTING NOTES Beneath the rind of this unusual ring of goat cheese covered with a creeping wrinkled grey mould lies a pure white curd with deliciously complex lingering nutty flavours.

HOW TO ENJOY Perfect with crusty bread and a glass of Sauvignon Blanc, La Luna also bakes and grills well.

AUSTRALIA Sutton Grange, Victoria		
Age 4–6 weeks		
Weight and Shape 1.4kg (3lb), disc		
Size D. 23cm (9in), H. 4cm (1½in)		
Milk Goat		
Classification Aged fresh		
Producer Holy Goat Organic Cheeses		

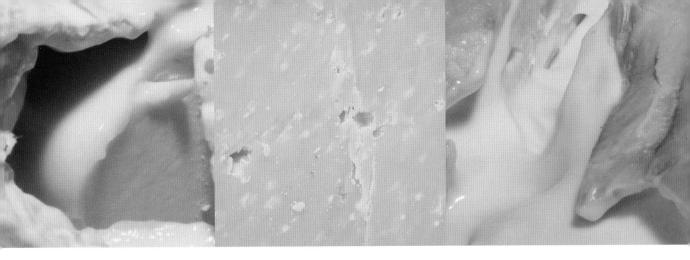

Holy Goat Pandora

The name says it all. This small drum is ripened under a cocktail of moulds. It was created by Carla Meurs and Anne-Marie Monda to be enjoyed at one sitting, and customers claim it pairs with everything and never fails to please.

TASTING NOTES The chalky centre has an irresistibly soft, creamy texture that rarely fails to satisfy with its luxurious feel and refreshingly mild goat flavour.

HOW TO ENJOY Cut off the lid, dig out the centre in large dollops like clotted cream, and enjoy with a glass of Sauvignon Blanc or rosé.

Australia Sutton Grange, Victoria	
Age 2–3 weeks	
Weight and Shape 200g (7oz), cylinder	
Size D. 5cm (2in), H. 5cm (2in)	
Milk Goat	
Classification Aged fresh	
Producer Holy Goat Organic Cheeses	

Ironstone Extra

After studying overseas, Steven Brown returned home to the family farm near Neerim South in Gippsland to set up a small dairy. Ironstone is based on a traditional Dutch Boerenkaas recipe. The cheese is made between spring and autumn from the farm's small herd of Holstein Friesians to ensure the rich pastures are reflected in the cheese.

TASTING NOTES Matured for up to two years, Ironstone Extra develops a sensational rich, buttery caramel flavour reminiscent of custard creams.

HOW TO ENJOY It makes a wonderful addition to any cheeseboard, or serve it in chunks with an apéritif.

AUSTRALIA Drouin West, Victoria	
Age 18–24 months	
Weight and Shape 5kg (11lb), boulder	
Size D. 23cm (9in), H. 11cm (4½in)	
Milk Cow	
Classification Hard	
Producer Piano Hill	

Jensen's Red Washed Rind

This bulging soft cheese from Tarago River near Neerim South in Gippsland, Victoria, is named after one of the dairy founders – cheesemaker Laurie Jensen. Made on the farm using Holstein Friesian milk, it is matured on wooden shelves and hand-washed until it develops a bright orange rind.

TASTING NOTES Beneath the smelly rind, which has hints of yeast and eucalyptus, lies a rich fudgy texture with a mild and creamy flavour.

HOW TO ENJOY Serve on a cheeseboard, with or without the rind, with crusty bread and sparkling white wine.

AUSTRALIA Neerim South, Victoria	
Age 4–5 weeks	
Weight and Shape 1.3kg (3lb), round	
Size D. 20cm (8in), H. 3cm (1in)	
Milk Cow	
Classification Semi-soft	
Producer Tarago River Cheese	

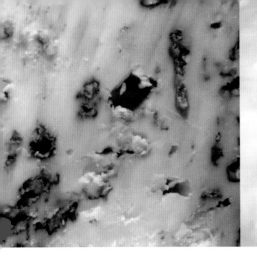

Meredith Blue

The first Australian ewe's milk blue was created in 1990 on the Cameron family dairy, using milk from the largest pack of dairy ewes in Australia. This handmade cheese is still matured in old shipping containers next to the dairy, which has an enviable reputation for its goat's and ewe's milk cheeses and yogurt.

TASTING NOTES As ewe's milk is highly seasonal, it is at its best in early spring, when the soft ivory interior texture of the cheese develops dark pockets of salty blue moulds.

HOW TO ENJOY Serve with toasted walnut bread or drizzled with local honey.

AUSTRALIA Meredith, Victoria	
Age 8–12 months	
Weight and Shape 1kg (2¼lb), drum	
Size D. 14cm (5½in), H. 7cm (3in)	
Milk Ewe	
Classification Blue	
Producer Meredith Dairy	

Richard Thomas Fromage Blanc

This soft, tender hand-ladled cow's milk curd from Richard Thomas is fresh cheese at its simple best. Using milk from the Yarra Valley, it is beautifully presented in self-draining containers that ensure that the whey does not sour the cheese.

TASTING NOTES Its delicate, silky, and exceptionally moist texture has the unmistakable sweet lactic perfume of a dairy, with a refreshingly mild lemony acidity.

HOW TO ENJOY At its best when served cold as it comes, or with homemade preserves or fresh berries for a breakfast treat.

AUSTRALIA Yarra Valley, Victoria	
Age 1–2 days	
Weight and Shape 100g (3½oz), pot	
Size D. 7cm (3in), H. 8cm (3in)	
Milk Cow	
Classification Fresh	
Producer Richard Thomas	

Roaring Forties

This full-flavoured blue cheese is aptly named for the strong westerly winds that buffet King Island, which lies in Bass Strait and is famous for the many shipwrecks along its isolated coast. Straw mattresses washed up from the wrecks are said to be responsible for the island's grasses and, ultimately, the quality of the milk.

TASTING NOTES The combination of rich creamy milk, blue *roqueforti* moulds, and a coating of dark blue wax ensures this dependable cheese is always very moist in texture with a sweet salty tang.

HOW TO ENJOY Serve with dark rye bread, matched with a sweet fortified wine.

AUSTRALIA Loorana, King Island, Tasmania	
Age 10–12 weeks	
Weight and Shape 1.3kg (3lb), drum	
Size D. 19cm (7½in), H. 4cm (1½in)	
Milk Cow	
Classification Blue	
Producer King Island Dairy	

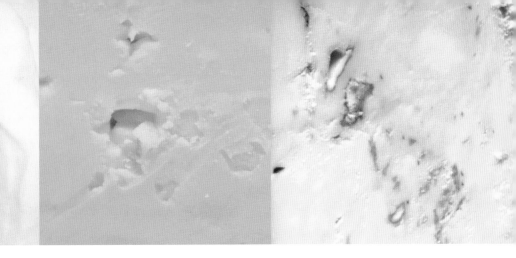

Shaw River Buffalo Mozzarella

Roger Haldene imported the first dairy buffalo into Australia in 1996, in spite of the odds and red tape. The herd grazes on the lush coastal pastures beside the Shaw River, and son-in-law Andrew Royal is the cheesemaker.

TASTING NOTES Unlike in Europe, the herd is pasture-based year-round, with the richest, sweetest milk produced during the warmer months, especially late summer and early autumn.

HOW TO ENJOY The slightly firm texture makes it ideal for pizza. It is also delicious with vine-ripened tomatoes, fresh basil, and extra virgin olive oil.

AUSTRALIA Yambuk, Victoria	
Age Within a few days of production	
Weight and Shape 50g (1oz), ball	
Size D. 9cm (3½in), H. 6.5cm (2½in)	
Milk Buffalo	
Classification Fresh	
Producer Shaw River Buffalo Cheese	

Stormy

Another great Australian washed rind cheese, this is named after Stormy Bay on the windswept coast of King Island, Tasmania, renowned for its rich and creamy cheeses. Stormy was originally created by cheesemaker Frank Beurain using techniques borrowed from the traditional washed-rind cheeses of Northern Europe.

TASTING NOTES The soft, buttery paste beneath the "whiffy" tangerine-coloured rind has a very mild creamy flavour and slightly salty sea-breeze finish.

HOW TO ENJOY Great on a cheeseboard, melted on pizza with cracked pepper, or served with baked potatoes and beer.

AUSTRALIA Loorana, King Island, Tasmania	
Age 4–5 weeks	
Weight and Shape 150g (5½oz), brick	
Size L. 10cm (4in), W. 4cm (1½in), H. 3cm (1in)	
Milk Cow	
Classification Semi-soft	
Producer King Island Dairy	

Strzelecki Blue

Pawel Strzelecki was the first person to discover gold in Australia in 1835, and it seems appropriate that his name is now attached to this striking blue. It uses milk from a nearby single farm and is matured in underground cellars beneath the dairy.

TASTING NOTES A seasonal cheese at its optimum with spring or autumn milk, it is quick to mature and best when its soft creamy interior is threaded with steely blue veins and the slightly sweet flavour has a distinct savoury tang.

HOW TO ENJOY It is perfect for a cheeseboard accompanied by a glass of dessert wine or a Gippsland Pinot.

AUSTRALIA Neerim South, Victoria	
Age 2–3 months	
Weight and Shape 2kg (4½lb), drum	
Size D. 20cm (8in), H. 19cm (7½in)	
Milk Goat	
Classification Blue	
Producer Tarago River Cheese	

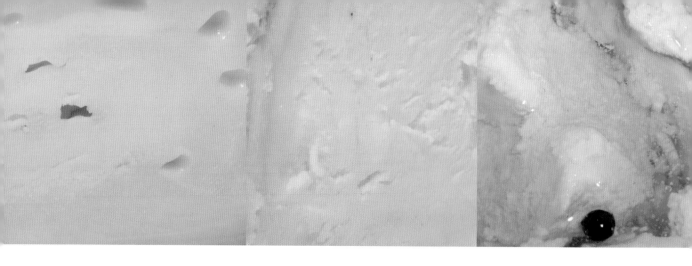

Washington Washrind

Victoria McClurg established Barossa Valley Cheese Company on Angaston's main street in 2003, after extensive winemaking travels in Europe. The dairy makes a range of washed-rind cheeses using cow's and goat's milk. The strongest is Washington.

TASTING NOTES This small orange disc has a very distinct and indiscreet aroma. Beneath the sticky rind lies a smooth silky paste with a mild creamy flavour.

HOW TO ENJOY Perfect on a cheeseboard, the yeasty flavours in the rind match well with the local Coopers ale and wood-fired sourdough bread. Use sparingly when cooking.

AUSTRALIA Angaston, South Australia	
Age 4–5 weeks	
Weight and Shape 220g (8oz), round	
Size D. 10cm (4in), H. 3cm (1in)	
Milk Cow	
Classification Semi-soft	
Producer Barossa Valley Cheese Company	

Woodside Edith

Kris Lloyd makes several dozen original cheeses; Edith is one of the oldest and takes its name from the Frenchwoman who provided the original recipe. Its secrets include the milk quality, and the slow overnight fermentation, during which it is smothered in black vine ash and ripened.

TASTING NOTES Deliciously nutty when young, it ages gracefully as the chalky centre gradually breaks down to a smooth, clotted texture. It has a peppery rind when fully mature.

HOW TO ENJOY It is ideal on a cheeseboard, or with crusty bread and Sauvignon Blanc.

AUSTRALIA Woodside, South Australia	
Age 3–4 weeks	
Weight and Shape 200g (7oz), drum	
Size D. 6cm (2½in), H. 4cm (1½in)	
Milk Goat	
Classification Aged fresh	
Producer Woodside Cheese Wrights	

Yarra Valley Dairy Persian Fetta

There are dozens of marinated feta-style cheeses in Australia, but the first was created by Richard Thomas in 1994, inspired by a Persian recipe and using milk collected from Yarra Valley Dairy's herd of Holstein Friesian cows.

TASTING NOTES Creamy chunks of curd are marinated in a powerful garlicky blend of oils, infused with crushed garlic, fresh thyme, and spices.

HOW TO ENJOY This surprisingly versatile cheese can be enjoyed straight from the jar on toast or biscuits, drizzled over steamed vegetables, or as an instant dressing for a salad.

AUSTRALIA Yarra Valley, Victoria	
Age 1–2 months	
Weight and Shape 250g (9oz), tin	
Size D. 7.5cm (3in), H. 8cm (3in)	
Milk Cow	
Classification Fresh	
Producer Yarra Valley Dairy	

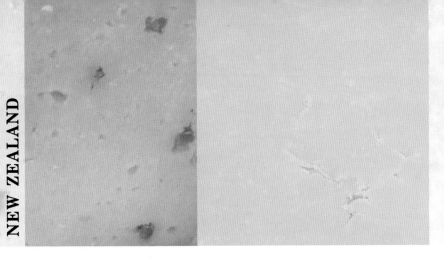

Aroha with Fenugreek

John and Jeanne van Kuyk make artisan cheese near Mount Te Aroha, using organic milk from their flock of Saanen and Nubian goats that browses freely on various herbs and shrubs. They are the first in New Zealand to be certified to produce raw milk cheese.

TASTING NOTES Using a classic Gouda recipe, the small dumpling-shaped cheeses come in various flavours including fenugreek, with its flavour reminiscent of curry and fresh walnuts that goes well with the creamy cheese.

HOW TO ENJOY The curry flavour lends itself well to salads, grilled over potatoes or vegetables, or grated into soups.

NEW ZEALAND	Te Aroha, Waikato
Age	3–5 weeks
Weight and Shape	950g (2lb). boulder
Size	D. 13cm (5in), H. 6cm (2.5in)
Milk	Goat
Classification	Hard
Producer	Aroha Organic Goat Cheese

Barry's Bay Cheddar

In 1989, the Walkers started making clothbound cheddar on Banks Peninsular. In 2008, the Careys stepped into their shoes, keeping alive the tradition. It is one of only 3 traditionally made cheddars in the country. They have a viewing gallery and small shop.

TASTING NOTES The hefty 36kg (79lb) cylinders are waxed or clothbound and matured for up to five years. At their best, they are hard and granular, with a strong, hot bite to finish.

HOW TO ENJOY Best with bread and chutney or an apple. Pair with handmade Canterbury beer or Canterbury red wine.

NEW ZEALAND	Barry's Bay, Canterbury
Age	2–5 years
Weight and Shape	1.5kg (3lb 3oz) and 4.5kg (9½lb), truckle; 36kg (79lb), cylinder
Size	truckle: D. 11cm (4½in) and 17cm (6½in), H. 14cm (5½in) and 17cm (6½in); round: D. 40cm (15½in), H. 35cm (14in)
Milk	Cow
Classification	Hard
Producer	Barry's Bay Cheese

Buffalo Mozzarella

In 2007, Clevedon Valley Buffalo, on the shores of the Hauraki Gulf, imported 65 Australian water buffaloes, which have now grown to over 170. They sell their wide range of buffalo milk cheeses and yoghurt in New Zealand, Australia and at the local farmers market, where ricotta and fresh mozzarella are the most popular.

TASTING NOTES They have perfected the art of trapping the milky whey.

HOW TO ENJOY Serve fresh with ripe tomatoes, basil, balsamic vinegar, and grassy olive oil.

NEW ZEALAND	Clevedon, South Auckland
Age	1–4 days old
Weight and Shape	80g (3oz)–125g (4½oz), ball
Size	Various
Milk	Buffalo
Classification	Fresh
Producer	Clevedon Valley Buffalo

Burrata

Massimo Lubisco fell in love with New Zealand while on holiday in 2004 and recognised the growing demand for quality food and the lack of fresh mozzarella. In 2010, he followed his dream and set up his own cheesemaking business in Auckland.

TASTING NOTES It is cream and strips of mozzarella (*Fior di latte* when made with cow milk), stuffed inside a mozzarella shell then squeezed shut. It is rich, buttery, yet feather light with the fresh sweetness of the organic milk.

HOW TO ENJOY Use in salads or dishes that involve tomatoes, fresh herbs, olive oil and cracked black pepper.

NEW ZEALAND Auckland	
Age 1–2 days	
Weight and Shape 125g (4½oz), money pouch	
Size D. 6cm (2⅜in), H. 7cm (2¾in)	
Milk Cow, Organic	
Classification Fresh	
Producer Massimo's Italian Cheeses	

Cilantro Fresh Chèvre

Mônica Salerno, a Brazillian with Italian heritage, and Jenny Oldham from the King Country, were both research scientists at Ruakura when they decided to make cheese. Their efficient handling ensures that none of the Billy goat notes taint the curd.

TASTING NOTES Bright white whipped curd with a smooth, mousse-like feel in the mouth that melts like ice cream releasing lemony fresh acidity and subtle aromatic, herbaceous notes.

HOW TO ENJOY It spreads easily, bakes superbly, and the subtle taste lends itself to many brochette or canapé ideas, with a glass of New Zealand Sauvignon.

NEW ZEALAND Ruakura Campus, Hamilton	
Age A few days	
Weight and Shape 140–180g (5-6oz), log	
Size L. 9cm (3½in), W. 6cm (2⅜in), H. 5cm (2in)	
Milk Goat	
Classification Fresh	
Producer Cilantro Cheese	

Coppermine

Jill and Ade Walcroft make a range of soft cheeses from organic milk sourced from Pohangina Valley in the Manawatu. Washed in brine, it is named after a stream in the Ruahine Range where copper was discovered in 1887.

TASTING NOTES The thin, copper-coloured washed rind, dusted with white *Penicillium candidum*, hints of farmyards and mushrooms. It has a warm-yellow interior which is velvety smooth with savoury notes to finish.

HOW TO ENJOY On a cheeseboard with a glass of Pohangina Valley Estate Pinot Gris or a hoppy Pilsner, or grilled over potatoes, onions and smoked bacon.

NEW ZEALAND Pohangina, Palmerston North	
Age 8–10 weeks	
Weight and Shape 180g (6½oz), round	
Size D. 9.5cm (4in), H. 2.5cm (1in)	
Milk Cow, Organic	
Classification Semi-soft	
Producer Cartwheel Creamery	

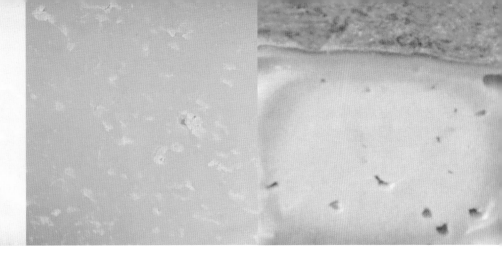

Crescent Dairy Farmhouse

Jan Walter, one of New Zealand's finest cheese makers, and husband John, have just 25 goats, yet this simple hard cheese is a consistent winner, year after year, at the New Zealand Cheese Awards.

TASTING NOTES It varies from one day to the next. Sometimes, coconut milk is discernible, sometimes cinnamon and thyme, but they all develop a fresh, earthy, goaty flavour. It is best when still moist and slightly soft.

HOW TO ENJOY Too precious as a mere sandwich filling, it should be savoured with a good Sauvignon Blanc.

NEW ZEALAND Auckland	
Age 6–12 months	
Weight and Shape 2kg (4½lb), round	
Size D. 17cm (6½in), H. 8cm (3¼in)	
Milk Goat	
Classification Hard	
Producer Crescent Dairy Goats	

Curio Bay Pecorino

Blue River sources milk from 3,000 crossbred East Friesians ewes on its own farms. This cheese, along with Tussock Feta and other cheeses, is the result of the unique grazing and head cheesemaker Maxi Robertson's talent and commitment to quality.

TASTING NOTES Dense, smooth when young with a sweetness like salted caramel, becoming granular, almost crumbly with age. It develops a slightly gamey taste with a salty edge on the finish

HOW TO ENJOY Eat in chunks with crusty bread and quince paste. Grate onto pasta, risotto, or polenta, or shave onto salads. Pair with fruity red wines.

NEW ZEALAND Invercargill, Southland	
Age 10–14 months	
Weight and Shape 2kg (4½lb), round	
Size D. 13cm (5in), H. 10cm (4in)	
Milk Ewe	
Classification Hard	
Producers Blue River Dairy Products	

Dirty Devil

It was almost inevitable that a talented cheesemaker like Jan Walter would be tempted to try her hand at making a washed rind cheese, despite the fact that they are difficult to make and are not to everyone's taste.

TASTING NOTES This small cone is hand washed with brine every few days for three weeks, then finished with French brandy. Beneath its farmyard aroma, its taste is savoury, rich and meaty.

HOW TO ENJOY Extremely popular on cheeseboards in many of New Zealand's top restaurants and best served with a dry Riesling or cool beer.

NEW ZEALAND Kumeu, Auckland	
Age 30–40 days	
Weight and Shape 200g (7oz), truncated cone	
Size D. 7cm (2¾in), H. 7cm (2¾in)	
Milk Goat	
Classification Semi-soft	
Producer Crescent Dairy Goats	

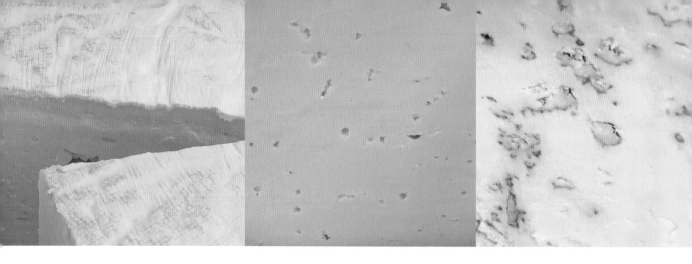

Evansdale Farmhouse Brie

Set up in 1979 by schoolteacher Colin Dennison to utilize excess milk from the family's house cow, and managed by son Paul, Evansdale remains small, hands-on, and quirky. Its Farmhouse Brie has become a New Zealand icon.

TASTING NOTES Smaller and twice as thick as the traditional Brie, with a white *penicillium candidum* rind and a smooth, buttery centre. It tastes of the sweetness of milk and the acidity of yogurt.

HOW TO ENJOY: Excellent with Chardonnay or sparkling wine. Try with a fresh fruit platter of Otago apricots, nectarines, and peaches.

NEW ZEALAND Waikouaiti, Otago	
Age 5–10 weeks	
Weight and Shape 1.3kg (3lb), round	
Size D. 16cm (6in), H. 7cm (3in)	
Milk Cow	
Classification Soft white	
Producer Evansdale Cheese	

Hohepa Danbo

Hohepa offers curative education and social therapy to people with intellectual disabilities. It is an amazing place with a masterpiece of a cheese, that is made with 'biodynamic' milk which gives complexity and character to the final product.

TASTING NOTES The deep yellow interior, scattered with tiny holes, is chewy yet creamy. When young, it has a savoury taste that carries hints of warm bread, thyme, and raw onion. The aged cheese has a deeper colour and more flavour.

HOW TO ENJOY Serve with a glass of fresh apple juice or Gimblett Gravels Pinot Noir.

NEW ZEALAND Clive, Hawkes Bay	
Age 4–9 months	
Weight and Shape 6.5kg (14lb), boulder	
Size D. 27cm (11in), H. 13cm (4in)	
Milk Cow	
Classification Hard	
Producer Hohepa Hawkes bay	

Kallarney Blue

Kelvin Haigh set up The Cheese Barn near Thames in 1996 where he makes and sells at the cafe a wide range of cheese and dairy products, mostly from their small herd of organic cows. Kallarney is their only blue.

TASTING NOTES The texture is pleasantly crumbly and drier than most New Zealand blues with streaks of crunchy blue, that have a spicy tang. It gradually becomes creamy in the mouth and has a light salty finish.

HOW TO ENJOY Can be crumbled into salads with fresh walnuts and apples or try it with a light beer or dry Riesling.

NEW ZEALAND Matatoki, Thames	
Age 4–5 months	
Weight and Shape 2.5kg (5½lb), drum	
Size D. 18cm (7in), H. 10cm (4in)	
Milk cow	
Classification Blue	
Producer The Cheese Barn	

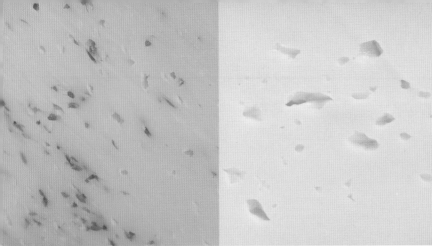
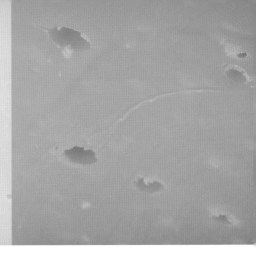

Karikaas Vintage Leyden

In 1984, Rients and Karen Rypma established Karikaas Dairy and helped resurrect traditional Dutch cheesemaking. In 2004, two families, the Lamers and the Hawkins, bought the business and now and continue to make traditional Dutch cheeses.

TASTING NOTES Leyden is a classic gouda scattered with cumin seeds, giving it a sweet taste with a hint of curry. At two years old, it is drier, sharper, and caramel-sweet.

HOW TO ENJOY Melt over potatoes, or try with cured meats. The cumin works well with mulled red wine, dark ales, and stout.

NEW ZEALAND Loburn, Canterbury	
Age 6–36 months	
Weight and Shape 10kg (22lb), boulder	
Size D. 32cm (12⅛in), H. 12cm (5in)	
Milk Cow	
Classification Flavour-added	
Producer Karikaas Dairy	

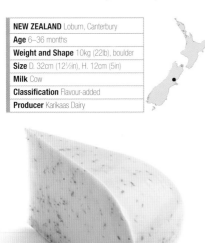

Kinzell Creek

Tucked away in the Tui Valley, the Trafford family farm has around 80 cows and make a wide range of dairy products. They have a holistic approach to their business and believe it produces content, robust disease-resistant animals, top quality milk, and great cheese.

TASTING NOTES Beneath a slightly sticky dark rind dotted with white and red moulds it has a supple, smooth texture and a salty butter taste with hints of damp leaves and meadow hay.

HOW TO ENJOY Serve with nuts, fresh apples, and chutney alongside a local woody chardonnay or pale ale.

NEW ZEALAND Tapawera, Nelson	
Age 6–8 weeks	
Weight and Shape 2.5kg (5½lb), round	
Size D. 14cm (6in), H. 3.5cm (1in)	
Milk Cow	
Classification Semi-soft	
Producer Wangapeka Family Dairy	

Mahoe Vintage Edam

New Zealand's most northern cheesemakers are situated in lush Oromahoe in the Bay of Islands. The Rosevears have been making cheese from their cows' milk since 1986. Made with semi-skimmed milk, it is as authentic as any made under that name in the Netherlands.

TASTING NOTES With tastes of butterscotch and caramel, a lactic tang, and a finish with a savoury bite; it has a supple texture when young, but like a Parmesan with crunchy crystals, when aged.

HOW TO ENJOY Excellent with white or dessert wines, it pairs well with a full-bodied red or trappiste beer.

NEW ZEALAND Kerikeri, Northland	
Age 18–24 months	
Weight and Shape 5kg (11lb) and 10kg (22lb), round	
Size D. 23cm (9in) and 33cm (13in), H. 10cm (4in) and 11cm (4½in)	
Milk Cow	
Classification Hard	
Producer Mahoe Farmhouse Cheese	

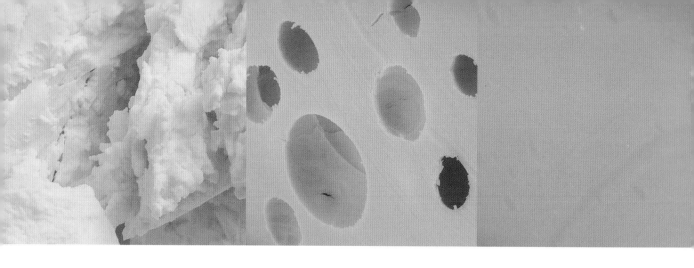

Meadowcroft Farm Goat's Curd

Tim and Kylie Connell took over from Averill Turnbull in 2013 and continue to make simple but delicious goat cheeses. Based in Golden Bay, their 60 goats graze on free-range pastures overlooking the sea, giving the milk its herbaceous, sweet flavour.

TASTING NOTES Whether it is plain, rolled in fresh herbs, or marinated in oil, the curd possesses a finely tuned balance of acidity and salt, and a texture that is moist and very slightly granular.

HOW TO ENJOY Perfect on crusty bread with Sauvignon Blanc or champagne, or spooned over fresh fruit and honey.

NEW ZEALAND Golden Bay, Tasman
Age Up to 5 weeks
Weight and Shape Various, pots
Size Various
Milk Goat
Classification Fresh
Producer Meadowcroft Farm

Mercer Maasdam

Maasdam is made by several of New Zealand's Dutch cheesemakers, including Albert Alfrink of Mercer Cheese. He sells it from his small shop, which is packed with hundreds of the redoubtable Dutch-style cheeses.

TASTING NOTES Special bacteria are added to the milk to produce the small holes in the deep yellow, supple interior and the fermenting fruit sweetness that mellows out with age, when it becomes more like an Emmental.

HOW TO ENJOY Excellent with cured meats, particularly ham, it melts beautifully making it ideal on pizza or in a fondue. Lovely with a malty beer or cider.

NEW ZEALAND Mercer, Waikato
Age 4–7 months
Weight and Shape 10kg (22lb), fat boulder
Size D. 33cm (13in), H. 11cm (4½in)
Milk Cow
Classification Semi-soft
Producer Mercer Cheese

Meyer Vintage Gouda

Named the "Cheese of the Decade" by the author in 2003, this vintage Gouda has been handmade by the Meyer family since the 1980s. Next generation Miel, and his brother Geert, took over in 2007, and continue to make outstanding cheeses using the original recipe.

TASTING NOTES Smooth, chewy, and caramel-sweet, with a savoury tang and a sprinkling of calcium crystals. At three years, it is as dark, intense, and rock-hard as any Dutch Boerenkaas.

HOW TO ENJOY Eat it in generous chunks with sourdough bread, or in a toasted sandwich with onions. Match with lighter red wines or lager.

NEW ZEALAND Hamilton, Waikato
Age 18–24 months
Weight and Shape 10kg (22lb), boulder
Size D. 33cm (13in), H. 12cm (5in)
Milk Cow
Classification Hard
Producer Meyer Gouda Cheese

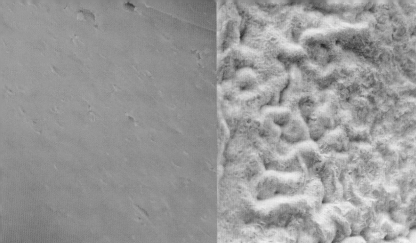

Mt Eliza Red Leicester

Cheesemakers Chris and Jill Whalley started making cheese in 2007. The Red Leicester curd is finely cut and twice-milled to give it a uniquely authentic close texture, while the annatto gives it the bright orange colour. They also make excellent handmade, clothbound traditional Cheddar.

TASTING NOTES This cheese is dense, smooth, and slightly sweet, with a strong bite at the back of the tongue. It is earthy and deep-flavoured near the rind.

HOW TO ENJOY Pair with darker beers and real ale; it is perfect in a sandwich with raw onion or peppery watercress, and makes a good Welsh rarebit.

NEW ZEALAND Katikati, Bay of Plenty	
Age 8–10 months	
Weight and Shape 8kg (17½lb), wheel	
Size D. 24cm (9½in), H. 16cm (6in)	
Milk Cow	
Classification Hard	
Producer Mount Eliza Cheese	

Mt Tamahunga

Annie and Phil Armstrong have 16 buffaloes that graze the wild pastures near Matakana. Phil looks after the herd and Annie makes the cheese. Together they produce some exceptional cheeses. "Tama" means youthful and "hunga" eruption.

TASTING NOTES A caramel-coloured pyramid with a soft, tightly wrinkled rind, dusted with fine white mould. It has a nutty and mushroomy aroma and taste, with hints of vanilla and thyme in the finish.

HOW TO ENJOY Pair with a rosé and a loaf of fresh crusty bread from the Matakana Farmers Market

NEW ZEALAND Whangaripo, Matakana	
Age 2–4 weeks	
Weight and Shape 250g (9oz), pyramid	
Size L. 8cm (3in), W. 5cm (2in), H 6cm (2½in),	
Milk Buffalo	
Classification Aged Fresh	
Producer Whangaripo Buffalo Cheese	

Neudorf Richmond Red

New Zealand's first ewe's milk cheese, this was created by Kate Light in the late 1990s. Brian Beuke, her original milk supplier, has now taken up the mantle and continues to make this great cheese.

TASTING NOTES At ten months it is firm with a nutty, and caramelised onion sweetness. At 20 months, it has a harder feel and more intense flavours but less salty than Italian Pecorino.

HOW TO ENJOY When young, it is wonderful with sliced pear or quince paste, and the aged is ideal grated on risotto or spaghetti. Serve with a red or white wine from the Neudorf vineyard.

NEW ZEALAND Upper Moutere, Nelson	
Age 10–20 months	
Weight and Shape 1.5kg (3lb 3oz), round	
Size D. 13cm (5in), H. 6cm (2½in)	
Milk Ewe	
Classification Hard	
Producer Neudorf Dairy	

Parihaka

Grinning Gecko, owned by Catherine and James McNamara, is a small artisan producer. They source organic milk, from two local farms: one milking Ayrshire cows and the other from Jersey cows, to create a range of unique, handcrafted cheeses.

TASTING NOTES Dense, supple, elastic textured, and deep yellow, it has the aroma and taste of fermenting pears with hints of sweetness and meadow flowers characteristic of Ayrshire milk.

HOW TO ENJOY Serve with preserved fruit or chutney or grill over your favourite roast vegetables. Its strong flavour means you won't need too much.

NEW ZEALAND Whangerei, Northland	
Age 5–6 months	
Weight and Shape 5kg (11lb), wheel	
Size D. 27cm (11in), H. 9cm (3½in)	
Milk Cow	
Classification Semi-soft	
Producer Grinning Gecko Cheese	

Pink & White Terraces

Joanie and Richard Williams started in 2011 with the aim of creating unique quality cheeses using beautiful fresh, organic milk that can be traced back to the farm and the animals. It is their shared fascination with cheese that has made this modern New Zealand classic.

TASTING NOTES Washed in brine, it is named for the pale pink, ridged rind dusted with white and patches of blue mould. Creamy, salty with hints of blue cheese, marmite, umami and peanuts – spectacular as the original terraces.

HOW TO ENJOY With dry Riesling or Viognier from Blackbarn Winery or any other dry aromatic Hawkes Bay white.

NEW ZEALAND Havelock North, Hawkes Bay	
Age 4–6 weeks	
Weight and Shape 200g (7oz), square	
Size L. 50cm (20in), W. 50cm (20in), H.25cm (10in)	
Milk Cow	
Classification Semi-soft	
Producer Organic Earth Cheese	

St Benedict the Black

Cheesemaking is not about following a recipe but about following your instincts and your curiosity. So rather than making mozzarella, Annie decided to create something different. After searching the length of New Zealand for charcoal, she made her first batch of St Benedict and hasn't stopped since.

TASTING NOTES A fine black layer of charcoal can be seen beneath the thin white rind, revealing the white interior that tastes of vanilla and mushrooms with the earthy freshness of the milk.

HOW TO ENJOY Enjoy lightly grilled on sourdough, or at a picnic by the river with a glass of rosé.

NEW ZEALAND Whangaripo Valley, Matakana	
Age 2–4 weeks	
Weight and Shape 200g (7oz), log	
Size L.12cm (5in), H. 5cm (2in)	
Milk Buffalo	
Classification Soft white	
Producer Whangaripo Buffalo Cheese	

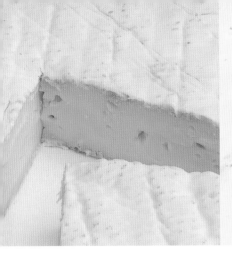
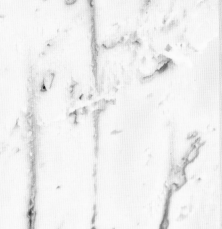
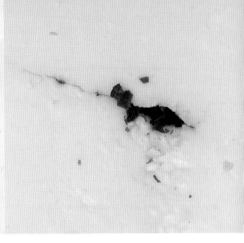

Waimata Camembert

Established in 1995, Rick and Carol Thorpe's Waimata Cheese Company is one of the largest independent cheesemaker, in New Zealand, producing more than 300 tonnes of cheese a year. Their huge range includes numerous blues, soft whites, double cream cheeses, Feta and Halloumi.

TASTING NOTES When young, it is mild and milky, but once ripe, it develops into a light runny vanilla cream style soft white cheese. Others can be nurtured to become more savoury, almost meaty.

HOW TO ENJOY Serve in a warm freshly baked croissant with apple chutney and a sparkling wine or crisp Chardonnay.

NEW ZEALAND Gisborne, East Cape
Age 4–7 weeks
Weight and Shape 800g (1¾lb), round
Size D. 19cm (7½in), H. 2.5cm (1in)
Milk Cow
Classification Soft white
Producer Waimata Cheese Company

Whitestone Windsor Blue

Set up in the mid 1980s by Bob Berry, Whitestone is another early pioneer of the country's cheese renaissance in the 1990s. They make a wide range of cheese but Windsor Blue is still their flagship blue.

TASTING NOTES The added cream gives an almost butter-like texture; while the taste is fruity and sharp when young, becoming sweet, salty, and spicier with age.

HOW TO ENJOY Spread on crackers or a baguette, toss into hot pasta, or serve with pears and gingerbread for dessert. Match with a slightly sweet, spritzy white wine.

NEW ZEALAND Oamaru, Otago
Age 3–8 months
Weight and Shape 3.8kg (8⅓lb), round
Size D. 21cm (8in), H. 12cm (5in)
Milk Cow
Classification Blue
Producer Whitestone Cheese

Zany Zeus Halloumi

Mike Matsis's passion for cheese started when his Cyprus-born mother taught him to make Halloumi. Fascinated by the process, he decided to become a cheesemaker, and now makes a range of authentic Mediterranean dairy products including yogurts, feta, smoked cheeses, all available in their Lower Hutt cafe.

TASTING NOTES When cooked, Halloumi tastes deliciously salty, feels slightly squeaky like a dense mozzarella and the milk sugars or lactose taste sweet, like caramelised onion as they cook.

HOW TO ENJOY Fry or barbeque on skewers, it will be crisp outside and melt inside. Serve with fruity white or red wines.

NEW ZEALAND Lower Hutt, Wellington
Age From a few days to 6 months
Weight and Shape 250g (9oz), block
Size L. 6cm (2½in), W. 4cm (1½in), H. 4 cm (1½in)
Milk Cow
Classification Fresh
Producer Zany Zeus

343

Glossary

ANNATTO
Orange-red dye, obtained from the natural pigments in the seeds of the Annatto tree (*Bixa orellana*).

BACTERIA LINENS
Formally known as *bacillus linens*, this bacteria is used to create the sticky orange rind on washed-rind cheeses.

BRINE
A strong salt solution used to seal the outside of some cheeses and prevent unwanted mould from growing.

BUTTERMILK
The slightly sour liquid left behind after butter has been churned.

CAROTENE
The yellow to red natural colorant that comes from grasses and is converted through the liver into Vitamin A.

CASEIN
Milk's chief and particular protein, precipitated in cheesemaking by acid development and by rennin enzyme, becoming curd.

COAGULATION
Also known as curdling, this refers to the separation of the solids and liquids in milk caused by acid and enzyme activity and heat. It is the fundamental process in cheesemaking.

COOKED CHEESES
Cheeses in which the just cut curd is heated or "cooked" in the whey, rendering the curd more elastic and expelling more whey.

CURDS
The solid protein that forms when milk coagulates. This is the basis of cheese. (See also Whey.)

ESTERS
The fatty acids and glycerides in plants. Aromatic esters from flora that is consumed by animals give aroma and flavour to cheeses.

EYES
The small eye-shaped holes that form in the body of some cheeses during fermentation. Most are small and uniform, except in the Gruyère-style cheeses, such as Emmentaler, where they are round and more often referred to as "holes".

FAT CONTENT
Fat is a carrier of flavour and feels soft and creamy in the mouth. If the fat is reduced or removed from milk, it will change its depth of flavour and texture or "mouth feel". The recipes for cheeses that have always been made with skimmed or semi-skimmed milk, however, have been developed to bring out the best in the milk, and consumers can rarely tell they are lower in fat.

FERMENTATION
During ripening, the fat, protein, and carbohydrates in cheese are broken down by biochemical changes, with the help of temperature, humidity, bacteria, and enzymes, which affect the texture, flavour, and aroma of the ripe cheese.

FULL FAT
Indicates that the milk has not been skimmed before being turned into cheese. Most cheeses are made from full-fat milk. It should be noted, however, that the fat content of milk ranges from only 3.8 per cent for cow's milk to 16 per cent for reindeer's milk, and the fat content of cheese ranges from 20–34 per cent, significantly lower than most people realise.

GLOBULES
Form in which fat is present in milk. Fat globules vary in size depending on the breed of animal.

HOOP
The container into which fresh curd is packed after salting, it typically has a perforated base and sides, and an open top. It is open-ended. (See also Mould.)

LACTATION
The period of time covering the milk production season of a cow, from calving to drying out.

LACTIC ACID
Formed by the bacterial action on lactose in milk. Within three months, the natural acidity of a cheese will kill off the remaining bacteria, leaving the enzymes to continue the ripening.

LACTIC FERMENTATION
The curdling of milk from lactose to lactic acid using only a starter culture (when rennet is not used), traditionally made by souring the previous day's milk or whey. Today, it is mostly carried out in laboratories. Also known as Lactic Cheese.

LACTOSE
Soluble sugar, specific to the milk of all mammals. Converted to lactic acid by the enzyme action of some micro-organisms in the Lactic Fermentation.

MARBLING
See Veining.

MOULD
1. The container into which fresh curd is packed after salting, it typically has a perforated base but an open top with perforations on the walls. The end is fixed. (See also Hoop.)
2. Micro-organisms belonging to the *mycota* family that grow on the outside or inside of cheeses and come from the *aspergillus*, *mucor*, and *penicillium* genus.

MOULD-RIPENING
The process by which moulds on the rind of cheeses, typically white, grey-blue, and orange coloured, speed up the breakdown of the curd.

ORGANIC CHEESES
Cheeses produced on farms approved by an official government scheme that adheres to the principles of organic production, such as no pesticides or chemicals on the land, in the dairy, or for the animals.

PASTA FILATA
Also known as Stretched Curd, a technique whereby curd is immersed in hot acid whey to make it elastic, then kneaded or stretched in hot water. Examples include Mozzarella and Provolone.

PASTEURIZATION
The heat treatment of raw milk for at least one minute at 73°C (163°F) to destroy any potential harmful micro-organisms. Unfortunately, it also destroys many flavour-enriching micro-organisms.

PASTE
Used in European cheeses to refer to the interior of a cheese. Also known as Pâte.

PENICILLIUM CANDIDUM
A white mould with a mushroom aroma and taste that grows on soft white cheeses such as Camembert and Brie.

PIERCING
Inserting of needles into a cheese to facilitate the entry and development of blue moulds.

PROCESSED CHEESE
Cheese that is heated along with an emulsifying agent, oil, and water, and shaped when hot and immediately sealed in its final pack.

PROTEOLYSIS
Breakdown of proteins by enzymes, acids, alkalis or heat.

RANCID
Used as a general term for unpleasant flavours in fats.

RAW MILK
Term used to refer to milk in its natural state (not subjected to pasteurization).

RENNET
An enzyme extracted from the stomach lining of a milk-fed animal, which breaks down the solids in milk into a digestible form, helping coagulation.

RIPENING
1. (of milk) Natural maturing of milk through rising acidity before renneting, without addition of a starter culture.
2. (of cheese) Continuing enzyme action of rennet and completion of bacterial action on curd, and consequent enzyme action.

SERUM
See Whey.

SILAGE
Grasses and legumes preserved by air-free storage, with limited fermentation.

SMEAR-RIPENED
A cheese whose rind is rubbed or smeared with a solution of brine and *bacillus linens,* usually with a cloth that forms a sticky orange rind.

STARTER CULTURE
Typically a combination of lactic bacterial cultures used to start transformation of lactose to lactic acid, which causes the milk to curdle. Mostly used in conjunction with rennet.

TABLE CHEESE
A term used in Italy to describe a hard cheese that can be used as an eating or snacking cheese, as well as in cooking, and was traditionally left on the table.

THERMIZED CHEESES
Cheeses whose curd has been heated to 54°C (129°F) in the whey – lower than pasteurization.

TURNING
The process of regularly turning a whole cheese while maturing, it ensures that the moisture in a cheese is evenly distributed and the mould grows evenly.

VAT
A container in which milk is contained for cheesemaking.

VEGETARIAN CHEESES
Cheeses in which a non-animal alternative to rennet is used to curdle the milk, in place of the more traditional animal rennet. The difference in taste in most cheeses is barely distinguishable.

VEINING
Also known as Marbling, this refers to the streaks or lines of blue mould found in the body of all blue cheeses. The Italians use the word *erborinatura* and the French use the term *persille* (both mean "parsley") to describe the scattered veining in their traditional cheeses.

WASHED RIND
Cheeses that are washed regularly over a period of time (not just once or twice) in a brine solution, often mixed with spices or alcohol, creating a sticky orange rind.

WHEY
The liquid residue of milk after most of the solids, including the fats, have been coagulated into curd. It is sometimes referred to as Serum.

Cheese-tasting terms

The following terms are commonly used to describe the aroma, texture and flavour of cheese:

Acidity In a cheese, like wine, this can be a positive attribute if it is not excessive – it leaves a refreshing, sometimes tingly, sensation in the mouth.

Aromatic A sensation of varied and interesting aromas – it could be spicy, perfumed, herbaceous, or fruity.

Bite A distinct, sharp, intense initial flavour, usually carried through to the finish.

Bitter A characteristic taste of some cheeses; can be a positive attribute as in strong Cheddar or a fault when used to describe Brie.

Body The sensation of weight and substance in the mouth, like red wine or Port.

Burnt Caramel A sweet flavour with just a hint of overcooked caramelised sugar, or roasted onions. Typically associated with hard ewes' milk cheeses.

Dry A feeling of lack of moisture in the mouth.

Earthy An aroma of freshly tilled soil.

Farmyard A term used to describe manure or animals. It is used to describe the rind or a wine, and literally means they smell a bit stinky. However, it is usually a good thing not bad.

Elastic A firm but flexible texture that returns to its original shape after gentle pressure, often with a tearable layered texture.

Finish The aftertaste, or sensation left on the palate after the last mouthful.

Friable The tendency of a cheese to crumble into small grainy fragments.

Fruity A flavour reminiscent of both the odour and taste of fresh fruit picked at its optimum stage of ripeness, such as pears, apples, melons, and mangoes.

Grainy A texture in which barely detectable small particles can be discerned – these are usually salt or crystals of calcium lactate.

Grassy Characteristic flavour of freshly cut grass.

Green Grass A fresh, pleasantly sharp grassy flavour.

Herbaceous The leafy fragrance of wild flowers, hedgerows, and grasses.

Lactic The taste of slightly soured milk.

Lactose The sugar in milk that is converted to lactic acid as the milk sours.

Metallic The mould in blue cheeses can be mild and slightly fruity, reminiscent of tarragon and thyme or when strong develops a distinct sharp mineral or metallic taint.

Moist Used in contrast to "dry", as in the texture of some cakes.

Pungent A forceful, pleasant, sometimes almost bitter flavour reminiscent of chicory, or fresh young grass.

Rubbery A bouncy springy feel and a rippable, rather than breakable, texture.

Smooth An absence of any structure, like double cream or custard.

Soft A yielding texture like mashed potato or cheesecake.

Squeaky When curd is washed it becomes very smooth and feels shiny and "squeaky" clean.

Supple More dense than "rubbery", as it has an underlying structure.

Tangy A tart or acidic flavour that causes the mouth to pucker and tingle. Often associated with mature hard cheeses such as Cheddar.

Umami This describes the yeasty, meaty savoury notes of many washed rind and Gruyère-type cheeses.

Unctuous Fatty and greasy to English speakers but creamy rich and luxurious when used by some Europeans.

Velvety Thick but soft, smooth, and without structure, such as processed cheese.

Index

350

INDEX

Contributors

FRANCE: As a native of Southern France, **Stéphane Blohorn** is the product of a Provençal education, which shows in his love of the outdoors, of animals, and of the gifts of the land. In 2005, Stéphane took over Androuet's house, and in 2006, he was inducted into the Guilde des Fromagers (France's elite cheese brotherhood). He dreams of preserving and furthering the quality and diversity of cheeses for future generations.

ITALY: Vincenzo Bozzetti began his career as a dairy master in 1960, and after nearly 40 years in the industry, he began training and teaching cheese judges for commercial trades and cheese contests. Today, he is a manager and columnist for *Il Latte*, an Italian dairy magazine. Vincenzo has written several dairy books and many articles for Italian and international dairy magazines.

SPAIN AND PORTUGAL: Monika Linton founded Brindisa, a highly respected warehouse and shop that brings Spanish food to British customers, 21 years ago. Armed with years of instruction in the language and her experiences of living with Spanish and Catalan people, she has guided the shop from its beginning, when it carried only Spanish farmhouse cheeses, into the successful business it is today.

ENGLAND: Katie Jarvis's interest in cheese began at the age of eight, when she spent a year in Paris. As a supporter of artisan producers, she writes about food and reviews restaurants for *Cotswold Life* magazine, and has written two books on the Cotswolds. She is one of the judges at the British Cheese Awards.

SCOTLAND: Kevin John Broome took up a full apprenticeship in cooking and went on to achieve two Michelin stars for his cooking at both of his co-owned Channel Islands restaurants. Kevin has won many awards for his fresh, unique and locally sourced dishes.

WALES: As a food writer, food consultant and former chef to the rich and famous, **Angela Gray** has had a lot of food experience. Her passion for food has led her to present cookery series for the BBC, write books and participate in live cooking festivals.

IRELAND: Dianne Curtin is a freelance food writer, stylist, broadcaster and author with a special interest in Irish artisan food production. In 2006, she set up a weekly artisan food market, and in 2007, published her first book, *The Creators, Individuals of Irish Food*. Dianne works closely with several organizations to promote Ireland's regional produce.

BELGIUM, DENMARK, NORWAY, SWEDEN, FINLAND, GREECE, HUNGARY, SLOVAKIA, MEXICO, BRAZIL, AND ARGENTINA: Jim Davies has helped to run The Great British Cheese Festival and The British Cheese Awards. He has a passion for seasonal, high-quality, local foods, and is also a successful script writer and PR consultant.

THE NETHERLANDS: Aad Vernooij has been working in the Information Department of the Dutch Dairy Association since 1980. He is the author of a book on the history of fine Dutch cheeses.

GERMANY, AUSTRIA, AND SWITZERLAND: Hansueli Renz was born into a life of cheese, as both his father and grandfather specialized in making soft cheese. After attending the Commerical School in Neufchâtel, he progressed from apprentice to master to expert. After working for 15 years in his own soft cheese plant, which he sold in 1987, Hansueli started a cheese shop with his wife. In 2007 he sold the shop and retired.

TURKEY, CYPRUS, LEBANON, AND ISRAEL: Cheese expert and chef **Ran Buck** studied at the French Culinary Institute and specialized in cheese at the New York Ideal Cheese Shop. Returning to Israel, Ran established two cheese importing companies and a concept cheese shop. Ran wrote *Gvinot* – the most complete and encompassing guide to cheese written in Hebrew.

Sagi Cooper started his culinary writing career in 2002. He writes for several magazines as well as online portals, including Israel's www.ynet.co.il (where he co-writes a column about cheese with Ran Buck).

USA Kate Arding is an independent dairy consultant, co-founder of CULTURE magazine, and a regular judge at the ACS. In 2014, she started her own cheese shop, Talbott & Arding, in Hudson, New York. Kate's cheese career began at Neal's Yard Dairy in London from where she moved to California to help establish Tomales Bay Foods. She now specializes in affinage, and has been helping small cheesemakers, since 2003.

Sheana Davis, creator and owner of The Epicurean Connection, is celebrating 20 years as chef, caterer, and culinary educator. She offers a range of food experiences and services while travelling between Sonoma, California, and New Orleans, Louisiana.

Richard Sutton's life-long love of cheese led him to work at Paxton & Whitfield in London, where he acquired much of his cheese training. In 2006, he moved to New Orleans, Louisiana, where he and his wife attended university. Together, they founded St James Cheese Company, which supplies many of the city's restaurants and offers one of the largest selections of cheese in the southern United States.

CANADA: Gurth Pretty is the founder of www. CheeseofCanada.ca; author of *The Definitive Guide to Canadian Artisanal and Fine Cheese* (a World Gourmand Cookbook award winner); and co-author of *The Definitive Canadian Wine and Cheese Cookbook*. He is active within the Canadian cheese industry as chairman of the Ontario Cheese Society and as a member of La Société des fromages du Québec.

JAPAN: In 1986, **Rumiko Honma** established Fermier, a mostly French cheese company in Tokyo. Rumiko has always emphasized the origins of cheeses, and as such, has visited many places to see the cheeses being made. Rumiko has become one of the key figures spreading information about European culture through cheese in Japan.

Rie Hijikata began exploring cheese by studying the history, origin, making, and terroir of cheeses. That knowledge base was expanded during a stay at an organic cheesemaking farm in Switzerland. Rie now works for Fermier's import department.

AUSTRALIA: Will Studd has worked with specialist cheeses for more than three decades. After establishing delicatessens in London, he moved to Australia. Will has written several books, and he produces and presents the international TV show Cheese Slices. Following his campaign to allow the sale of raw-milk cheese in Australia, Will was made the only Ambassadeur of the Guilde des Fromagers and awarded the Ordre Mérite Agricole.

NEW ZEALAND: Martin Aspinwall started his cheese career during a one-year sabbatical from social work, which extended into several years at London's Neal's Yard Dairy. After emigrating to New Zealand, Martin and his Kiwi wife Sarah started selling cheeses at the markets in Christchurch, and in 2002, they opened Canterbury Cheesemongers, a community bakery and cheese shop.

Acknowledgments

About the author

Juliet Harbutt, one of the world's most highly respected cheese expert, founded the renowned Jeroboams Wine & Cheese Shop when she arrived in Britain from her native New Zealand. Her passion and expertise were recognized with membership to the Guilde des Fromagers, the Confrerie de Saint-Uguzon and the Confrerie des Chevaliers du Taste-Fromage de France.

In 1994, Juliet created the prestigious British Cheese Awards and the Great British Cheese Festival and was made a fellow of the Royal Society for the Encouragement of Arts, Manufactures and Commerce in 2005 in recognition of her work for British producers.

Now a writer, consultant, competition judge, and lecturer she regularly appears on TV and Radio from BBC Radio 4 Food Programme to The Hairy Bikers, and travels the world educating and inspiring a new generation of cheese lovers. Her latest project has been to establish a Cheese "School" and she is working on her own range of cheeses.

Juliet Harbutt's Acknowledgments

Writing, editing, researching, and publishing a book like this could not be achieved without a team effort from all concerned and a genuine commitment to achieving excellence, and the author would like to thank all those directly involved, particularly the contributors and the team at Dorling Kindersley in London.

However, I would like to say a special thank you to those people who were there to encourage, feed and cajole me when the task seemed insurmountable. Rory Goodman, Linda Slide, Sue Taylor and Winston from the Cotswold Consultancy, Katie Jarvis, freelance journalist, Jim Davis, script writer and researcher, Jon and Lisa Goodchild from the Cotswold Cheese Company, Miles and Emily Lampson of the Kingham Plough, Diana Tietjens and Sarah Aspinwall (New Zealand), Kate Arding, Richard Sutton, Murrays Cheese Shop [New York] and Cowgirl Creamery (USA), George Mewes Cheese Shop and Rory Stone (Scotland).

The knowledge and inspiration however for a book like this has come not only from working in the industry for nearly 30 years as a retailer, affineur, trainer, and speaker but from meeting my cheese heroes. The most influential and inspirational cheese experts of the 20th and 21st century whose common traits are a passion for cheese and a desire to share it. Patrick Rance, Pierre Androuet, James Aldridge, Eurwen Richards, Carole Faulkner, Val Bines, Mariano Sanchez, Eugene Burns, and all the wonderful cheesemakers who have shared their cheeses and their dreams with me.

Dorling Kindersley's Acknowledgments

Updated edition 2015: The publisher would like to thank Ligi John for editorial assistance, Claire Cross and Shalini Krishan for proofreading, Marie Lorimer for the index, Suresh Kumar for cartography, and Sachin Singh for illustrations.

And the following for helping with the images in the book: Androuet London, Old Spitalfields Market; Grafton Village Cheese; Sara Remington for pictures of Red Hawk cheese and St. Tam; Vera Chang for pictures of Shelburne Cheddar; Fromagerie La Station for pictures of Raclette de Compton au Poivre; and Yuanchang Wang for photographing Rubing cheese.

First edition 2009: Will Heap, Alex Havret, Sara Essex, Kelsie Parsons, Andrew Harris, Stephen Goodenough, Sean McDevitt, Oded Marom, and Cath Harries for photography; Danaya Bunnag, Mandy Earey, Pamela Shiels for design assistance; Amy Sutton and Todd Webb for illustrations; Dawn Bates, Siobhan O'Connor, Helena Caldon, Tarda Davison-Aitkins for editorial assistance; Jenny Faithfull for picture research; Susan Bosanko for the index; Rupert Linton and Katie Jarvis for food research and writing; Jane Ewart for art direction in Paris; Susan Varajanant for food styling in New York; François at Androuët's, Paris; Charles Martell at Dymock for allowing us to photograph the Stinking Bishop process; Rebecca Warren, Michelle Baxter, Liza Kaplan, of the New York office; Rita Costa and Cynthia Gilbert, of DK IPL; Rebecca Amarnani, Blaine Williams, Terri Moore, Gillian Morgan.

And the following for generously supplying cheese for photography: Rachael Sills at KäseSwiss, Jonas Aurell at Scandinavian Kitchen, Monika Linton at Brindisa, Rippon Cheese Stores, Neal's Yard Dairy, Harrods, Sue Cloke at Cheese at Leadenhall, Dominic at The Borough Cheese Company, Valio, Rick Stein's Delicatessen, Mr. Christian's Delicatessen, Jeroboam's, Rick Stein's Delicatessen, Swara Trading International Ltd, Cynthia Jennings at Pant Mawr Cheeses, Kathy Biss at West Highland Dairy, Kellys Organic, Mossfield Organic Farm, Silke Croppe at Corleggy Cheese, De Kaaskammer, Poncelet, Kaasaffineurs Michel Van Tricht & zoon, FrieslandCampina Cheese & Butter; Dries Debergh at Het Hinkelspel; Adbdij van Postel; Chimay Fromages; Murray's Cheese, New York; Luigi Guffanti, Italy; Jose Luis Martin, Spain; Rainha Santa; Iberica.

352